yah!!

Four Knights of the Apocalypse

the Apocalypse

Nakaba Suzuki Presents

3

Contents

Four Knights Of The Apocalypse

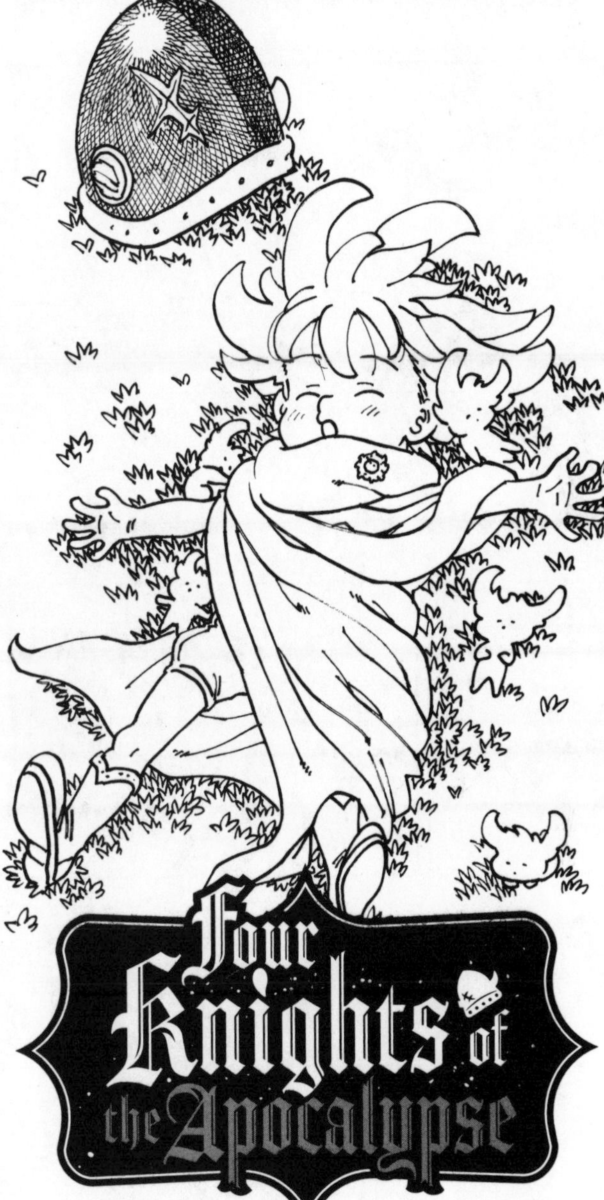
Four Knights of the Apocalypse

CHAPTER 15: ANGHALHAD AND HER DREAM

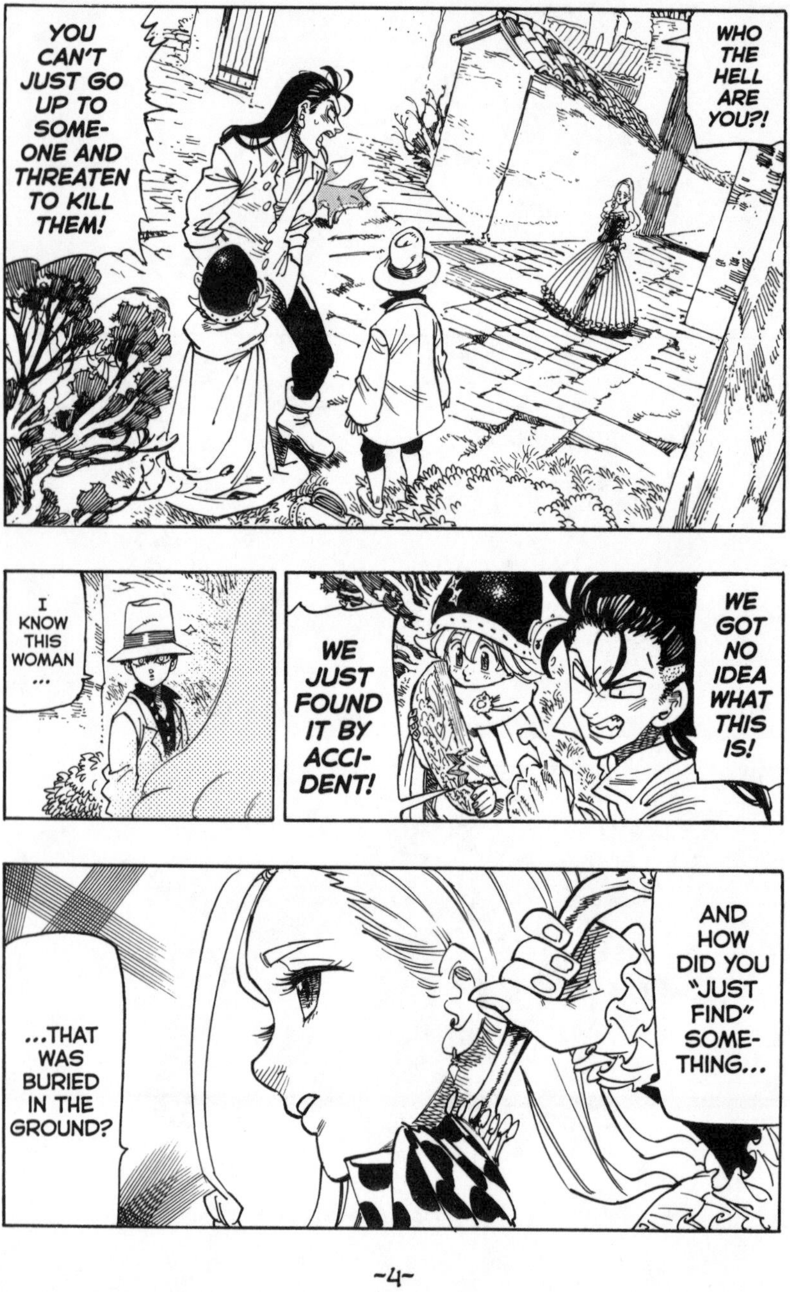
WHO THE HELL ARE YOU?!
YOU CAN'T JUST GO UP TO SOME-ONE AND THREATEN TO KILL THEM!
WE GOT NO IDEA WHAT THIS IS!
WE JUST FOUND IT BY ACCI-DENT!
I KNOW THIS WOMAN ...
AND HOW DID YOU "JUST FIND" SOME-THING...
...THAT WAS BURIED IN THE GROUND?

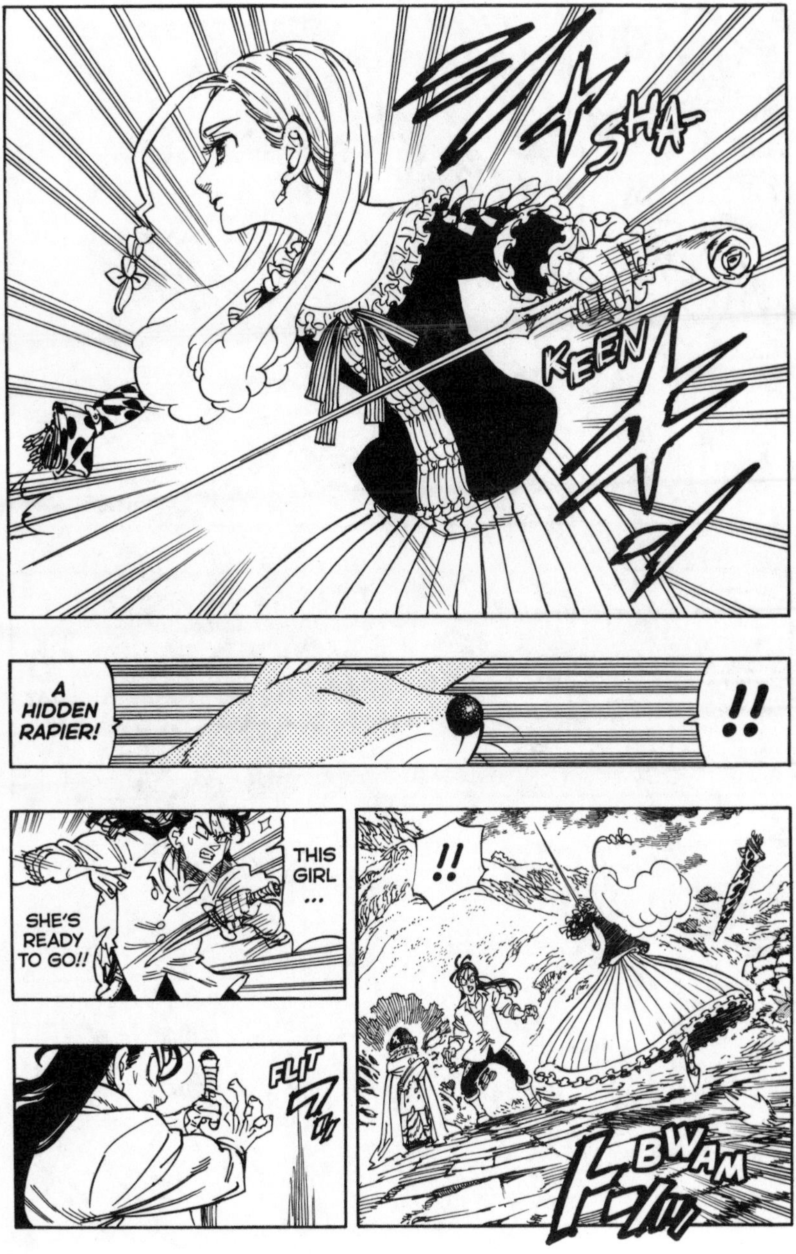
SHA
KEEN
!!
A HIDDEN RAPIER!
!!
BWAM
THIS GIRL ...
SHE'S READY TO GO!!
FLIT

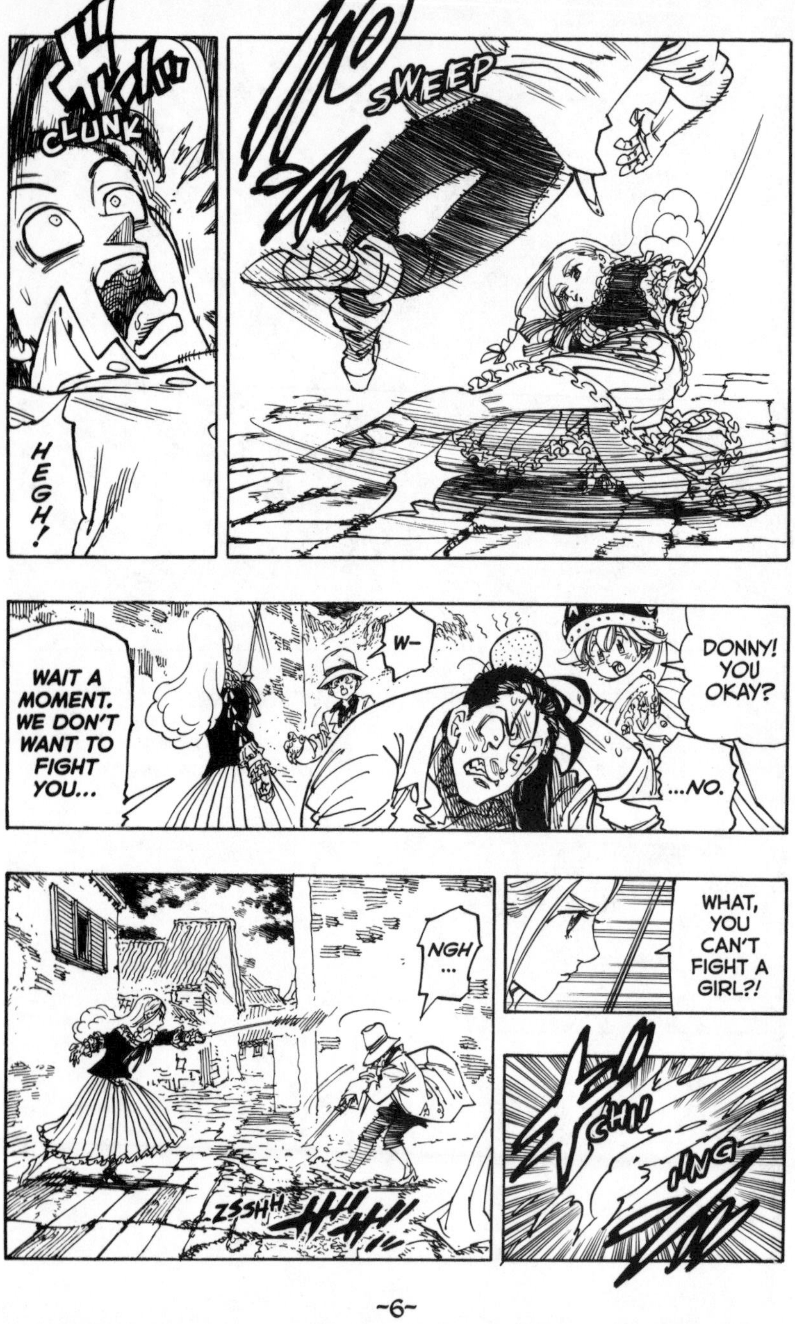
SWEEP
CLUNK
HEGH!
DONNY! YOU OKAY?
...NO.
W-
WAIT A MOMENT. WE DON'T WANT TO FIGHT YOU...
WHAT, YOU CAN'T FIGHT A GIRL?!
CHIIING
NGH...
ZSSHH

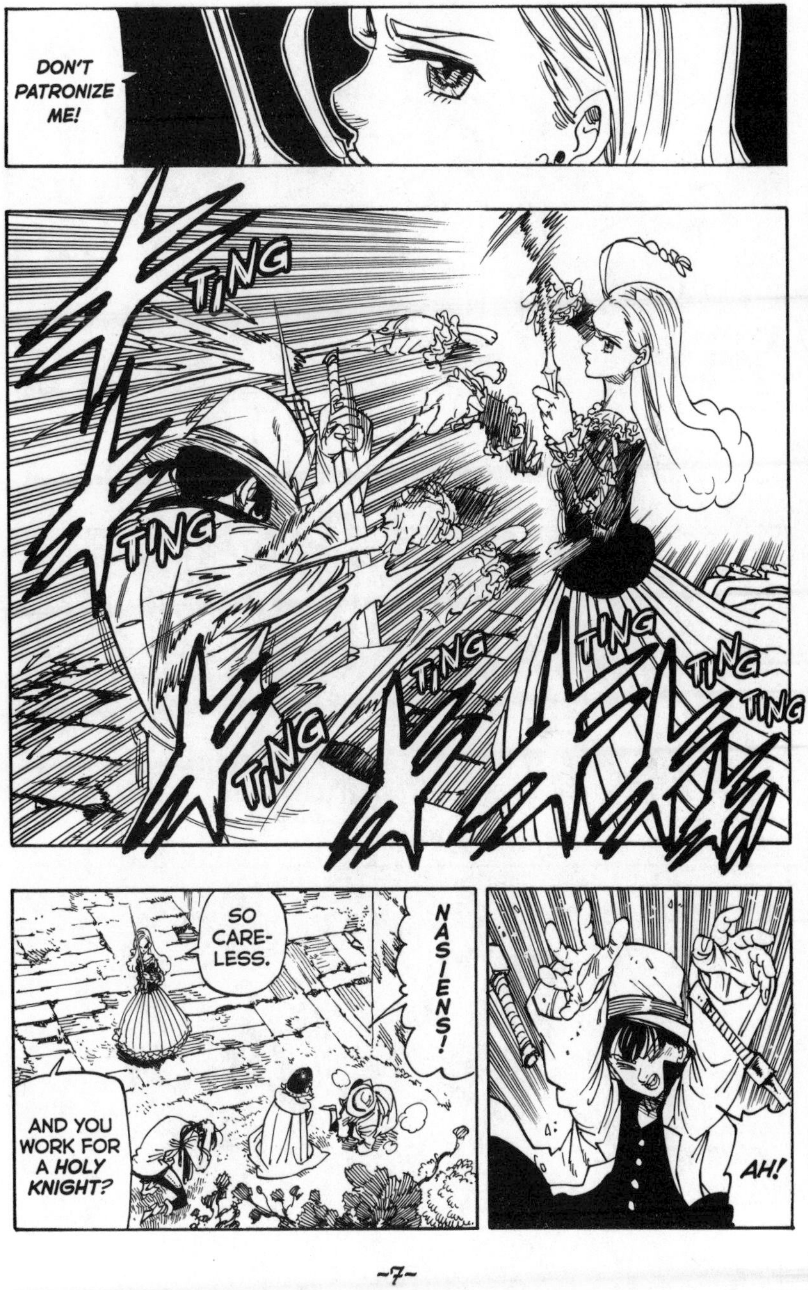
DON'T PATRONIZE ME!
TING
TING
TING
TING
TING
TING
TING
TING
AH!
NASIENS!
SO CARE-LESS.
AND YOU WORK FOR A HOLY KNIGHT?

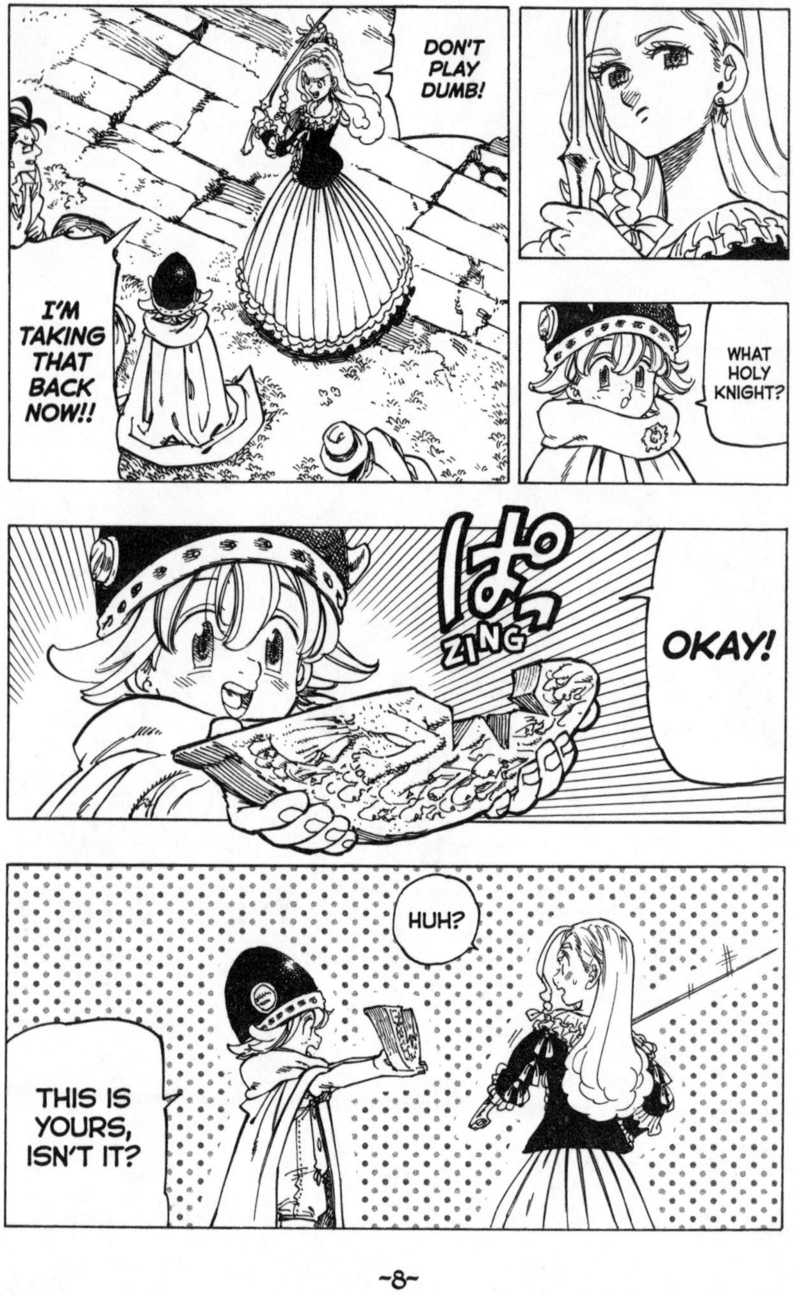
WHAT HOLY KNIGHT?
DON'T PLAY DUMB!
I'M TAKING THAT BACK NOW!!
ぱっ
ZING
OKAY!
HUH?
THIS IS YOURS, ISN'T IT?

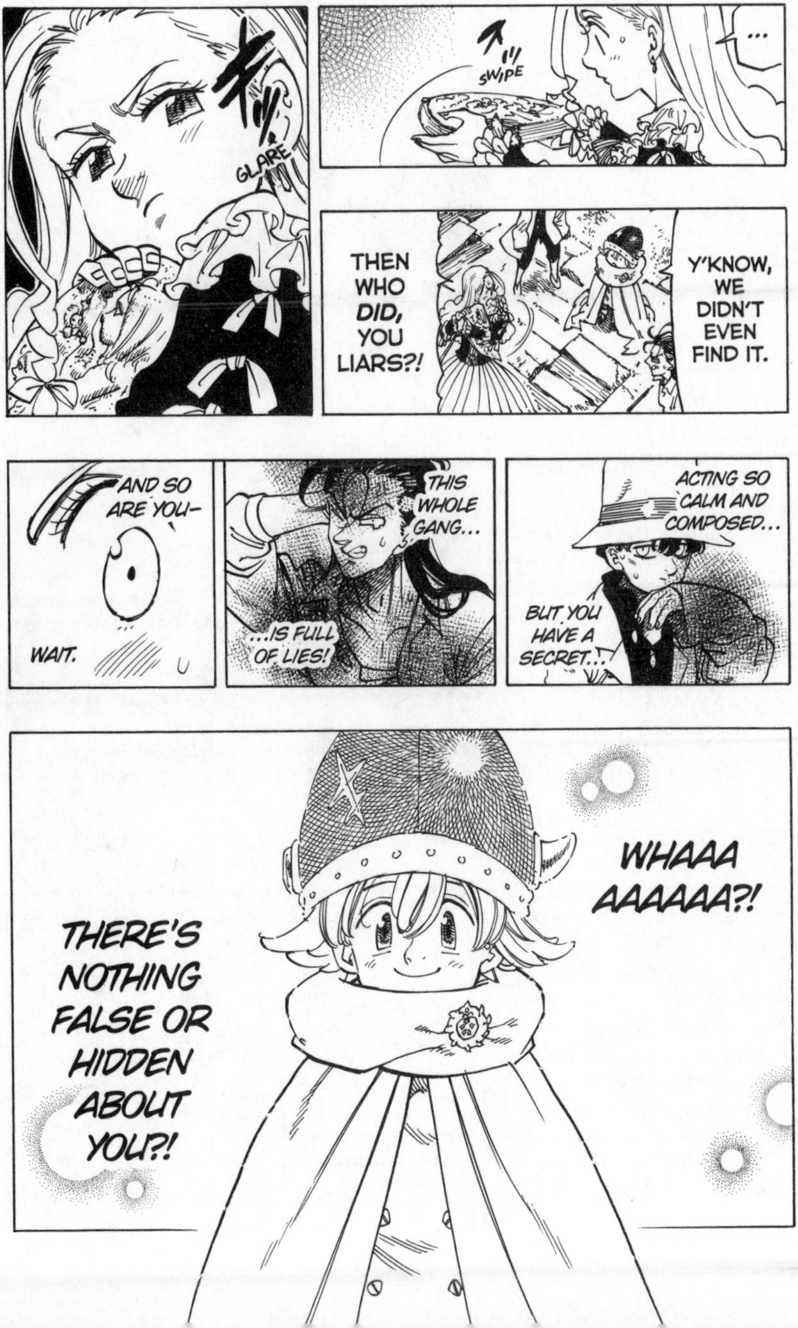
...
SWIPE
Y'KNOW, WE DIDN'T EVEN FIND IT.
THEN WHO DID, YOU LIARS?!
GLARE
ACTING SO CALM AND COMPOSED...
BUT YOU HAVE A SECRET...
THIS WHOLE GANG...
...IS FULL OF LIES!
AND SO ARE YOU-
WAIT.
WHAAA AAAAAA?!
THERE'S NOTHING FALSE OR HIDDEN ABOUT YOU?!

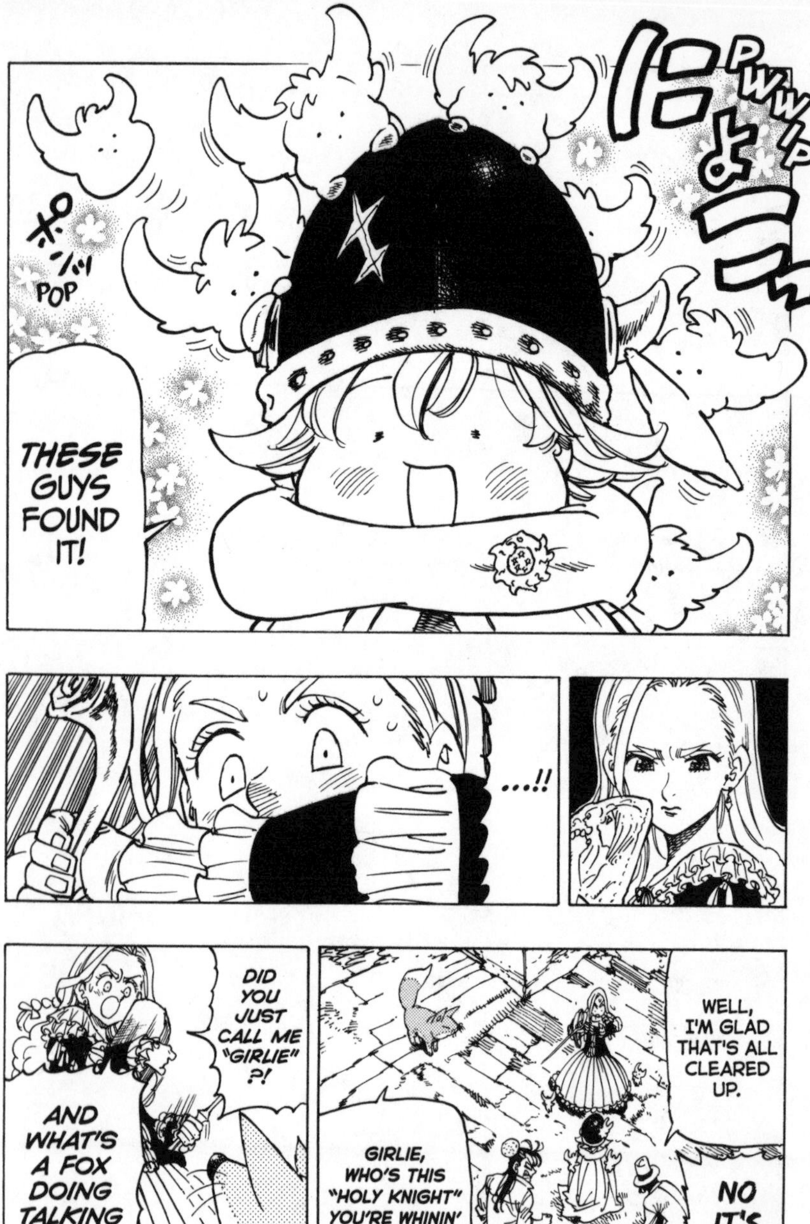

PWWP
POP
THESE GUYS FOUND IT!
...!!
WELL, I'M GLAD THAT'S ALL CLEARED UP.
NO IT'S NOT!!
GIRLIE, WHO'S THIS "HOLY KNIGHT" YOU'RE WHININ' ABOUT?
DID YOU JUST CALL ME "GIRLIE"?!
AND WHAT'S A FOX DOING TALKING AT ALL?!

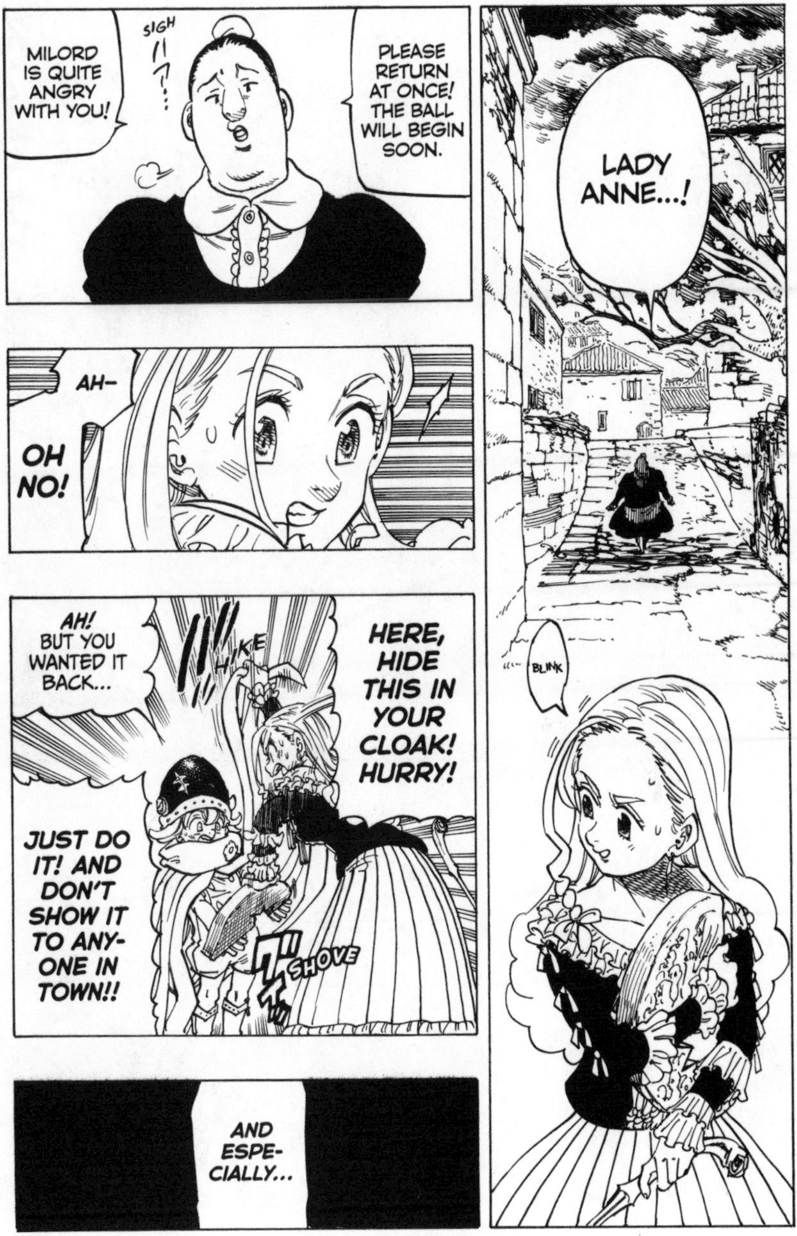
LADY ANNE...!
BLINK
PLEASE RETURN AT ONCE! THE BALL WILL BEGIN SOON.
SIGH
MILORD IS QUITE ANGRY WITH YOU!
AH–
OH NO!
HERE, HIDE THIS IN YOUR CLOAK! HURRY!
HIKE
AH! BUT YOU WANTED IT BACK...
JUST DO IT! AND DON'T SHOW IT TO ANY-ONE IN TOWN!!
SHOVE
AND ESPE-CIALLY...

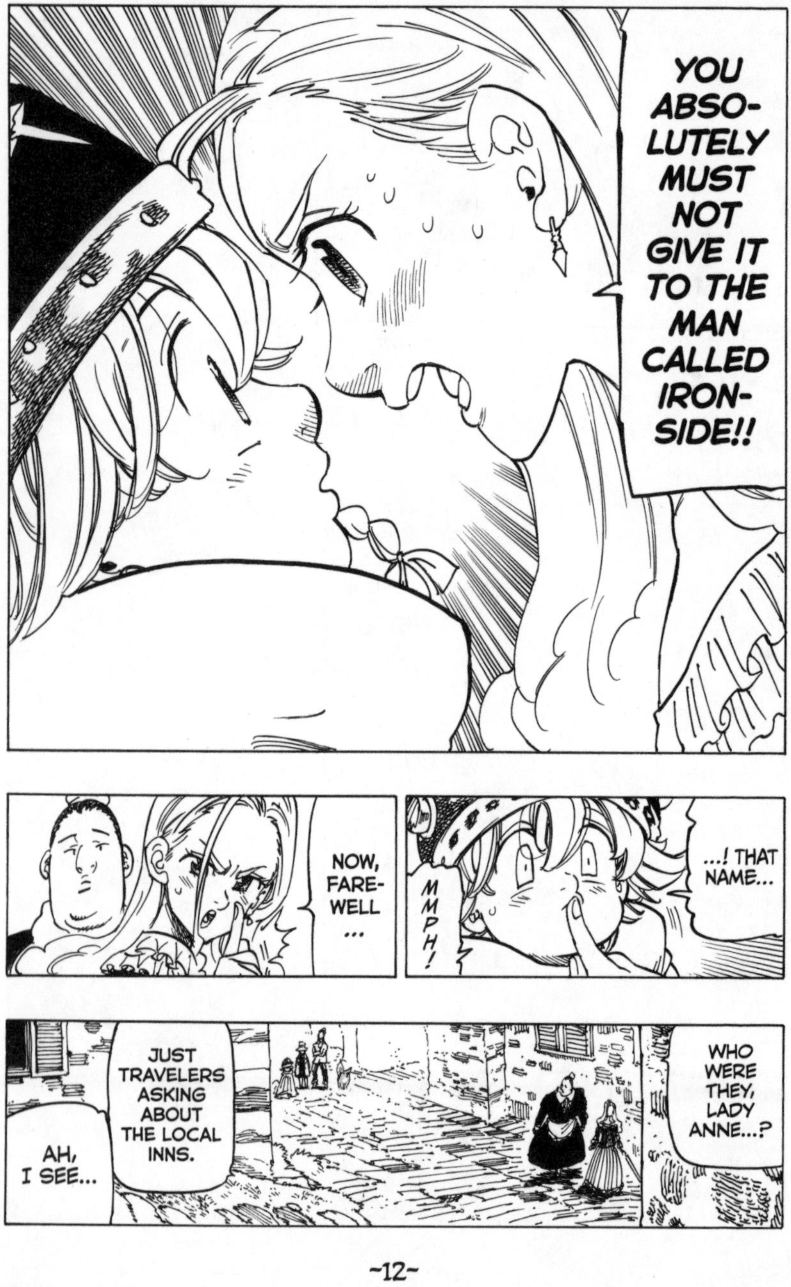
YOU ABSO-LUTELY MUST NOT GIVE IT TO THE MAN CALLED IRON-SIDE!!
...! THAT NAME...
MMPH!
NOW, FARE-WELL ...
WHO WERE THEY, LADY ANNE...?
JUST TRAVELERS ASKING ABOUT THE LOCAL INNS.
AH, I SEE...

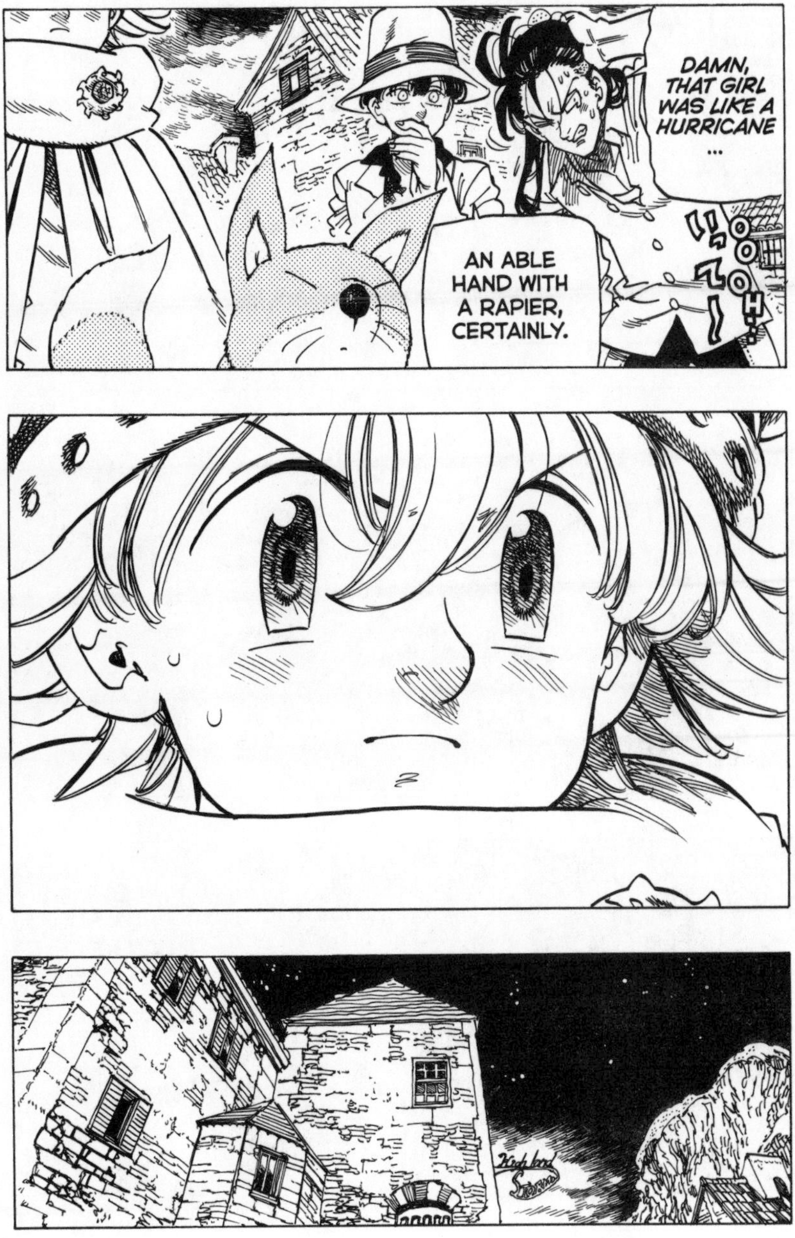
DAMN, THAT GIRL WAS LIKE A HURRICANE ...
OOOH!
AN ABLE HAND WITH A RAPIER, CERTAINLY.
Highland

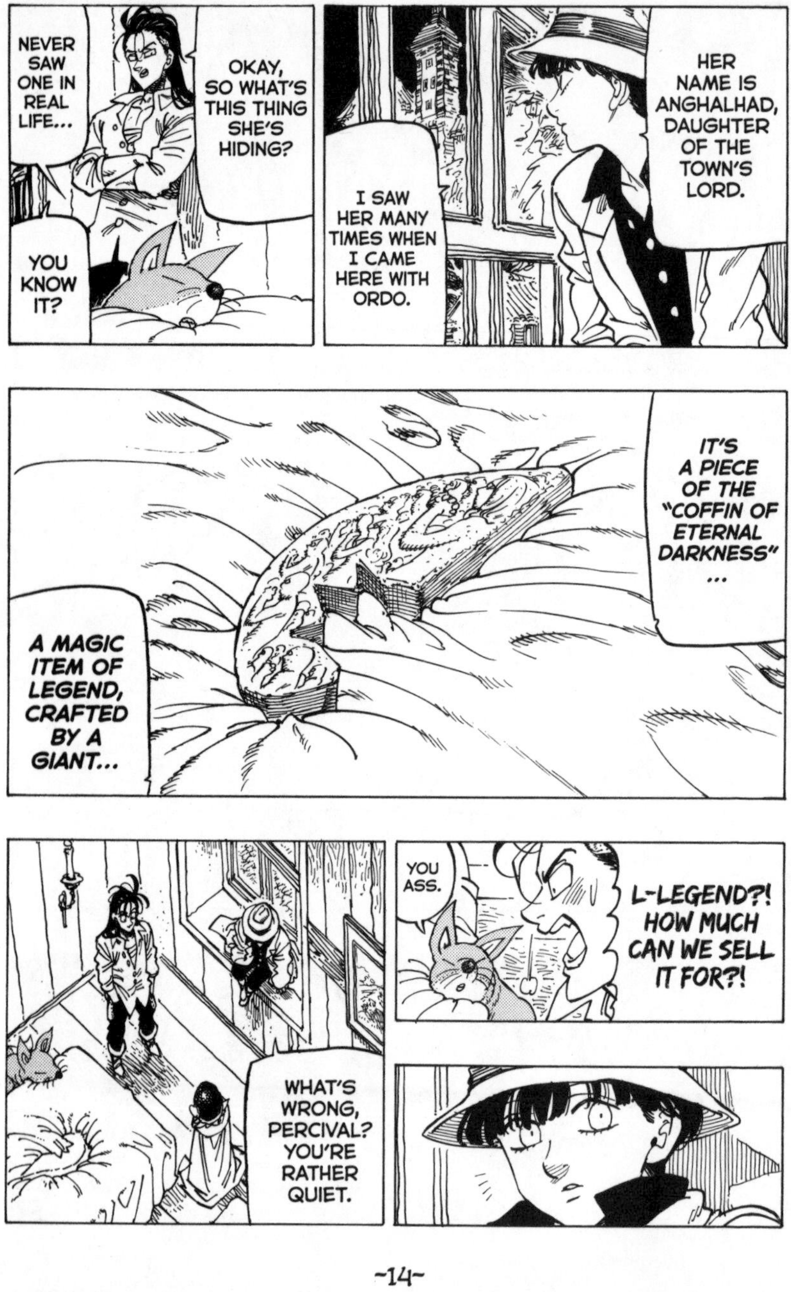
HER NAME IS ANGHALHAD, DAUGHTER OF THE TOWN'S LORD.
I SAW HER MANY TIMES WHEN I CAME HERE WITH ORDO.
OKAY, SO WHAT'S THIS THING SHE'S HIDING?
NEVER SAW ONE IN REAL LIFE...
YOU KNOW IT?
IT'S A PIECE OF THE "COFFIN OF ETERNAL DARKNESS"...
A MAGIC ITEM OF LEGEND, CRAFTED BY A GIANT...
L-LEGEND?! HOW MUCH CAN WE SELL IT FOR?!
YOU ASS.
WHAT'S WRONG, PERCIVAL? YOU'RE RATHER QUIET.

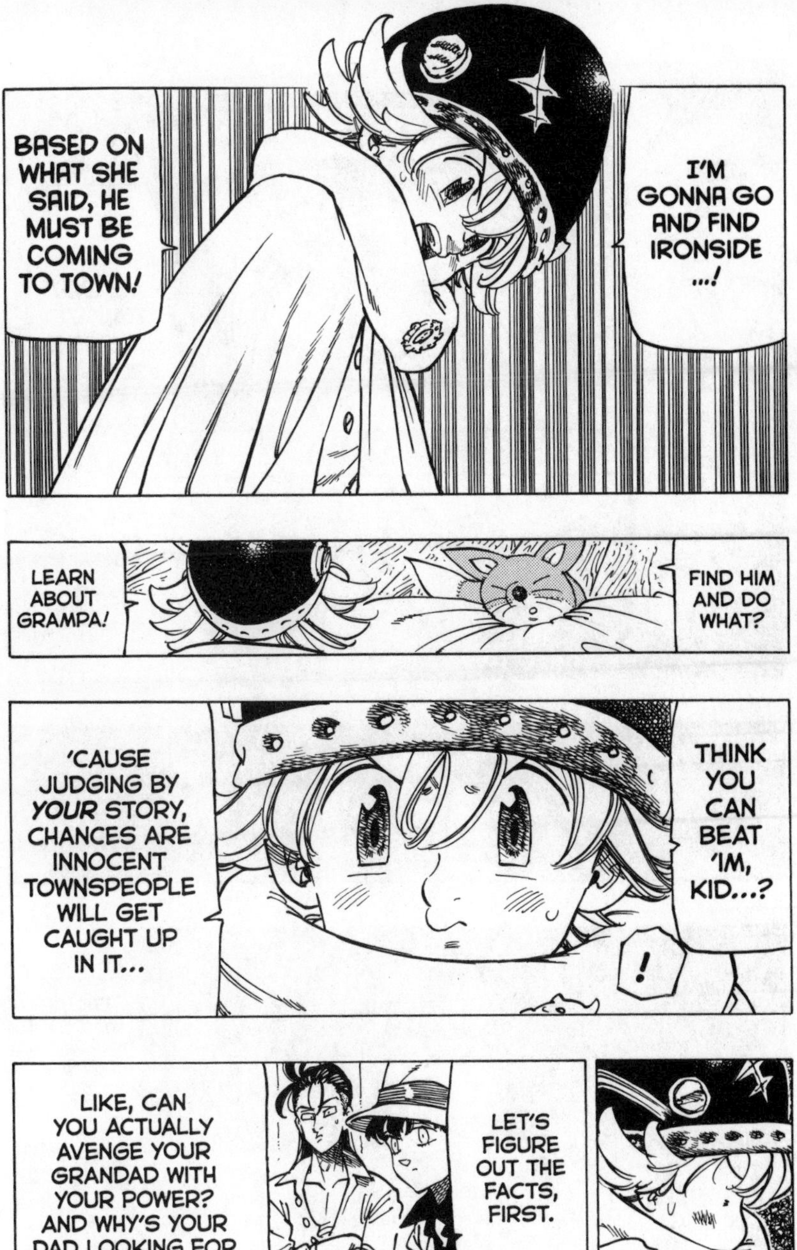
I'M GONNA GO AND FIND IRONSIDE ...!
BASED ON WHAT SHE SAID, HE MUST BE COMING TO TOWN!
FIND HIM AND DO WHAT?
LEARN ABOUT GRAMPA!
THINK YOU CAN BEAT 'IM, KID...?
!
'CAUSE JUDGING BY *YOUR* STORY, CHANCES ARE INNOCENT TOWNSPEOPLE WILL GET CAUGHT UP IN IT...
...
LET'S FIGURE OUT THE FACTS, FIRST.
LIKE, CAN YOU ACTUALLY AVENGE YOUR GRANDAD WITH YOUR POWER? AND WHY'S YOUR DAD LOOKING FOR THE COFFIN?

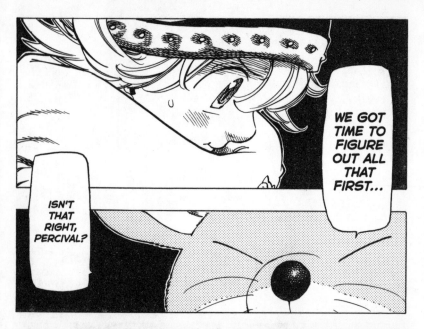

WE GOT TIME TO FIGURE OUT ALL THAT FIRST...

ISN'T THAT RIGHT, PERCIVAL?

ENOUGH WITH YOUR WANDERING OUTSIDE!

WE'VE NO IDEA WHAT DISASTER MAY BEFALL OUR TOWN!

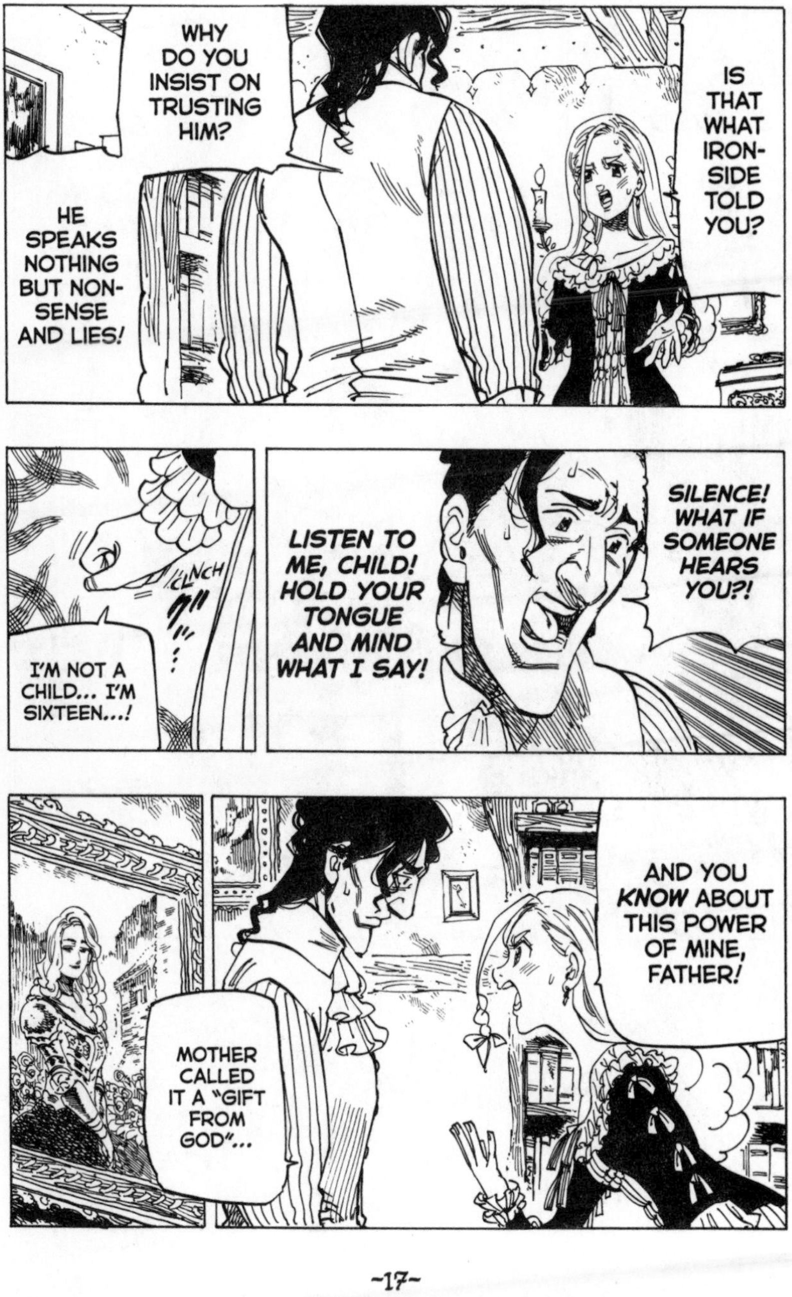
IS THAT WHAT IRON-SIDE TOLD YOU?
WHY DO YOU INSIST ON TRUSTING HIM?
HE SPEAKS NOTHING BUT NON-SENSE AND LIES!
SILENCE! WHAT IF SOMEONE HEARS YOU?!
LISTEN TO ME, CHILD! HOLD YOUR TONGUE AND MIND WHAT I SAY!
CLNCH
I'M NOT A CHILD... I'M SIXTEEN...!
AND YOU *KNOW* ABOUT THIS POWER OF MINE, FATHER!
MOTHER CALLED IT A "GIFT FROM GOD"...

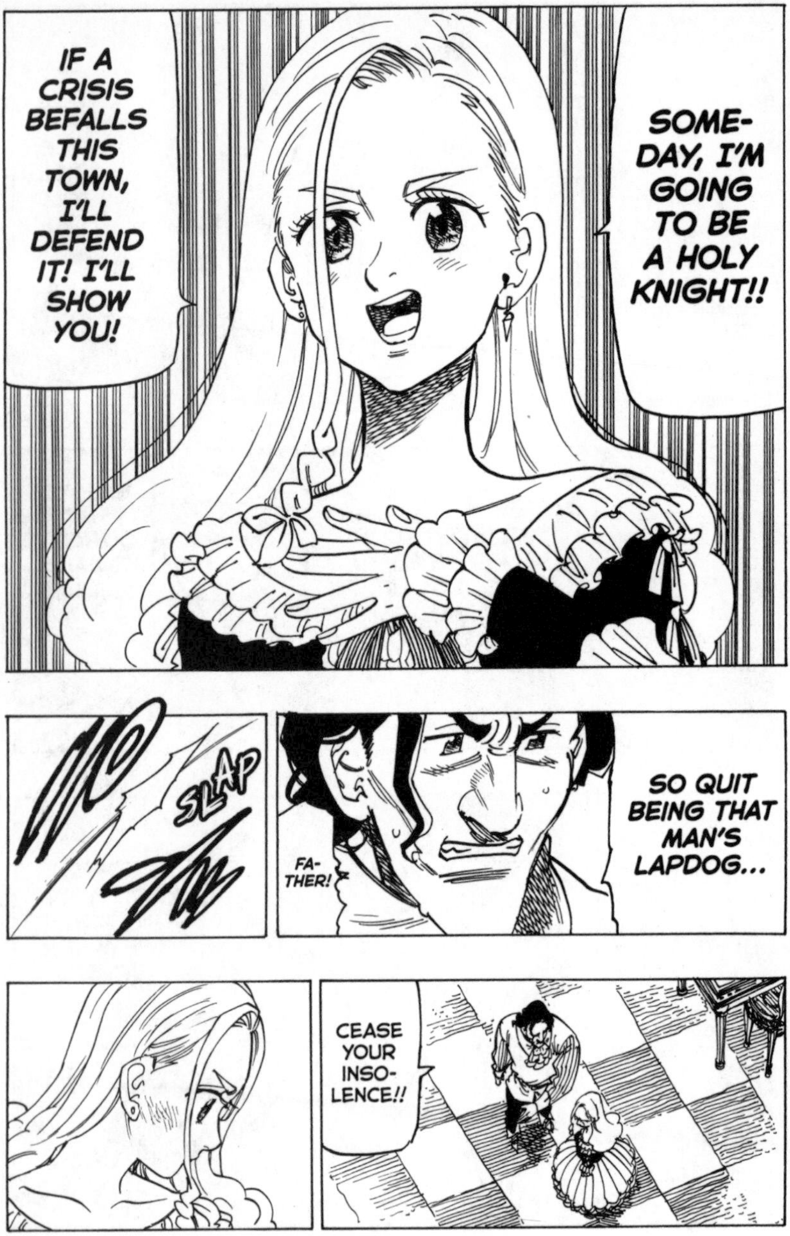
SOME-DAY, I'M GOING TO BE A HOLY KNIGHT!!
IF A CRISIS BEFALLS THIS TOWN, I'LL DEFEND IT! I'LL SHOW YOU!
SO QUIT BEING THAT MAN'S LAPDOG...
FA-THER!
SLAP
CEASE YOUR INSO-LENCE!!

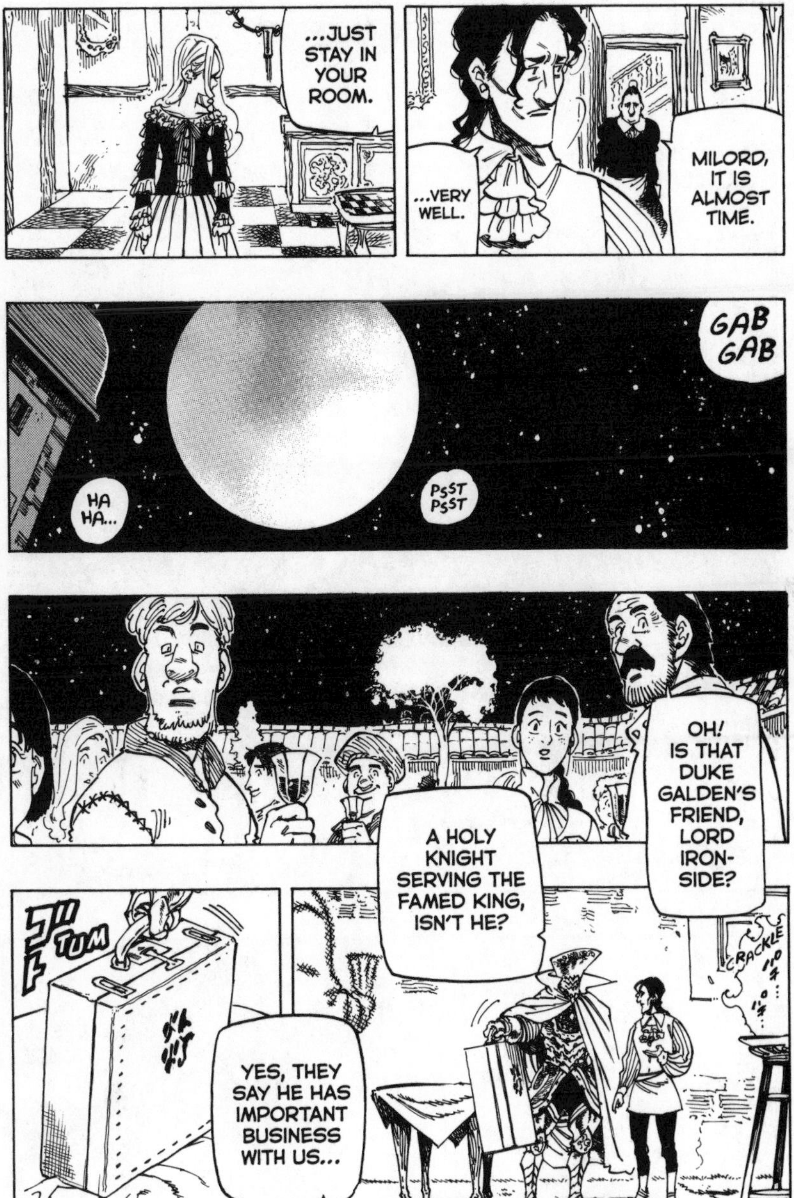
MILORD, IT IS ALMOST TIME.
...VERY WELL.
...JUST STAY IN YOUR ROOM.
GAB GAB
PSST PSST
HA HA...
OH! IS THAT DUKE GALDEN'S FRIEND, LORD IRON-SIDE?
A HOLY KNIGHT SERVING THE FAMED KING, ISN'T HE?
CRACKLE
YES, THEY SAY HE HAS IMPORTANT BUSINESS WITH US...
TUM

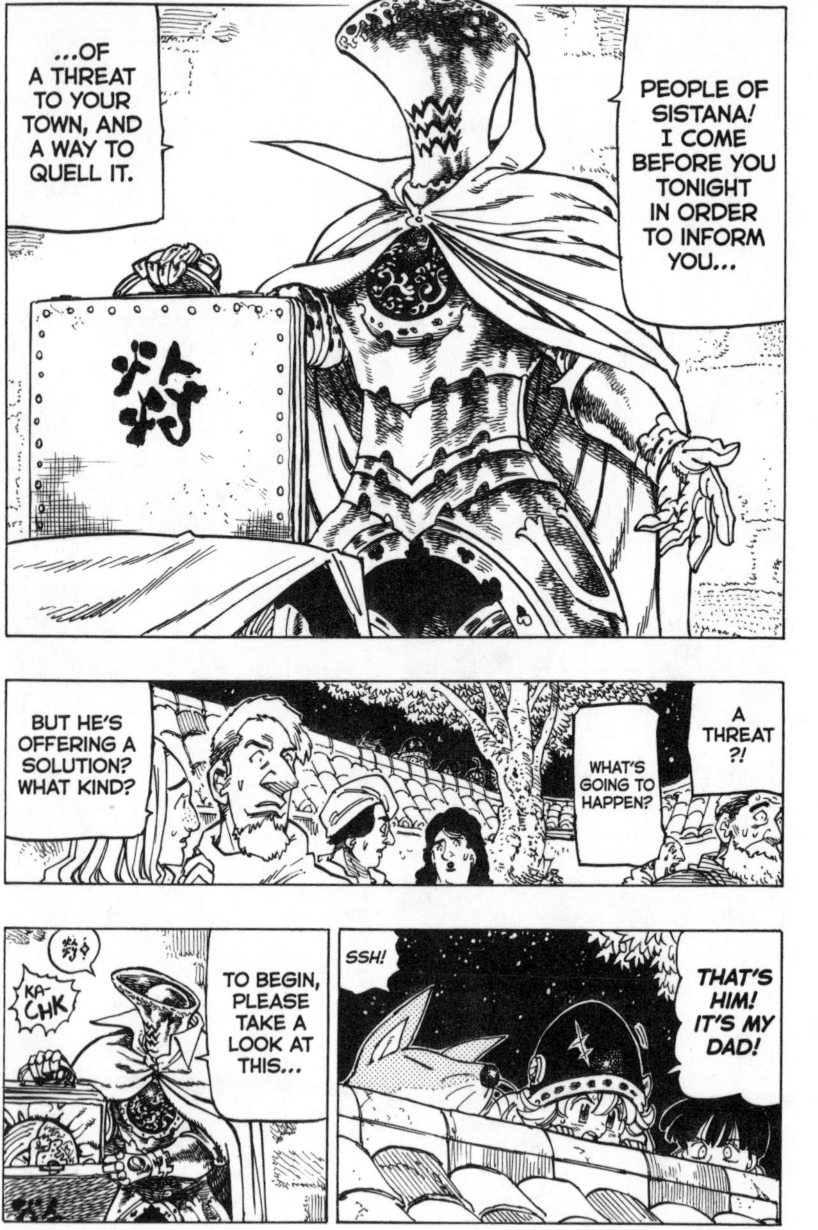
PEOPLE OF SISTANA! I COME BEFORE YOU TONIGHT IN ORDER TO INFORM YOU...
...OF A THREAT TO YOUR TOWN, AND A WAY TO QUELL IT.
A THREAT?!
WHAT'S GOING TO HAPPEN?
BUT HE'S OFFERING A SOLUTION? WHAT KIND?
THAT'S HIM! IT'S MY DAD!
SSH!
TO BEGIN, PLEASE TAKE A LOOK AT THIS...
KA-CHK

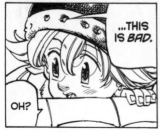

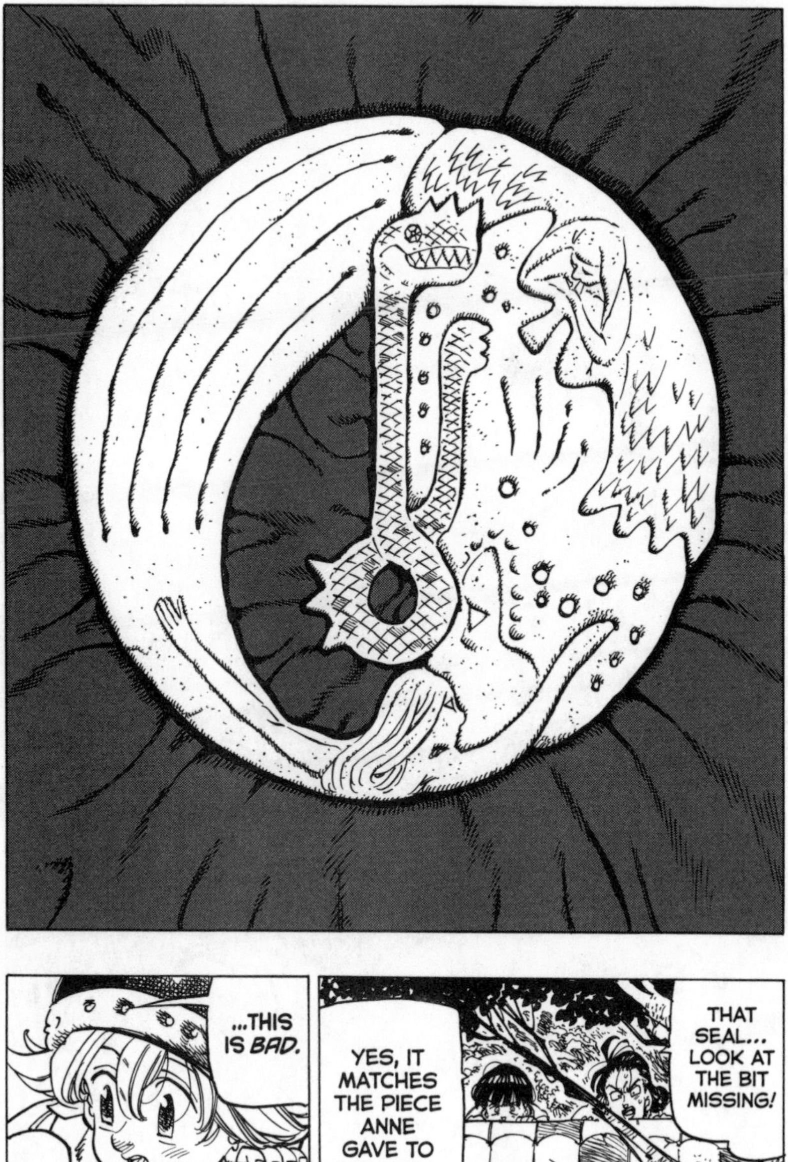
THAT SEAL... LOOK AT THE BIT MISSING!
YES, IT MATCHES THE PIECE ANNE GAVE TO PERCIVAL.
...THIS IS *BAD.*
OH?

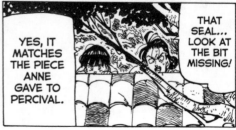

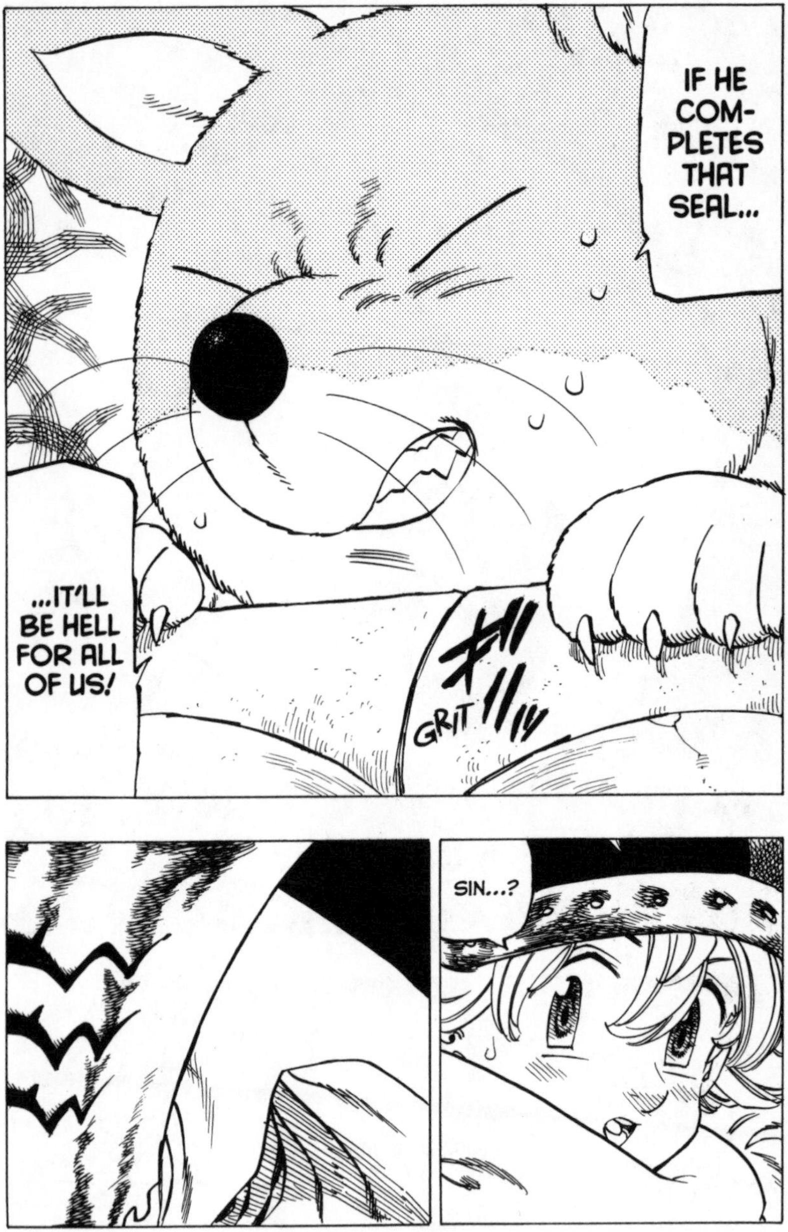
IF HE COMPLETES THAT SEAL...
...IT'LL BE HELL FOR ALL OF US!
GRIT
SIN...?

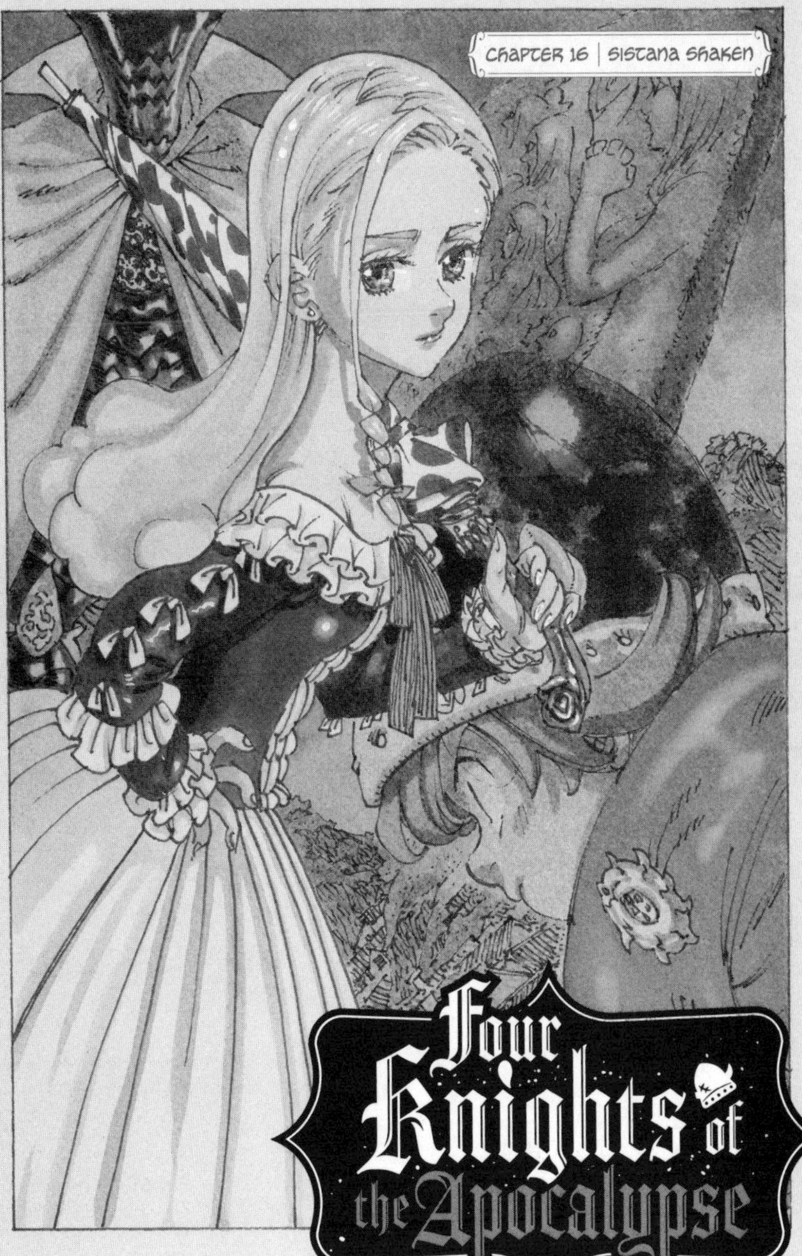

Chapter 16 | Sistana Shaken
Four Knights of the Apocalypse

On Magical Types

Magic is a mysterious power possessed by many living creatures in
Britannia. It can be subdivided into nine types. Rarely, a human may
possess two or more of the types—and supposedly, about one in 10,000
of those people may possess four or more. Such people are referred to
as the "Hero Type."

DESTROYER TYPE	Involves attacks using natural forces like fire or lightning, or the unnatural force known as Darkness.
SHIFTER TYPE	The ability to change the physical properties of an object. Lots of variety here: altering weight, making something harder or softer, or changing water into ice are all possible.
HEALER TYPE	The ability to heal wounds and illnesses. May have a variety of effects. Typically possessed by members of the Goddess Clan.
TRACKER TYPE	A number of powers have been demonstrated to be associated with this type, such as the ability to find the location of a given object or to "seek out" whether someone is telling the truth.
EMPATH TYPE	The power to control the hearts and minds of others, including manipulating memories. Potentially even more powerful than the Destroyer Type.
BEWITCHER TYPE	Magic that can induce visual or auditory hallucinations. Many members of the Fairy Clan possess this magic.
STEALTH TYPE	The power of the shadows: the ability to get close to people without them knowing it, or track a target's movements from afar.
ENCHANTER TYPE	Uses natural forces like fire or lightning, as well as unnatural forces—but unlike the Destroyer Type, this type imbues these powers into items and weapons.
ORACLE TYPE	The rarest of the nine powers, this grants the ability to foretell anything from the weather to future events.

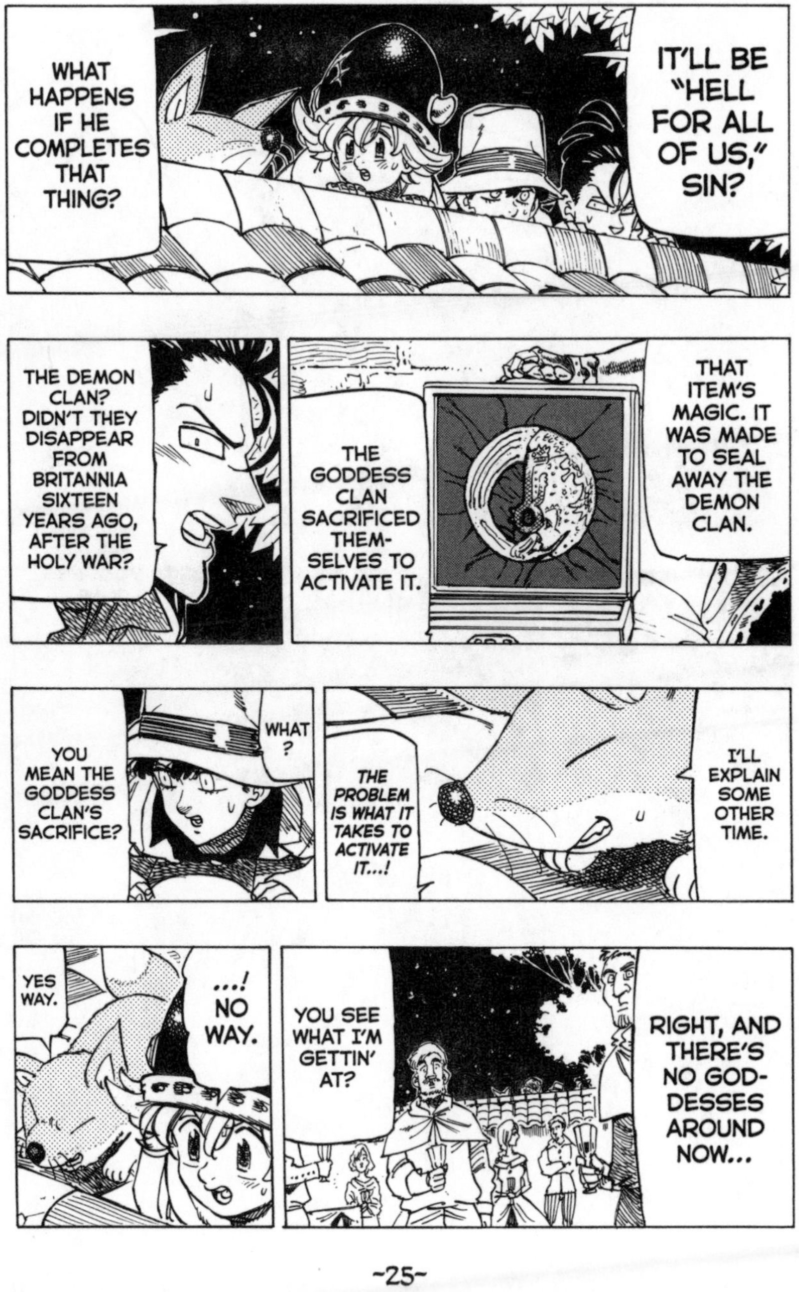
IT'LL BE "HELL FOR ALL OF US," SIN?
WHAT HAPPENS IF HE COMPLETES THAT THING?
THAT ITEM'S MAGIC. IT WAS MADE TO SEAL AWAY THE DEMON CLAN.
THE GODDESS CLAN SACRIFICED THEM-SELVES TO ACTIVATE IT.
THE DEMON CLAN? DIDN'T THEY DISAPPEAR FROM BRITANNIA SIXTEEN YEARS AGO, AFTER THE HOLY WAR?
I'LL EXPLAIN SOME OTHER TIME.
THE PROBLEM IS WHAT IT TAKES TO ACTIVATE IT...!
WHAT?
YOU MEAN THE GODDESS CLAN'S SACRIFICE?
RIGHT, AND THERE'S NO GOD-DESSES AROUND NOW...
YOU SEE WHAT I'M GETTIN' AT?
...! NO WAY.
YES WAY.

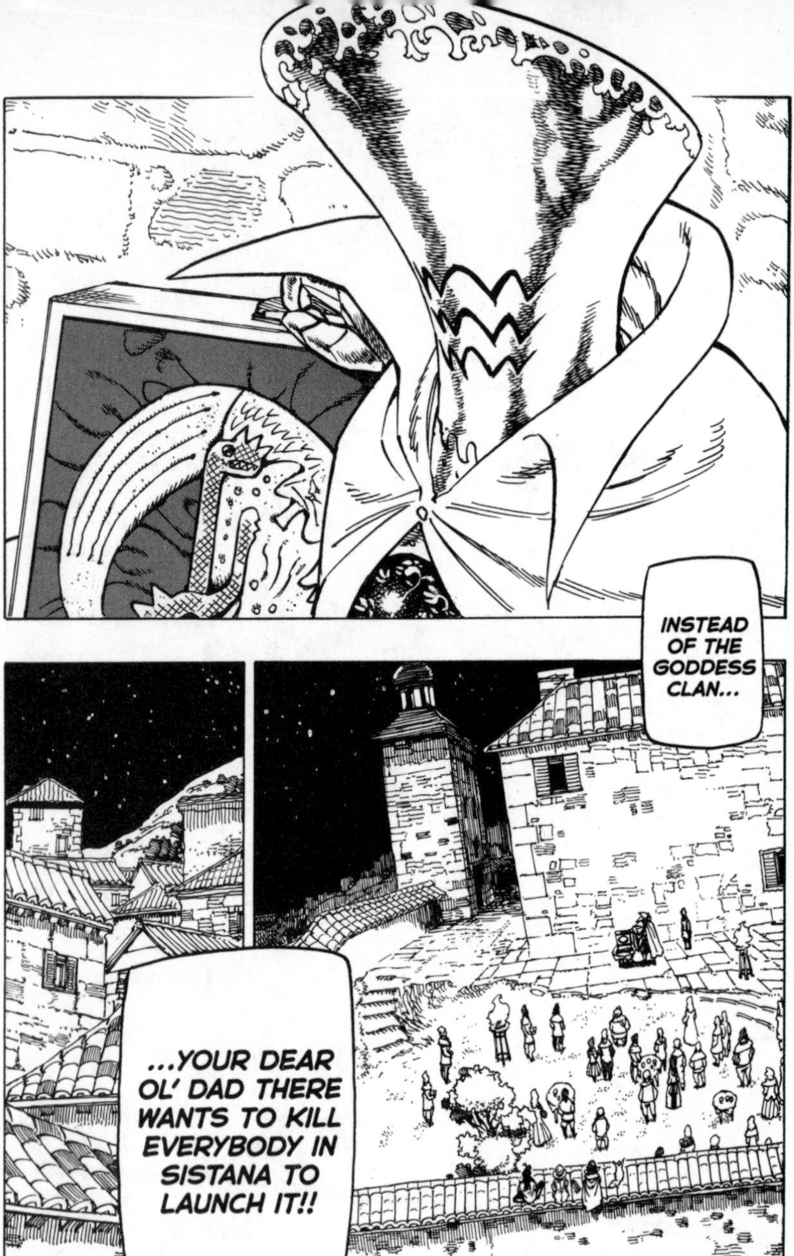
INSTEAD OF THE GODDESS CLAN...
...YOUR DEAR OL' DAD THERE WANTS TO KILL EVERYBODY IN SISTANA TO LAUNCH IT!!

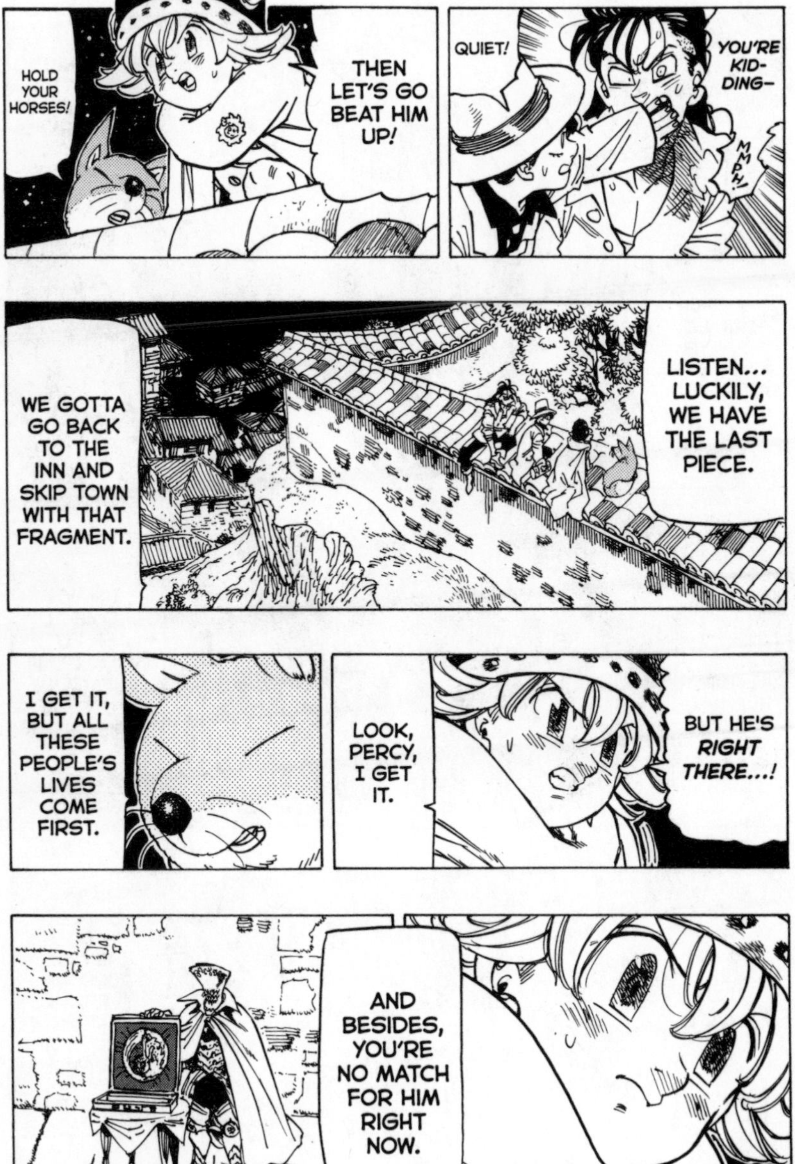
YOU'RE KIDDING—
QUIET!
MMPH!
THEN LET'S GO BEAT HIM UP!
HOLD YOUR HORSES!
LISTEN... LUCKILY, WE HAVE THE LAST PIECE.
WE GOTTA GO BACK TO THE INN AND SKIP TOWN WITH THAT FRAGMENT.
BUT HE'S *RIGHT THERE...!*
LOOK, PERCY, I GET IT.
I GET IT, BUT ALL THESE PEOPLE'S LIVES COME FIRST.
AND BESIDES, YOU'RE NO MATCH FOR HIM RIGHT NOW.

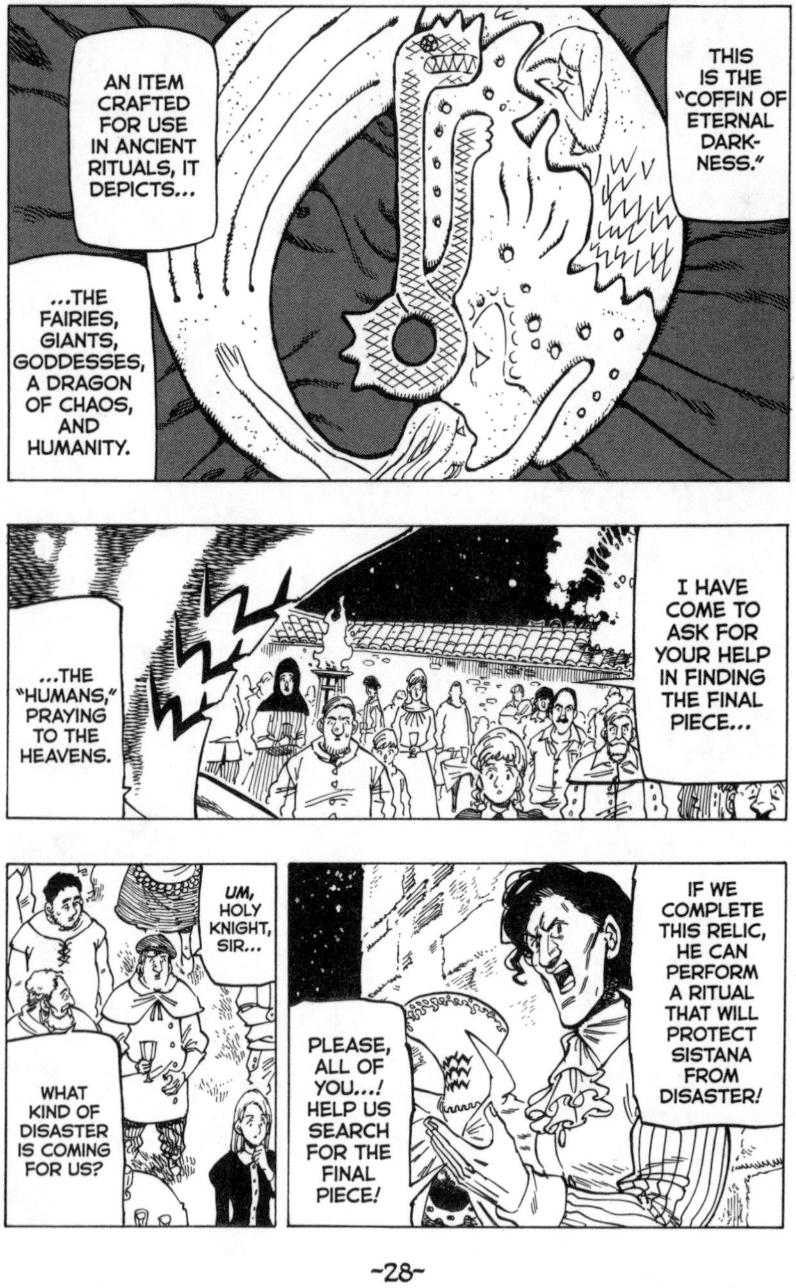
THIS IS THE "COFFIN OF ETERNAL DARK-NESS."
AN ITEM CRAFTED FOR USE IN ANCIENT RITUALS, IT DEPICTS...
...THE FAIRIES, GIANTS, GODDESSES, A DRAGON OF CHAOS, AND HUMANITY.
I HAVE COME TO ASK FOR YOUR HELP IN FINDING THE FINAL PIECE...
...THE "HUMANS," PRAYING TO THE HEAVENS.
IF WE COMPLETE THIS RELIC, HE CAN PERFORM A RITUAL THAT WILL PROTECT SISTANA FROM DISASTER!
PLEASE, ALL OF YOU...! HELP US SEARCH FOR THE FINAL PIECE!
UM, HOLY KNIGHT, SIR...
WHAT KIND OF DISASTER IS COMING FOR US?

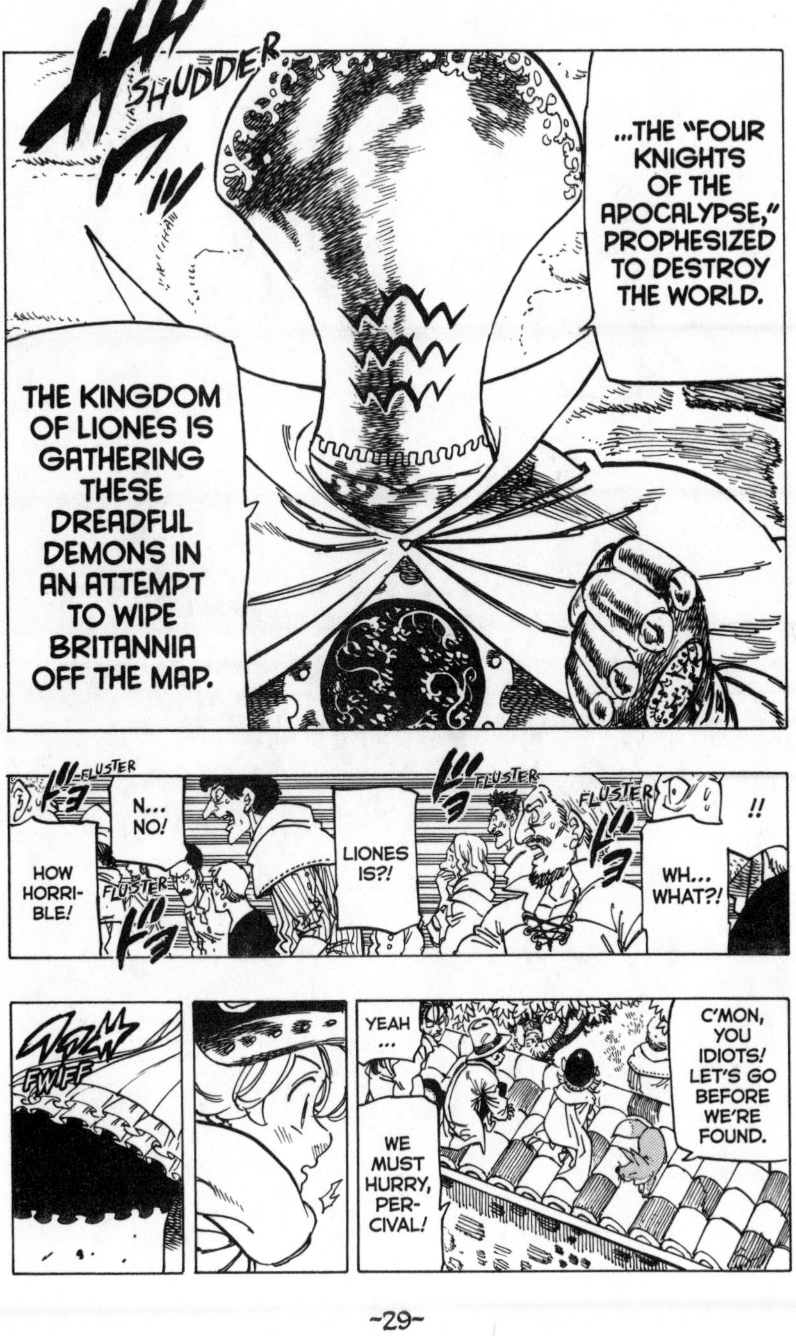
...THE "FOUR KNIGHTS OF THE APOCALYPSE," PROPHESIZED TO DESTROY THE WORLD.
SHUDDER
THE KINGDOM OF LIONES IS GATHERING THESE DREADFUL DEMONS IN AN ATTEMPT TO WIPE BRITANNIA OFF THE MAP.
!!
WH... WHAT?!
FLUSTER
FLUSTER
LIONES IS?!
N... NO!
FLUSTER
HOW HORRI-BLE!
FLUSTER
C'MON, YOU IDIOTS! LET'S GO BEFORE WE'RE FOUND.
YEAH ...
WE MUST HURRY, PER-CIVAL!
FWIFF

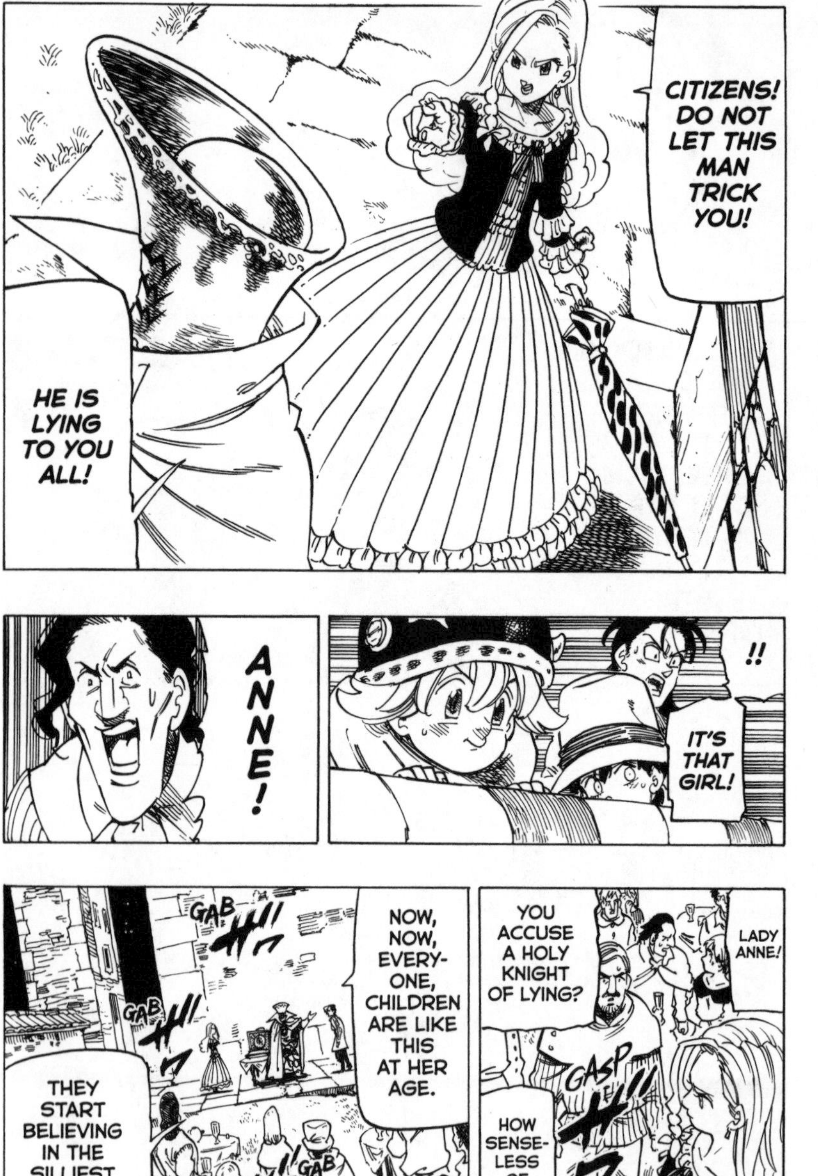
CITIZENS! DO NOT LET THIS MAN TRICK YOU!
HE IS LYING TO YOU ALL!
!!
IT'S THAT GIRL!
ANNE!
LADY ANNE!
YOU ACCUSE A HOLY KNIGHT OF LYING?
GASP
HOW SENSELESS OF YOU!
NOW, NOW, EVERYONE, CHILDREN ARE LIKE THIS AT HER AGE.
GAB
GAB
THEY START BELIEVING IN THE SILLIEST THINGS.
GAB

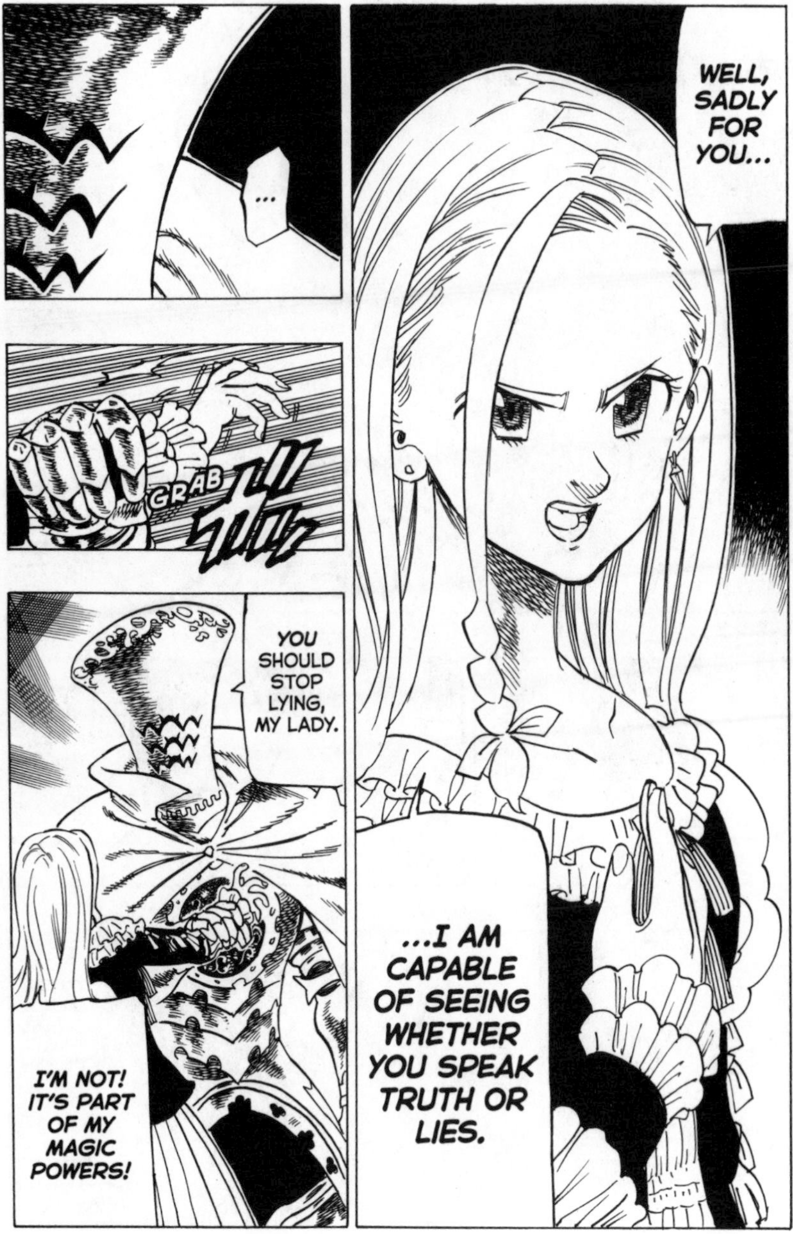
WELL, SADLY FOR YOU...
...I AM CAPABLE OF SEEING WHETHER YOU SPEAK TRUTH OR LIES.
...
GRAB
YOU SHOULD STOP LYING, MY LADY.
I'M NOT! IT'S PART OF MY MAGIC POWERS!

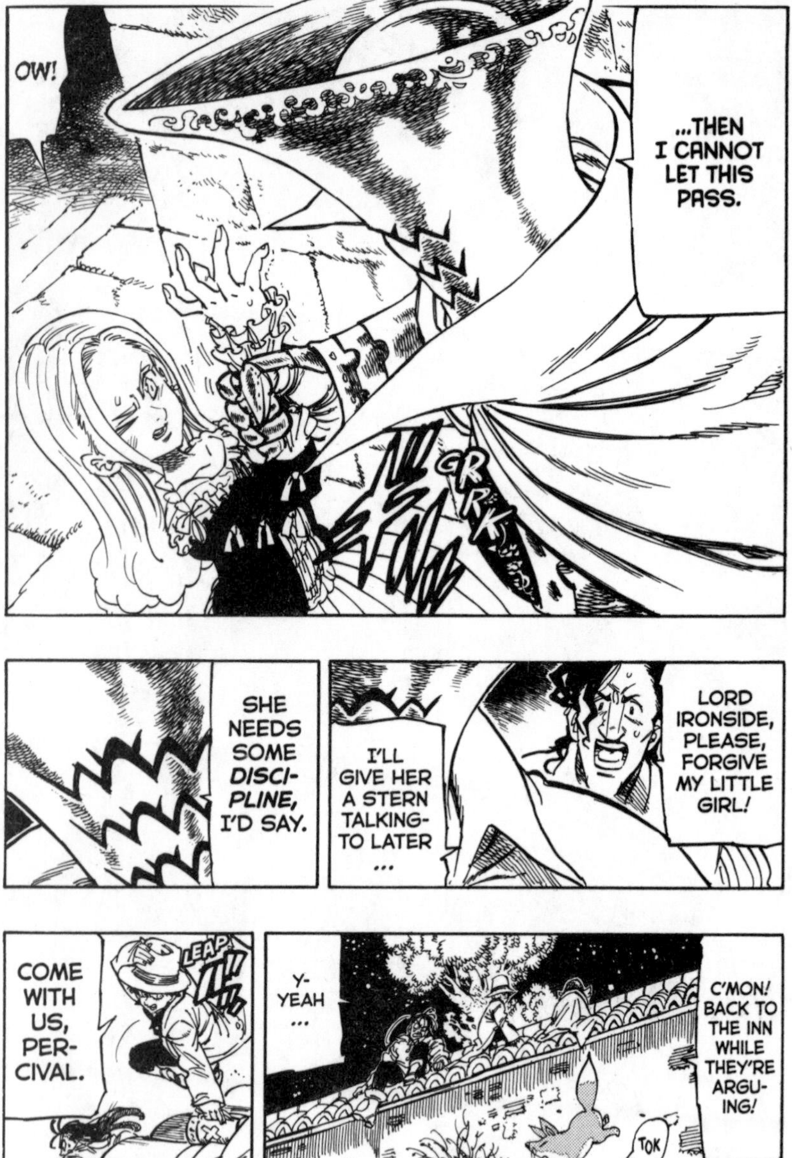
...THEN I CANNOT LET THIS PASS.
OW!
GRRK
LORD IRONSIDE, PLEASE, FORGIVE MY LITTLE GIRL!
I'LL GIVE HER A STERN TALKING-TO LATER ...
SHE NEEDS SOME *DISCIPLINE*, I'D SAY.
C'MON! BACK TO THE INN WHILE THEY'RE ARGUING!
Y-YEAH ...
TOK
LEAP
COME WITH US, PERCIVAL.

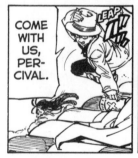

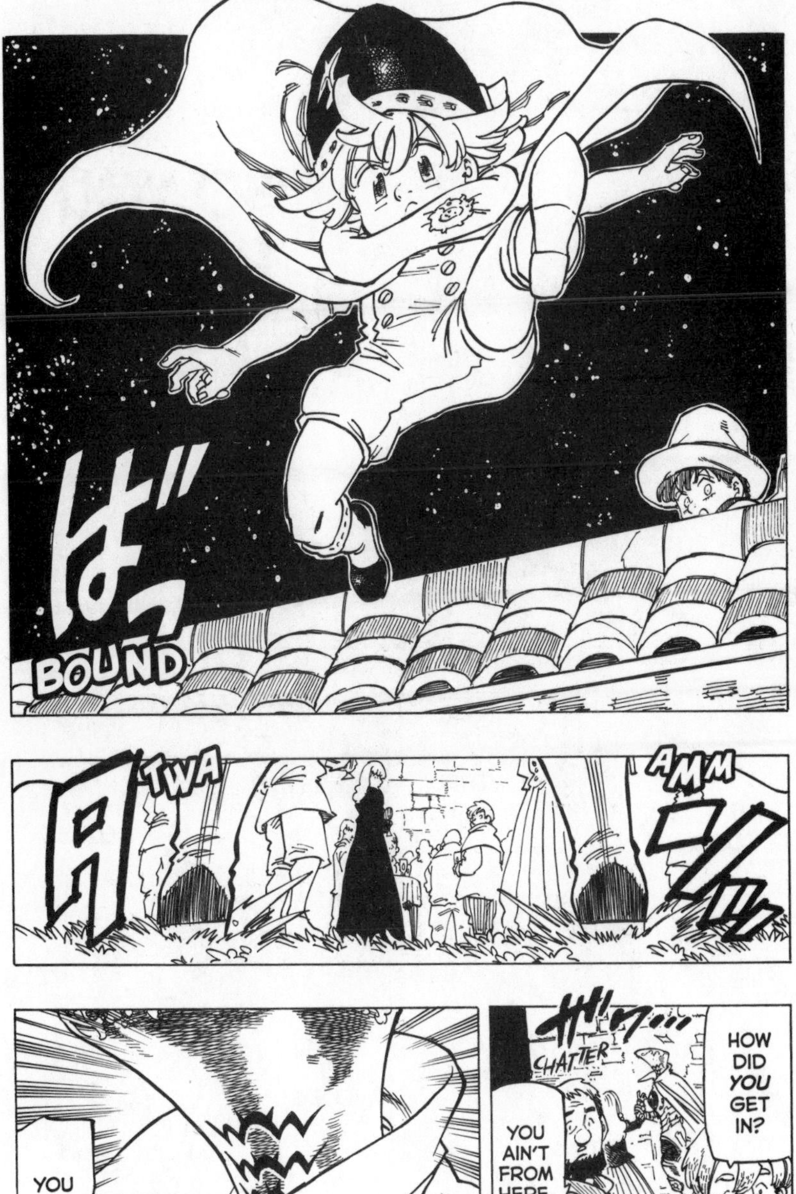
ばっ
BOUND
AMM
TWA
ザワ…
CHATTER
HOW DID *YOU* GET IN?
YOU AIN'T FROM HERE, EH?
YOU ...

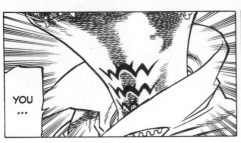

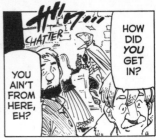

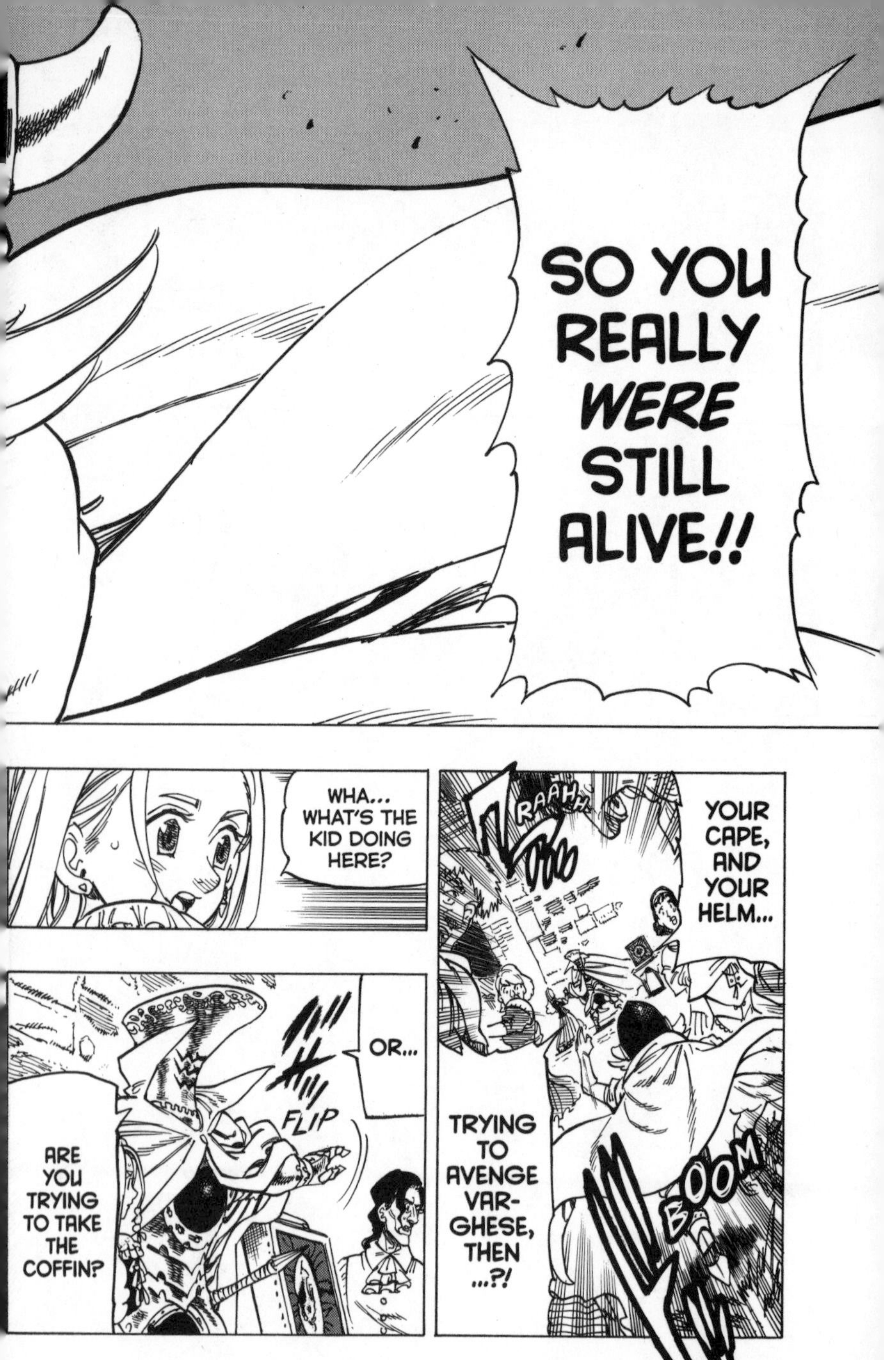
SO YOU REALLY *WERE* STILL ALIVE!!
RAAHH
YOUR CAPE, AND YOUR HELM...
TRYING TO AVENGE VAR-GHESE, THEN ...?!
BOOM
WHA... WHAT'S THE KID DOING HERE?
OR...
FLIP
ARE YOU TRYING TO TAKE THE COFFIN?

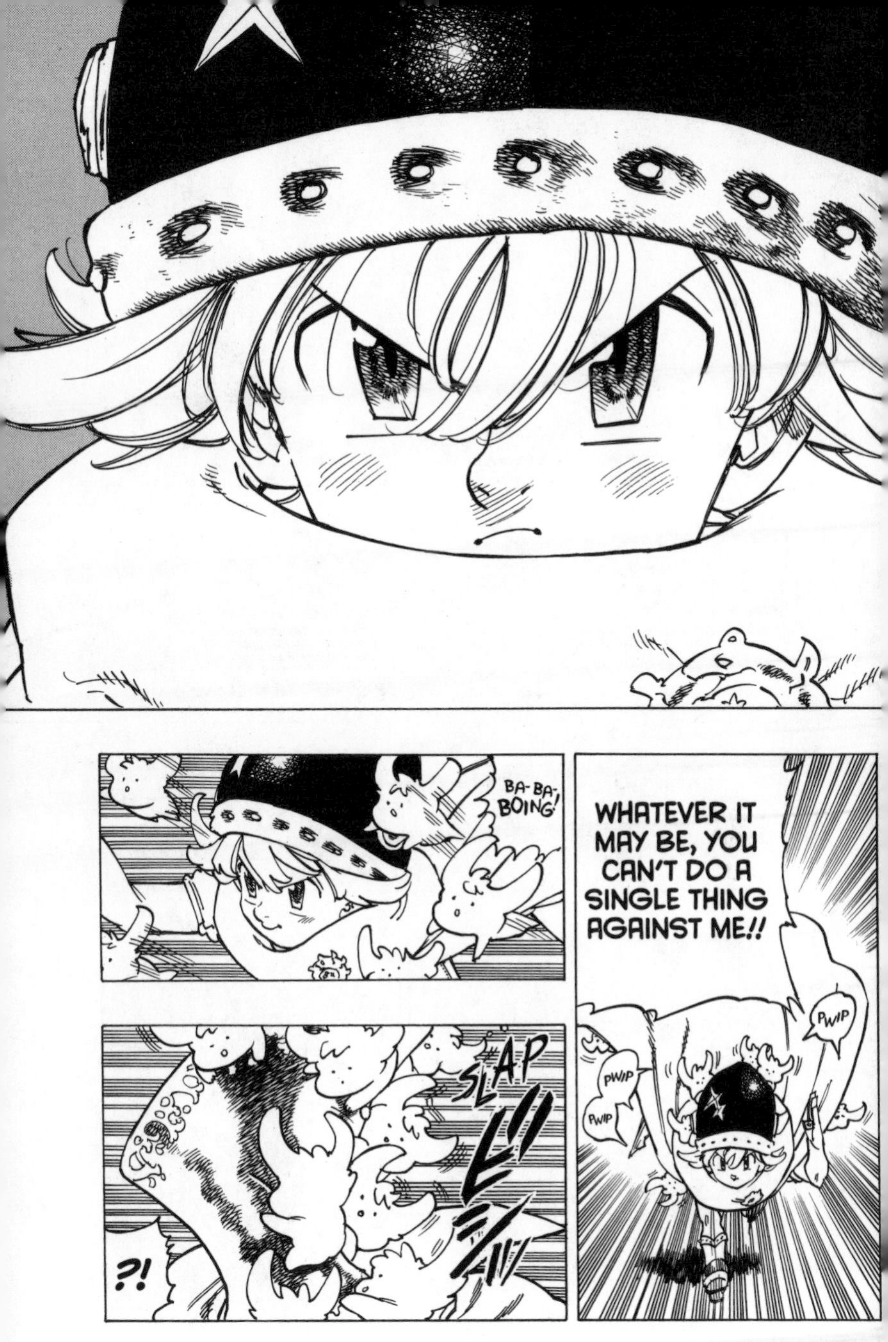
WHATEVER IT MAY BE, YOU CAN'T DO A SINGLE THING AGAINST ME!!
PWIP
PWIP
PWIP
BA-BA-BOING!
SLAP
?!

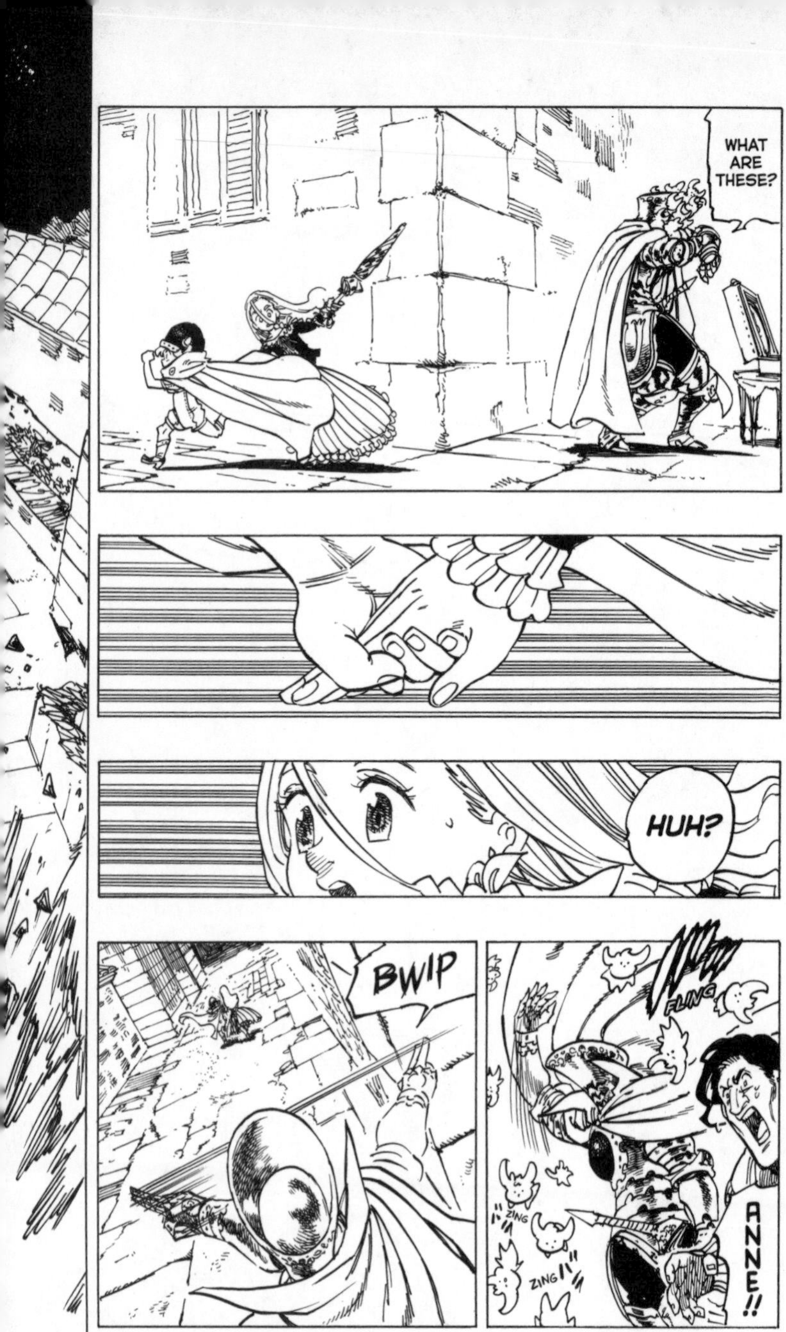
WHAT ARE THESE?
HUH?
FLING
ANNE!!
ZING
ZING
BWIP

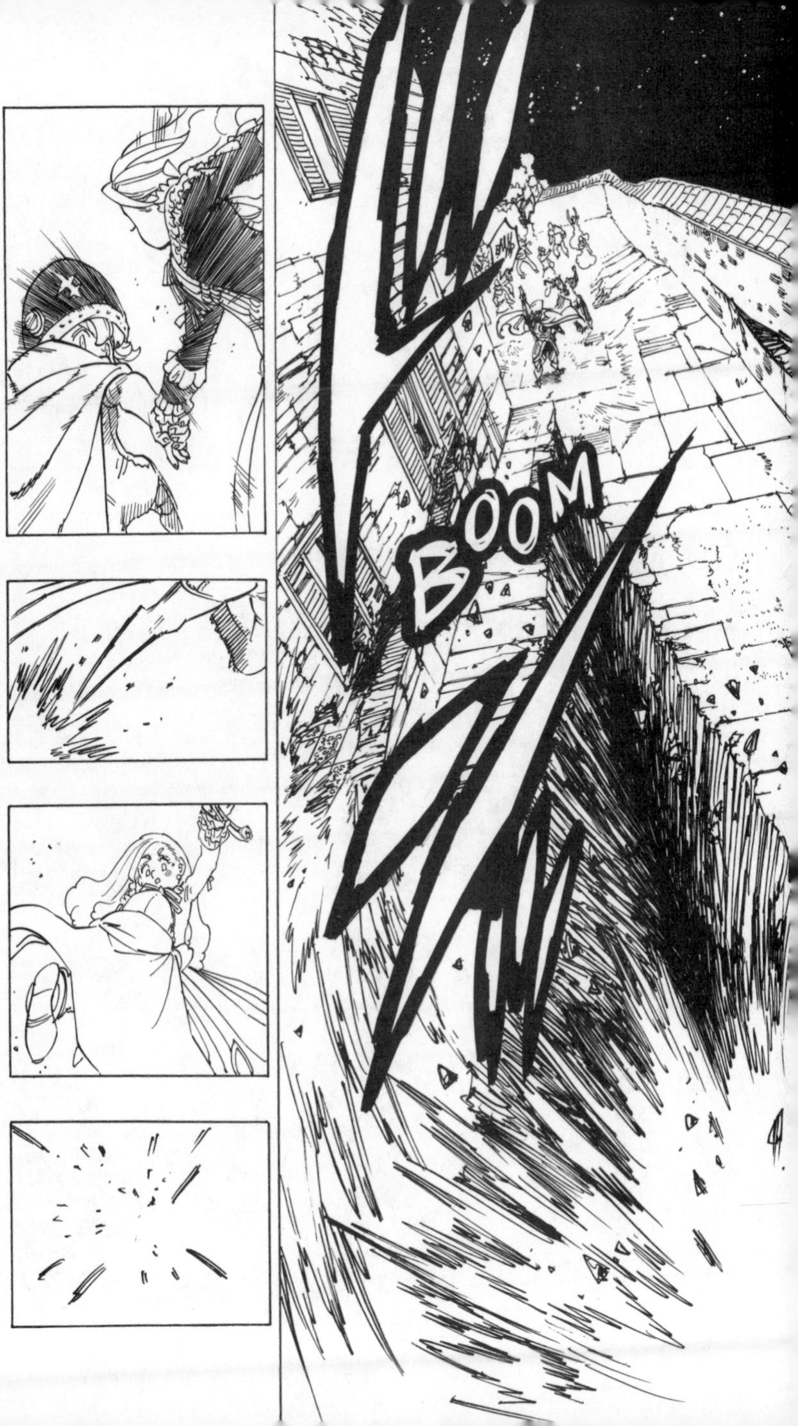
BOOM

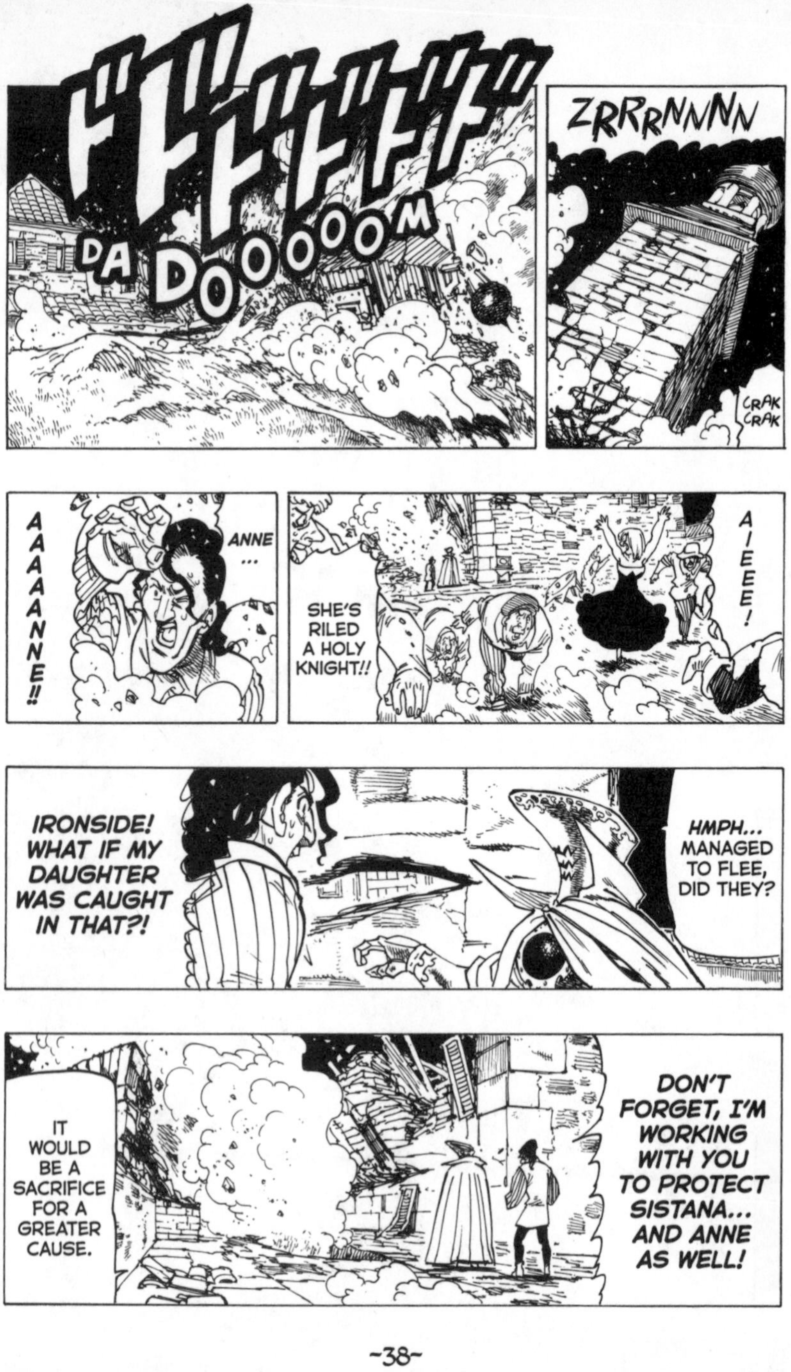
ZRRRNNNN
CRAK CRAK
DA DOOOOOM
AIEEE!
SHE'S RILED A HOLY KNIGHT!!
ANNE...
AAAAAANNE!!
HMPH... MANAGED TO FLEE, DID THEY?
IRONSIDE! WHAT IF MY DAUGHTER WAS CAUGHT IN THAT?!
DON'T FORGET, I'M WORKING WITH YOU TO PROTECT SISTANA... AND ANNE AS WELL!
IT WOULD BE A SACRIFICE FOR A GREATER CAUSE.

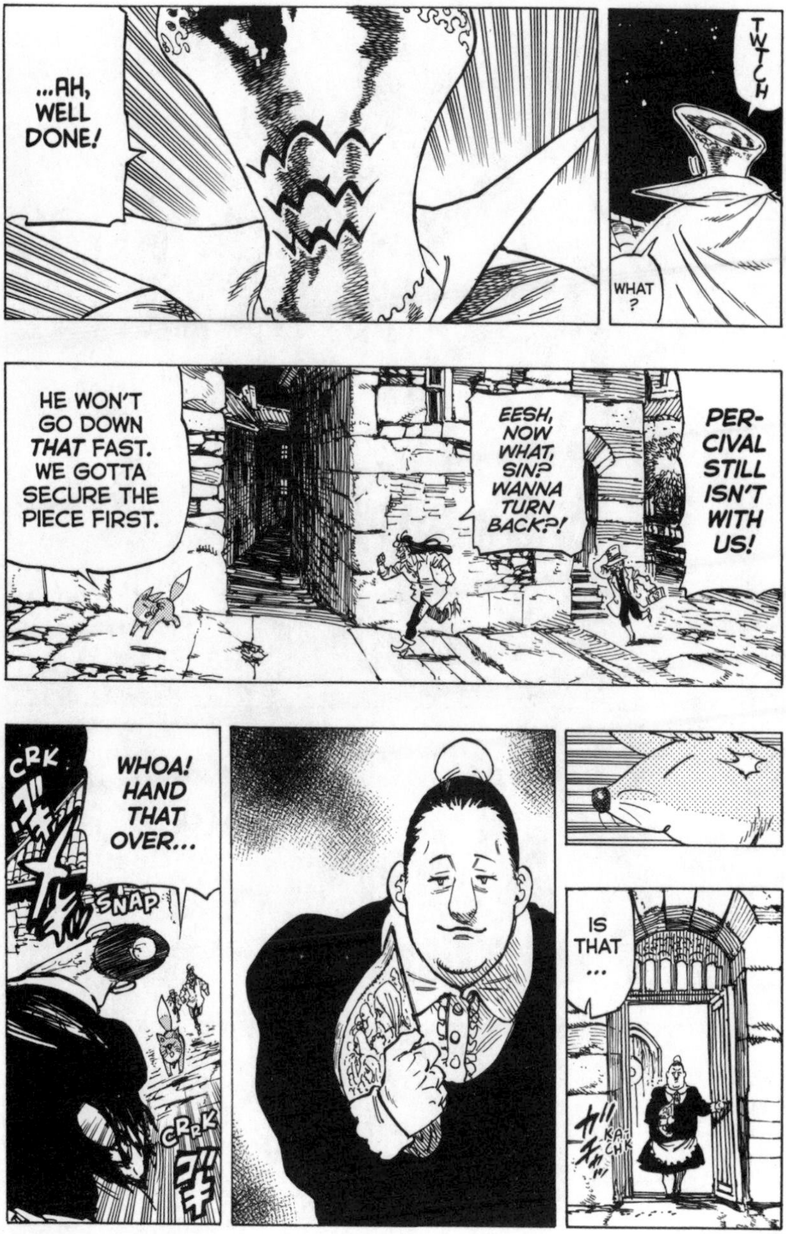
TWTCH
WHAT?
...AH, WELL DONE!
PERCIVAL STILL ISN'T WITH US!
EESH, NOW WHAT, SIN? WANNA TURN BACK?!
HE WON'T GO DOWN *THAT* FAST. WE GOTTA SECURE THE PIECE FIRST.
IS THAT ...
KA-CHK
WHOA! HAND THAT OVER...
CRK
SNAP
CRRK

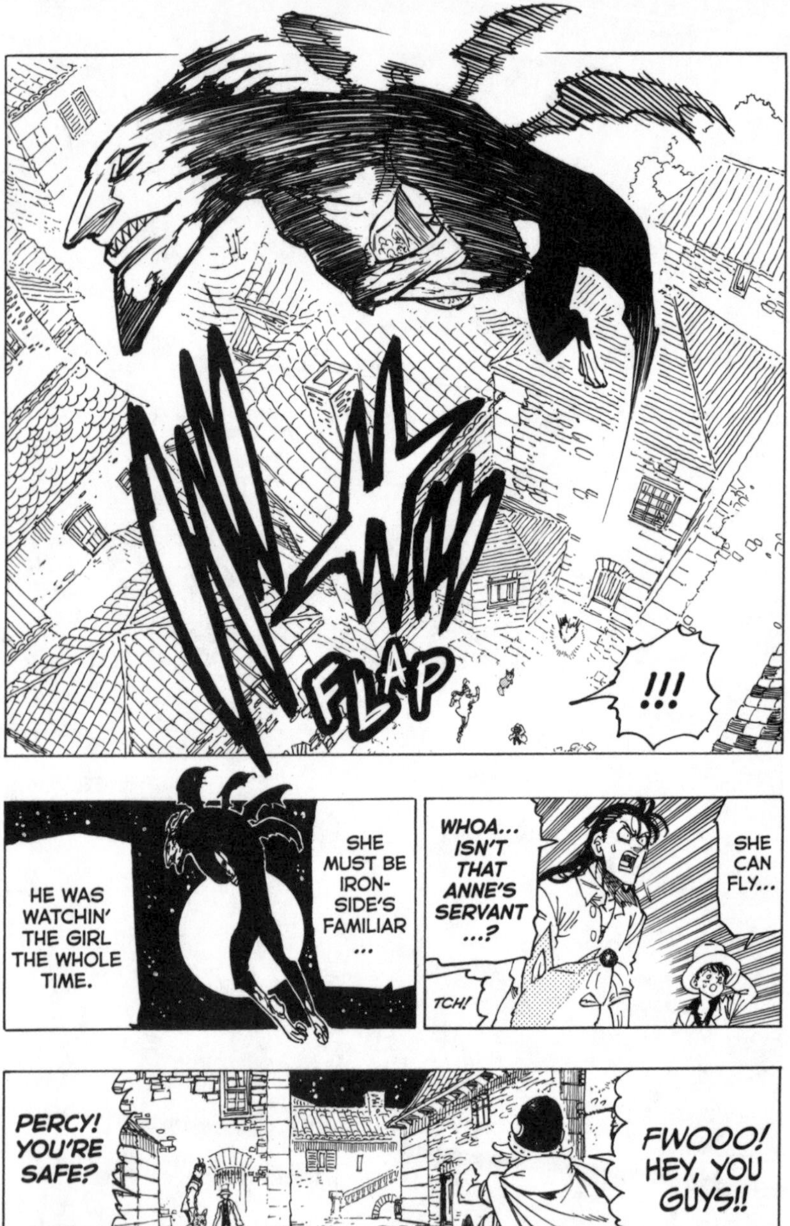
FLAP
!!!
SHE CAN FLY...
WHOA... ISN'T THAT ANNE'S SERVANT ...?
TCH!
SHE MUST BE IRON-SIDE'S FAMILIAR ...
HE WAS WATCHIN' THE GIRL THE WHOLE TIME.
FWOOO! HEY, YOU GUYS!!
PERCY! YOU'RE SAFE?

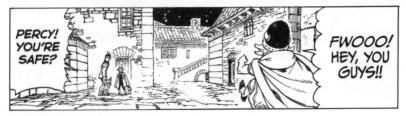

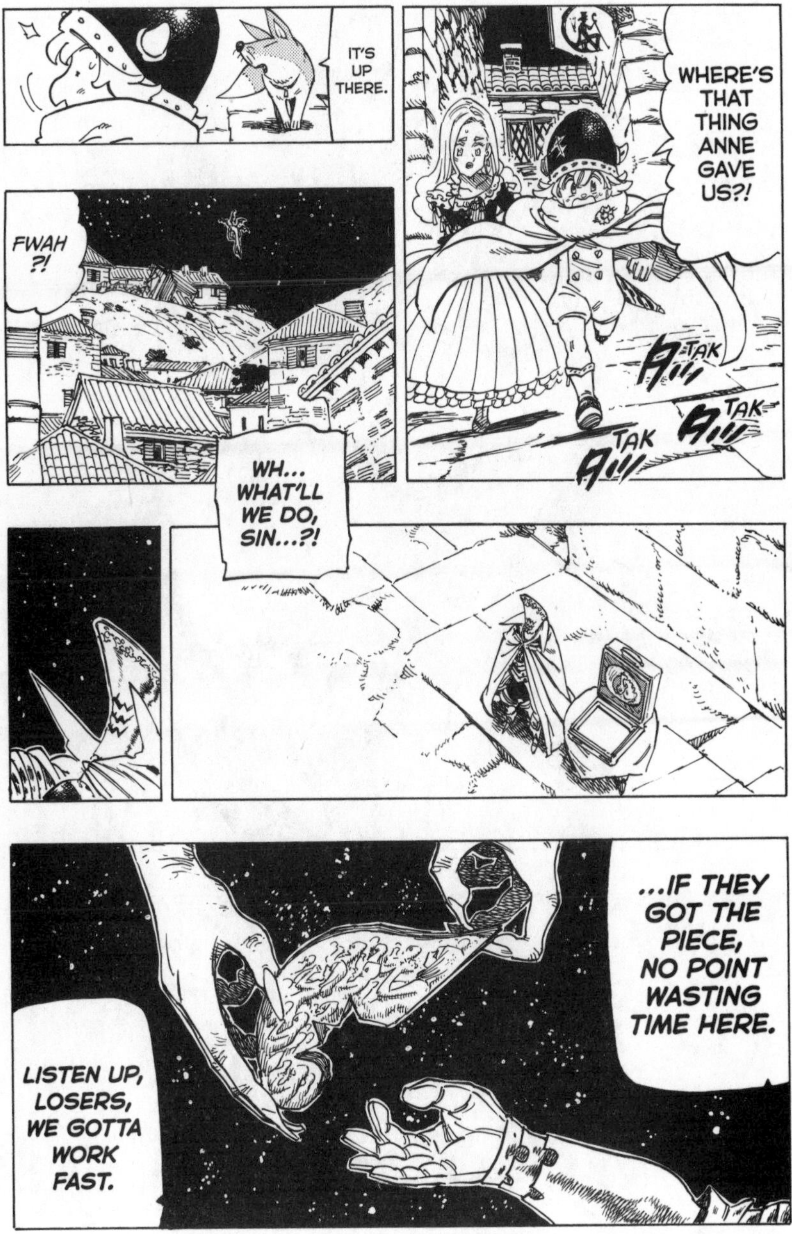
WHERE'S THAT THING ANNE GAVE US?!
TAK
TAK
TAK
IT'S UP THERE.
FWAH ?!
WH... WHAT'LL WE DO, SIN...?!
...IF THEY GOT THE PIECE, NO POINT WASTING TIME HERE.
LISTEN UP, LOSERS, WE GOTTA WORK FAST.

ACTIVATING THE RELIC REQUIRES A BLOOD SACRIFICE.

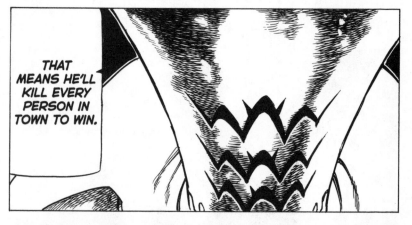

THAT MEANS HE'LL KILL EVERY PERSON IN TOWN TO WIN.

....!

CLENCH

EVERY PERSON ...?!

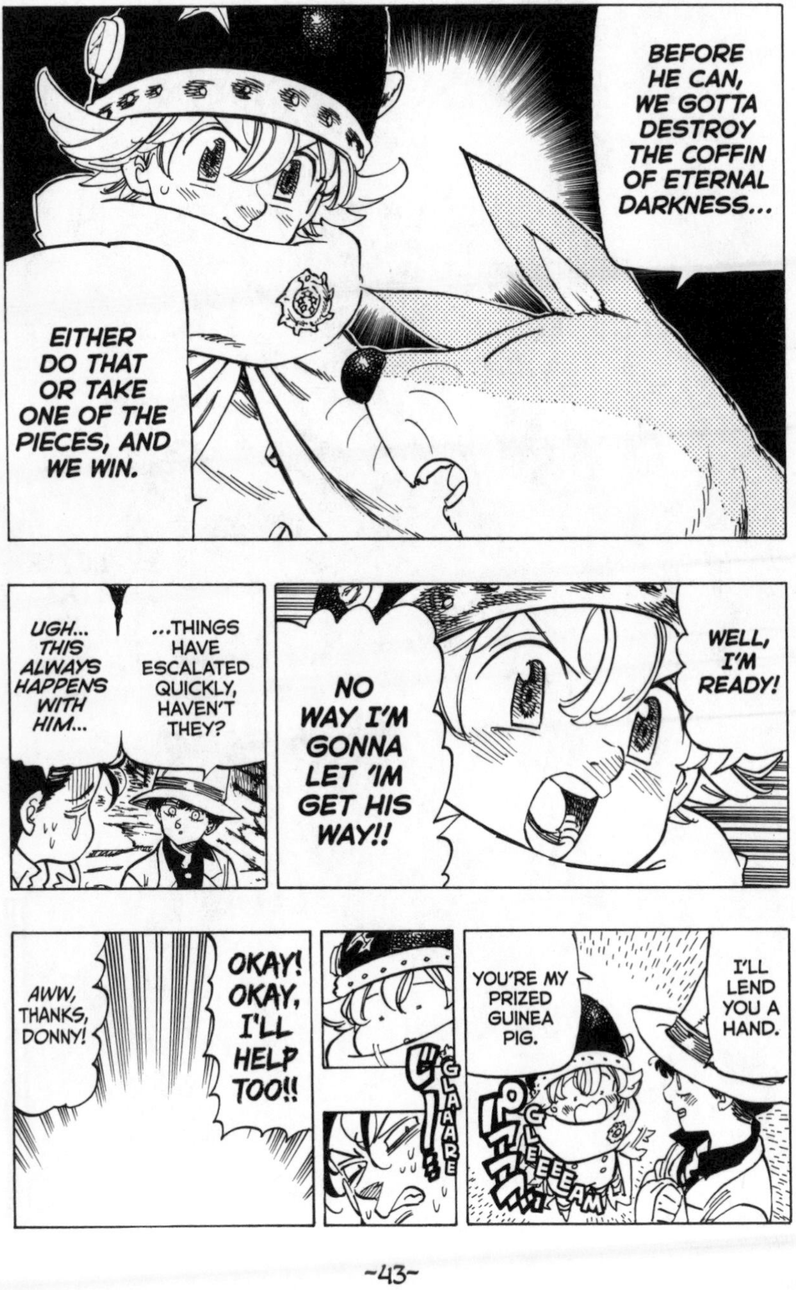
BEFORE HE CAN, WE GOTTA DESTROY THE COFFIN OF ETERNAL DARKNESS...
EITHER DO THAT OR TAKE ONE OF THE PIECES, AND WE WIN.
WELL, I'M READY!
NO WAY I'M GONNA LET 'IM GET HIS WAY!!
...THINGS HAVE ESCALATED QUICKLY, HAVEN'T THEY?
UGH... THIS ALWAYS HAPPENS WITH HIM...
I'LL LEND YOU A HAND.
YOU'RE MY PRIZED GUINEA PIG.
GLEEEAM
GLAARE
OKAY! OKAY, I'LL HELP TOO!!
AWW, THANKS, DONNY!

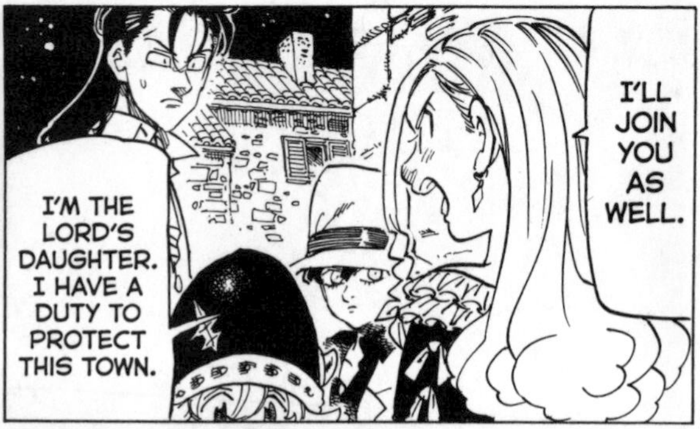
I'LL JOIN YOU AS WELL.
I'M THE LORD'S DAUGHTER. I HAVE A DUTY TO PROTECT THIS TOWN.

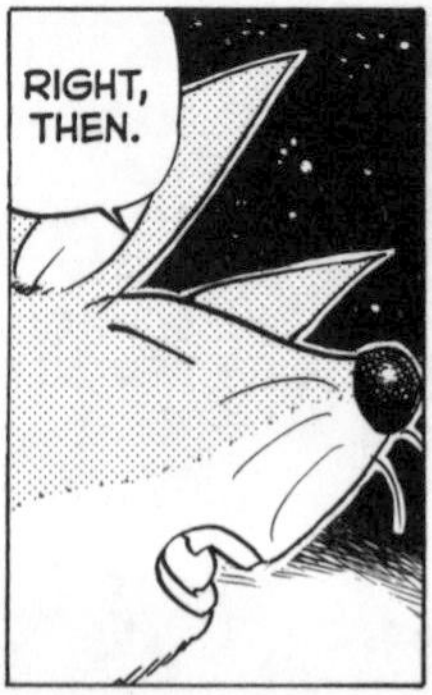
RIGHT, THEN.

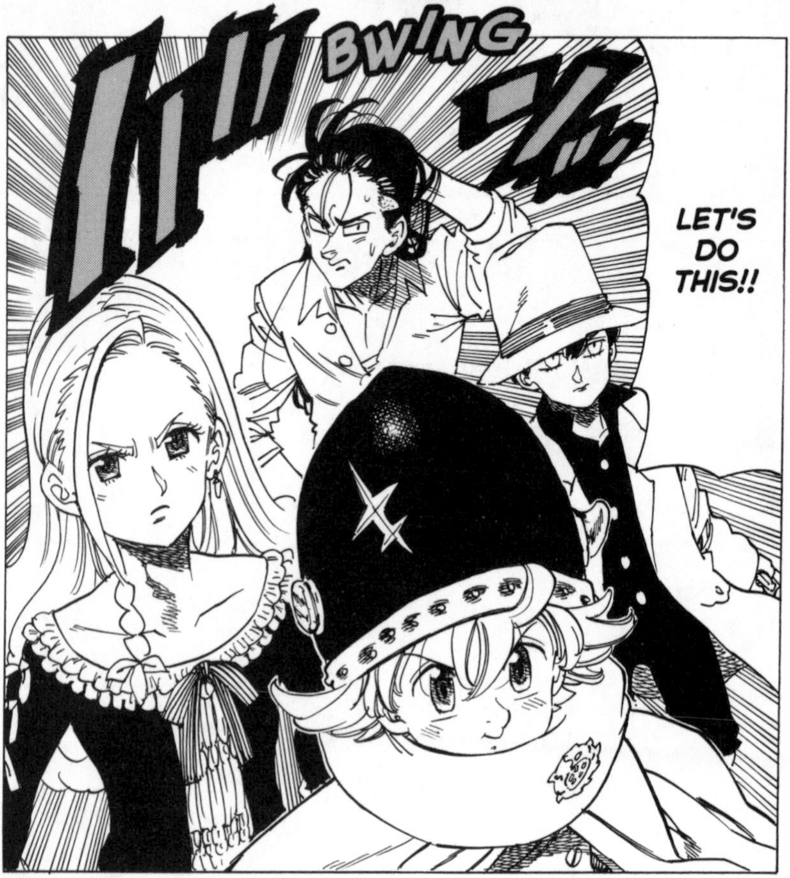
BWING
LET'S DO THIS!!

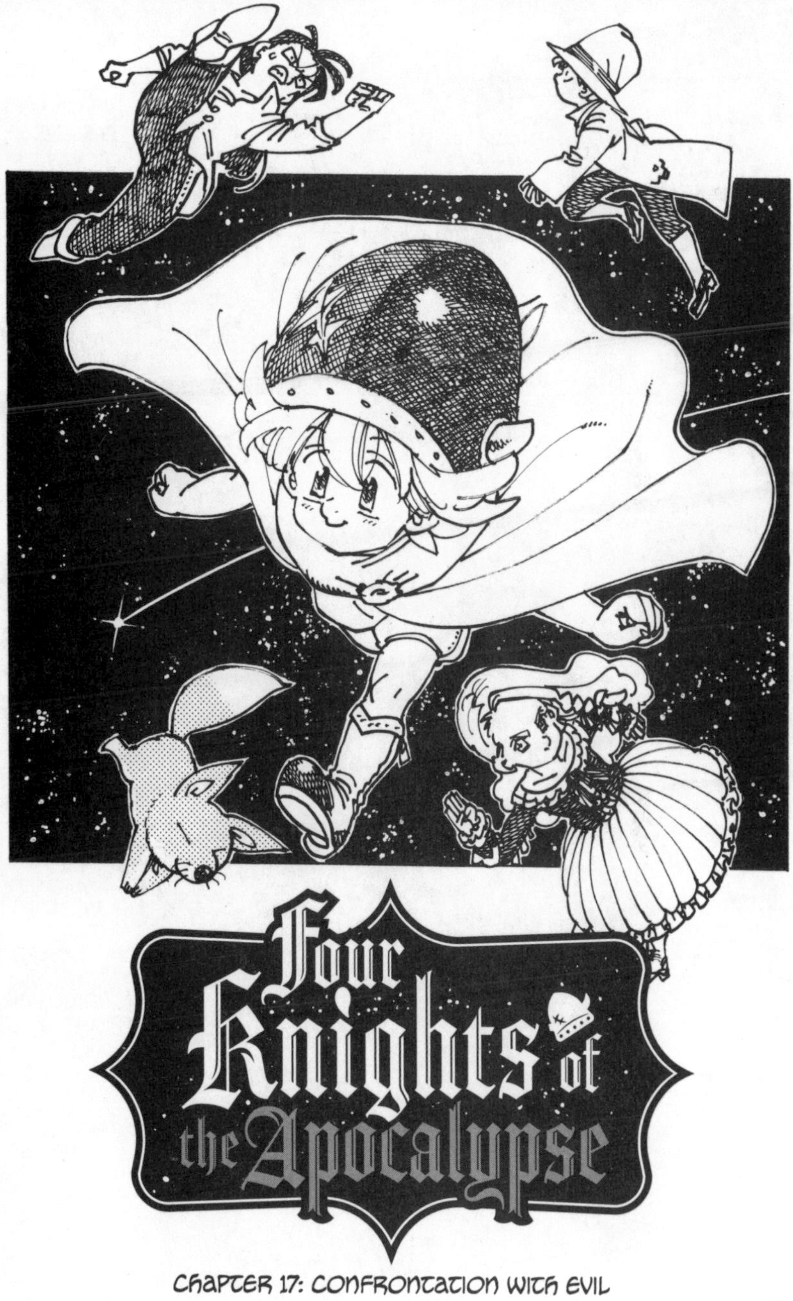

Four Knights of the Apocalypse

CHAPTER 17: CONFRONTATION WITH EVIL

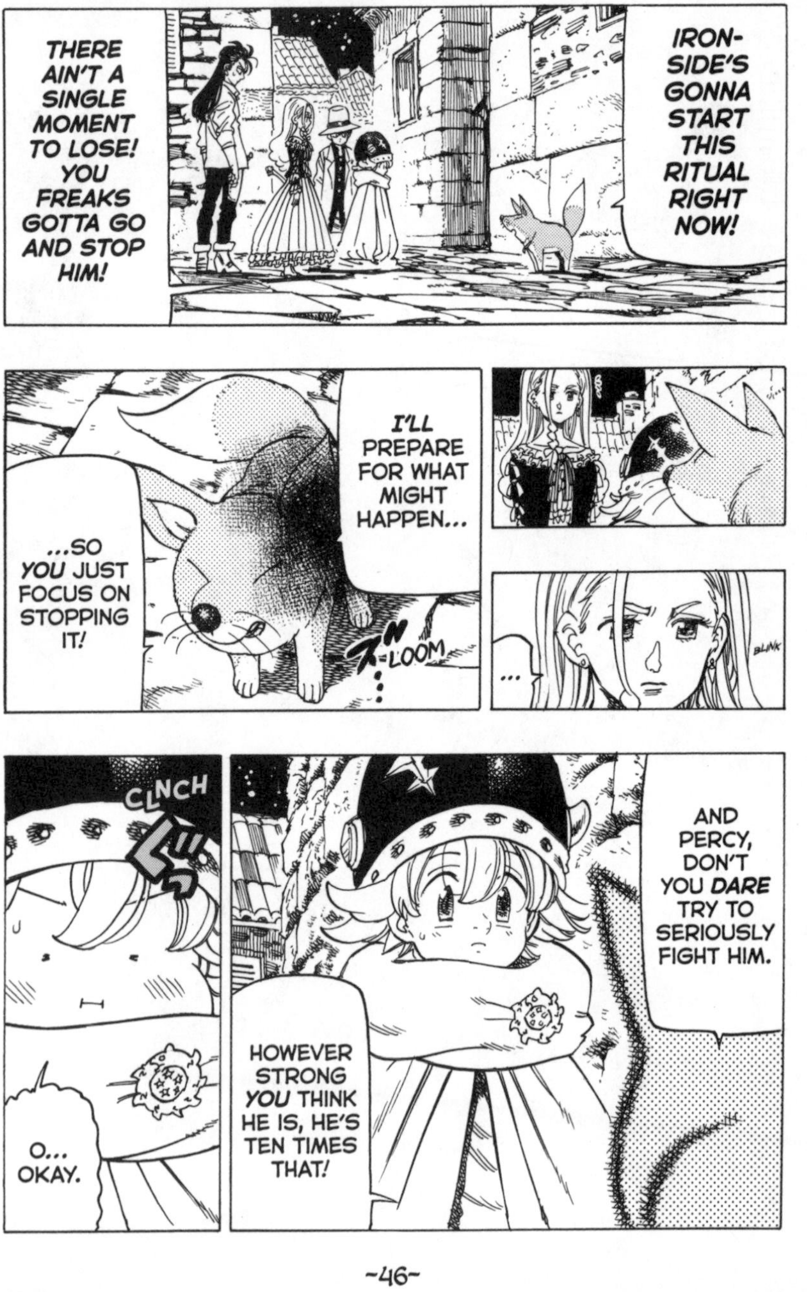
IRON-SIDE'S GONNA START THIS RITUAL RIGHT NOW!
THERE AIN'T A SINGLE MOMENT TO LOSE! YOU FREAKS GOTTA GO AND STOP HIM!
...
BLINK
I'LL PREPARE FOR WHAT MIGHT HAPPEN...
...SO YOU JUST FOCUS ON STOPPING IT!
LOOM
AND PERCY, DON'T YOU DARE TRY TO SERIOUSLY FIGHT HIM.
HOWEVER STRONG YOU THINK HE IS, HE'S TEN TIMES THAT!
CLNCH
O... OKAY.

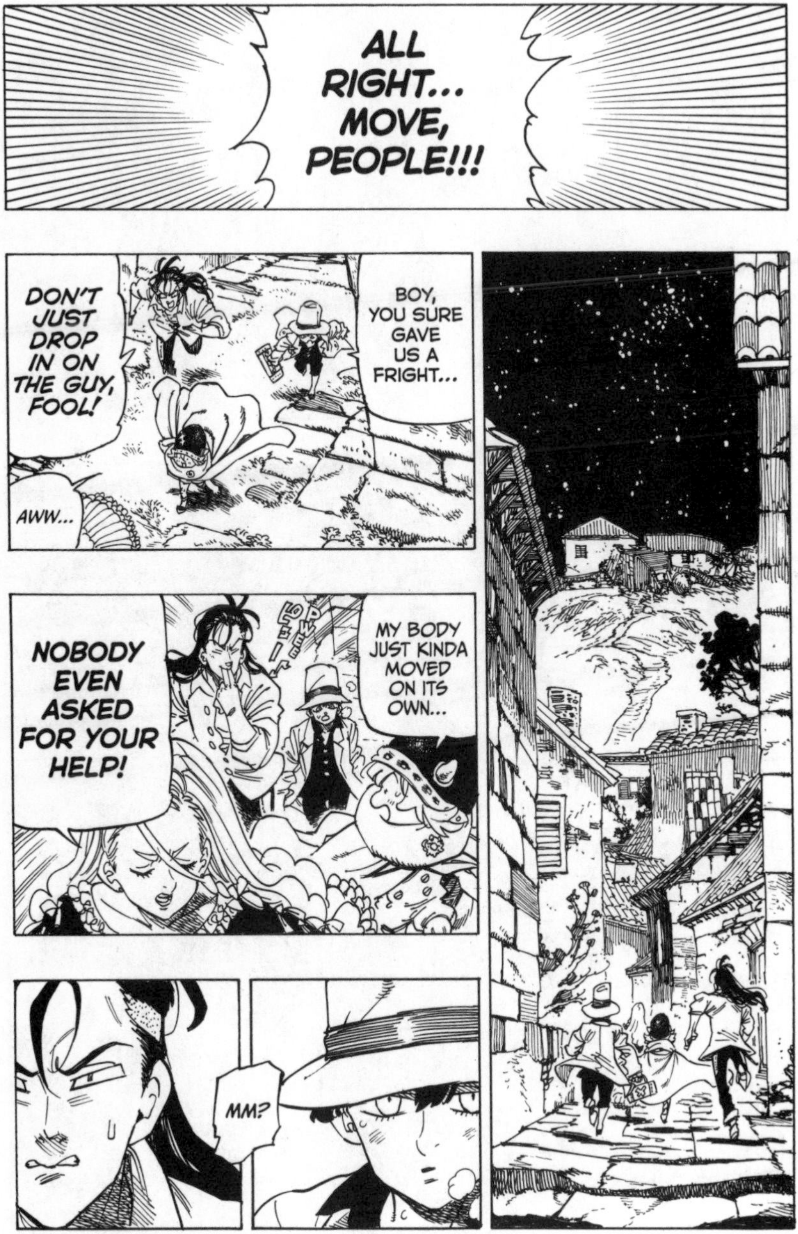
ALL RIGHT... MOVE, PEOPLE!!!
BOY, YOU SURE GAVE US A FRIGHT...
DON'T JUST DROP IN ON THE GUY, FOOL!
AWW...
MY BODY JUST KINDA MOVED ON ITS OWN...
NOBODY EVEN ASKED FOR YOUR HELP!
MM?

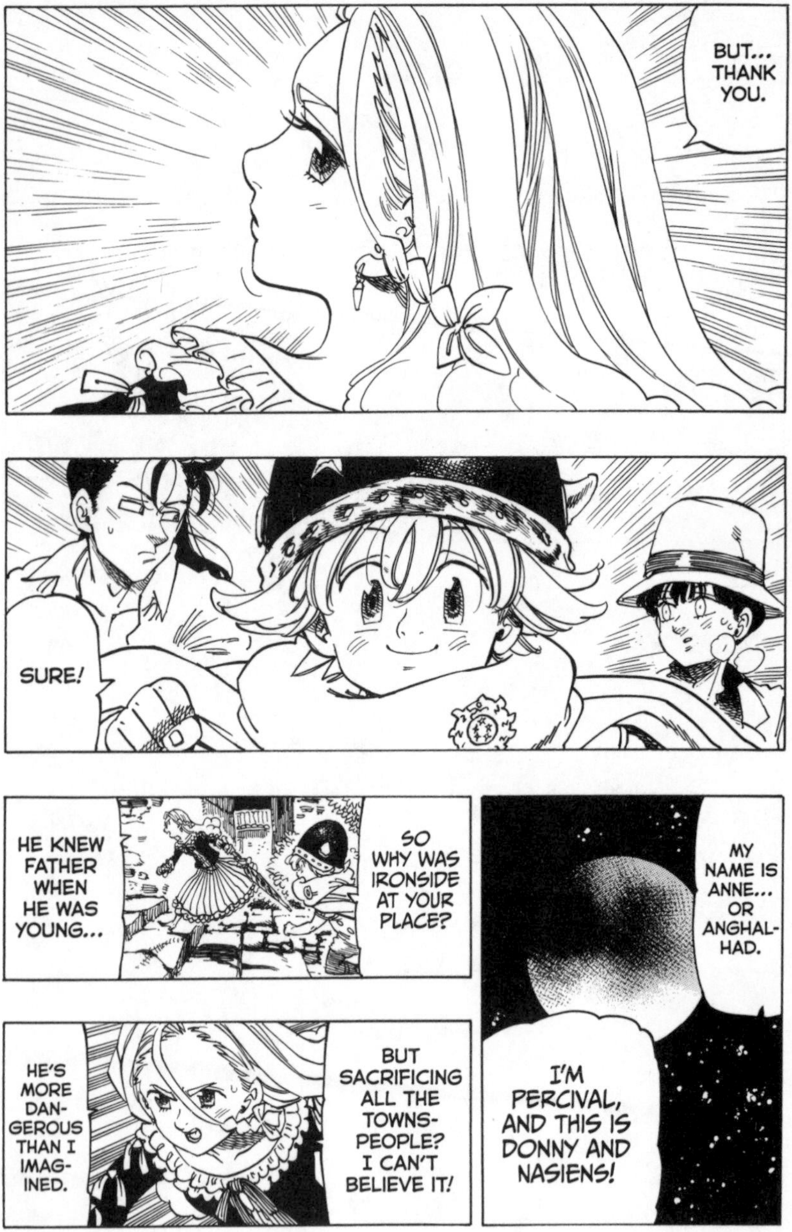
BUT... THANK YOU.
SURE!
MY NAME IS ANNE... OR ANGHAL-HAD.
I'M PERCIVAL, AND THIS IS DONNY AND NASIENS!
SO WHY WAS IRONSIDE AT YOUR PLACE?
HE KNEW FATHER WHEN HE WAS YOUNG...
BUT SACRIFICING ALL THE TOWNS-PEOPLE? I CAN'T BELIEVE IT!
HE'S MORE DAN-GEROUS THAN I IMAG-INED.

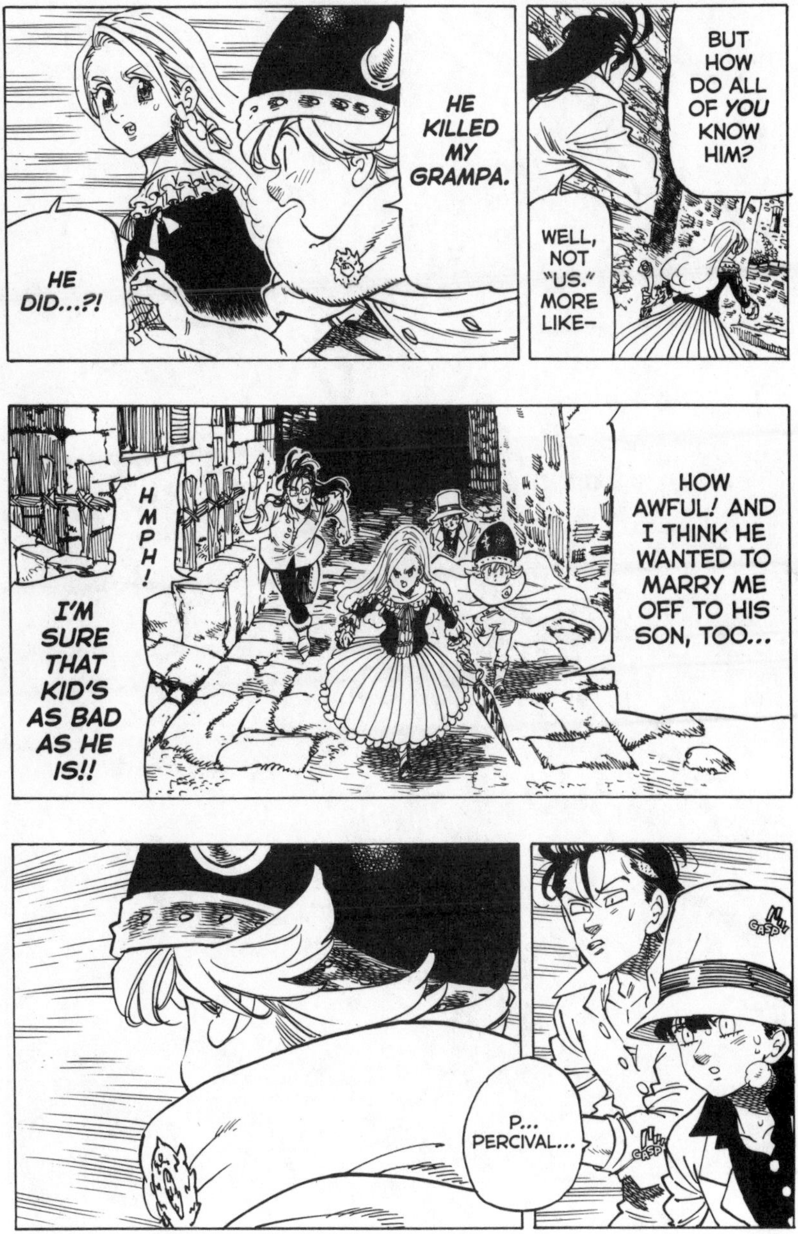
BUT HOW DO ALL OF *YOU* KNOW HIM?
WELL, NOT "US." MORE LIKE–
HE KILLED MY GRAMPA.
HE DID...?!
HOW AWFUL! AND I THINK HE WANTED TO MARRY ME OFF TO HIS SON, TOO...
HMPH!
I'M SURE THAT KID'S AS BAD AS HE IS!!
GASP
GASP
P... PERCIVAL...

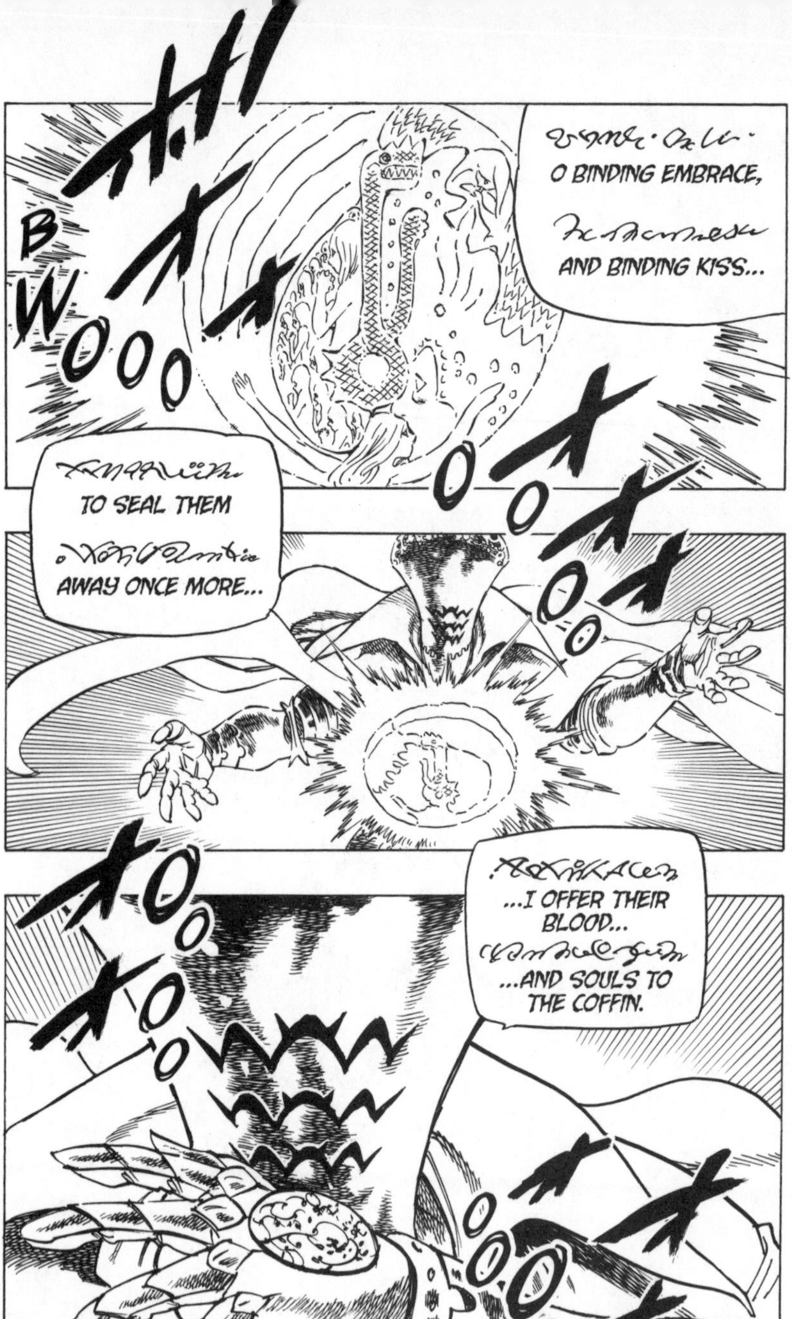
O BINDING EMBRACE,
AND BINDING KISS...
BWOOO
TO SEAL THEM
AWAY ONCE MORE...
...I OFFER THEIR BLOOD...
...AND SOULS TO THE COFFIN.

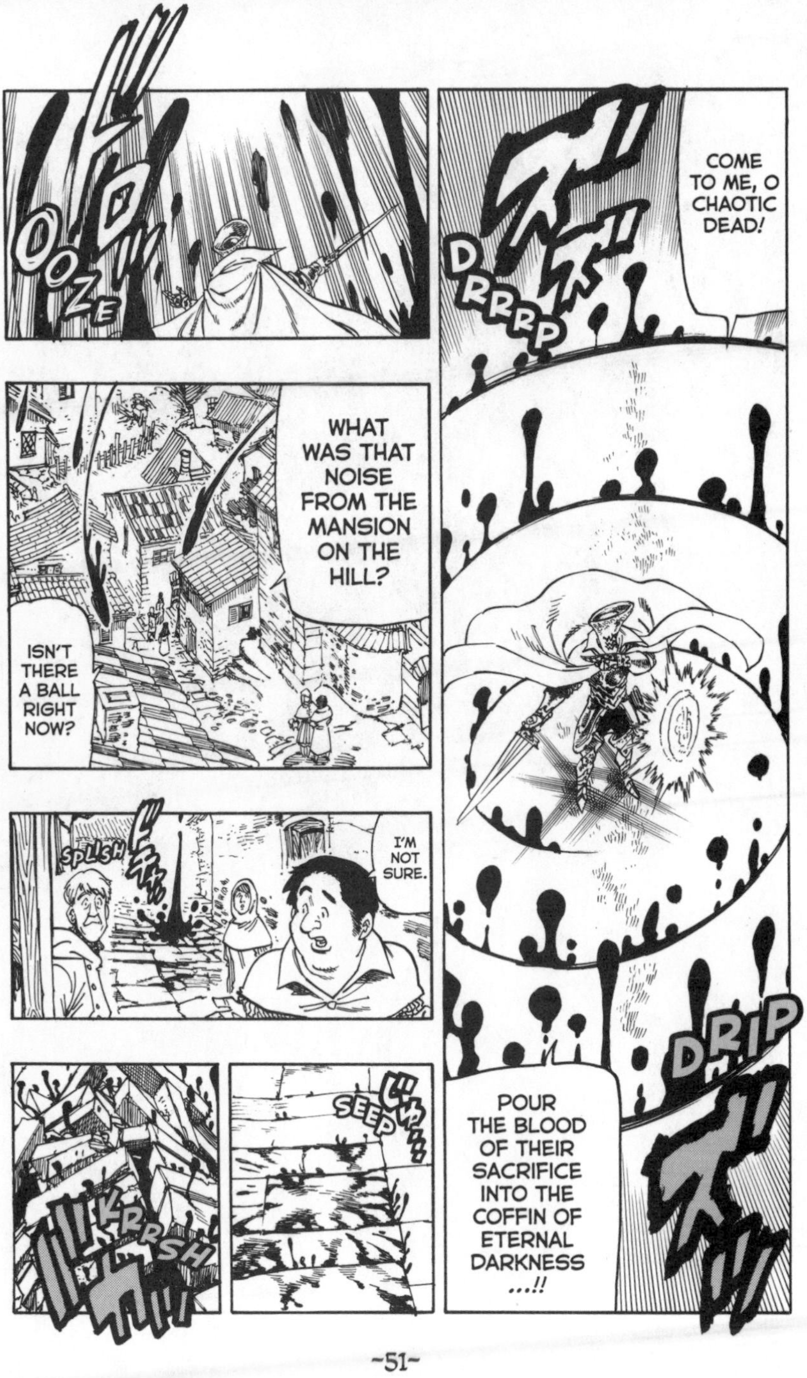
COME TO ME, O CHAOTIC DEAD!
DRRRP
DRIP
POUR THE BLOOD OF THEIR SACRIFICE INTO THE COFFIN OF ETERNAL DARKNESS ...!!
OOZE
WHAT WAS THAT NOISE FROM THE MANSION ON THE HILL?
ISN'T THERE A BALL RIGHT NOW?
I'M NOT SURE.
SPLISH
SEEP
KRRSH

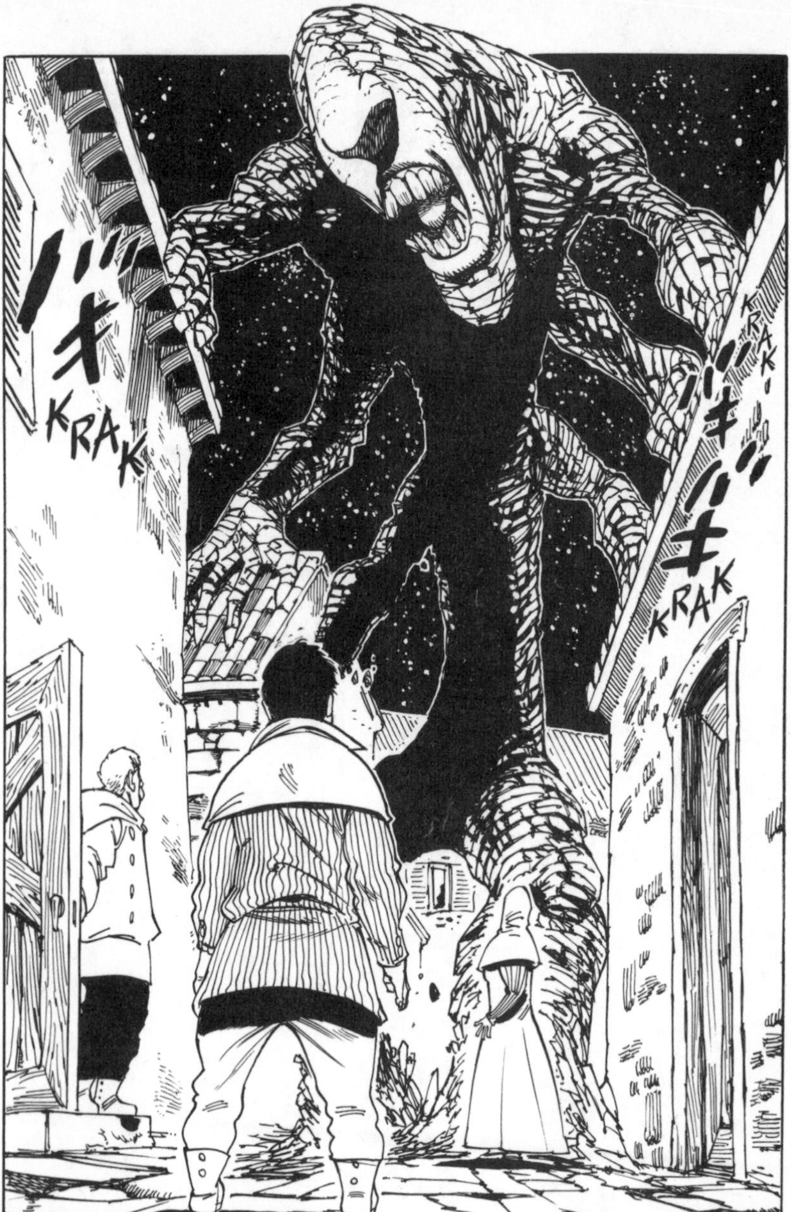
KRAK
バキバキ
KRAK
バキ
KRAK

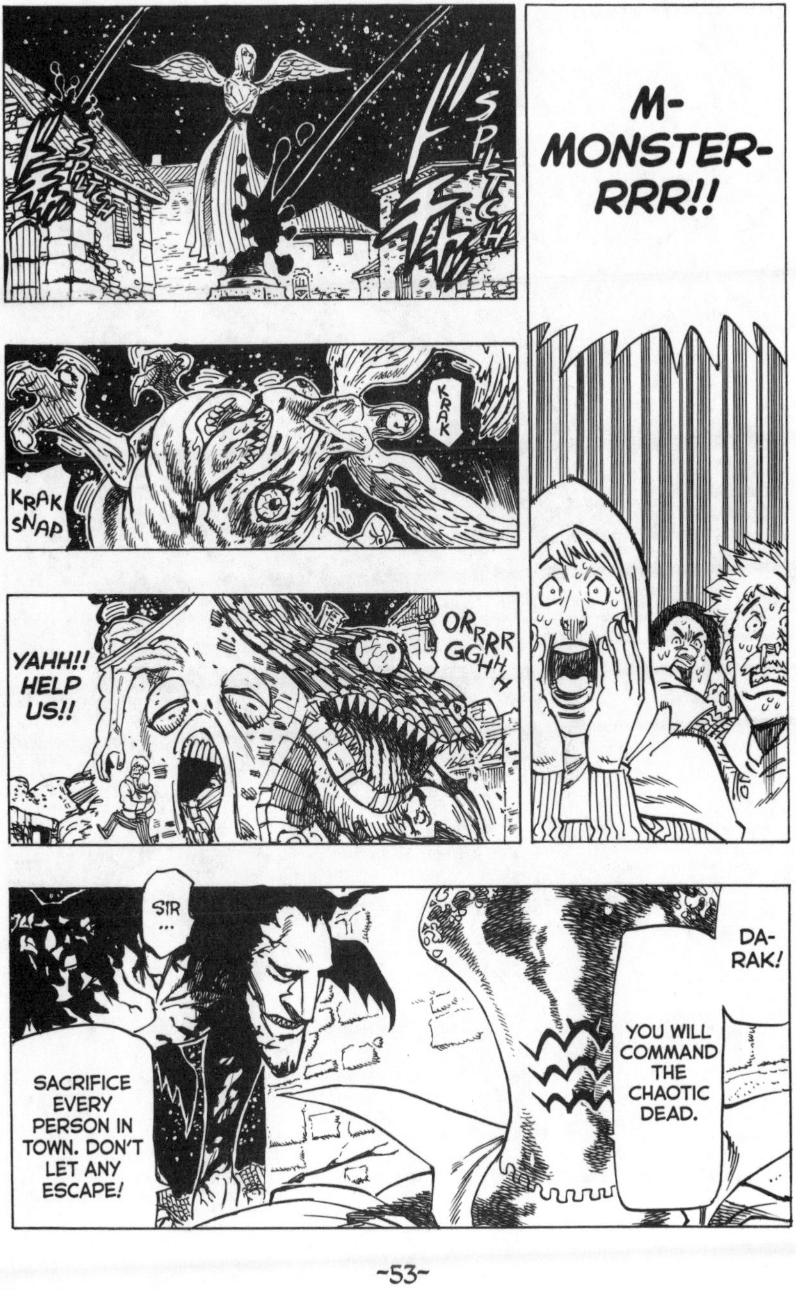
M-MONSTER-RRR!!
SPLTCH
SPLTCH
KRAK
KRAK SNAP
ORRRRGGHHH
YAHH!! HELP US!!
DA-RAK!
YOU WILL COMMAND THE CHAOTIC DEAD.
SIR...
SACRIFICE EVERY PERSON IN TOWN. DON'T LET ANY ESCAPE!

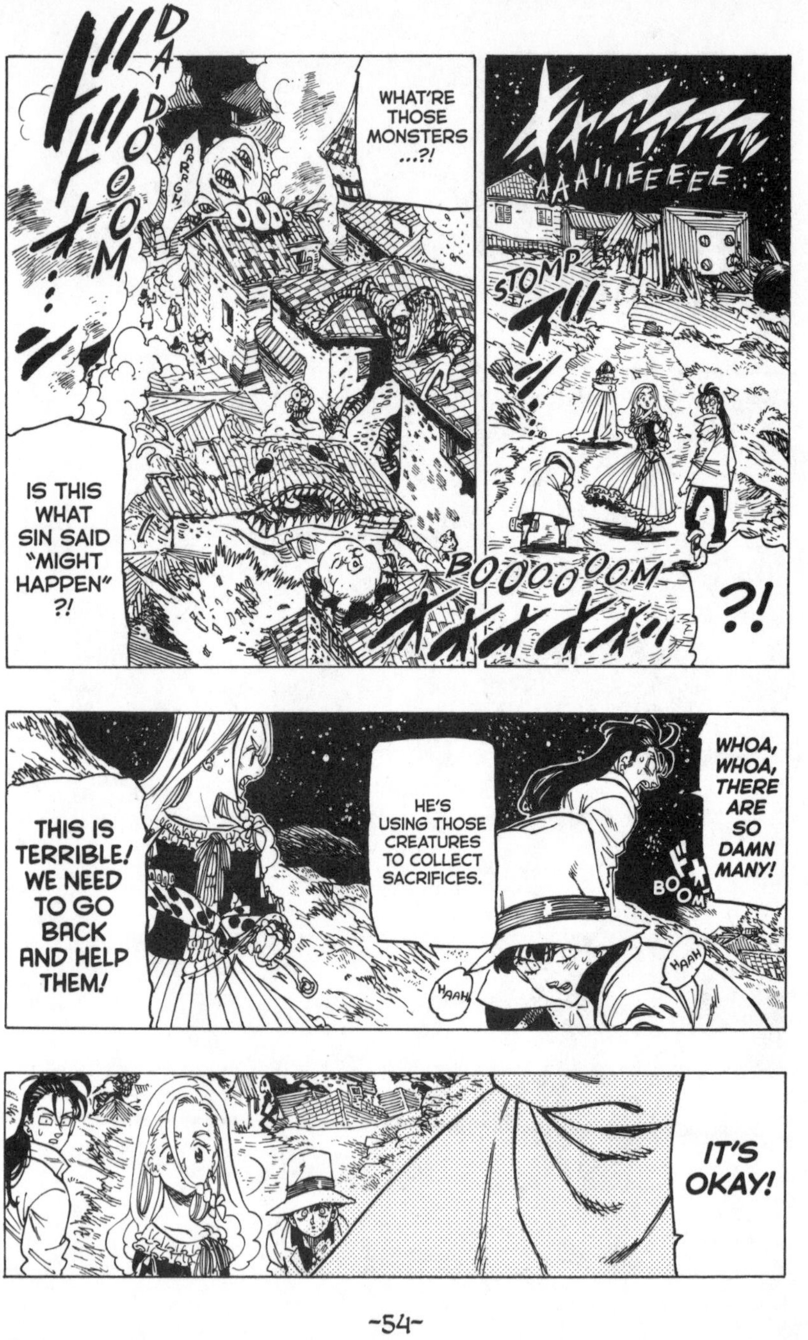
AAAIIIEEEEEE
STOMP
BOOOOOOOM
?!
WHAT'RE THOSE MONSTERS ...?!
ARRGH!
DAIDOOOOM
IS THIS WHAT SIN SAID "MIGHT HAPPEN"?!
WHOA, WHOA, THERE ARE SO DAMN MANY!
BOOM
HAAH
HE'S USING THOSE CREATURES TO COLLECT SACRIFICES.
HAAH
THIS IS TERRIBLE! WE NEED TO GO BACK AND HELP THEM!
IT'S OKAY!

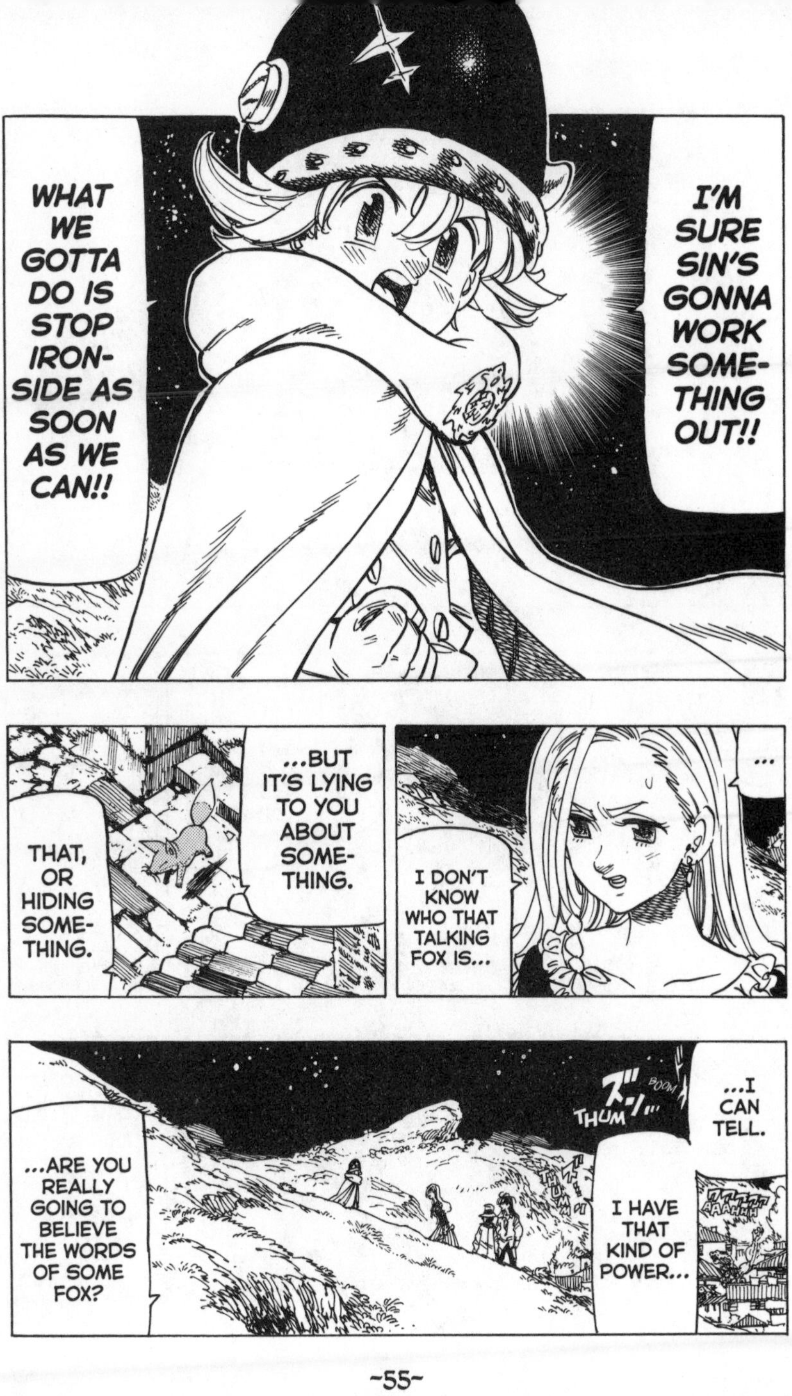
I'M SURE SIN'S GONNA WORK SOMETHING OUT!!
WHAT WE GOTTA DO IS STOP IRONSIDE AS SOON AS WE CAN!!
...
I DON'T KNOW WHO THAT TALKING FOX IS...
...BUT IT'S LYING TO YOU ABOUT SOMETHING.
THAT, OR HIDING SOMETHING.
...I CAN TELL.
I HAVE THAT KIND OF POWER...
AAAHHH
BOOM
THUM
THUM
...ARE YOU REALLY GOING TO BELIEVE THE WORDS OF SOME FOX?

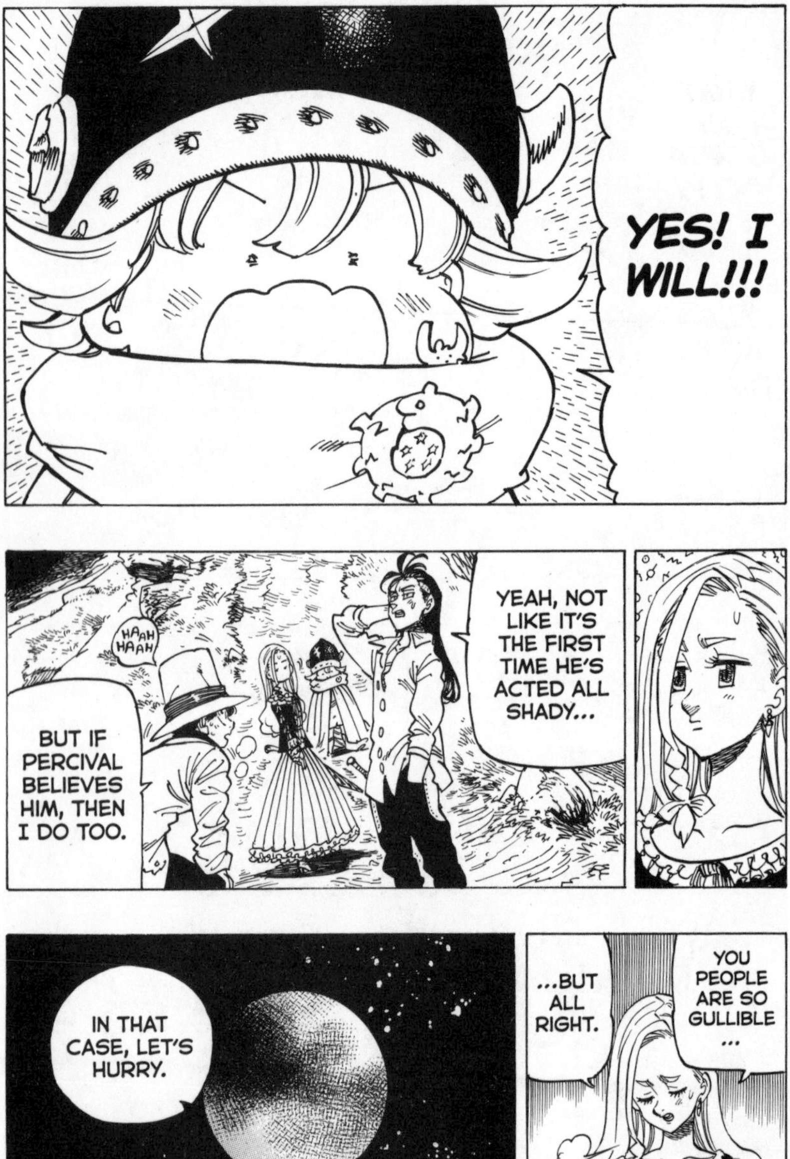
YES! I WILL!!!
YEAH, NOT LIKE IT'S THE FIRST TIME HE'S ACTED ALL SHADY...
HAAH HAAH
BUT IF PERCIVAL BELIEVES HIM, THEN I DO TOO.
YOU PEOPLE ARE SO GULLIBLE ...
...BUT ALL RIGHT.
IN THAT CASE, LET'S HURRY.

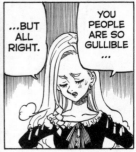

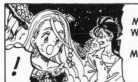

TAP
TAP
TAP
!
MAN, WHAT A MESS ...
FA-THER !!
FATHER, HANG IN THERE!
IT'S OKAY. HE'S JUST KNOCKED OUT...

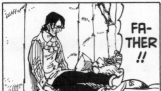

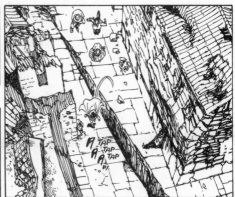

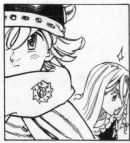

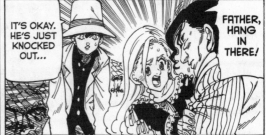

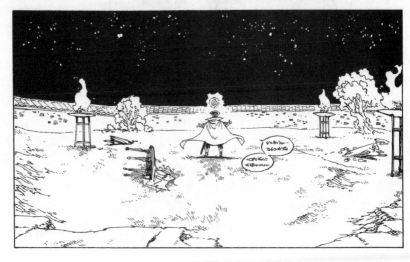

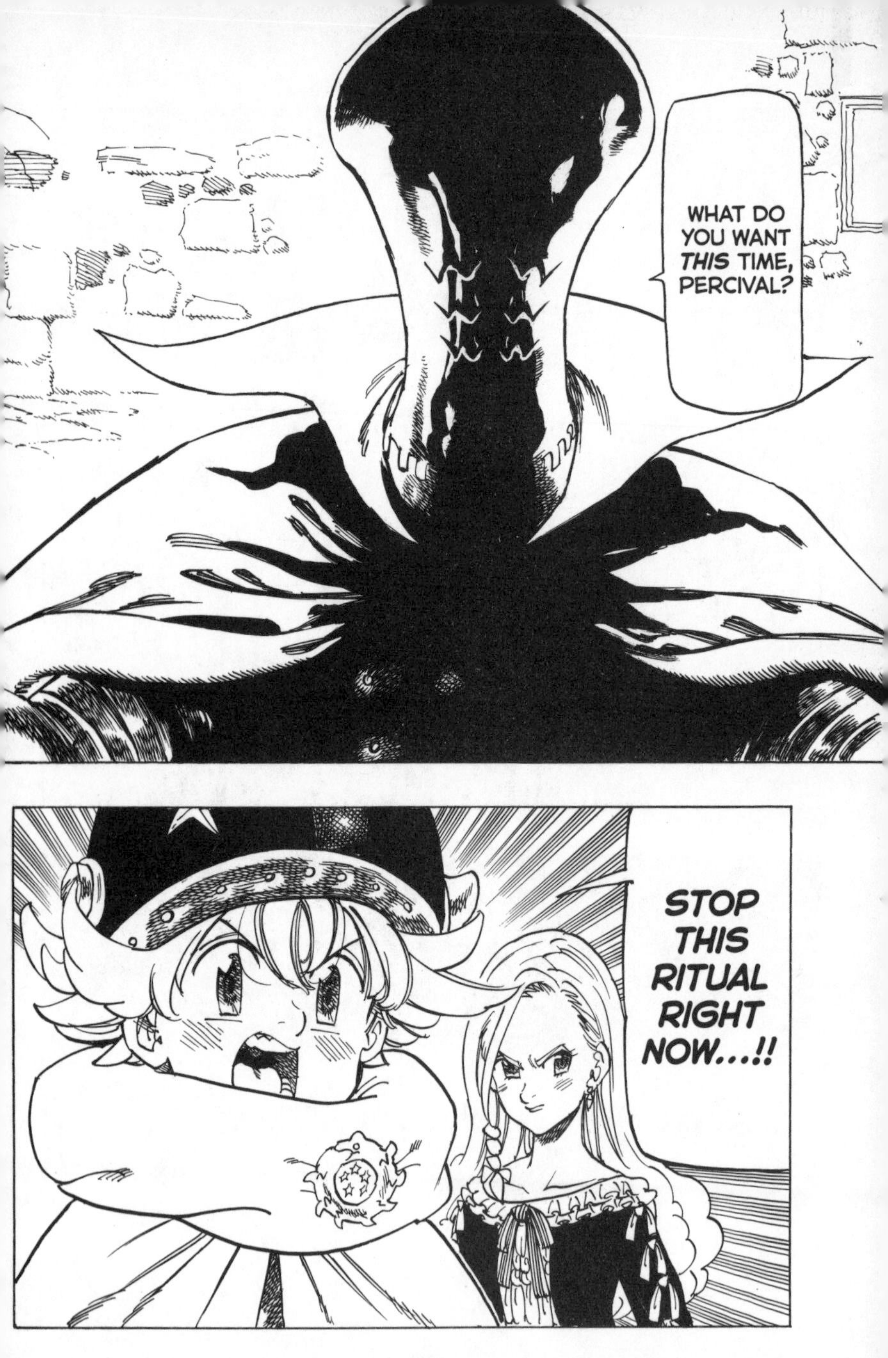
WHAT DO YOU WANT *THIS* TIME, PERCIVAL?
STOP THIS RITUAL RIGHT NOW...!!

NORMALLY, I WOULD TAKE THIS OPPORTUNITY TO SNUFF YOU OUT FOR GOOD...

...BUT I'M BUSY TONIGHT.

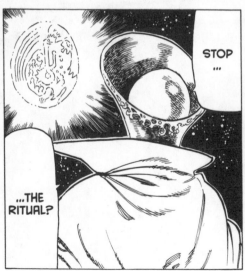

STOP...

...THE RITUAL?

HEH... THIS GUY MIGHT BE TOUGH, BUT ALL WE GOTTA DO IS GET THAT SEAL.

THE FOUR OF US CAN PULL IT OFF, RIGHT...?

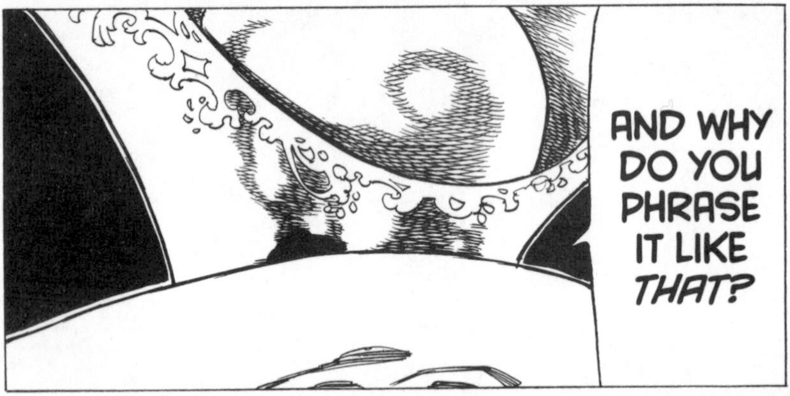
AND WHY DO YOU PHRASE IT LIKE *THAT?*
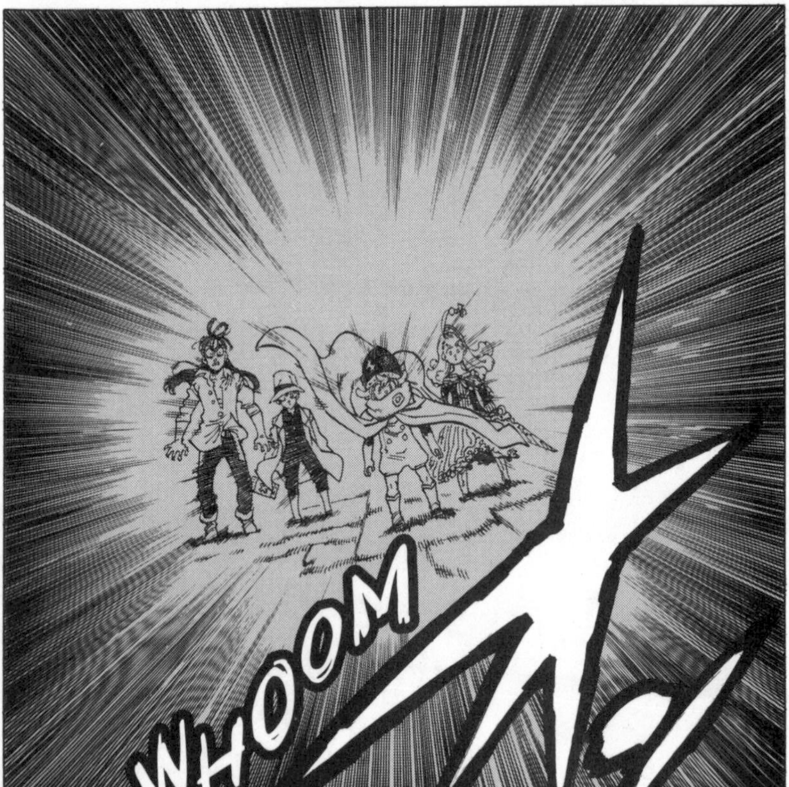
WHOOM

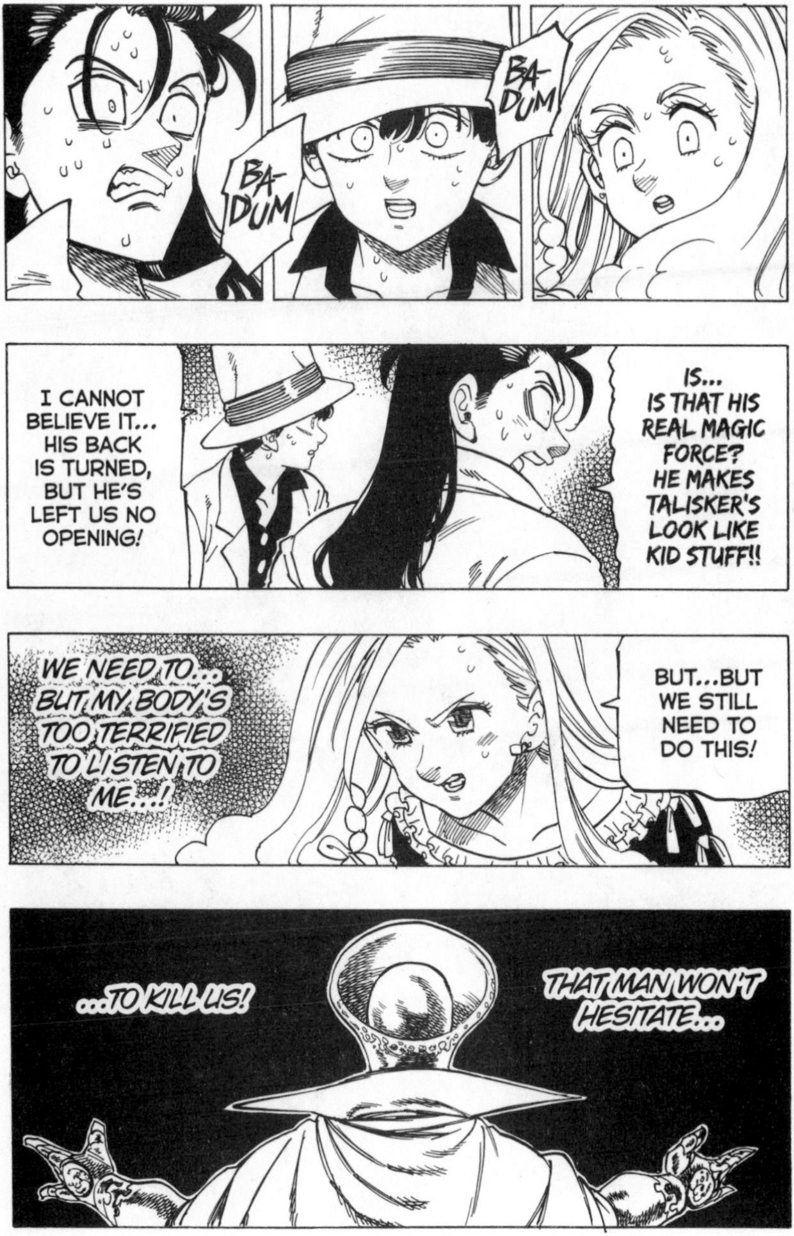
BA-DUM
BA-DUM
IS... IS THAT HIS REAL MAGIC FORCE? HE MAKES TALISKER'S LOOK LIKE KID STUFF!!
I CANNOT BELIEVE IT... HIS BACK IS TURNED, BUT HE'S LEFT US NO OPENING!
BUT...BUT WE STILL NEED TO DO THIS!
WE NEED TO... BUT MY BODY'S TOO TERRIFIED TO LISTEN TO ME...!
THAT MAN WON'T HESITATE...
...TO KILL US!

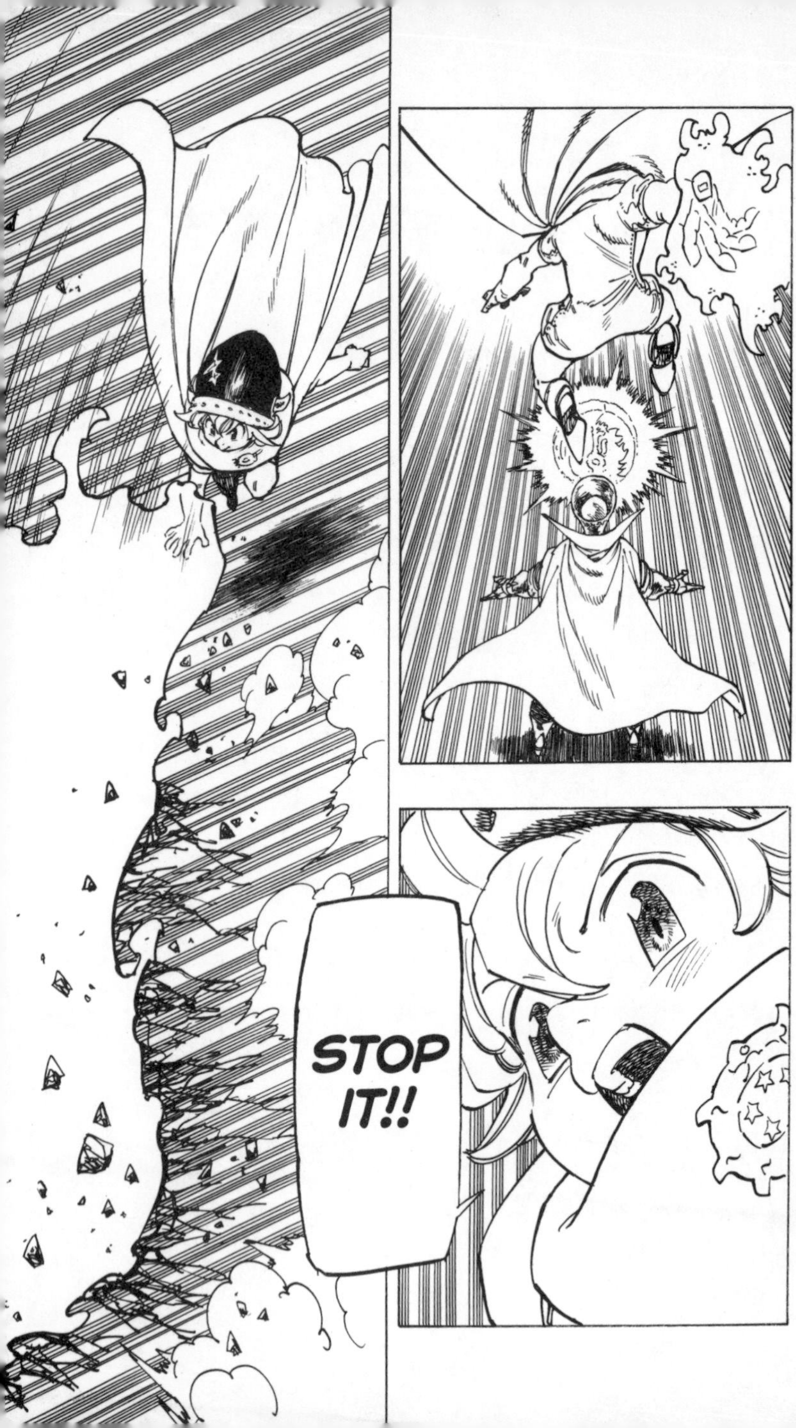
STOP IT!!

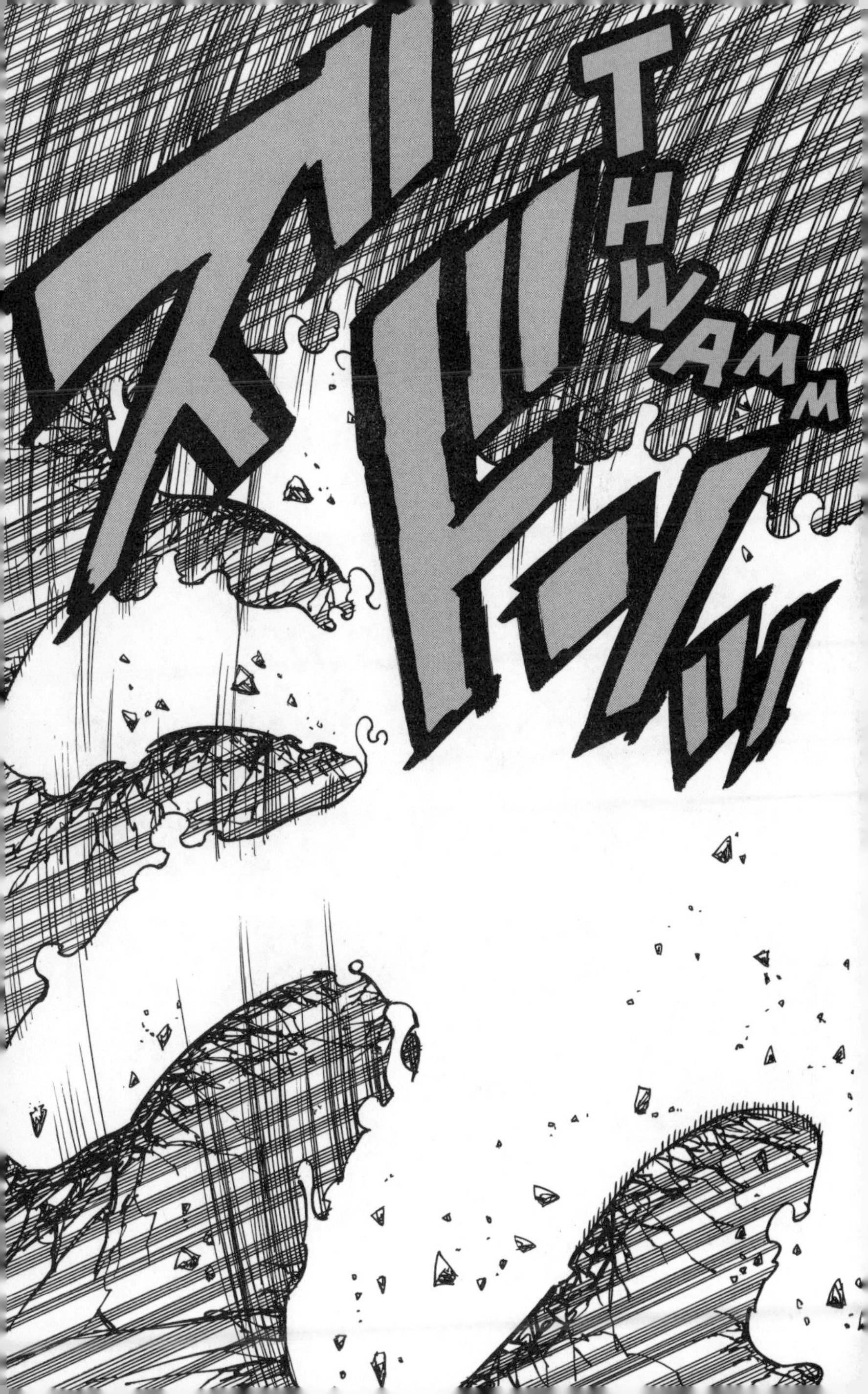
THWAMM

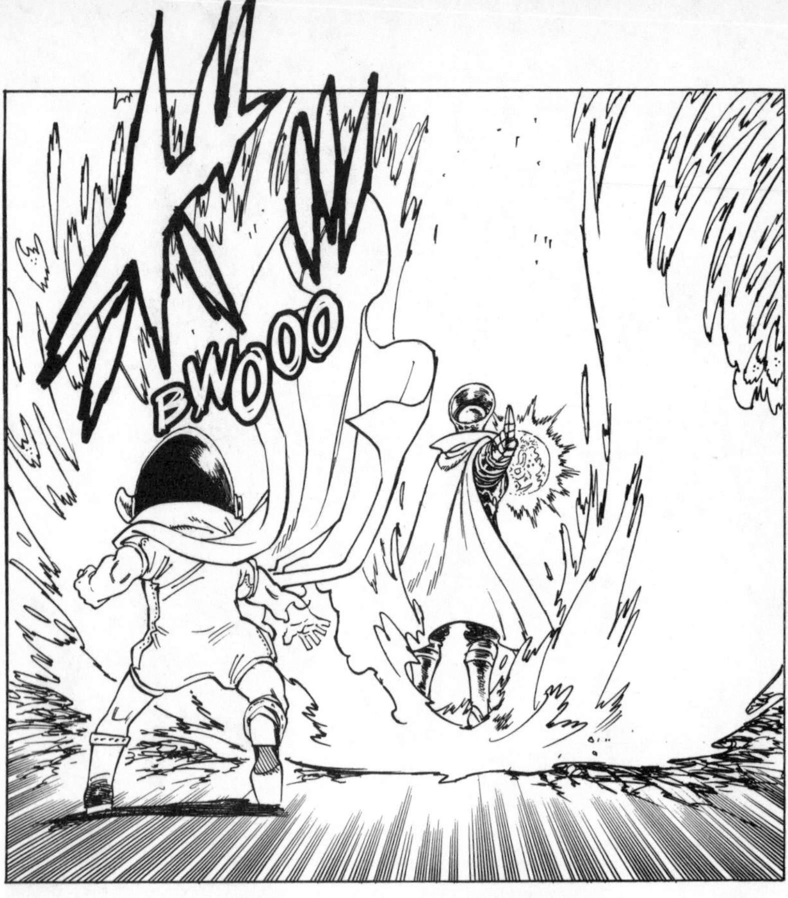
BWOOO

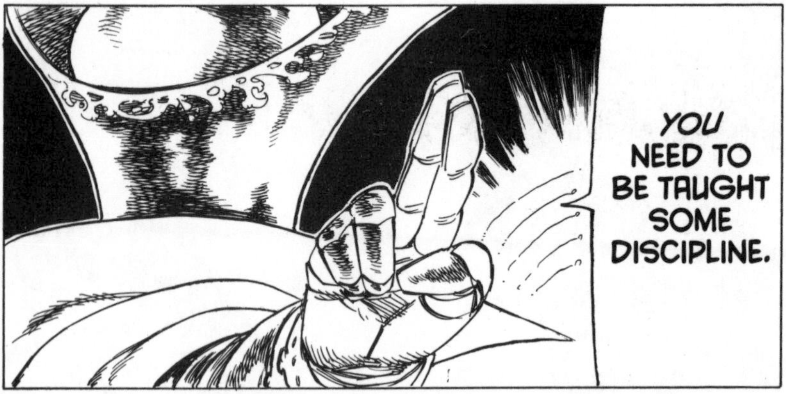
YOU NEED TO BE TAUGHT SOME DISCIPLINE.

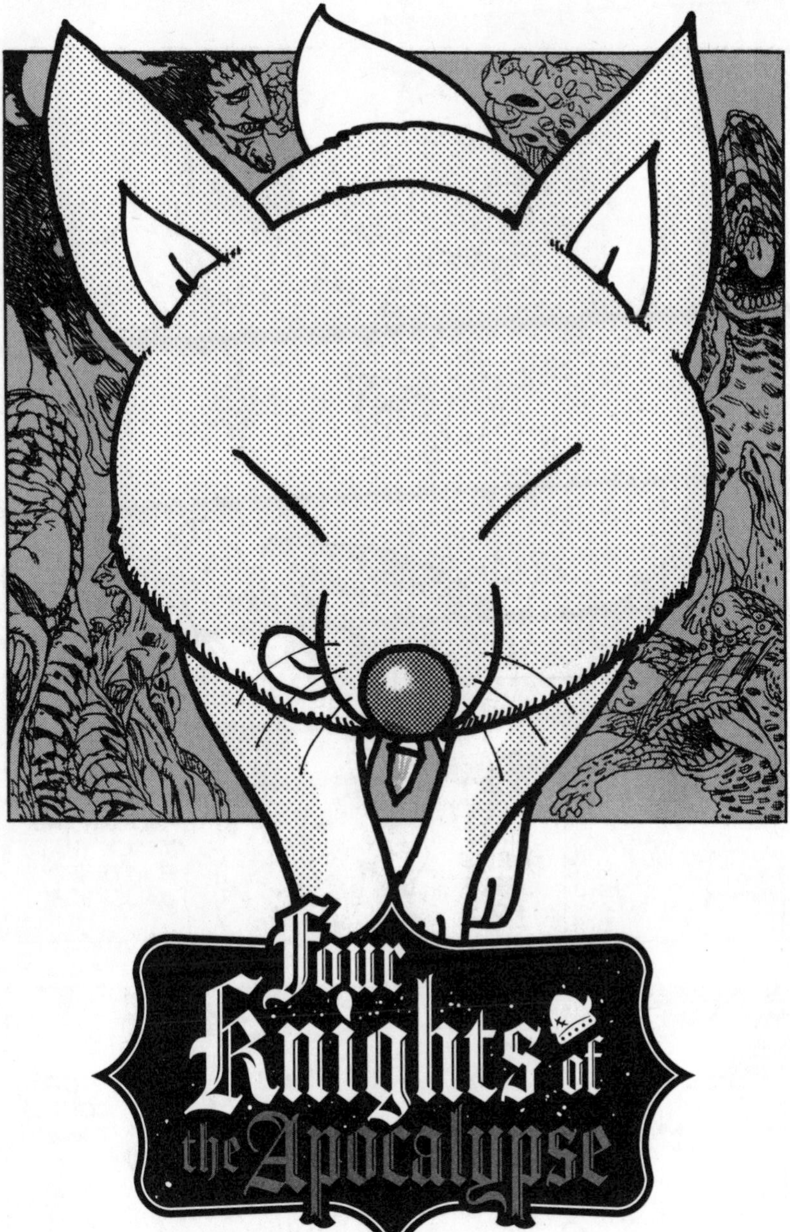
Four Knights of the Apocalypse

CHAPTER 18: RESOLVE FOR THE BATTLE

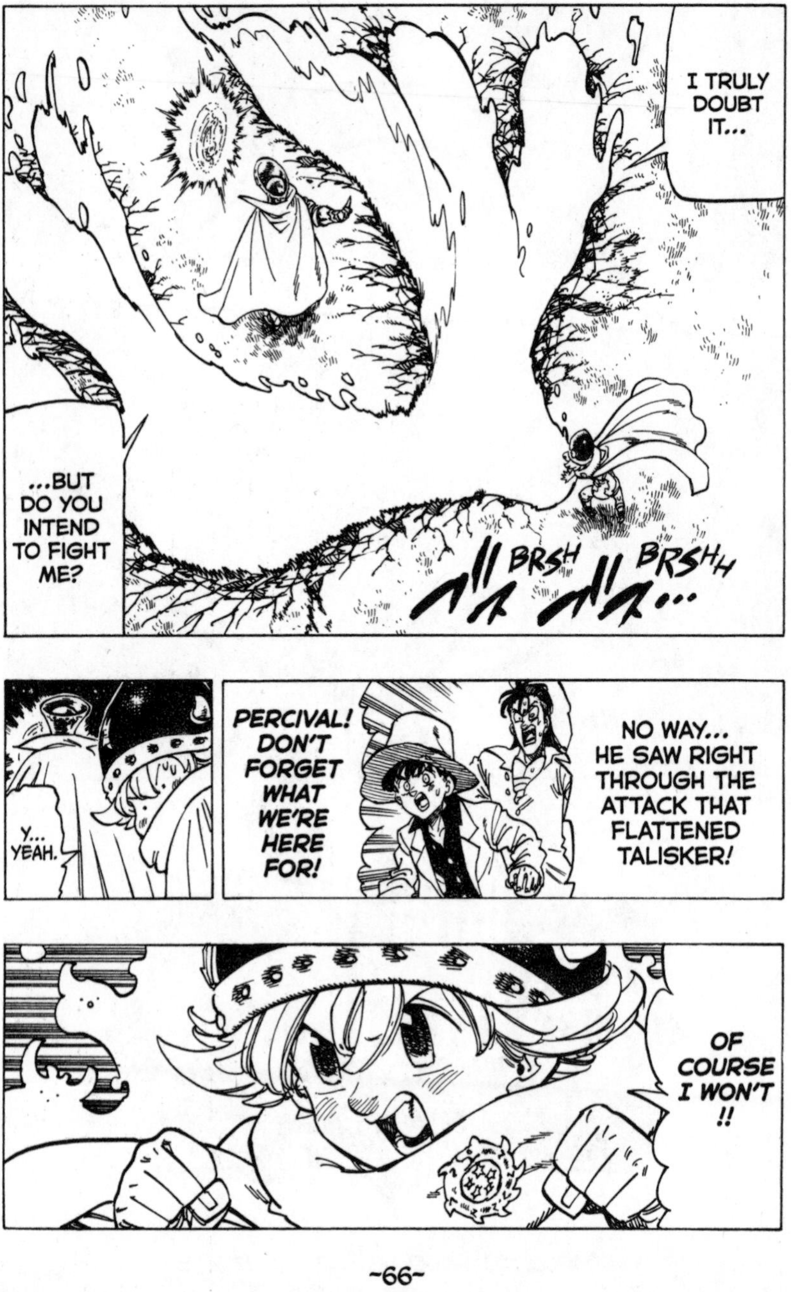
I TRULY DOUBT IT...
...BUT DO YOU INTEND TO FIGHT ME?
BRSH BRSHH
NO WAY... HE SAW RIGHT THROUGH THE ATTACK THAT FLATTENED TALISKER!
PERCIVAL! DON'T FORGET WHAT WE'RE HERE FOR!
Y... YEAH.
OF COURSE I WON'T !!

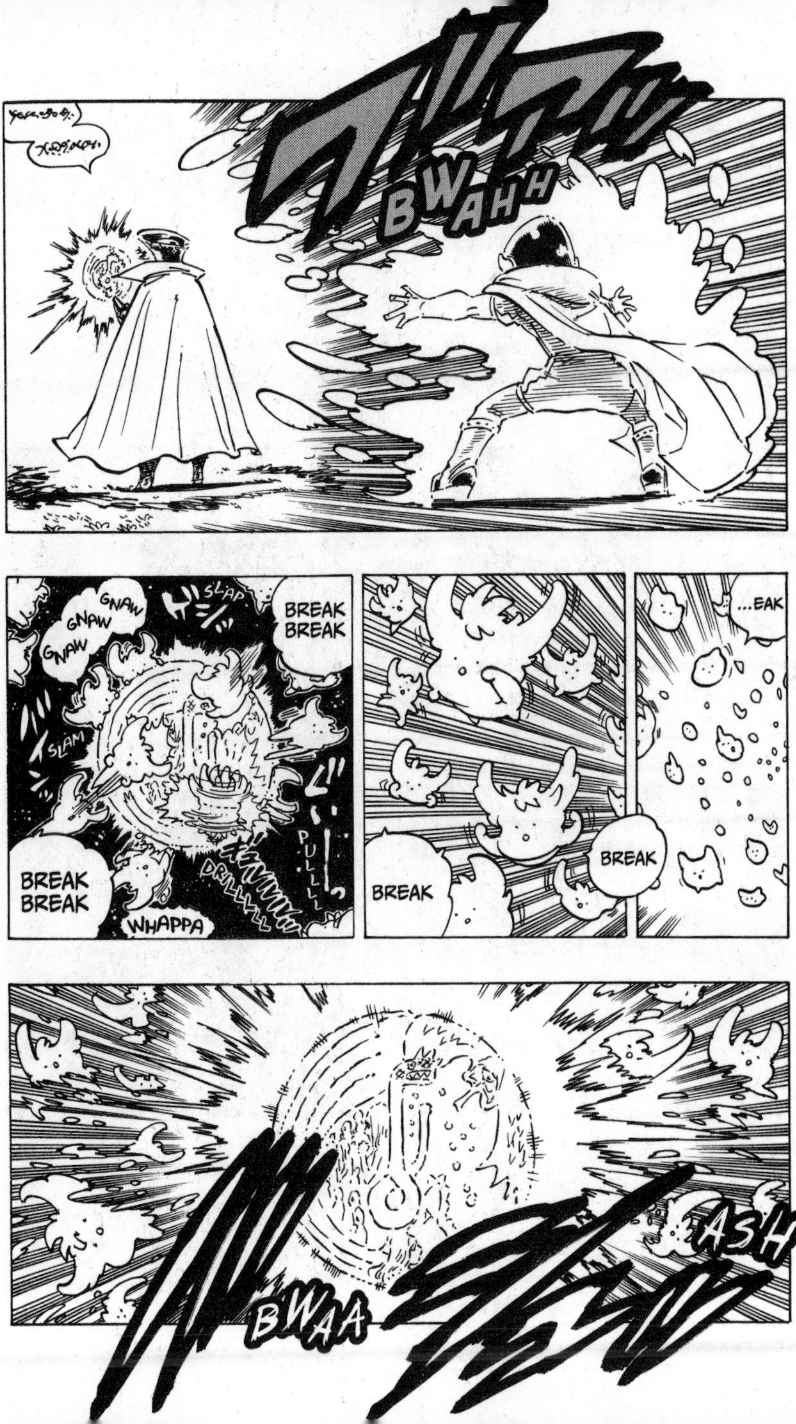
BWAHH
...EAK
BREAK
BREAK
BREAK
BREAK
GNAW
GNAW
GNAW
SLAP
SLAM
PULLLLL
DRILLLLL
WHAPPA
BREAK
BREAK
ASH
BWAA

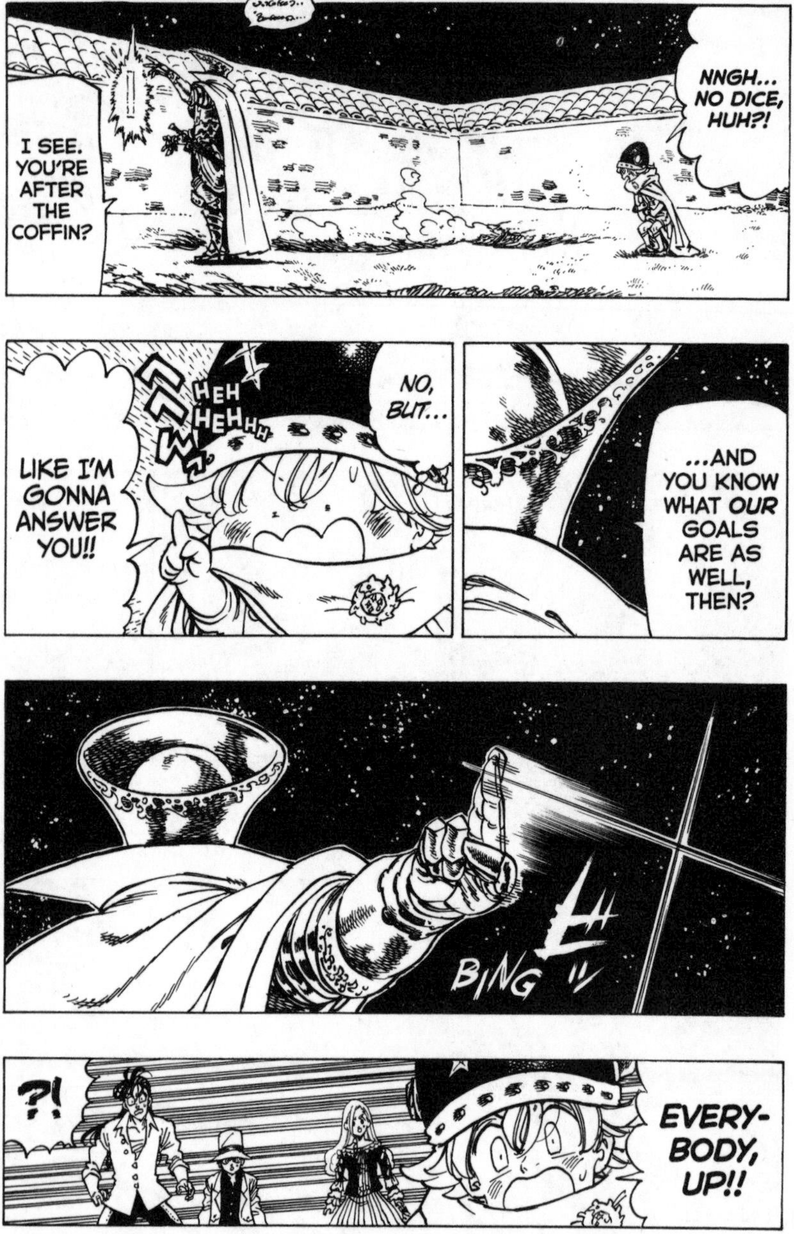
NNGH... NO DICE, HUH?!
I SEE. YOU'RE AFTER THE COFFIN?
...AND YOU KNOW WHAT OUR GOALS ARE AS WELL, THEN?
NO, BUT...
HEH HEHHHH
LIKE I'M GONNA ANSWER YOU!!
BING
EVERY-BODY, UP!!
?!

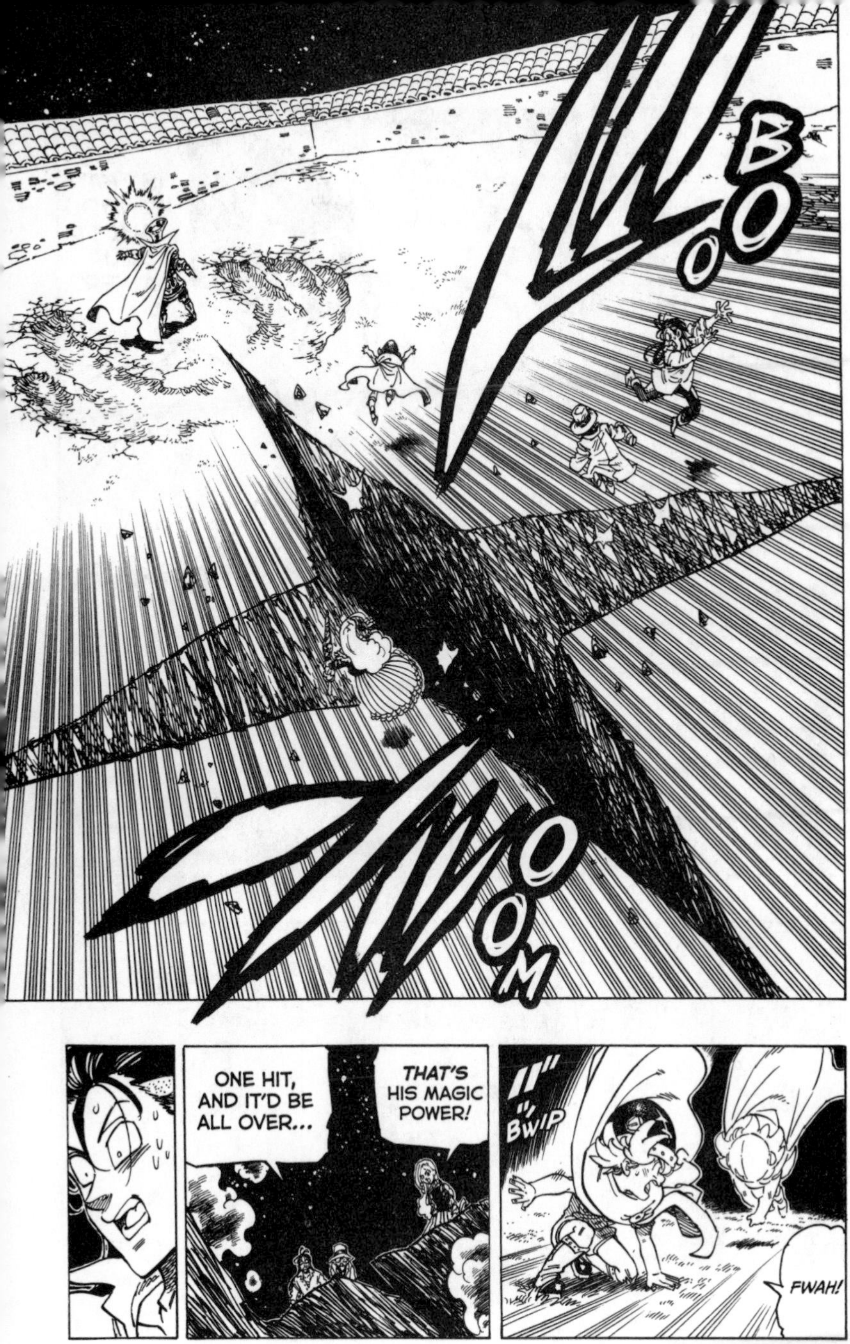
BOO
OOM
BWIP
FWAH!
THAT'S HIS MAGIC POWER!
ONE HIT, AND IT'D BE ALL OVER...

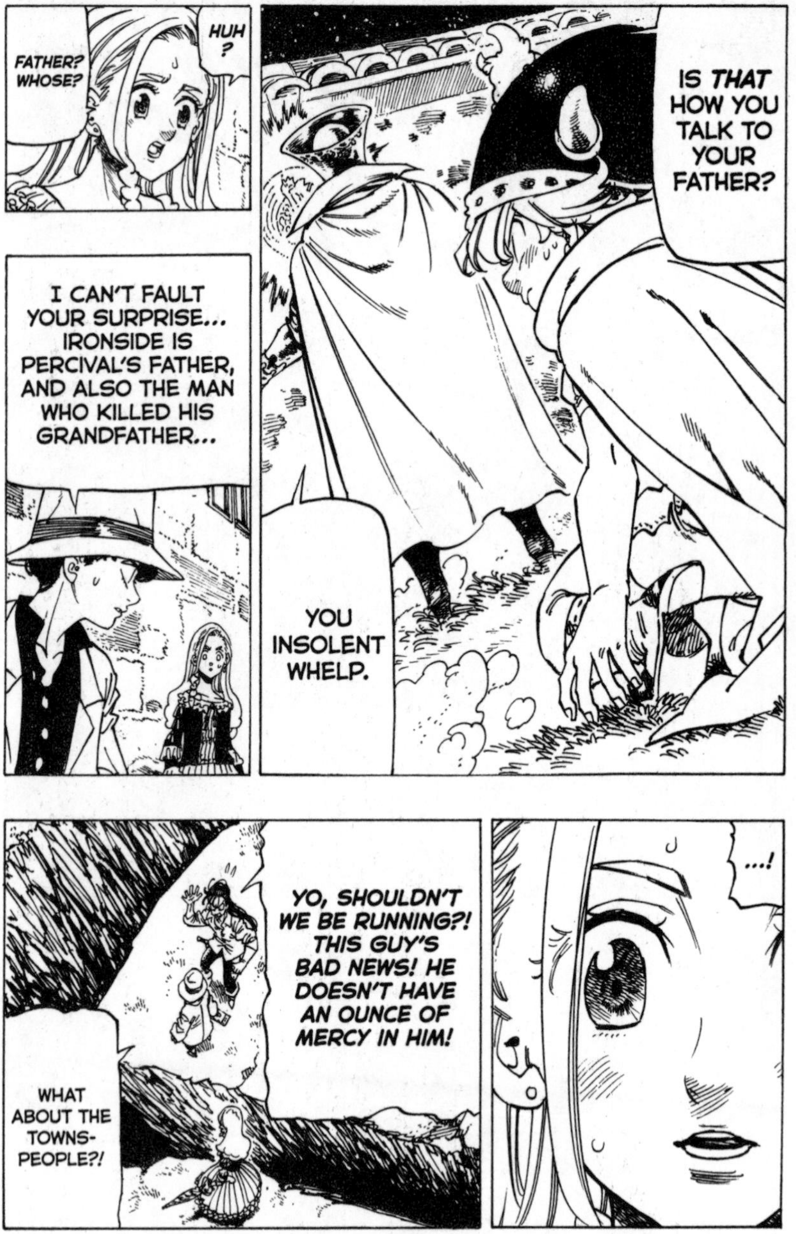
IS *THAT* HOW YOU TALK TO YOUR FATHER?
YOU INSOLENT WHELP.
HUH?
FATHER? WHOSE?
I CAN'T FAULT YOUR SURPRISE... IRONSIDE IS PERCIVAL'S FATHER, AND ALSO THE MAN WHO KILLED HIS GRANDFATHER...
...!
YO, SHOULDN'T WE BE RUNNING?! THIS GUY'S BAD NEWS! HE DOESN'T HAVE AN OUNCE OF MERCY IN HIM!
WHAT ABOUT THE TOWNS-PEOPLE?!

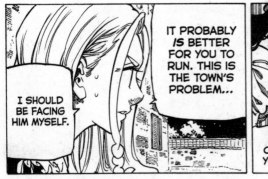

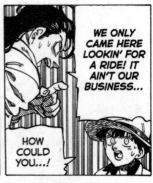

WE ONLY CAME HERE LOOKIN' FOR A RIDE! IT AIN'T OUR BUSINESS...
HOW COULD YOU...!
IT PROBABLY *IS* BETTER FOR YOU TO RUN. THIS IS THE TOWN'S PROBLEM...
I SHOULD BE FACING HIM MYSELF.
WELL, I'M NOT GOING. I KNOW TOO WELL WHAT IT'S LIKE TO WANT TO DEFEND YOUR HOME-LAND...
NA-SIENS...
WHAT...
WHATEVER! DO WHAT YOU WANT! I DON'T WANNA DIE!!
DASH
'CAUSE IF I DIE...
IT'LL BE ALL OVER THEN!!

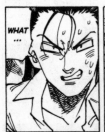

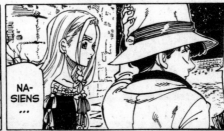

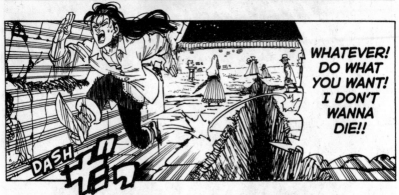

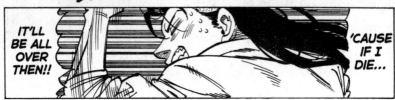

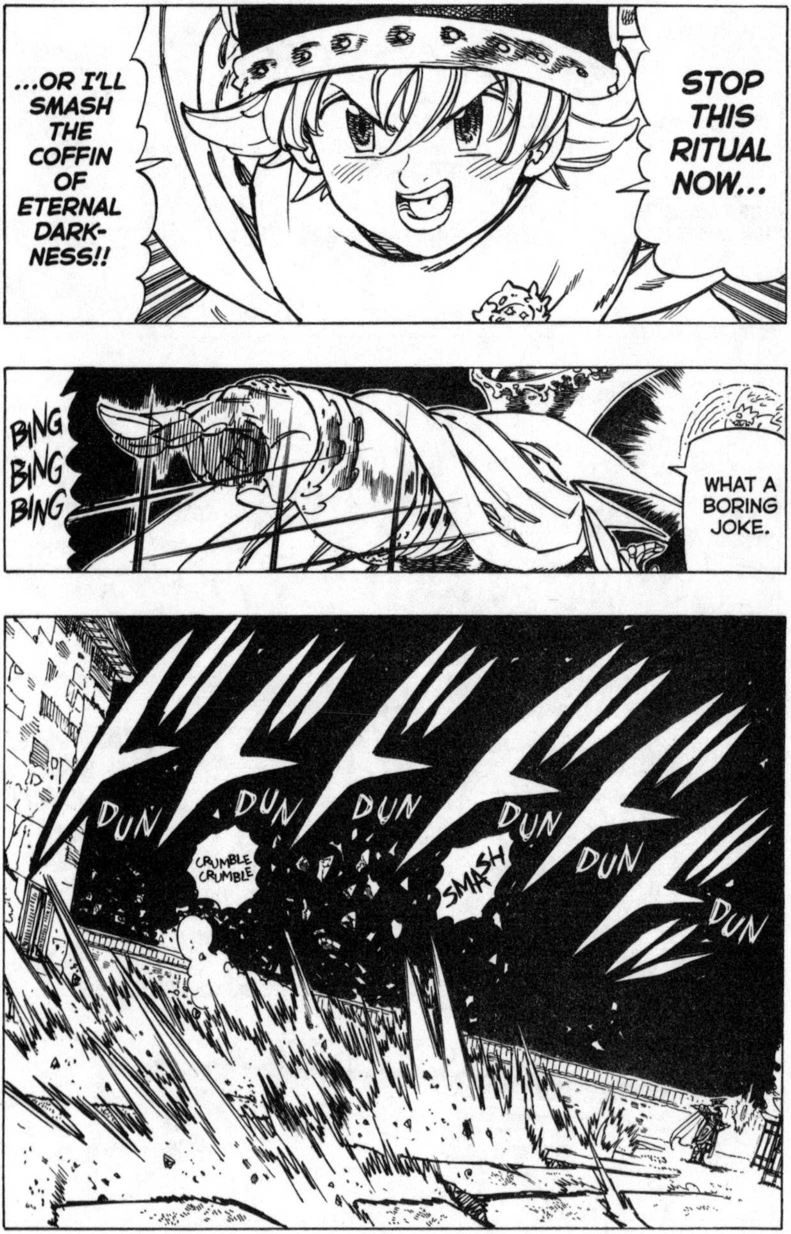
STOP THIS RITUAL NOW...
...OR I'LL SMASH THE COFFIN OF ETERNAL DARKNESS!!
WHAT A BORING JOKE.
BING BING BING
DUN DUN DUN DUN DUN DUN
SMASH
CRUMBLE CRUMBLE

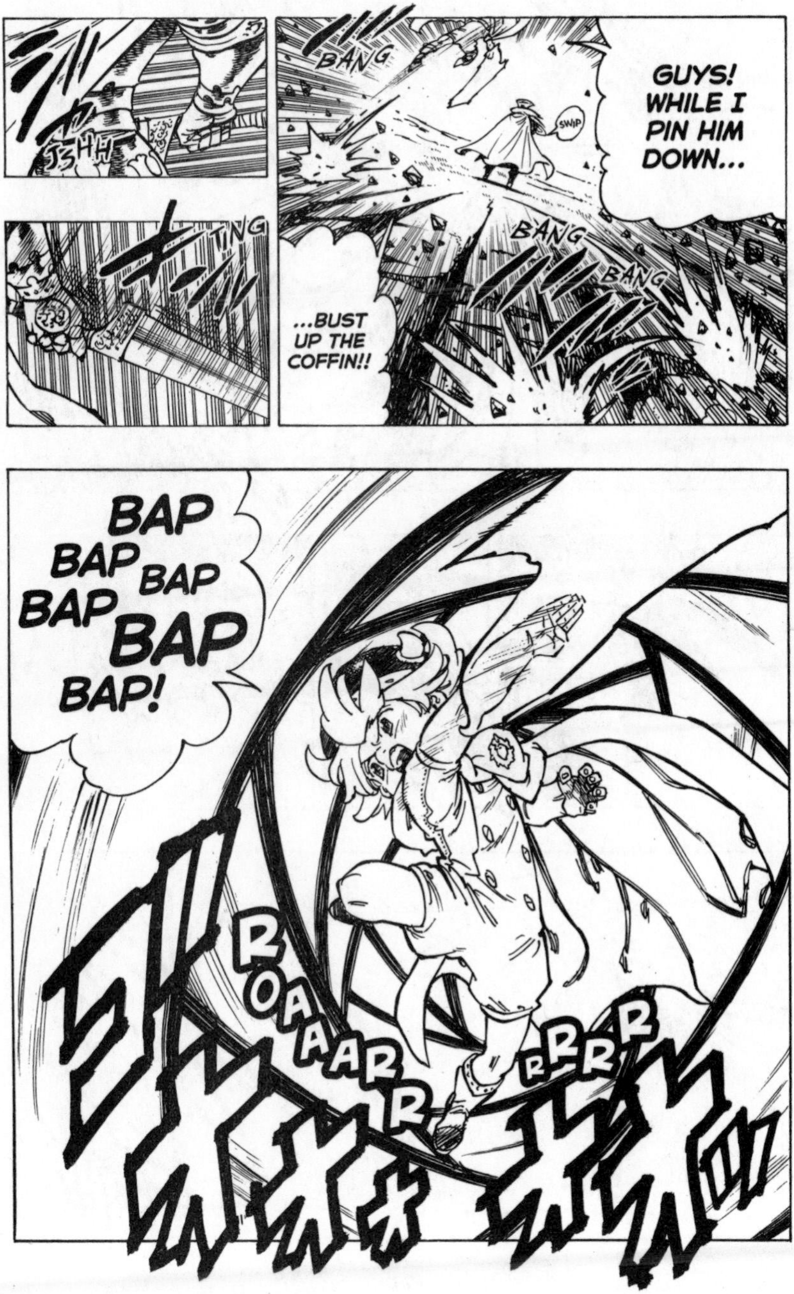
BANG
SWIP
GUYS! WHILE I PIN HIM DOWN...
BANG
BANG
...BUST UP THE COFFIN!!
JSHH
TING
BAP BAP BAP BAP BAP BAP!
ROAAAARR
RRRR

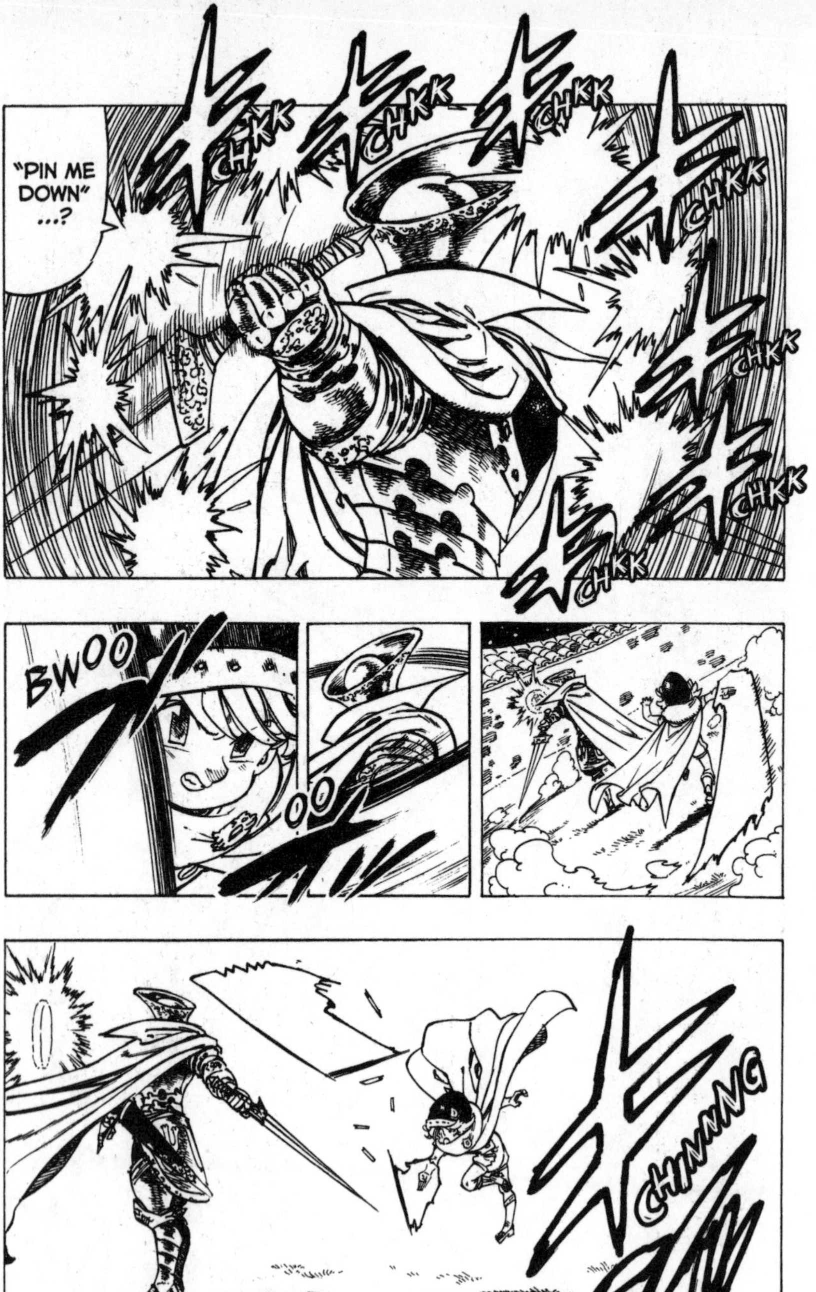
CHKK
CHKK
CHKK
CHKK
CHKK
CHKK
CHKK
"PIN ME DOWN" ...?
BWOO
CHINNNG

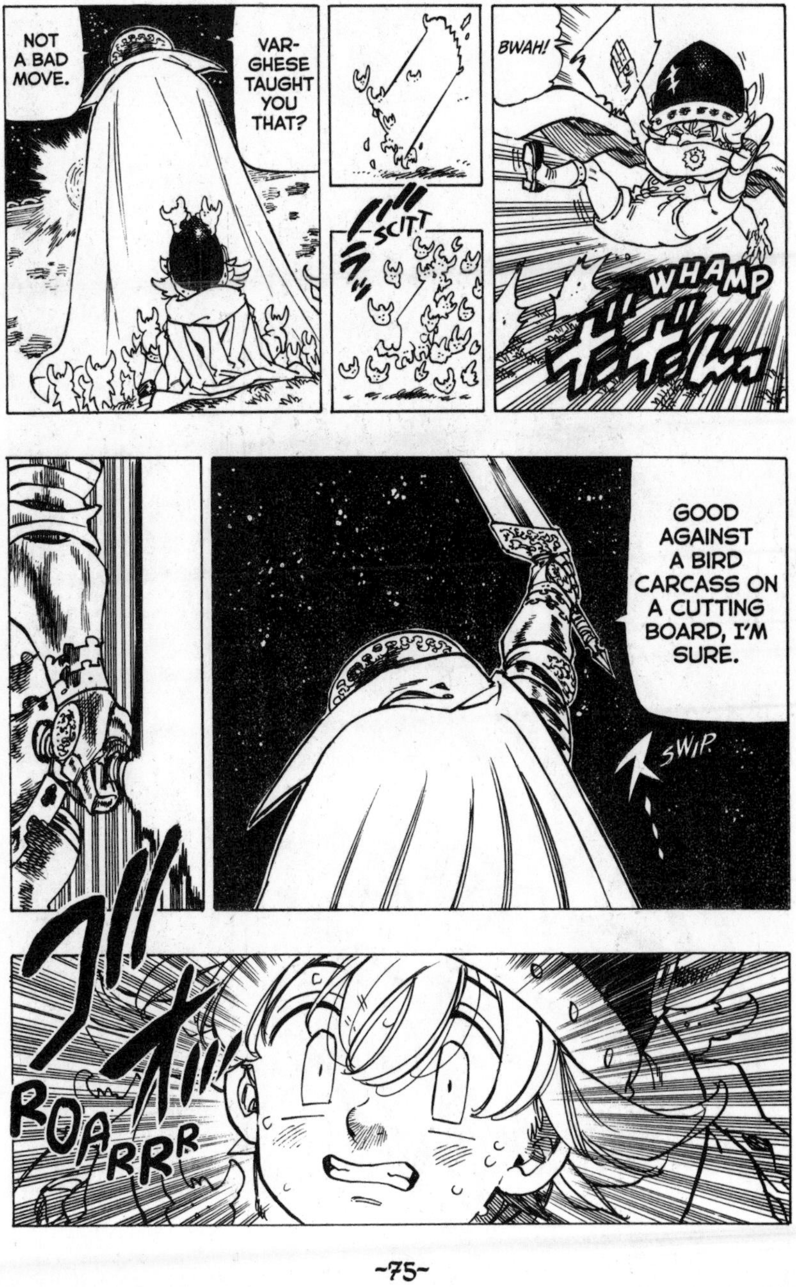
BWAH!
WHAMP
SCITT
VAR-GHESE TAUGHT YOU THAT?
NOT A BAD MOVE.
GOOD AGAINST A BIRD CARCASS ON A CUTTING BOARD, I'M SURE.
SWIP
ROARRR

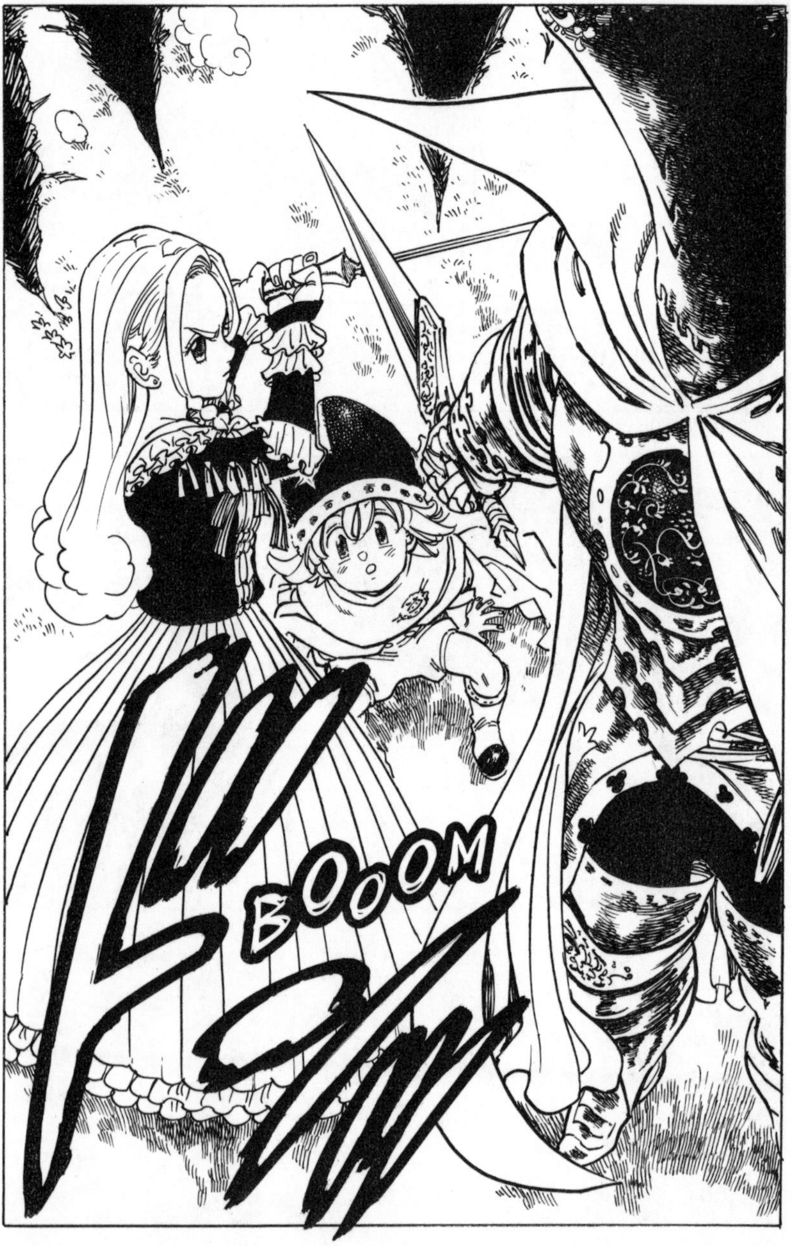
BOOOM

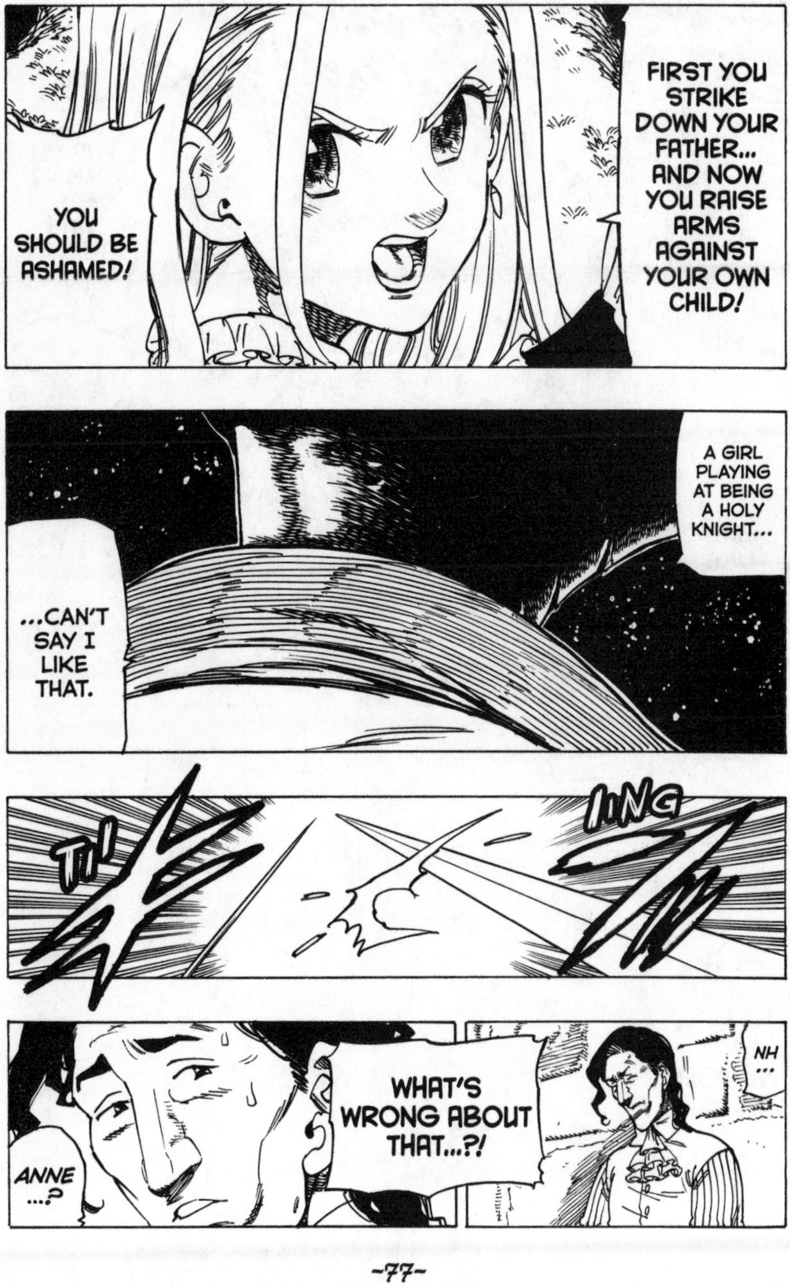
FIRST YOU STRIKE DOWN YOUR FATHER... AND NOW YOU RAISE ARMS AGAINST YOUR OWN CHILD!
YOU SHOULD BE ASHAMED!
A GIRL PLAYING AT BEING A HOLY KNIGHT...
...CAN'T SAY I LIKE THAT.
IING
TI'
NH...
WHAT'S WRONG ABOUT THAT...?!
ANNE...?

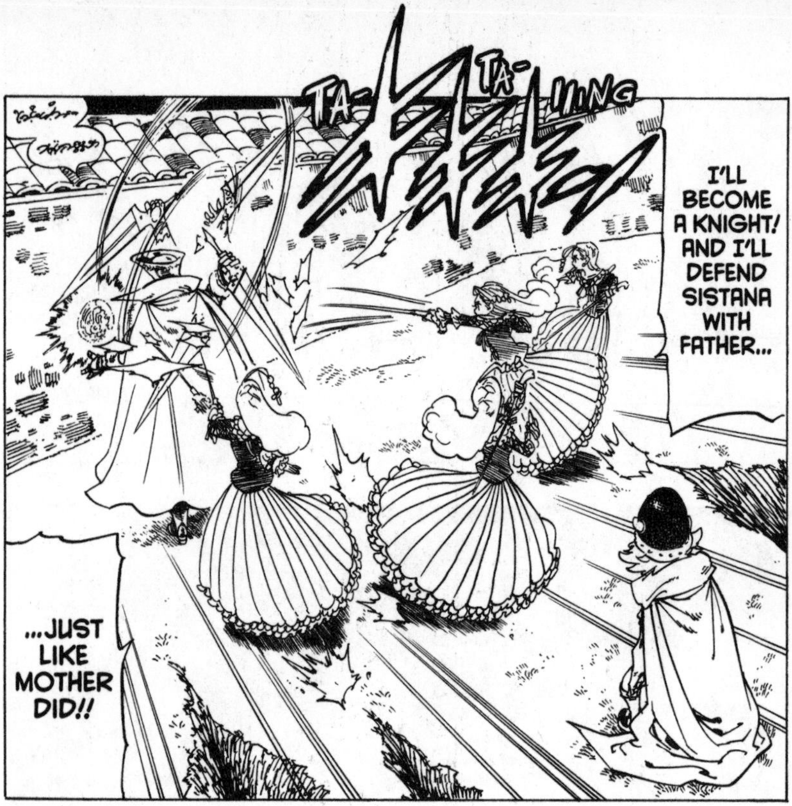
TA-TA-IIING
I'LL BECOME A KNIGHT! AND I'LL DEFEND SISTANA WITH FATHER...
...JUST LIKE MOTHER DID!!

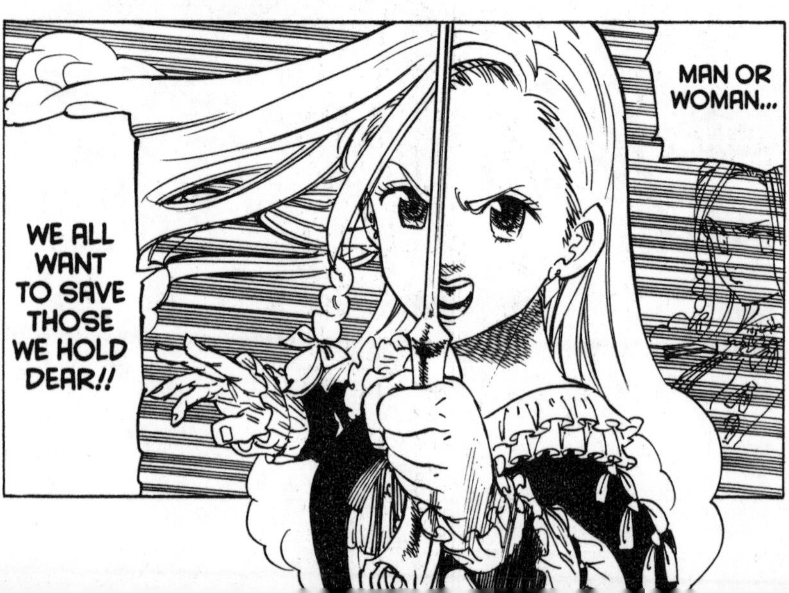
MAN OR WOMAN...
WE ALL WANT TO SAVE THOSE WE HOLD DEAR!!

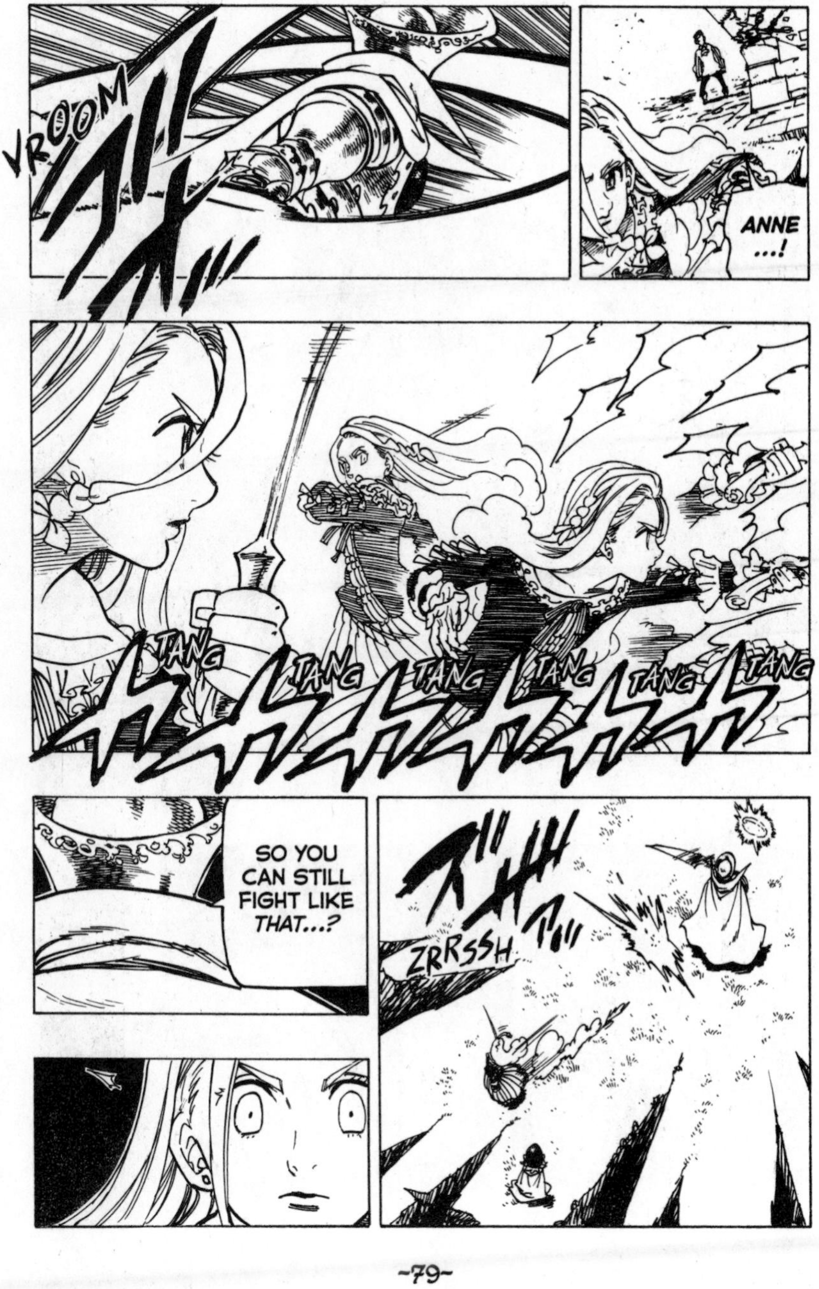
ANNE ...!
VROOM
TANG TANG TANG TANG TANG TANG
ZRRSSH
SO YOU CAN STILL FIGHT LIKE THAT...?

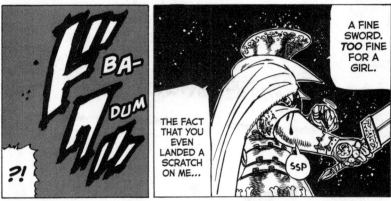

BSSH

BA-DUM

?!

A FINE SWORD. *TOO* FINE FOR A GIRL.

THE FACT THAT YOU EVEN LANDED A SCRATCH ON ME...

SSP

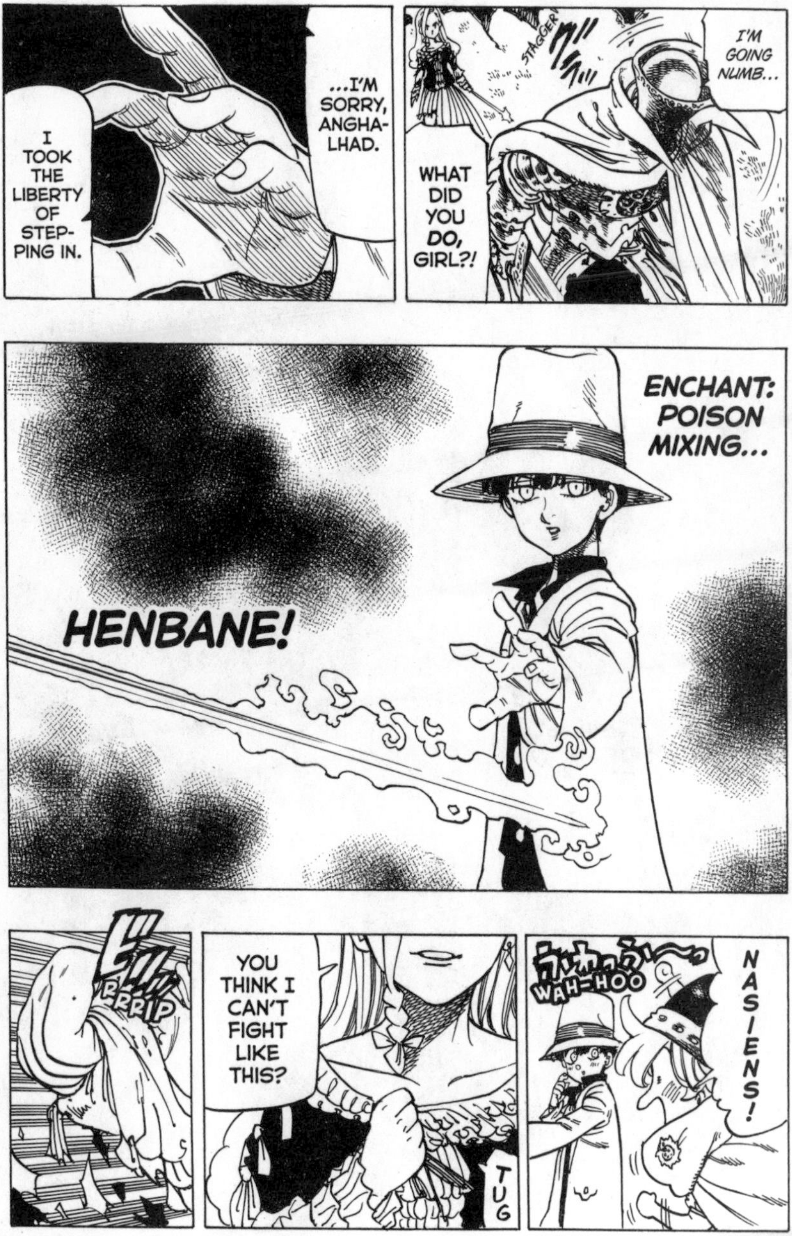
STAGGER
I'M GOING NUMB...
WHAT DID YOU *DO*, GIRL?!
...I'M SORRY, ANGHA-LHAD.
I TOOK THE LIBERTY OF STEP-PING IN.
ENCHANT: POISON MIXING...
HENBANE!
WAH-HOO
NASIENS!
YOU THINK I CAN'T FIGHT LIKE THIS?
TUG
RRRIP

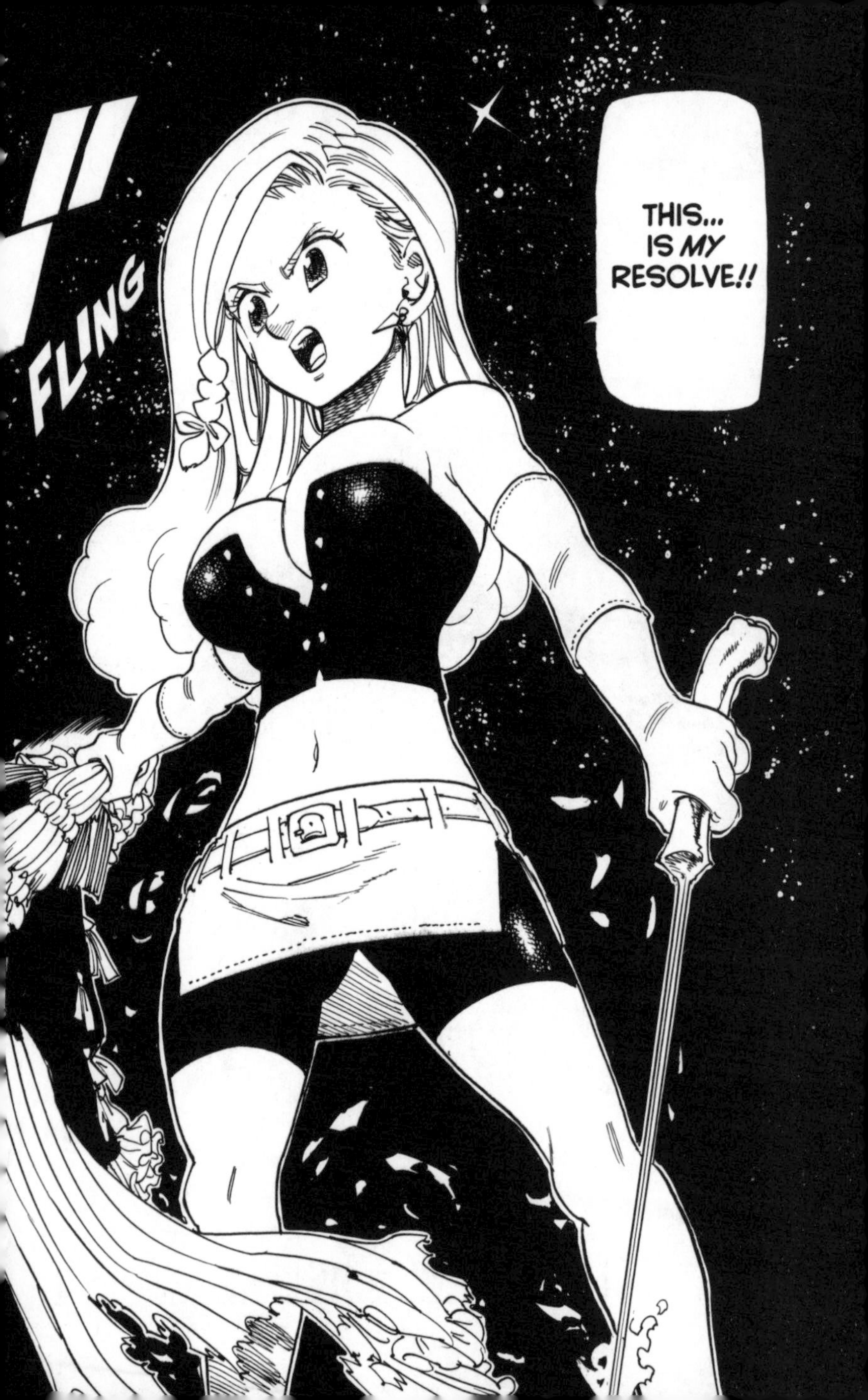
FLING
THIS... IS MY RESOLVE!!

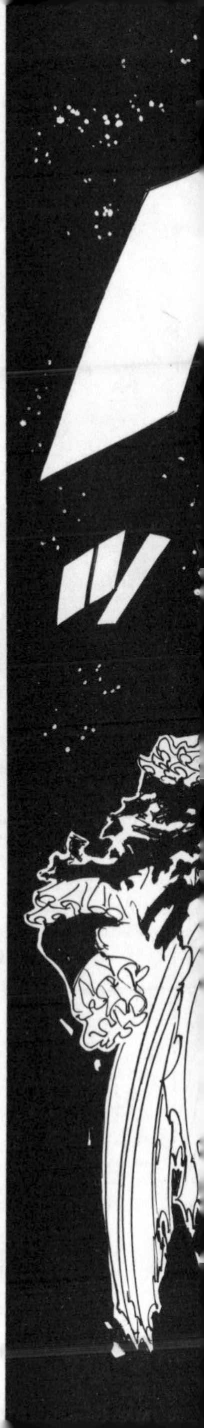

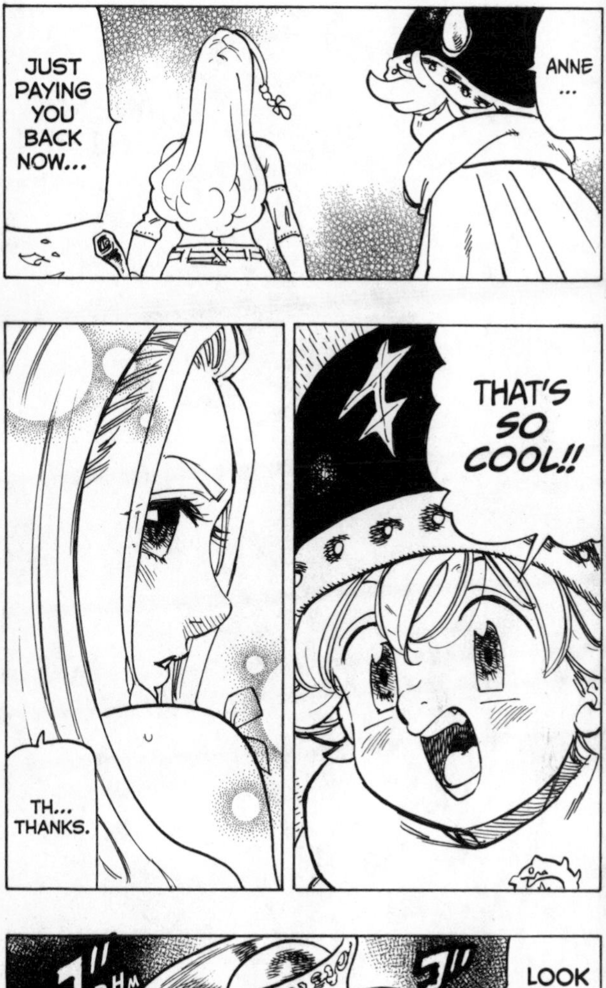
ANNE...
JUST PAYING YOU BACK NOW...
THAT'S SO COOL!!
TH... THANKS.
LOOK AT ALL OF YOU...
RHM
RHM
RHM
NO DISCIPLINE AT ALL.

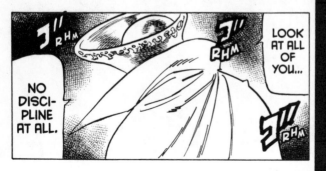

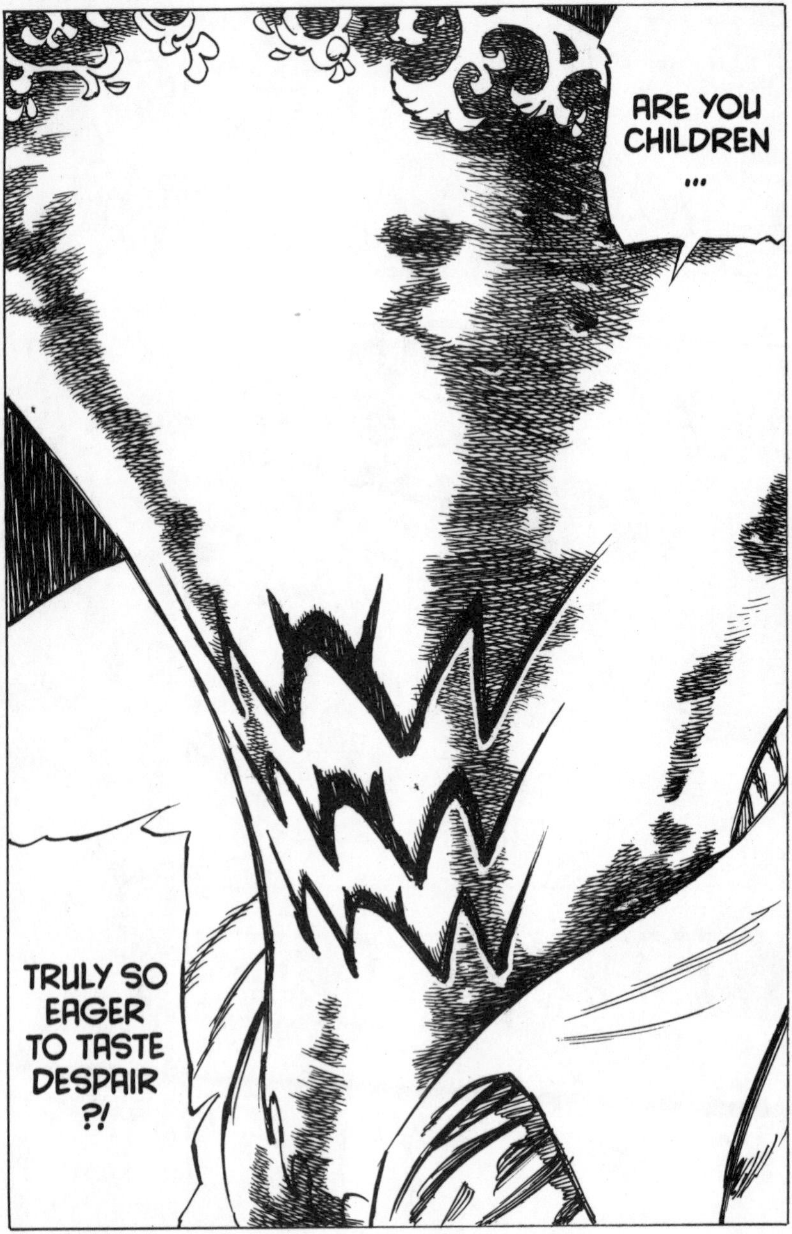
ARE YOU CHILDREN ...
TRULY SO EAGER TO TASTE DESPAIR ?!

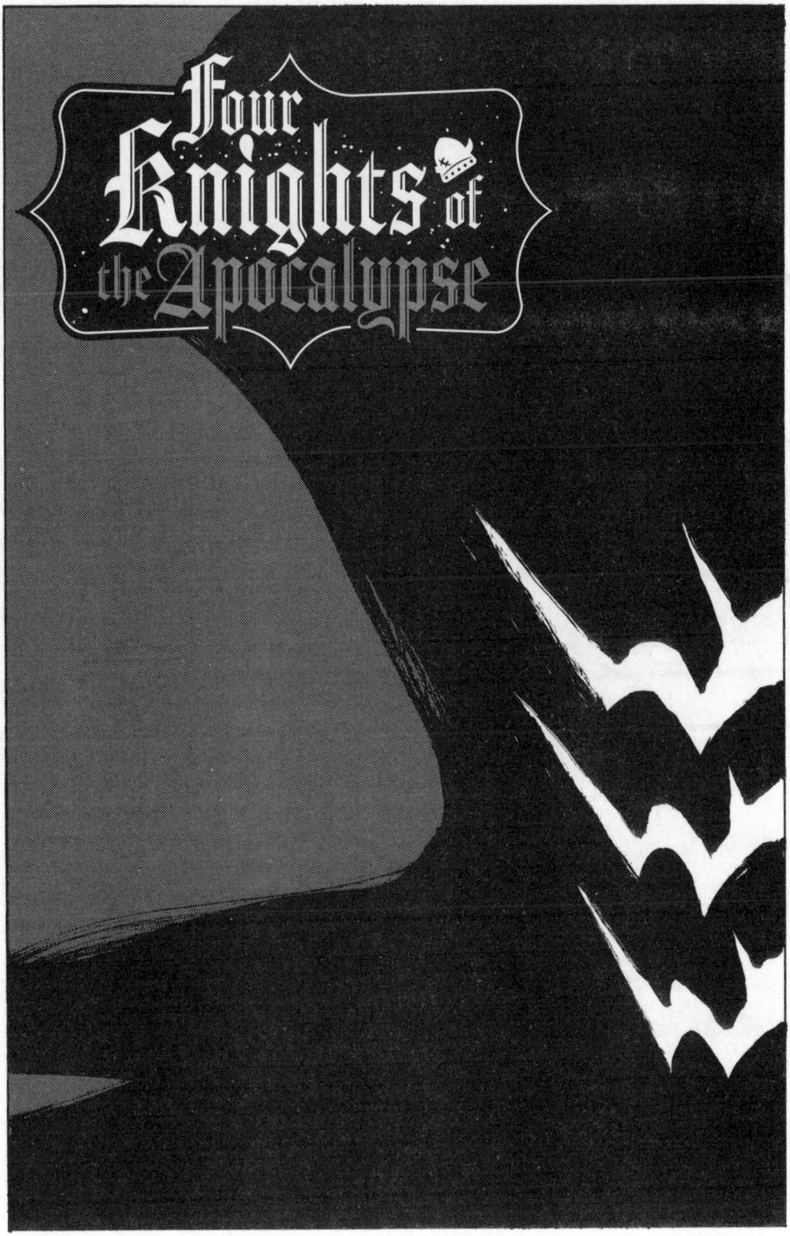
Four Knights of the Apocalypse

CHAPTER 19: AN ACT OF EVIL

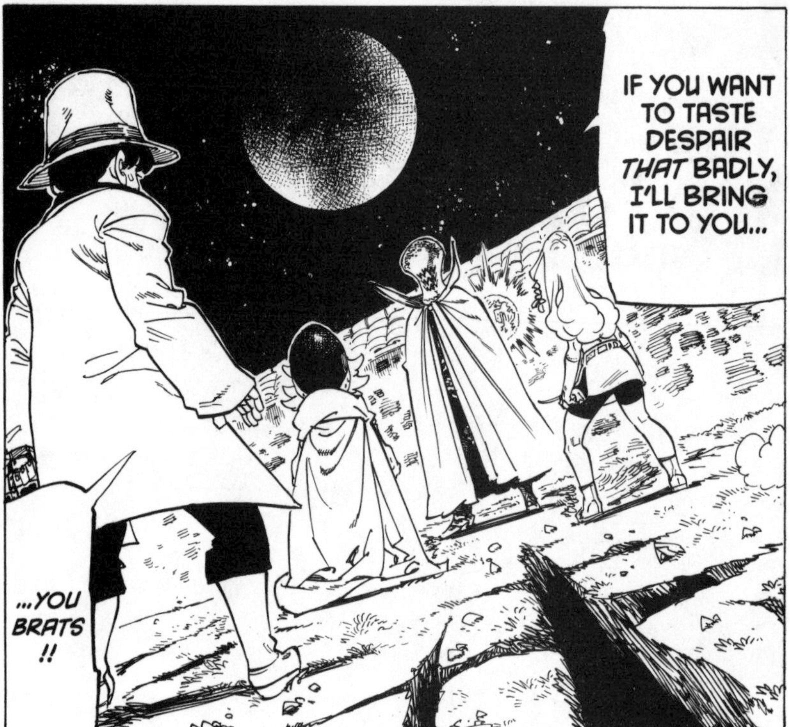
IF YOU WANT TO TASTE DESPAIR *THAT* BADLY, I'LL BRING IT TO YOU...
...YOU BRATS!!

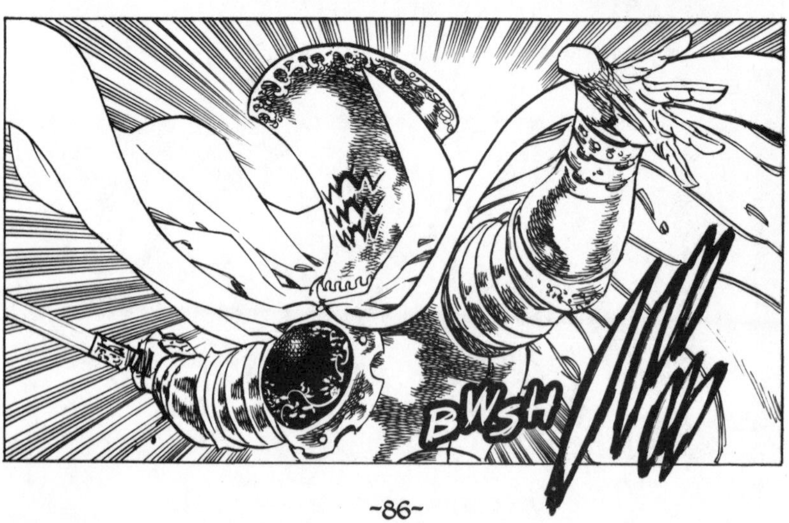
BWSH

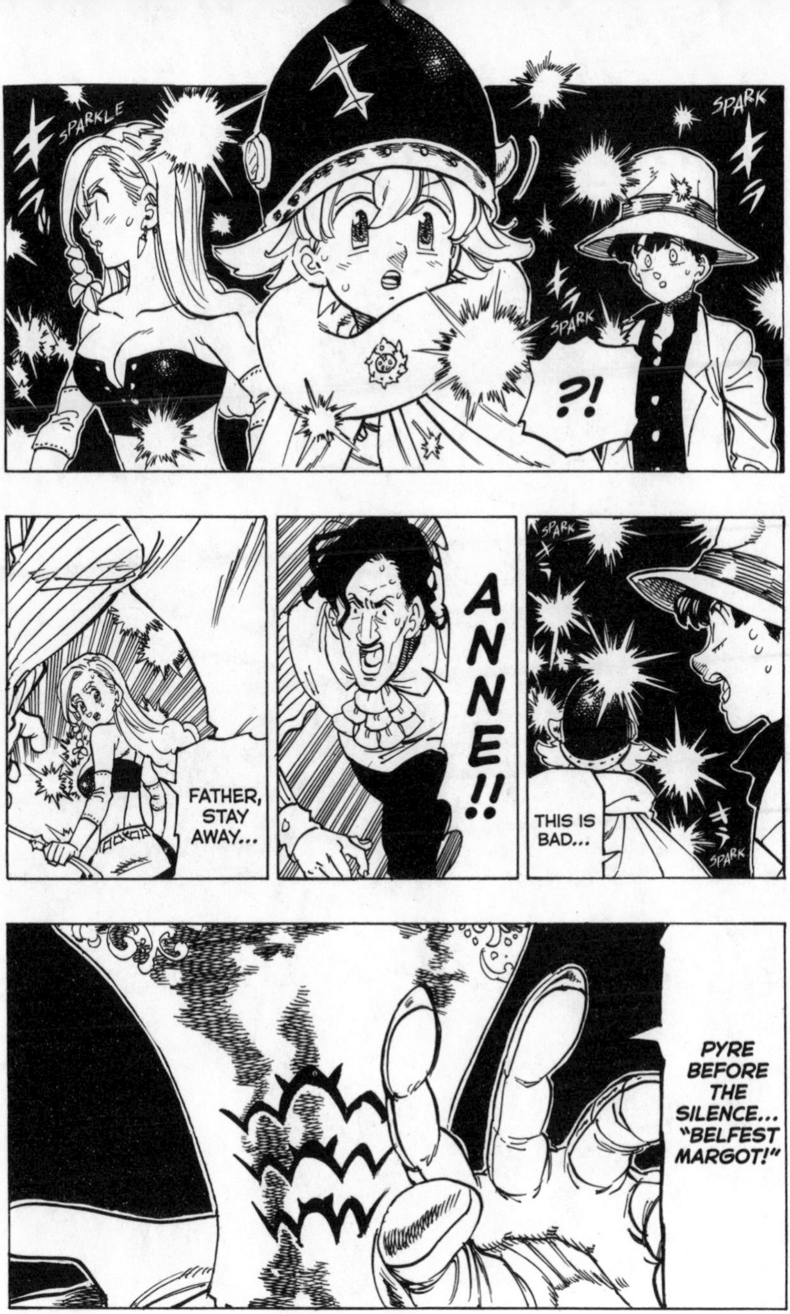
SPARK
SPARKLE
SPARK
?!
SPARK
THIS IS BAD...
SPARK
ANNE!!
FATHER, STAY AWAY...
PYRE BEFORE THE SILENCE... "BELFEST MARGOT!"

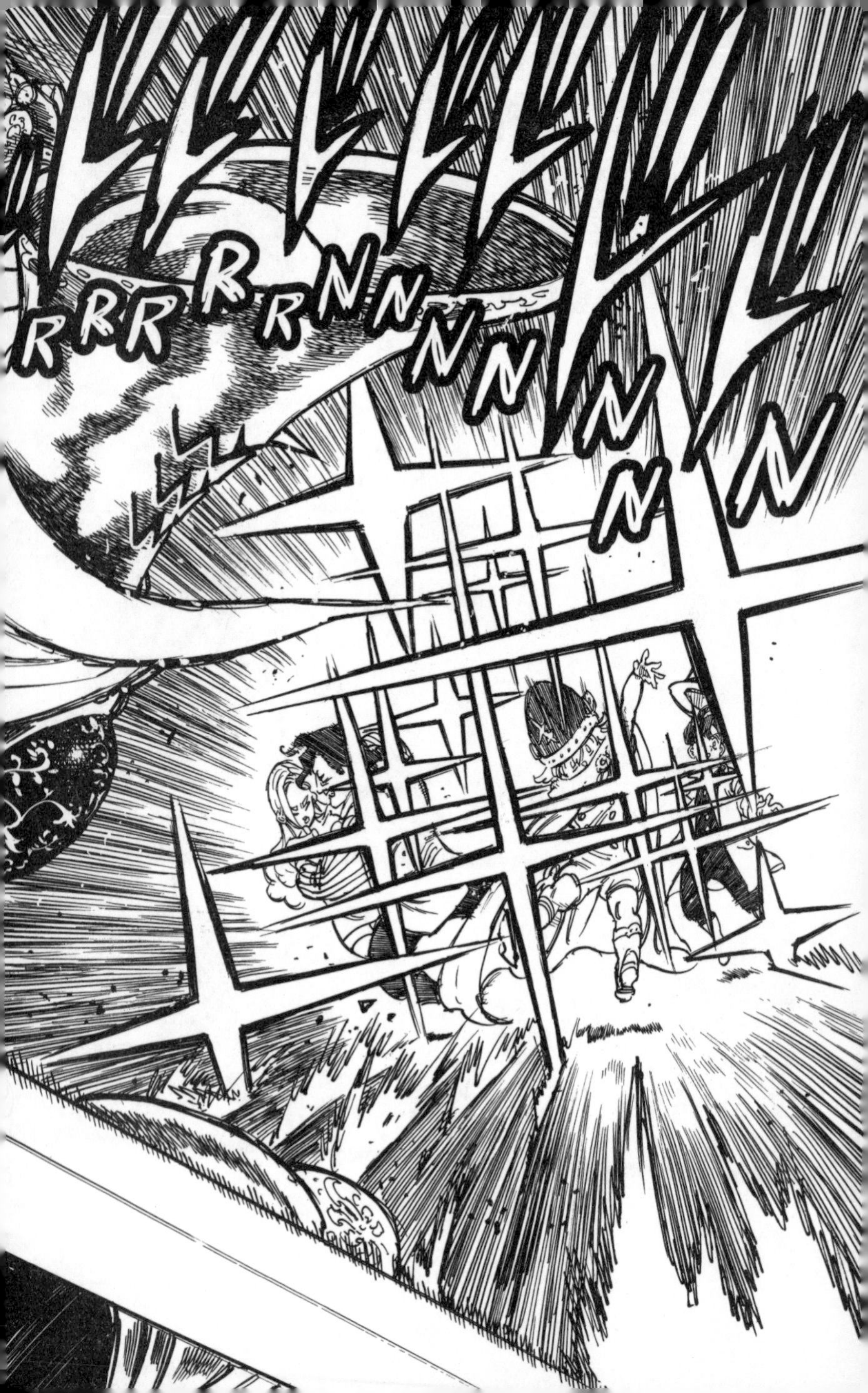
RRRRRRNNNNNNNN

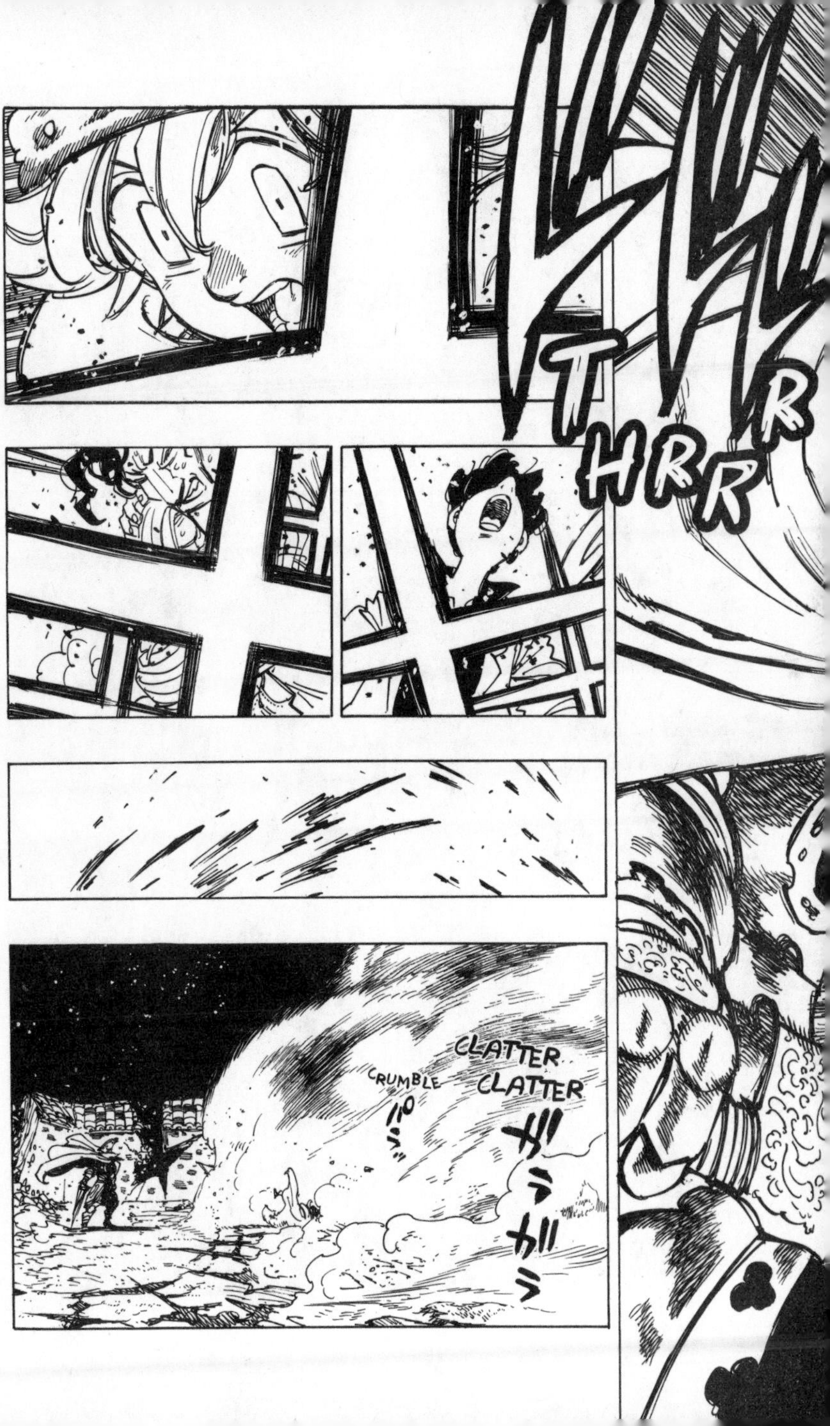
THRRR
CLATTER CLATTER
ガラガラ
CRUMBLE
ゴッ

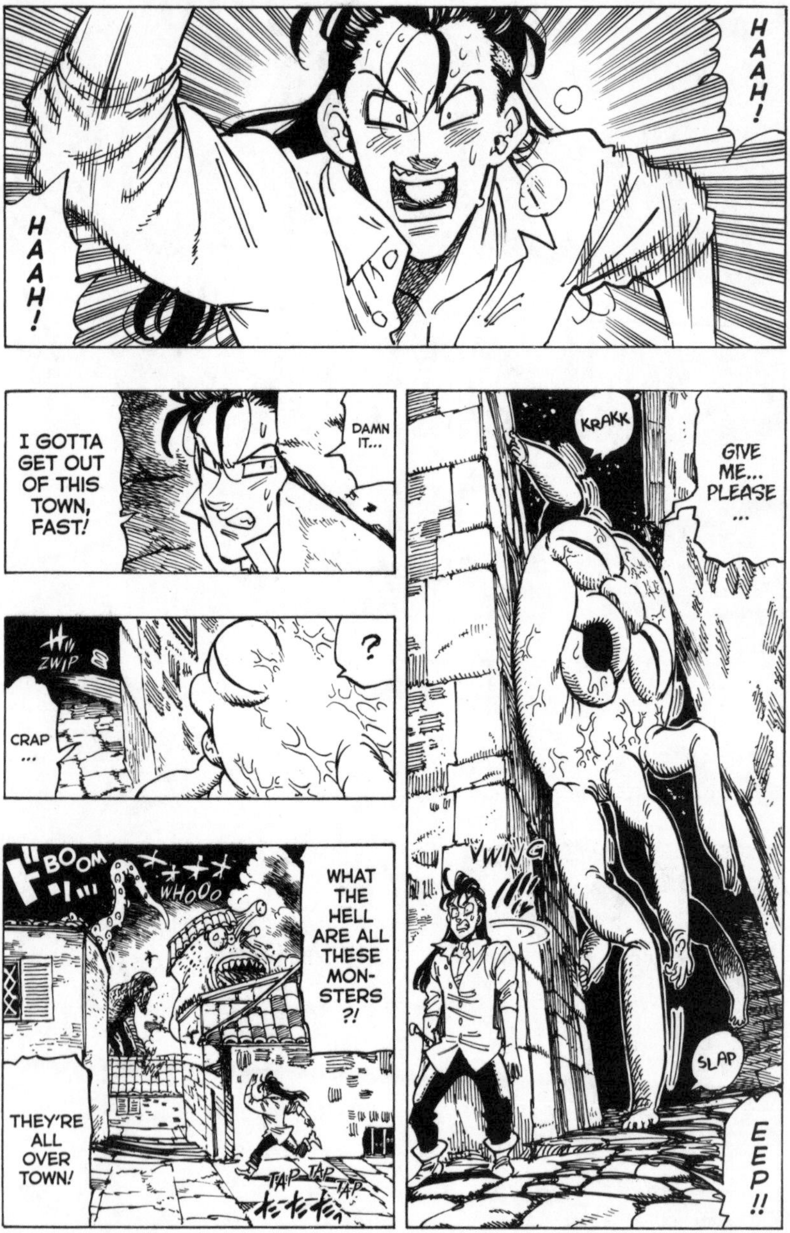
HAAAH!
HAAAH!
KRAKK
GIVE ME... PLEASE ...
VWING
SLAP
EEP!!
DAMN IT...
I GOTTA GET OUT OF THIS TOWN, FAST!
?
ZWIP
CRAP ...
WHAT THE HELL ARE ALL THESE MONSTERS ?!
BOOM
WHOOO
THEY'RE ALL OVER TOWN!
TAP TAP TAP

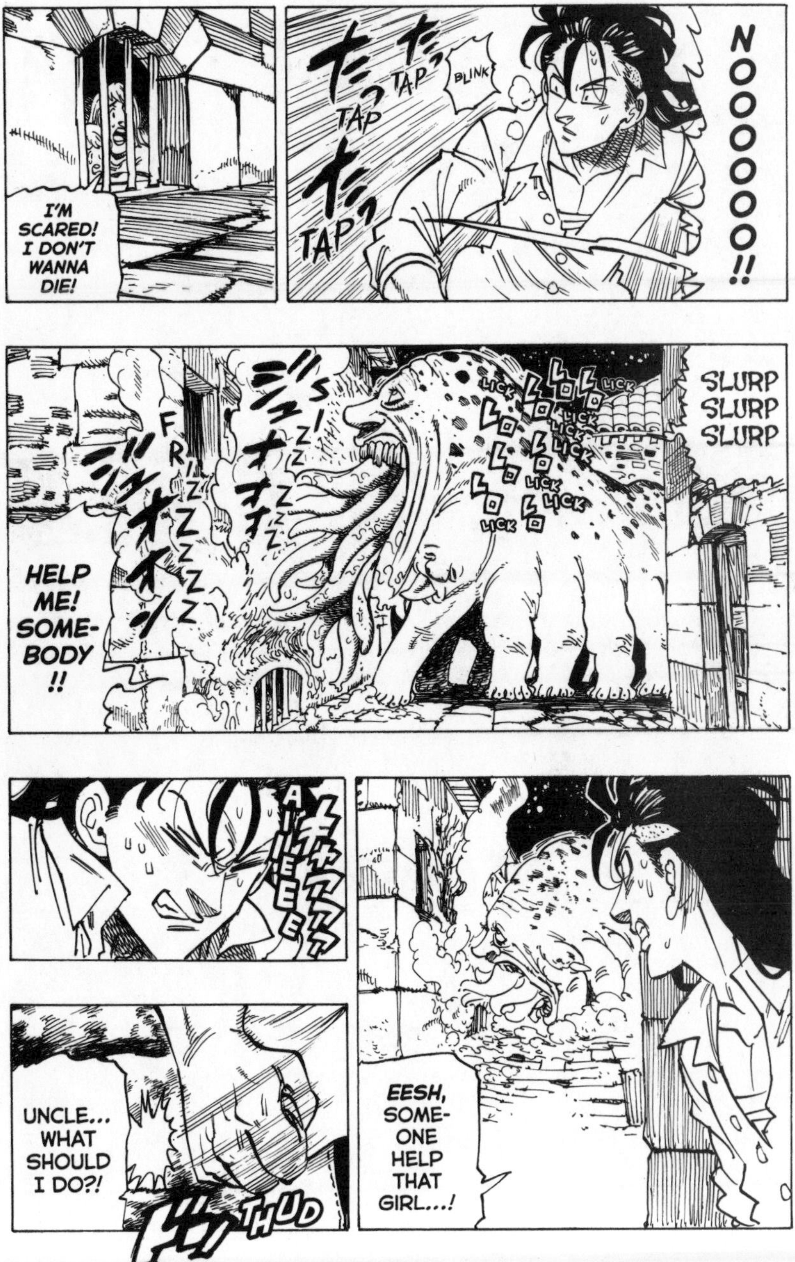
TAP
BLINK
TAP
TAP
NOOOOOOO!!
I'M SCARED! I DON'T WANNA DIE!
SLURP SLURP SLURP
LICK LICK LICK LICK LICK LICK LICK
FRIZZZZZZ
SIZZZZZZZ
HELP ME! SOMEBODY!!
EESH, SOMEONE HELP THAT GIRL...!
AIIIEEEE
UNCLE... WHAT SHOULD I DO?!
THUD

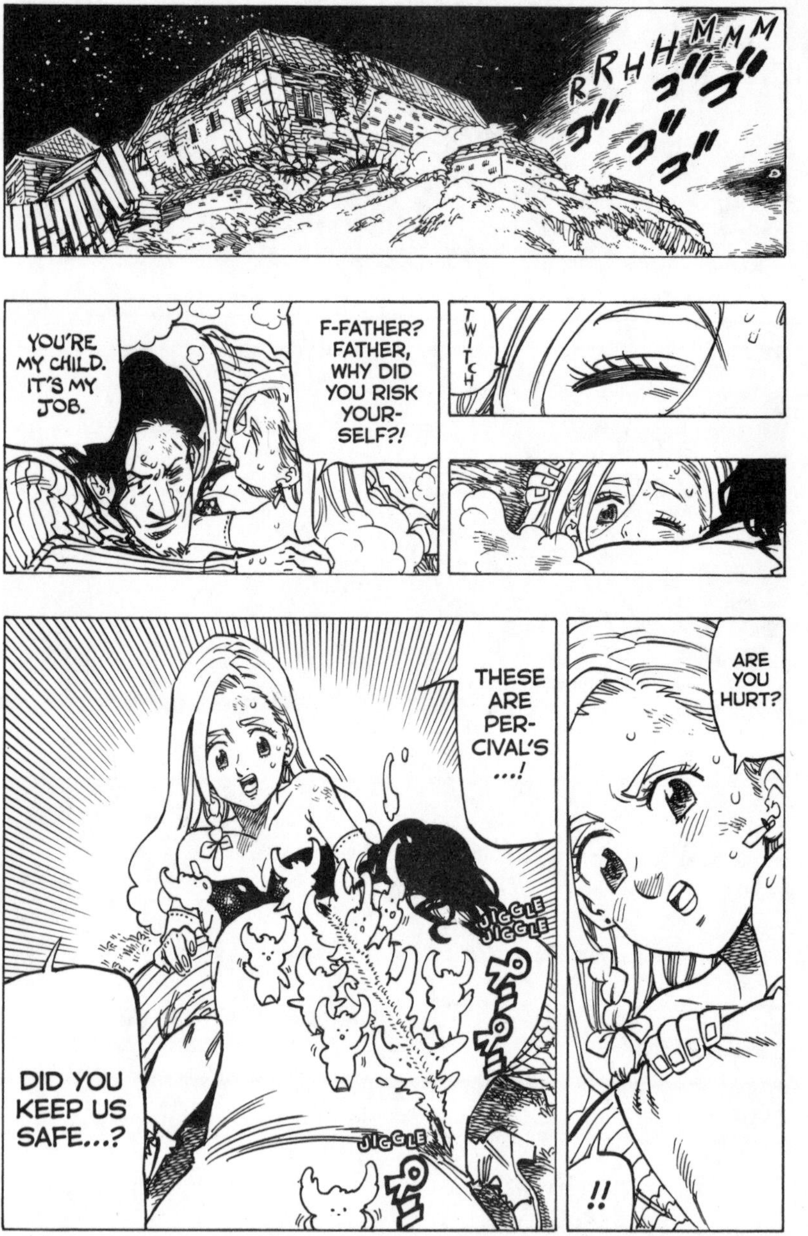
RRHHMMMM
TWITCH
F-FATHER? FATHER, WHY DID YOU RISK YOURSELF?!
YOU'RE MY CHILD. IT'S MY JOB.
ARE YOU HURT?
!!
THESE ARE PERCIVAL'S ...!
JIGGLE JIGGLE
DID YOU KEEP US SAFE...?
JIGGLE

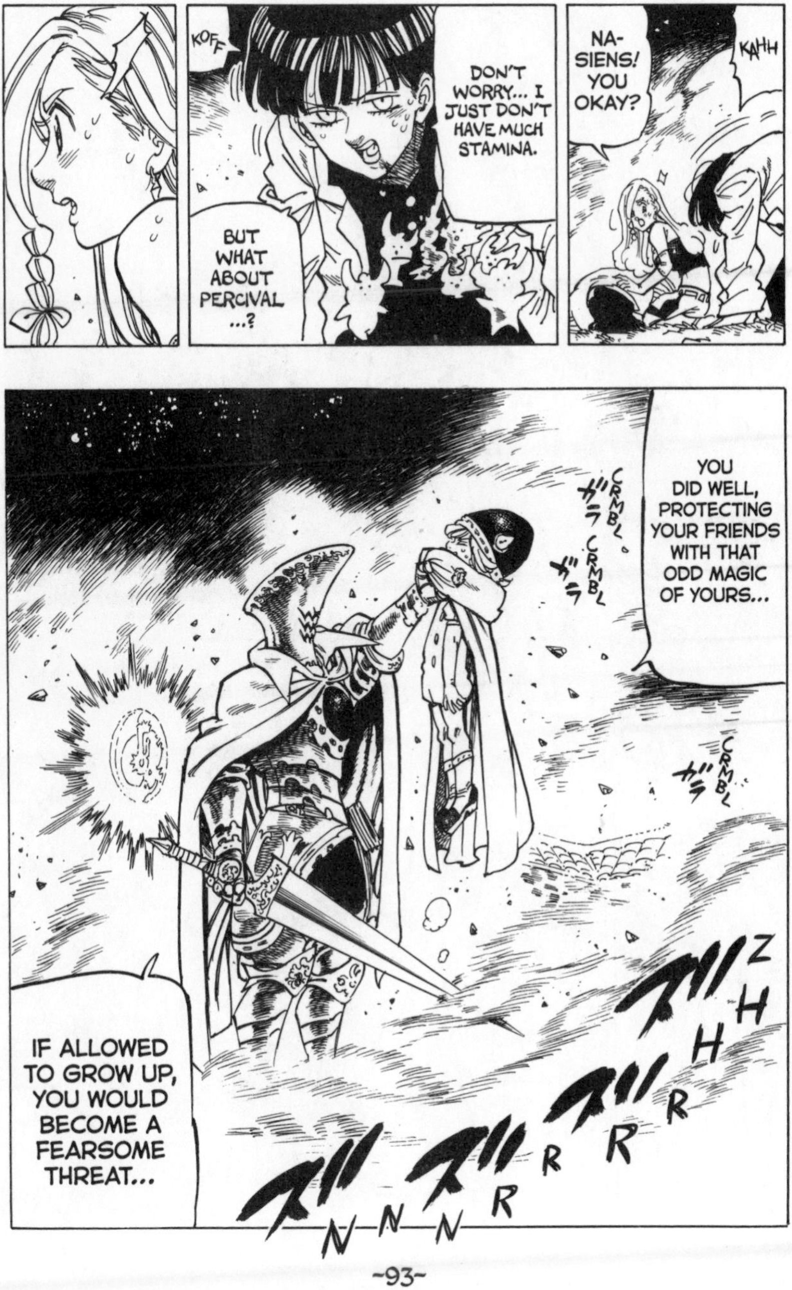
NA-SIENS! YOU OKAY?
KAHH
KOFF
DON'T WORRY... I JUST DON'T HAVE MUCH STAMINA.
BUT WHAT ABOUT PERCIVAL ...?
YOU DID WELL, PROTECTING YOUR FRIENDS WITH THAT ODD MAGIC OF YOURS...
CRMBL
CRMBL
CRMBL
IF ALLOWED TO GROW UP, YOU WOULD BECOME A FEARSOME THREAT...
ZHHH
RRRRR
NNN

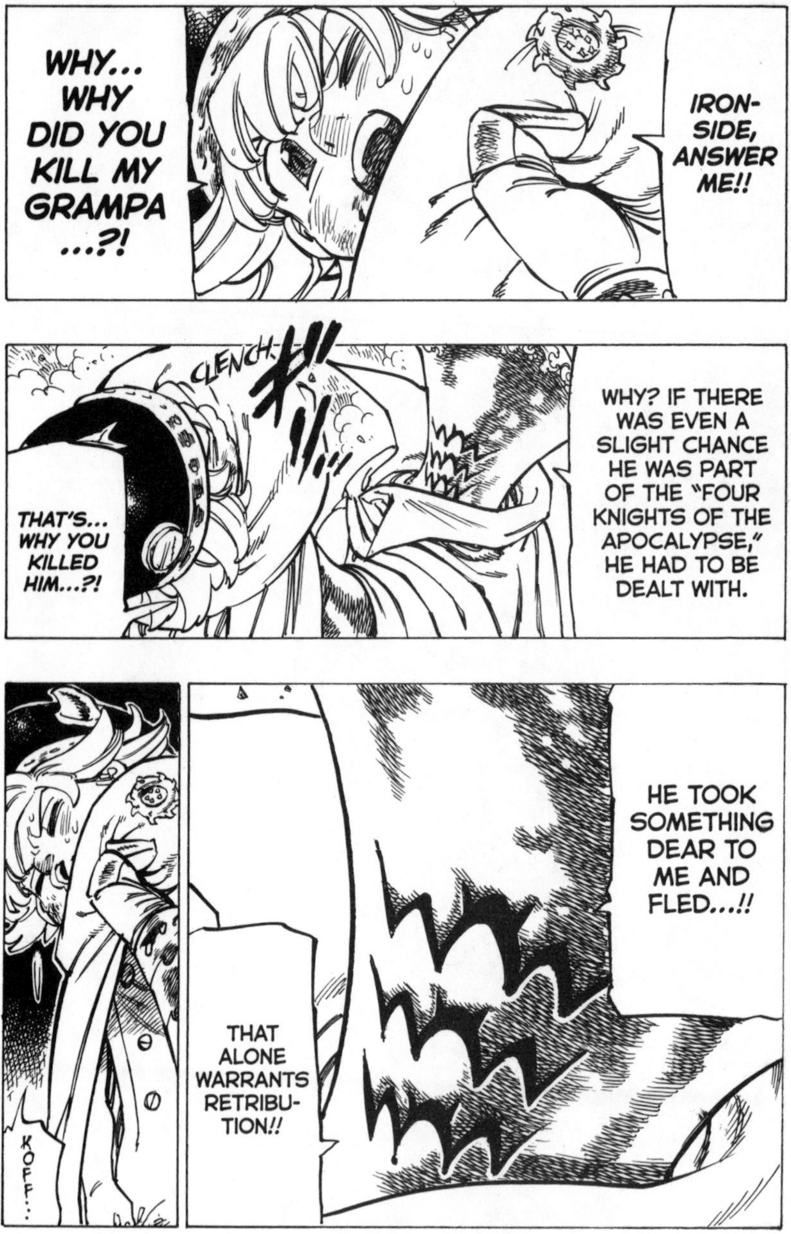
IRON-SIDE, ANSWER ME!!
WHY... WHY DID YOU KILL MY GRAMPA ...?!
WHY? IF THERE WAS EVEN A SLIGHT CHANCE HE WAS PART OF THE "FOUR KNIGHTS OF THE APOCALYPSE," HE HAD TO BE DEALT WITH.
CLENCH
THAT'S... WHY YOU KILLED HIM...?!
HE TOOK SOMETHING DEAR TO ME AND FLED...!!
THAT ALONE WARRANTS RETRIBU-TION!!
KOFF...

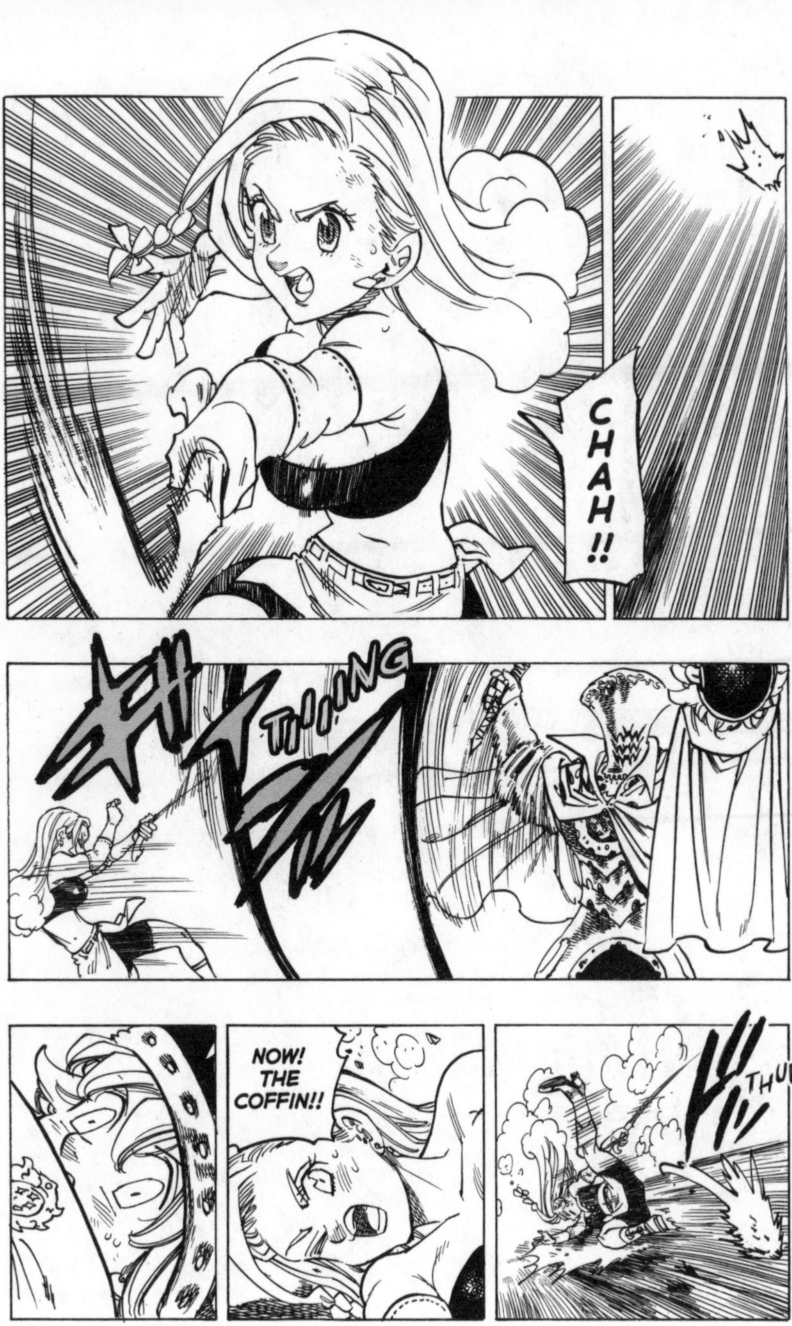
CHAH!!
ZZH
TI'I'I'ING
NOW! THE COFFIN!!
THUD

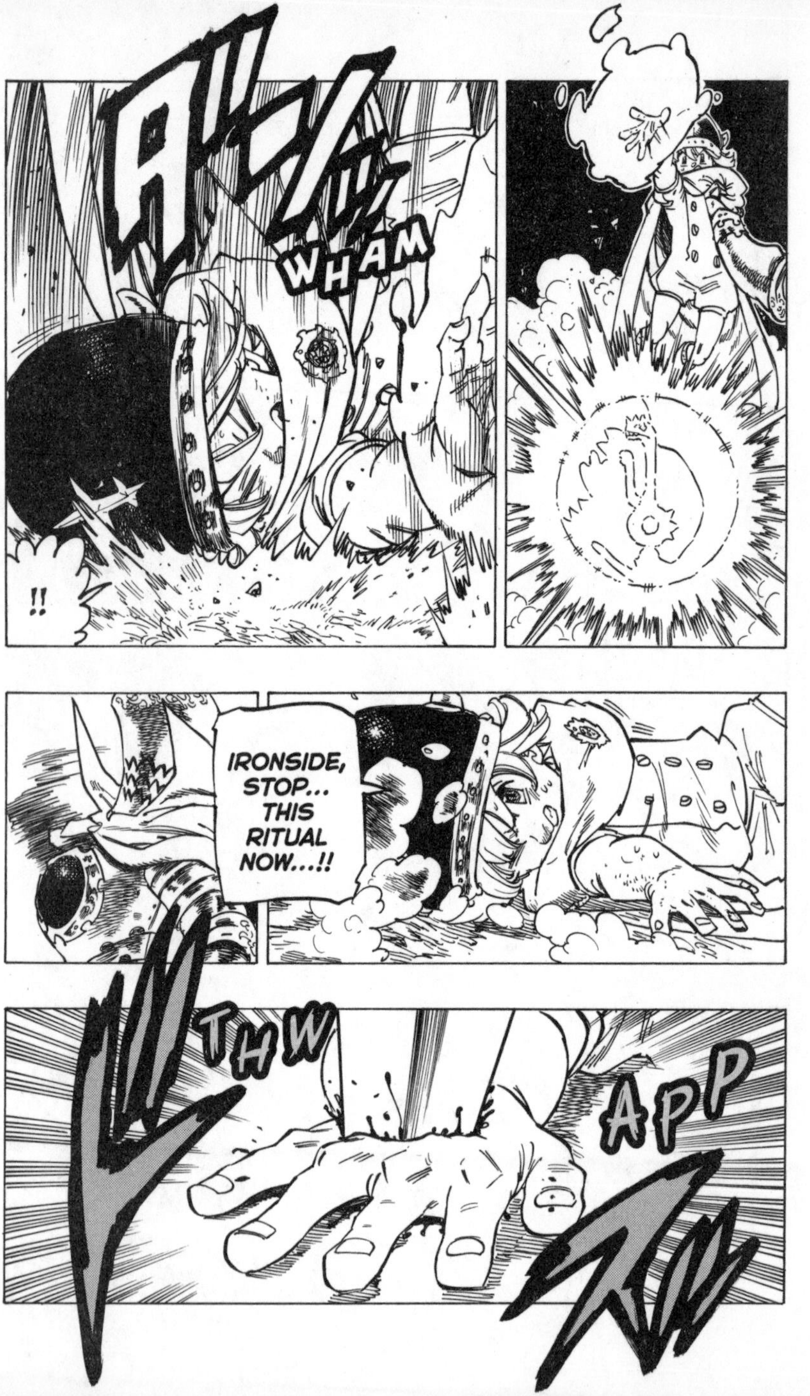
WHAM
!!
IRONSIDE, STOP... THIS RITUAL NOW...!!
THWAPP

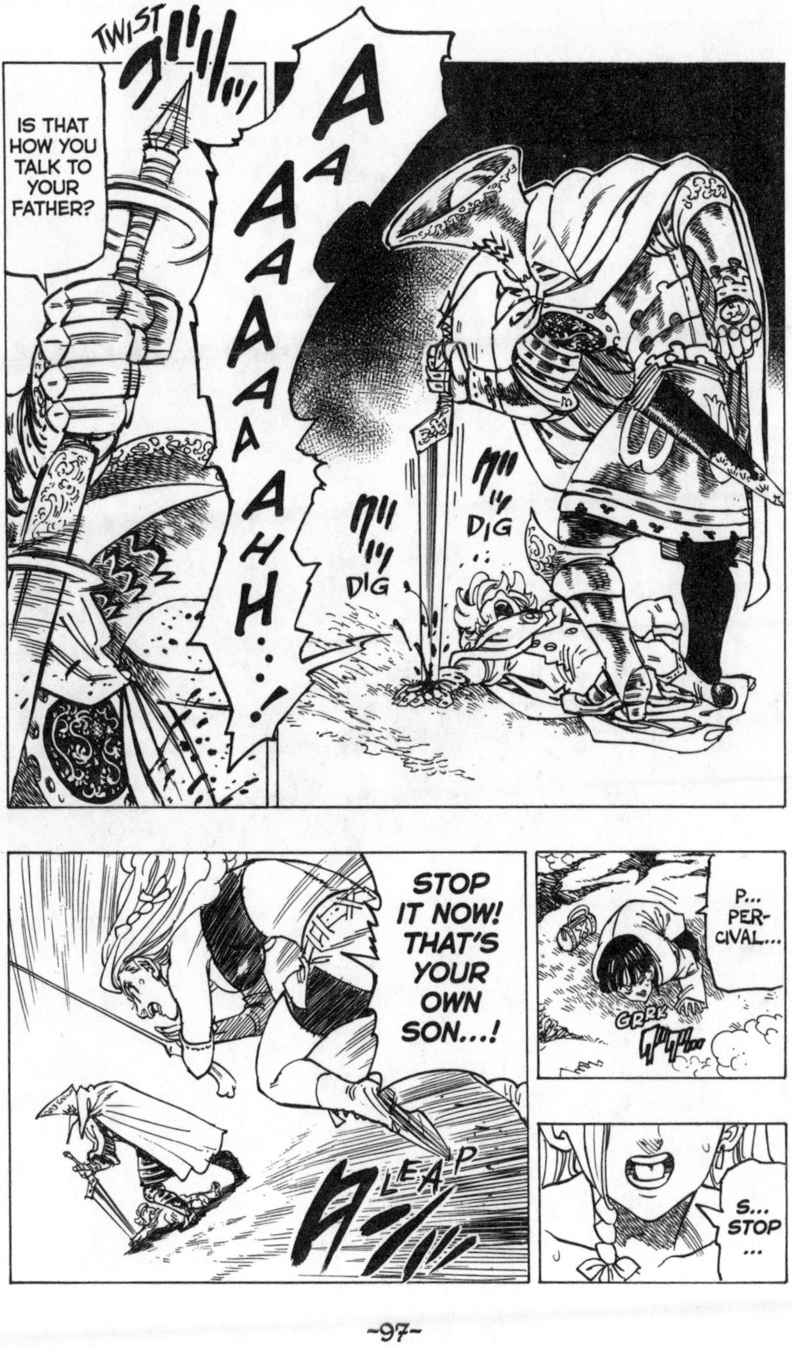
TWIST
IS THAT HOW YOU TALK TO YOUR FATHER?
AAAAAAAAAAAH...!
DIG
DIG
P... PERCIVAL...
GRRK
S... STOP ...
STOP IT NOW! THAT'S YOUR OWN SON...!
LEAP

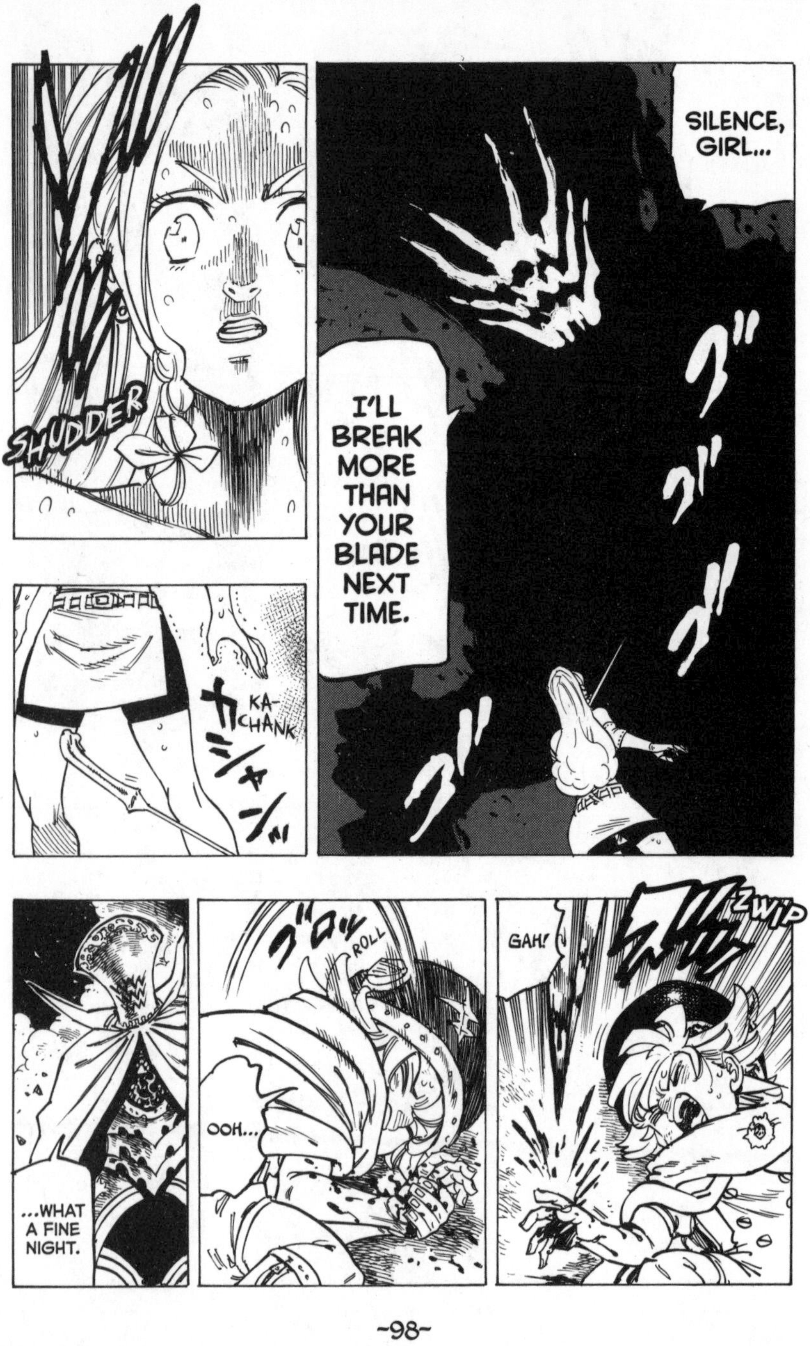
SILENCE, GIRL...
I'LL BREAK MORE THAN YOUR BLADE NEXT TIME.
SHUDDER
KA-CHANK
ZWIP
GAH!
ROLL
OOH...
...WHAT A FINE NIGHT.

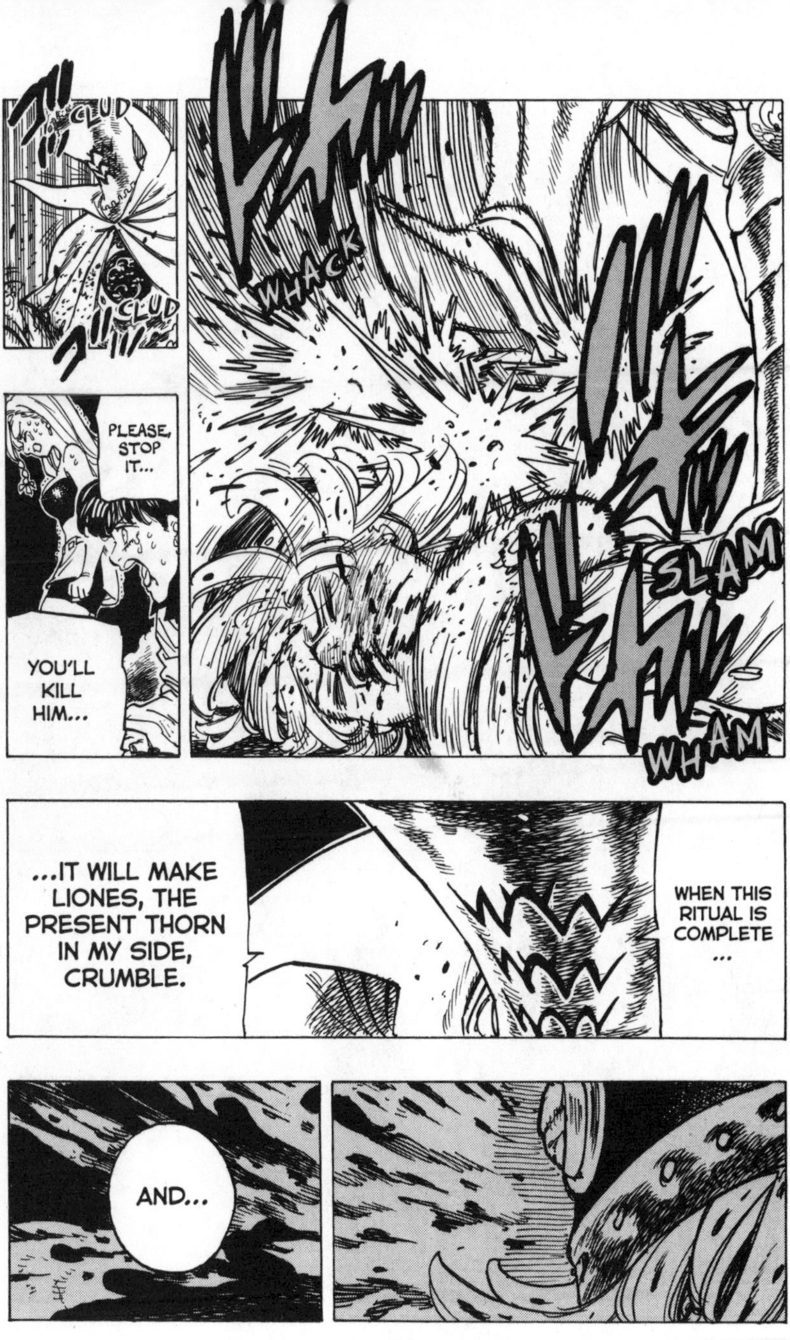
WHACK
SLAM
WHAM
CLUD
CLUD
PLEASE, STOP IT...
YOU'LL KILL HIM...
WHEN THIS RITUAL IS COMPLETE ...
...IT WILL MAKE LIONES, THE PRESENT THORN IN MY SIDE, CRUMBLE.
AND...

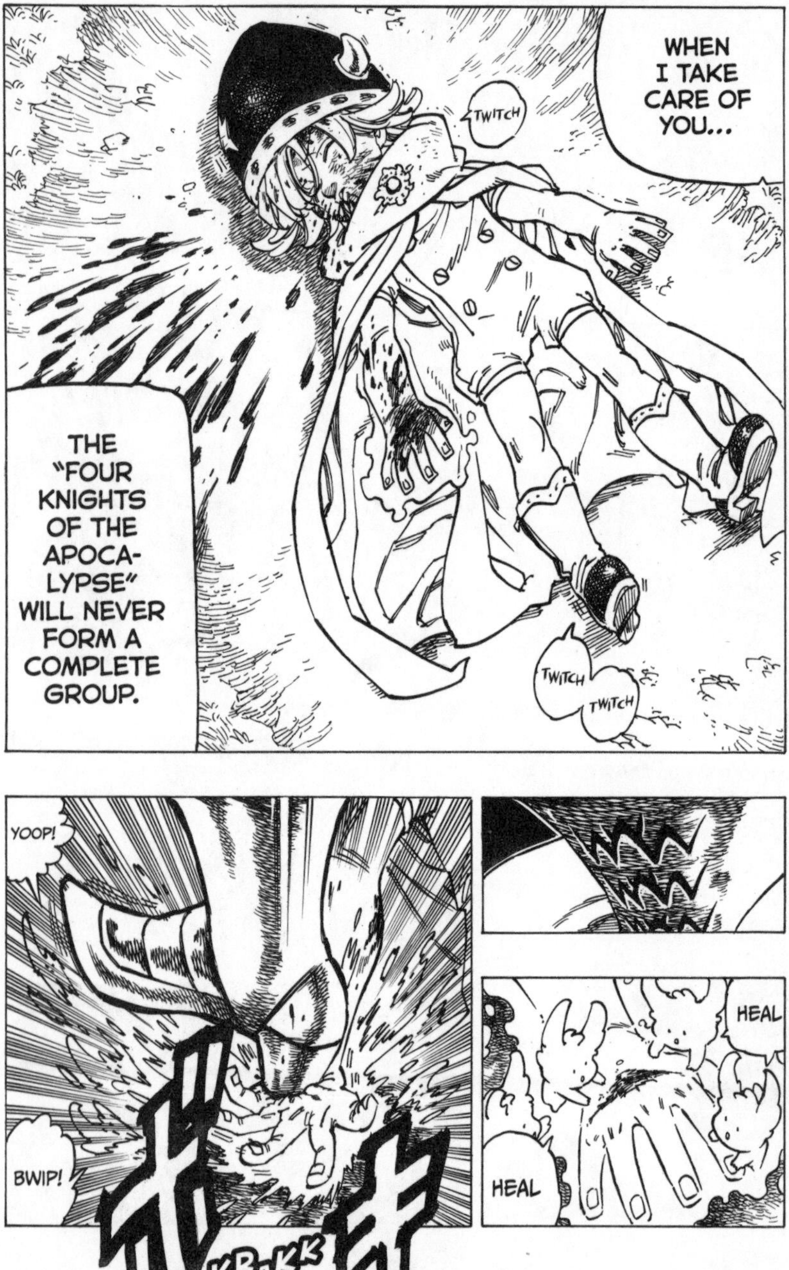
WHEN I TAKE CARE OF YOU...
TWITCH
THE "FOUR KNIGHTS OF THE APOCALYPSE" WILL NEVER FORM A COMPLETE GROUP.
TWITCH
TWITCH
HEAL
HEAL
YOOP!
BWIP!
KRAKK

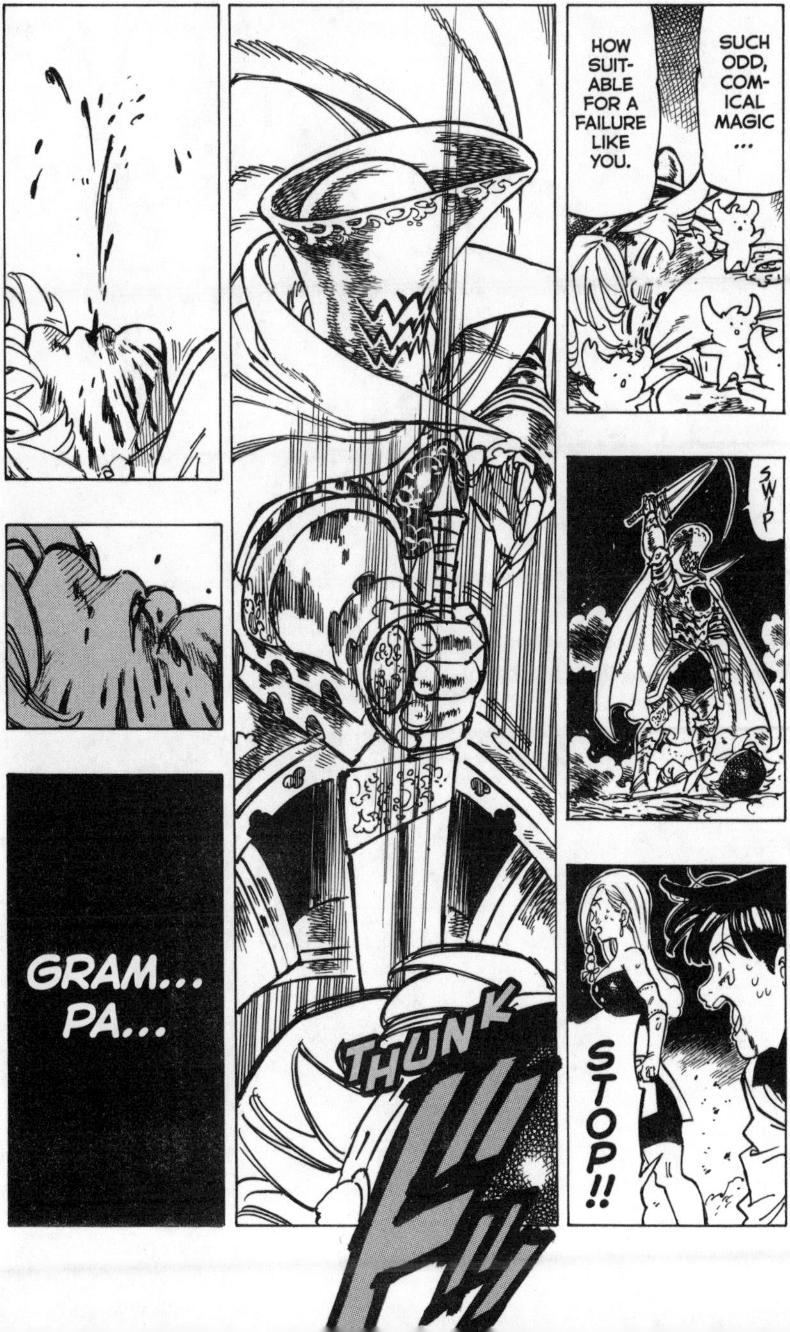
SUCH ODD, COMICAL MAGIC...
HOW SUITABLE FOR A FAILURE LIKE YOU.
SWIP
STOP!!
THUNK
GRAM... PA...

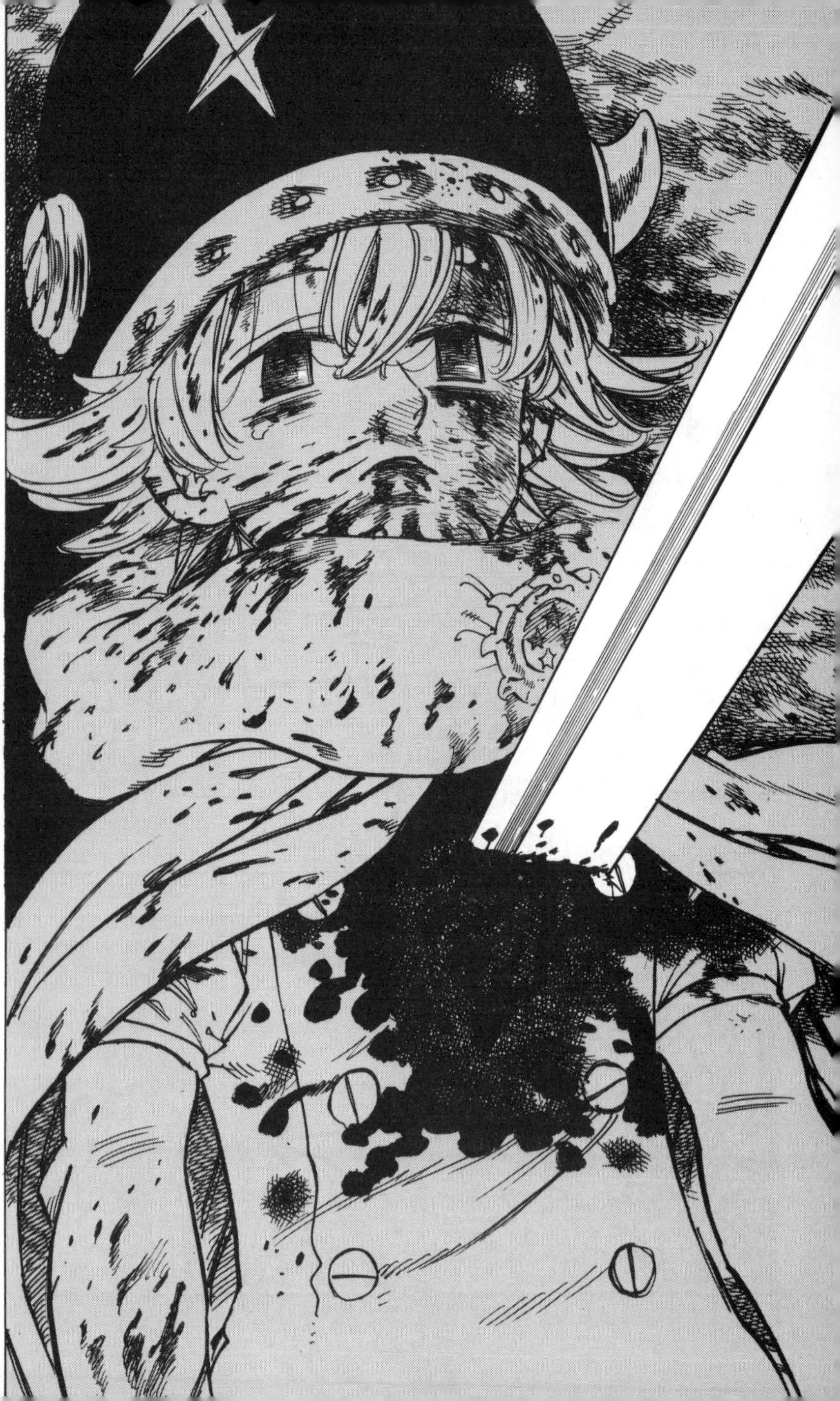

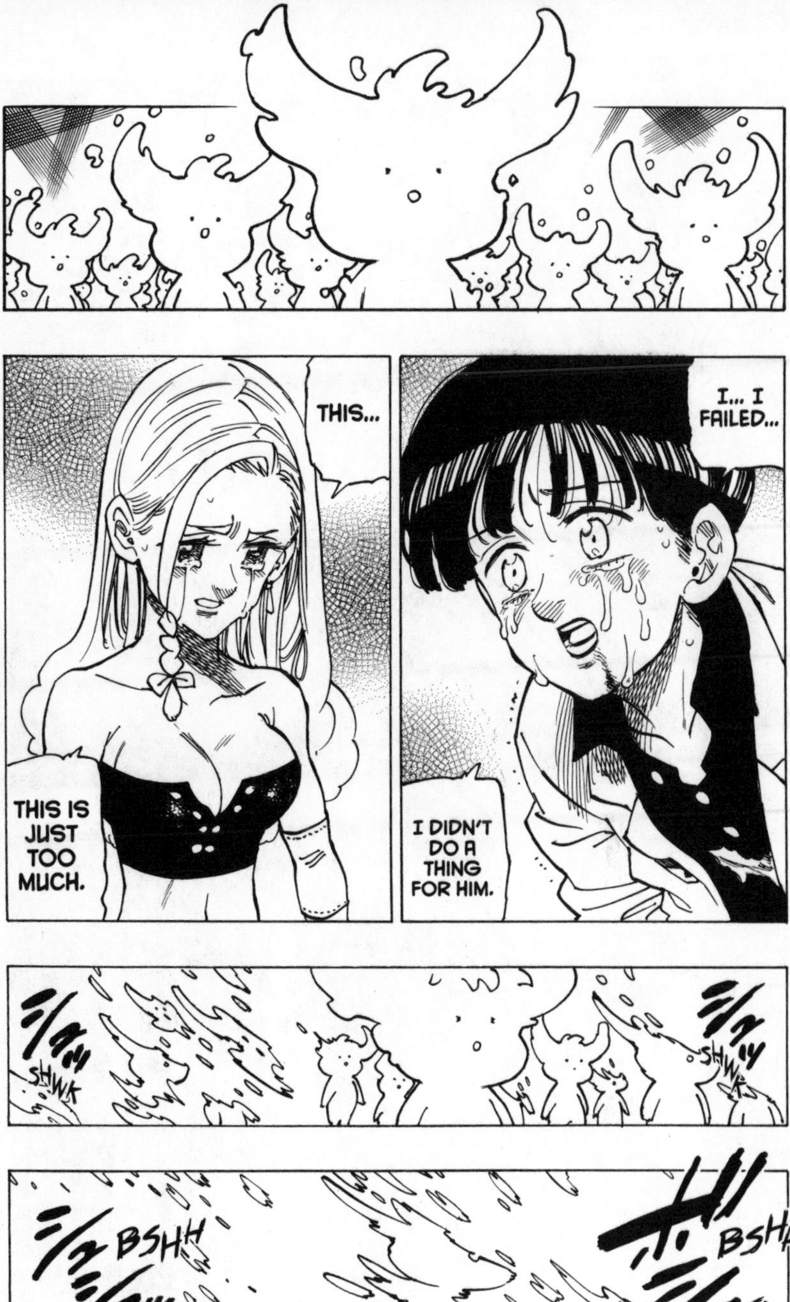
I... I FAILED...
I DIDN'T DO A THING FOR HIM.
THIS...
THIS IS JUST TOO MUCH.
SHWK
SHWK
BSHH
BSHH

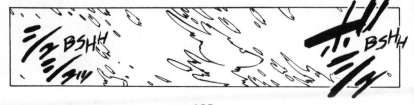

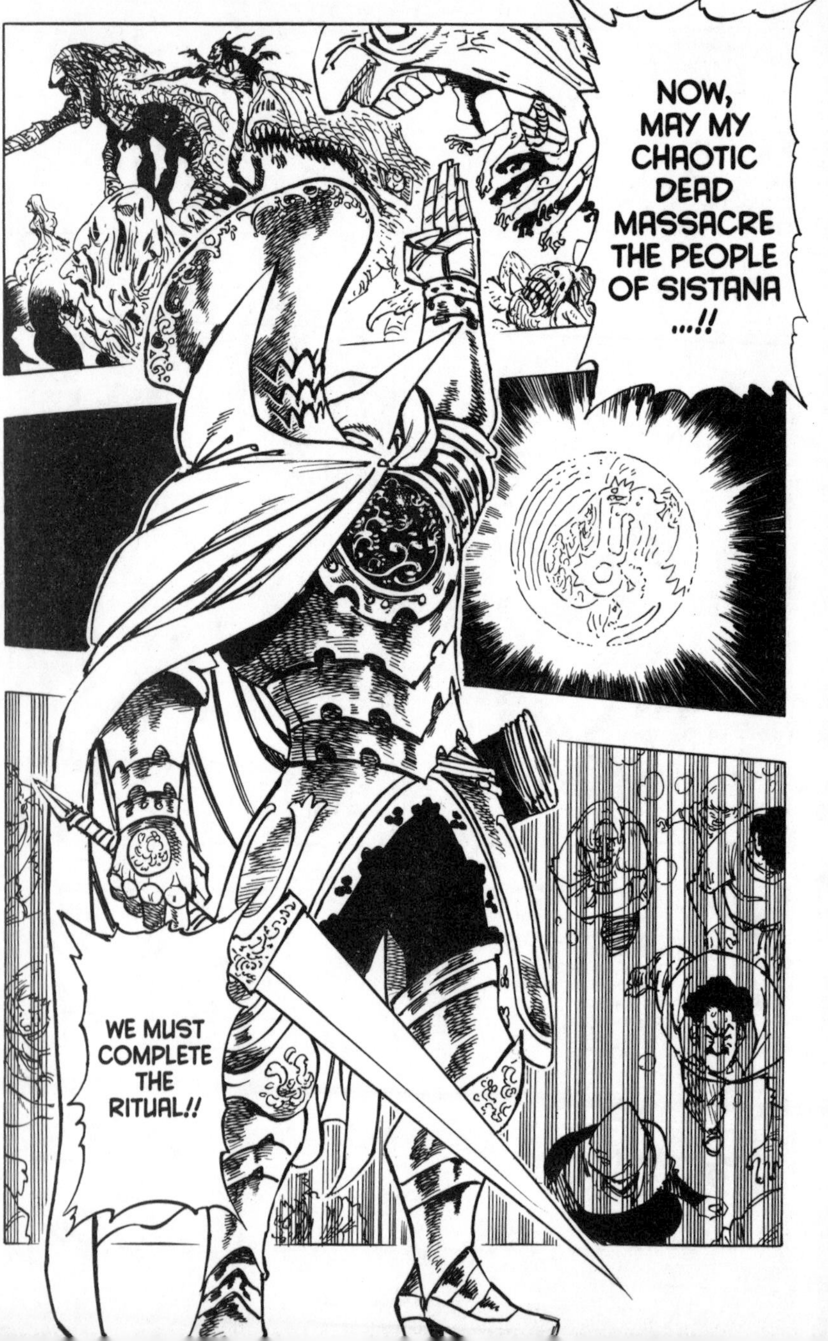
NOW, MAY MY CHAOTIC DEAD MASSACRE THE PEOPLE OF SISTANA ...!!
WE MUST COMPLETE THE RITUAL!!

NASIENS'S PRESCRIPTION (1)

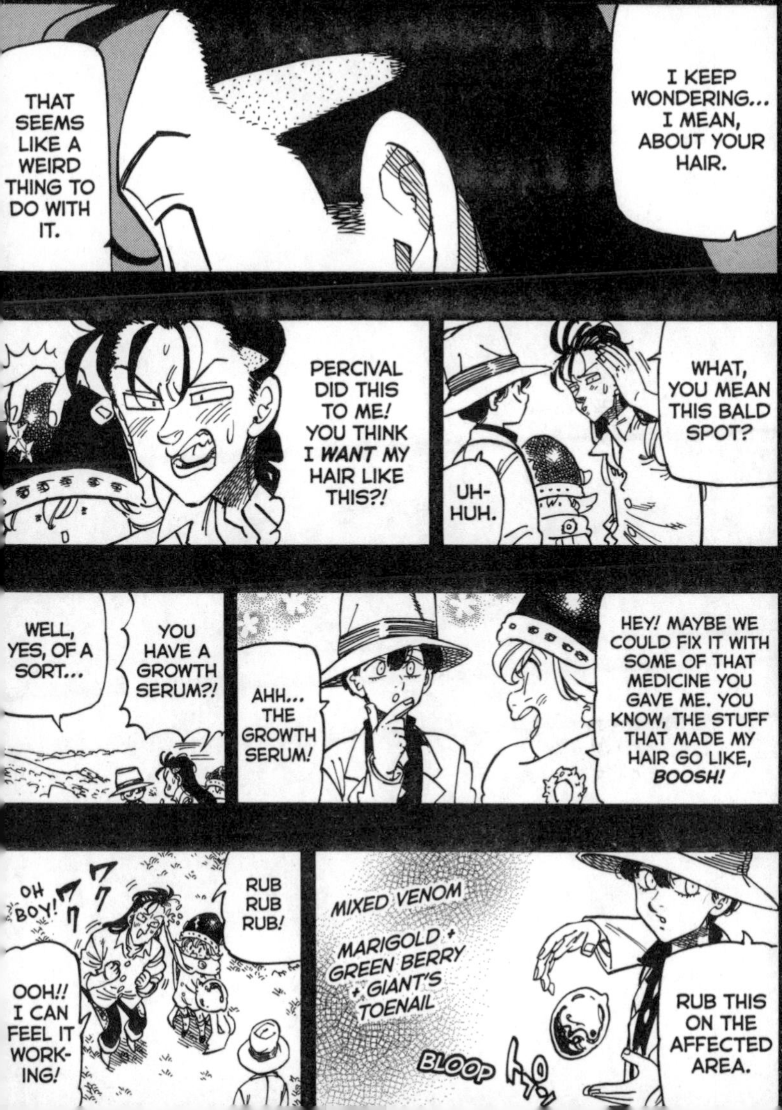

I KEEP WONDERING... I MEAN, ABOUT YOUR HAIR.
THAT SEEMS LIKE A WEIRD THING TO DO WITH IT.
WHAT, YOU MEAN THIS BALD SPOT?
UH-HUH.
PERCIVAL DID THIS TO ME! YOU THINK I *WANT* MY HAIR LIKE THIS?!
HEY! MAYBE WE COULD FIX IT WITH SOME OF THAT MEDICINE YOU GAVE ME. YOU KNOW, THE STUFF THAT MADE MY HAIR GO LIKE, *BOOSH!*
AHH... THE GROWTH SERUM!
YOU HAVE A GROWTH SERUM?!
WELL, YES, OF A SORT...
RUB THIS ON THE AFFECTED AREA.
MIXED VENOM
MARIGOLD + GREEN BERRY + GIANT'S TOENAIL
BLOOP
RUB RUB RUB!
OH BOY!
OOH!! I CAN FEEL IT WORKING!

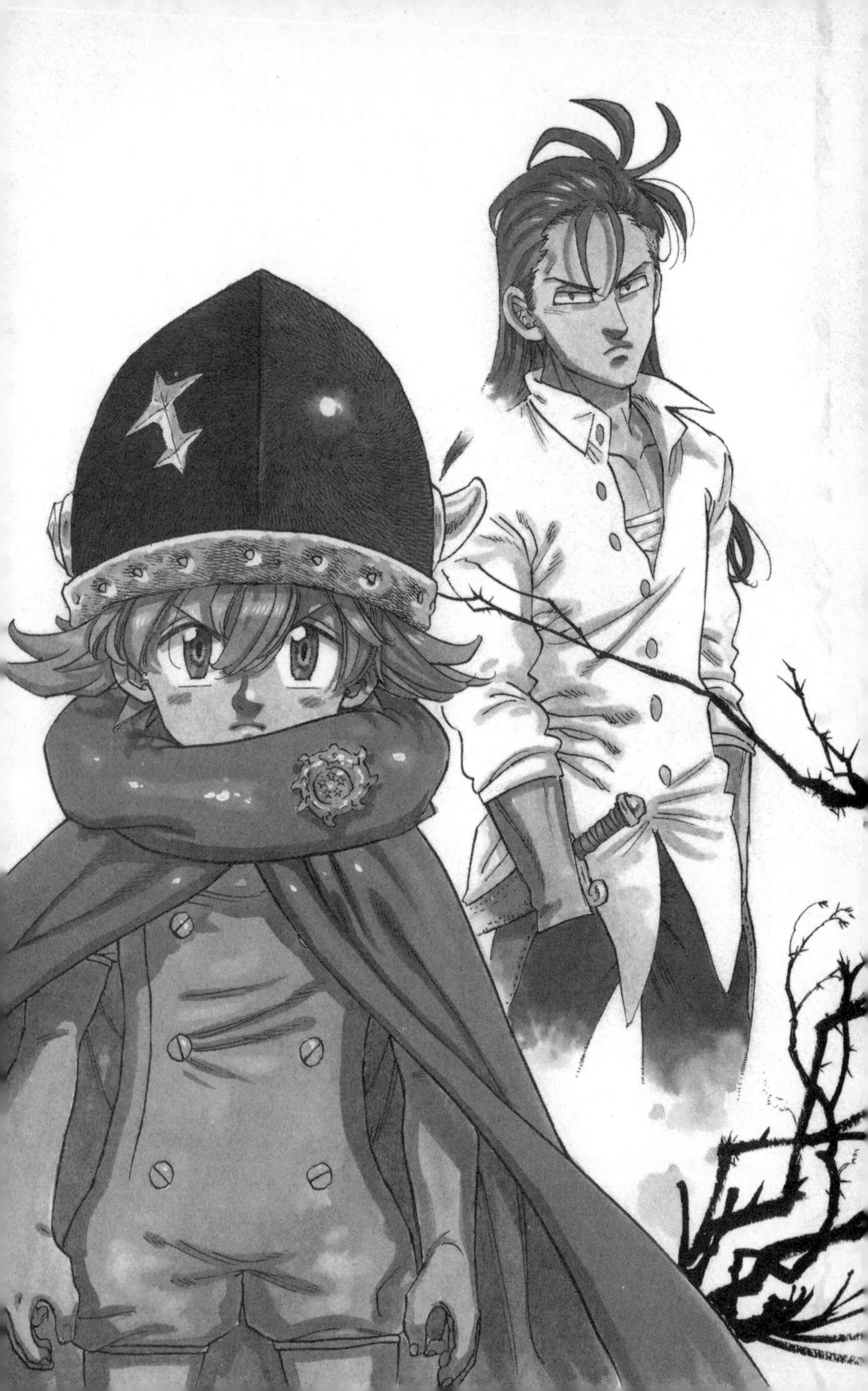

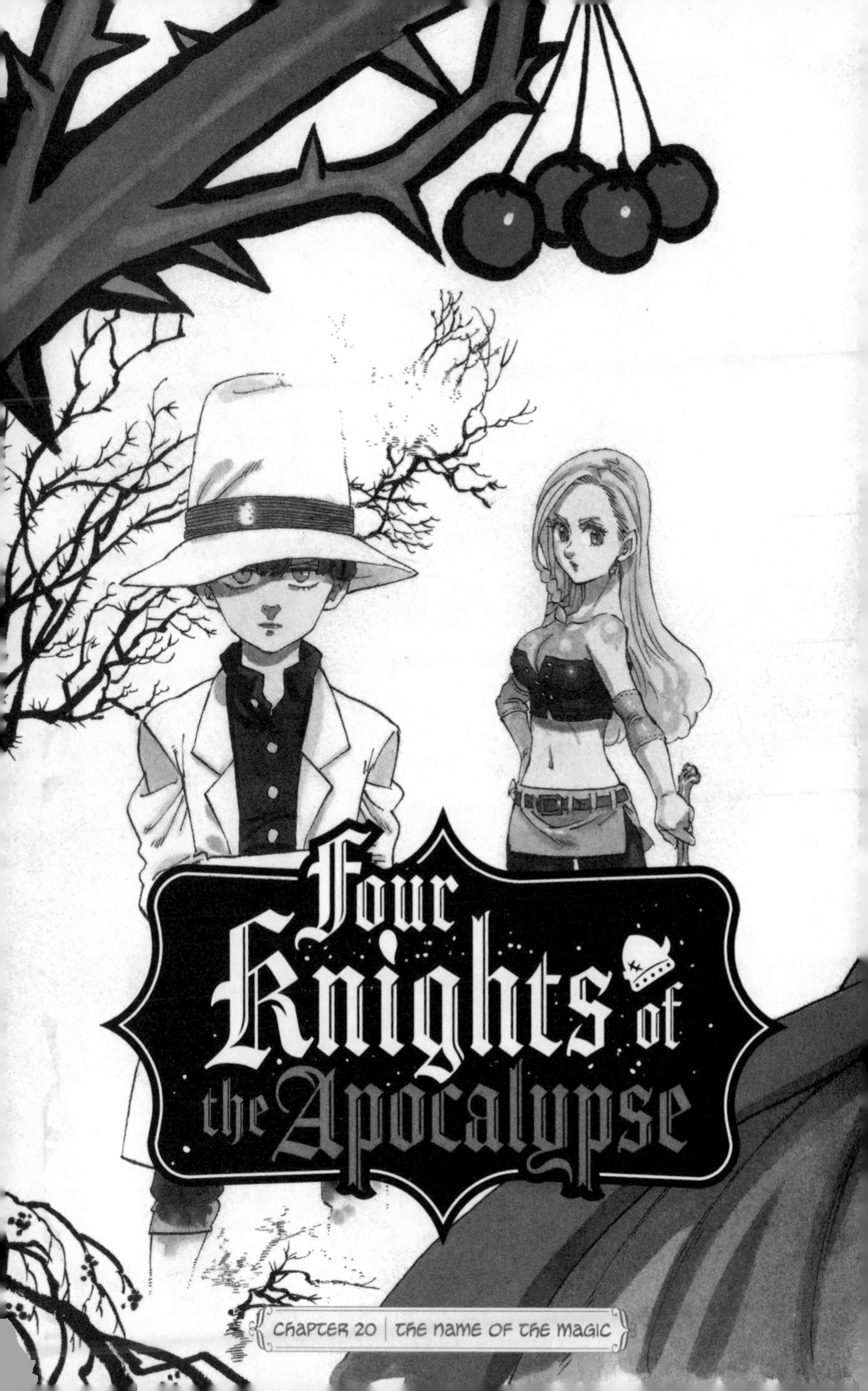
Four Knights of the Apocalypse
CHAPTER 20 | THE NAME OF THE MAGIC

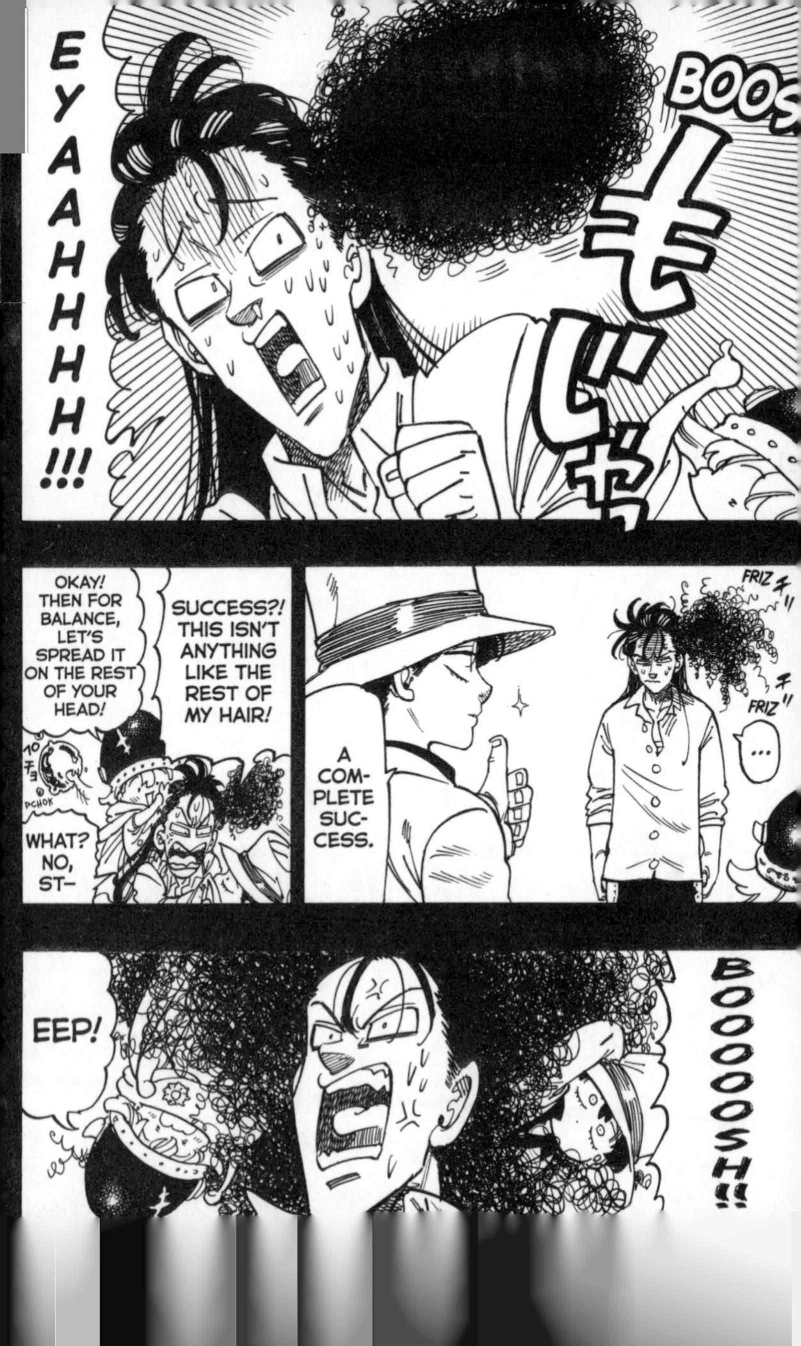
BOOS
もじ
EYAAHHHHH!!!
FRIZ
FRIZ
...
A COMPLETE SUCCESS.
SUCCESS?! THIS ISN'T ANYTHING LIKE THE REST OF MY HAIR!
OKAY! THEN FOR BALANCE, LET'S SPREAD IT ON THE REST OF YOUR HEAD!
PCHOK
WHAT? NO, ST–
BOOOOOOSH!!
EEP!

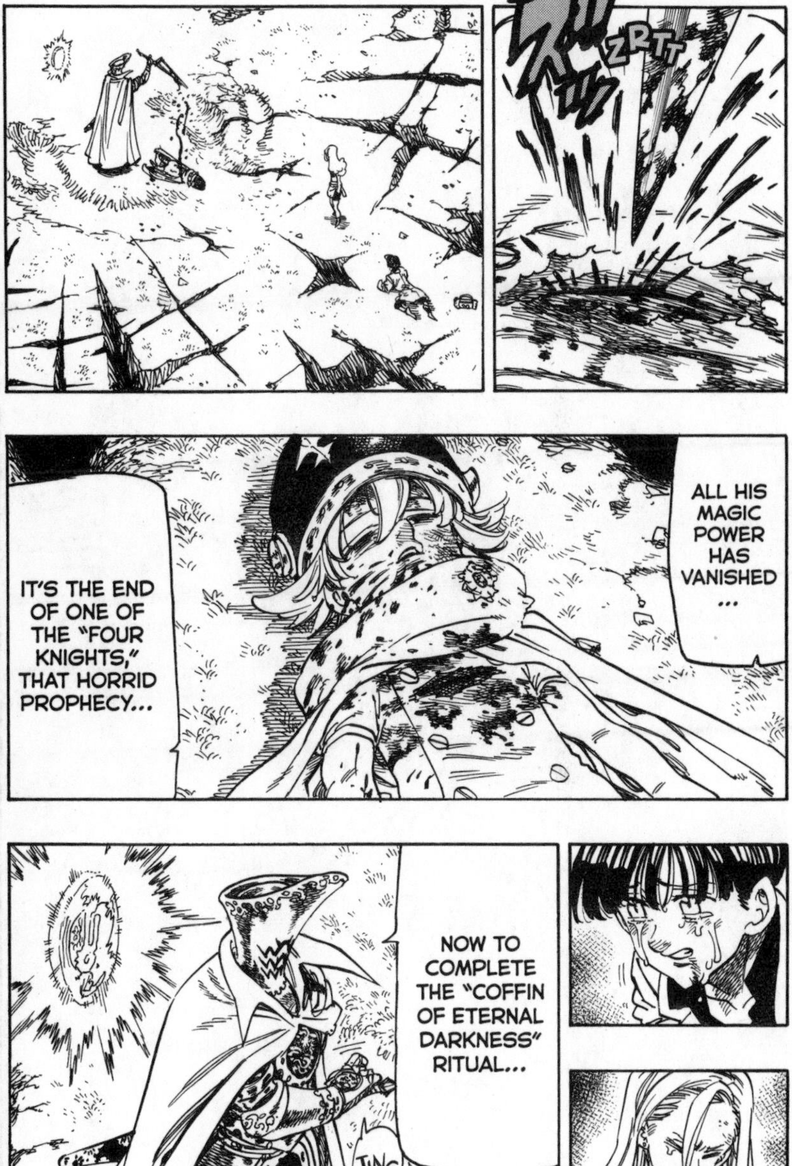
ZRTT
ALL HIS MAGIC POWER HAS VANISHED...
IT'S THE END OF ONE OF THE "FOUR KNIGHTS," THAT HORRID PROPHECY...
NOW TO COMPLETE THE "COFFIN OF ETERNAL DARKNESS" RITUAL...
TING

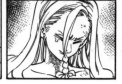

AAAHHH!
LUNGE
GRAB
HAAH! HAAH...
ZRRSSHHH
JUST GO HOME, CHILDREN...
HAAH...
HAAH...
PLEASE, OPEN YOUR EYES!

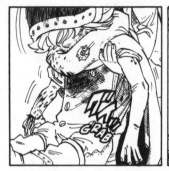

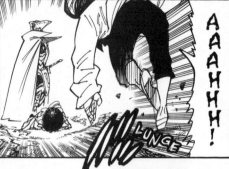

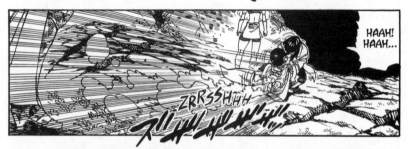

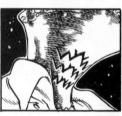

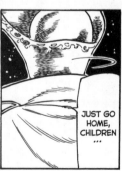

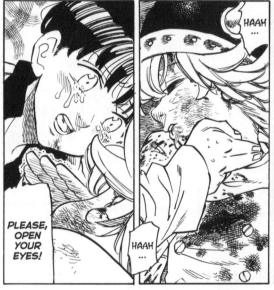

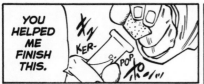

NASIENS...
WAIT! I HAVE THIS!
YOU HELPED ME FINISH THIS.
KER-
POP
DRINK IT UP! I'M SURE YOU'LL FEEL BETTER!
DRINK IT...
...!
PLEASE, JUST DO IT...
SPLSH
FWAP
MOVE!
WHAT...?
GLUG

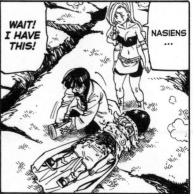

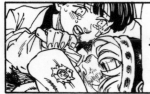

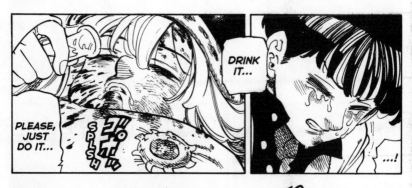

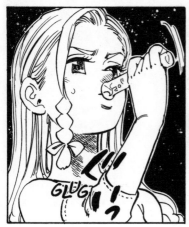

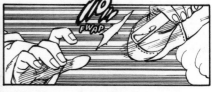

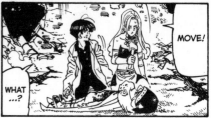

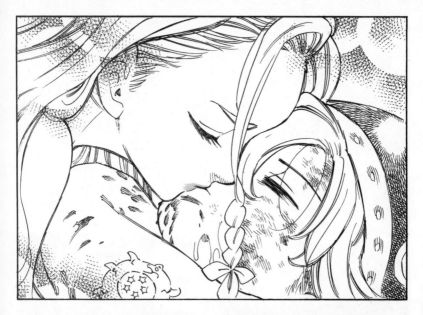

WHY...?!
WHY
WON'T HE
SWALLOW
IT?!

SPLIP

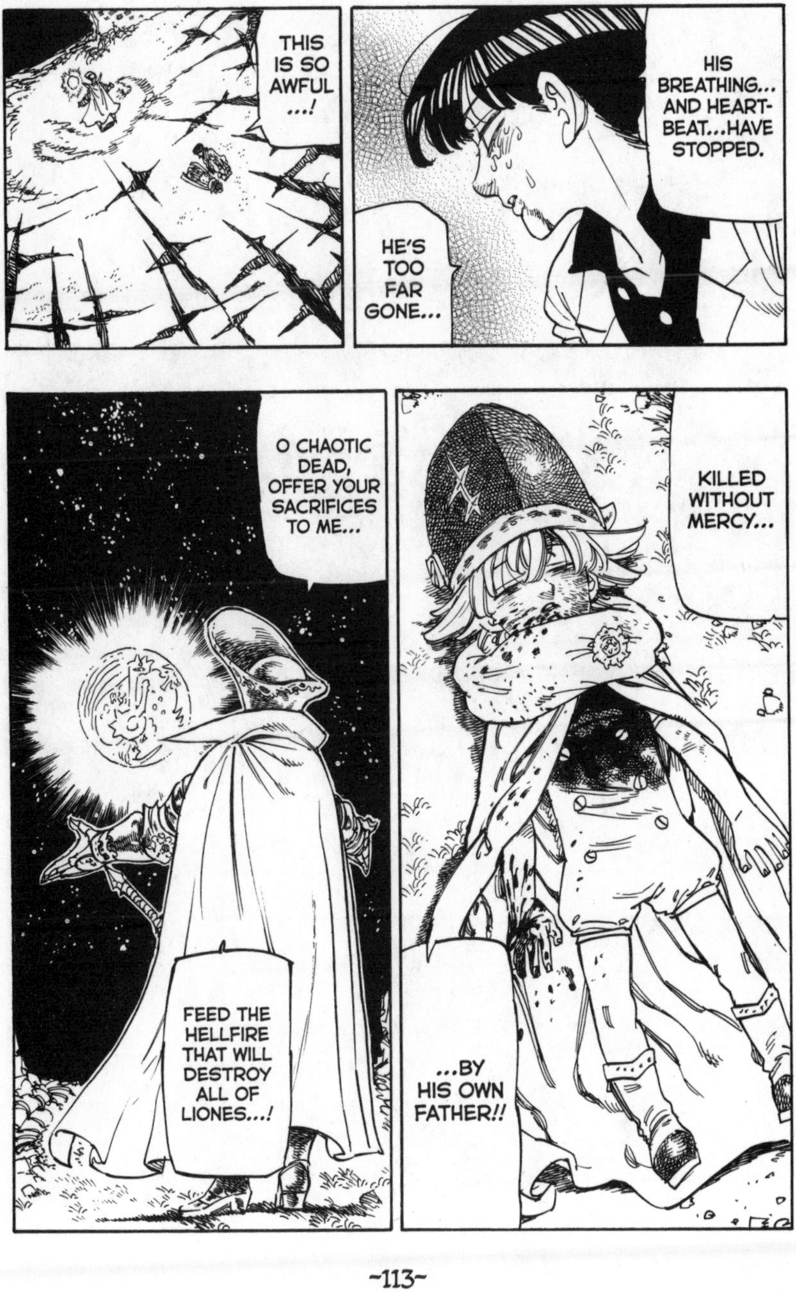
HIS BREATHING... AND HEART-BEAT...HAVE STOPPED.
HE'S TOO FAR GONE...
THIS IS SO AWFUL...!
KILLED WITHOUT MERCY...
...BY HIS OWN FATHER!!
O CHAOTIC DEAD, OFFER YOUR SACRIFICES TO ME...
FEED THE HELLFIRE THAT WILL DESTROY ALL OF LIONES...!

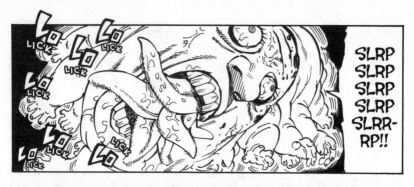

SLRP SLRP SLRP SLRP SLRR-RP!!
LO LICK
LO LICK
LO LICK
LO LICK
LO LICK
LO LICK
LO LICK
?
SLRP! SLRP! SLRR-RRP?
FLAP FLAP FLAP FLAP
BADOOM
AIEEE
AAHHHH
THAT MAN LIFTED THE MONSTER UP TO THE SKY!
LISTEN! I'LL FIGURE SOMETHING OUT BEFORE IT FALLS BACK DOWN, SO HOLD OUT FOR ME!
HE MUST BE A HOLY KNIGHT!
WE'RE ALL SAVED... HE'LL GUARD THIS TOWN FOR US!
TAK
TAK
TAK

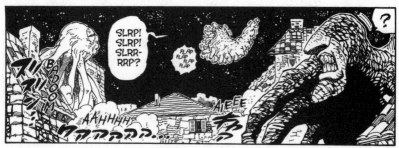

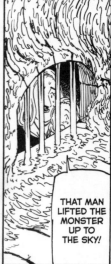

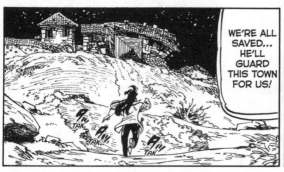

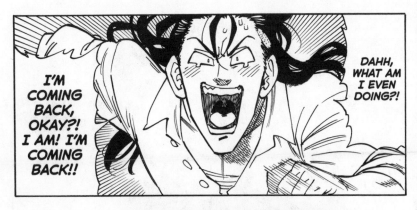

DAHH, WHAT AM I EVEN DOING?!
I'M COMING BACK, OKAY?! I AM! I'M COMING BACK!!
THIS TOWN'S TOO FULL OF MON- STERS TO ESCAPE.
AND EVEN IF I COULD, I'D NEVER LIVE IT DOWN...
THE ONLY WAY OUT IS TO BUST UP THAT "COFFIN!"
BUT IRONSIDE'S *SUCH* BAD NEWS! HE MIGHT KILL ME IF I GO BACK...
...
COME ON, DONNY! MAKE UP YOUR MIND!
THERE'S NO NEED TO TRY 'N FIGHT IRONSIDE!
ALL WE NEED'S THE COFFIN!
...AHH, BUT, MAN...
THIS'LL NEVER WORK...

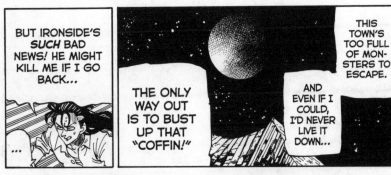

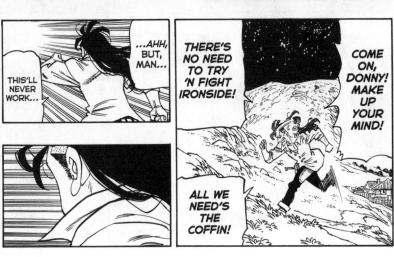

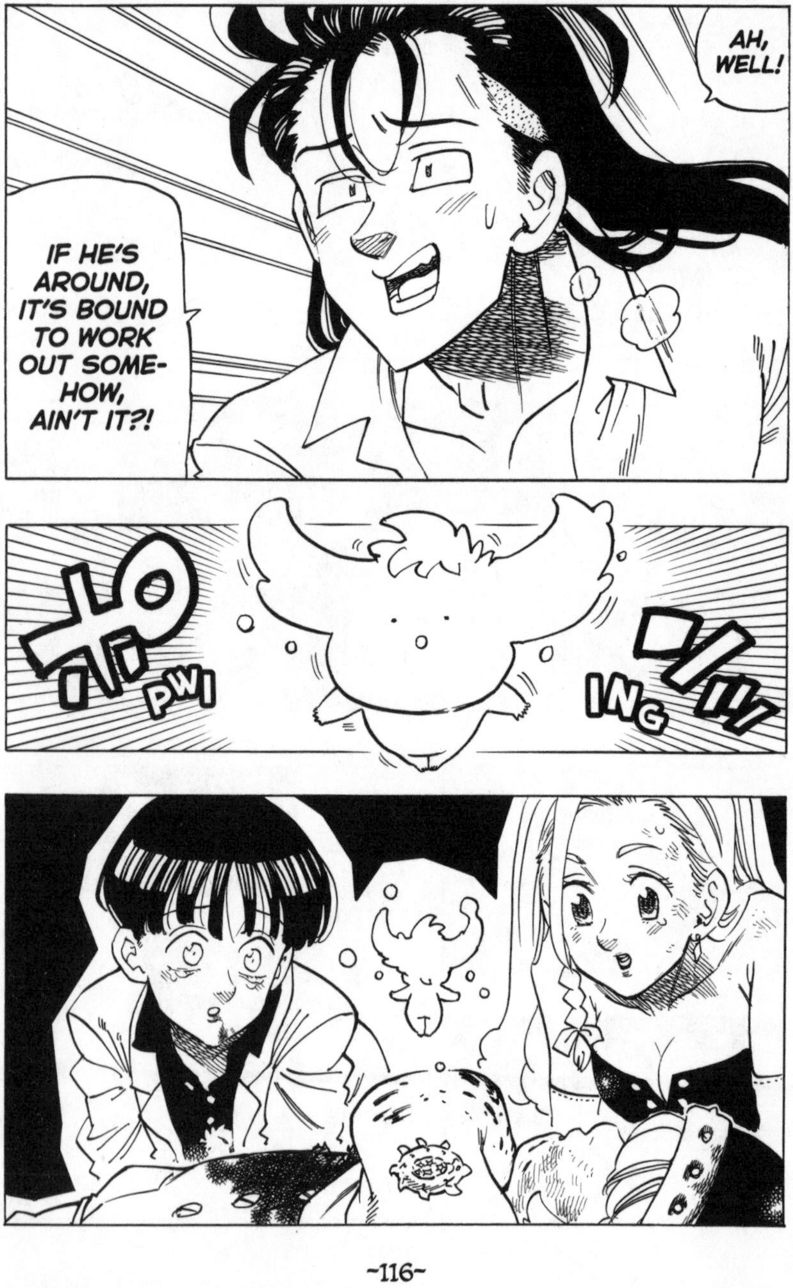
AH, WELL!
IF HE'S AROUND, IT'S BOUND TO WORK OUT SOME-HOW, AIN'T IT?!
PWI
ING

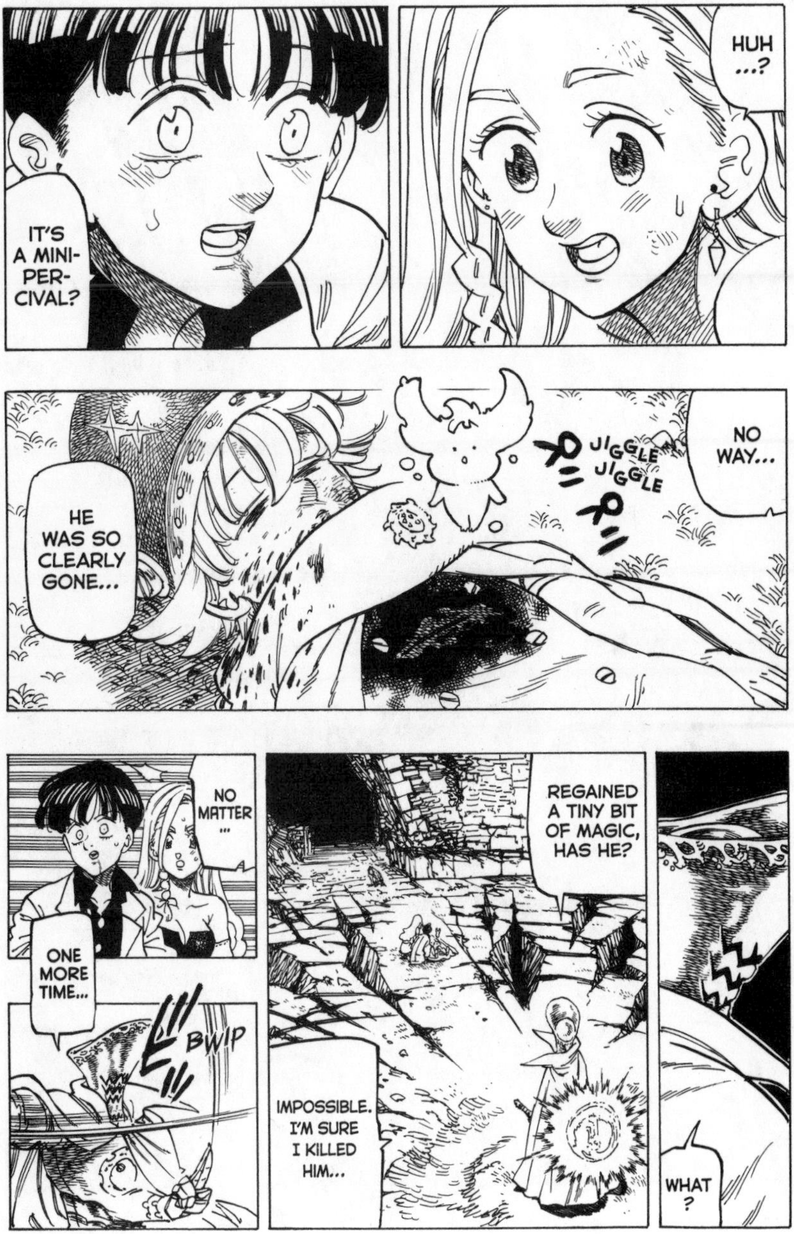
HUH ...?
IT'S A MINI-PERCIVAL?
NO WAY...
JIGGLE JIGGLE
HE WAS SO CLEARLY GONE...
WHAT ?
REGAINED A TINY BIT OF MAGIC, HAS HE?
IMPOSSIBLE. I'M SURE I KILLED HIM...
NO MATTER ...
ONE MORE TIME...
BWIP

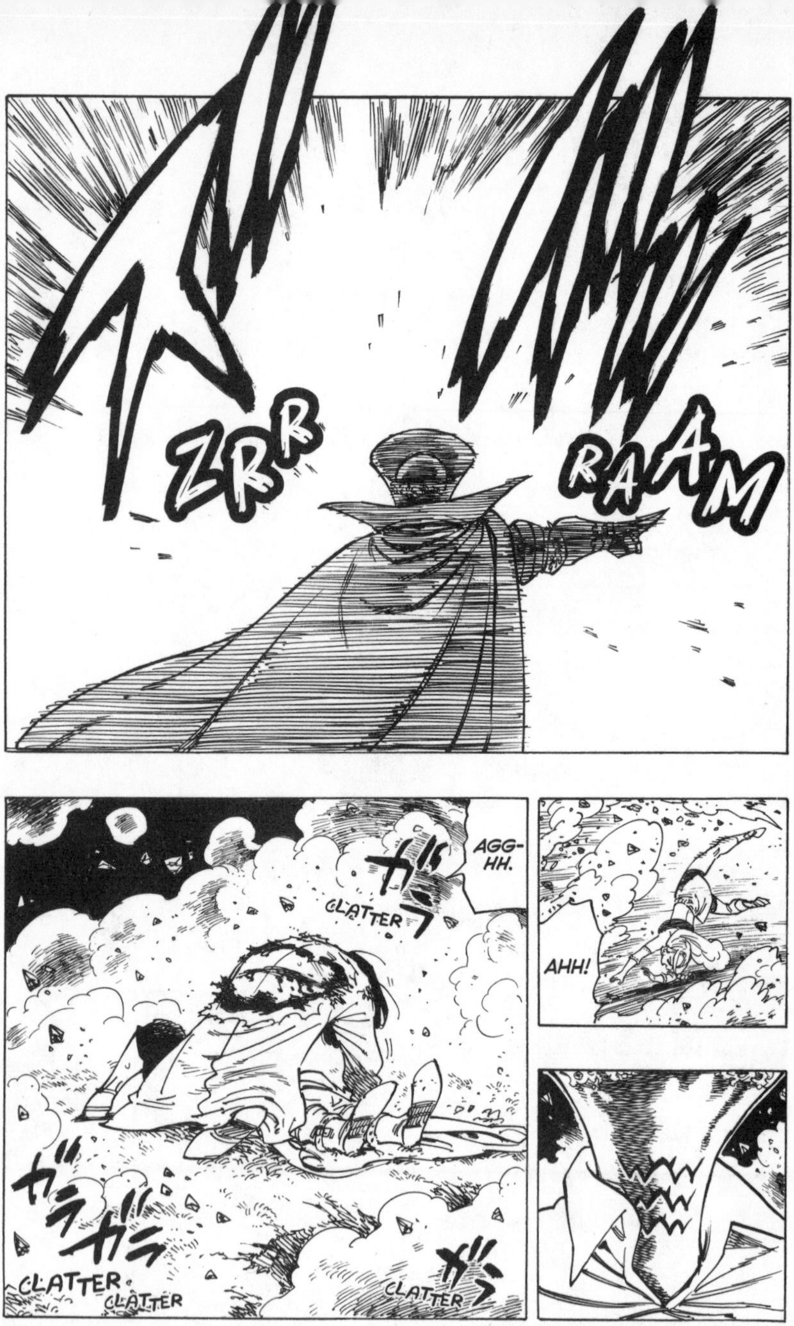
ZRR
RAAM
AHH!
AGG-HH.
ガラ
CLATTER
ガラ
CLATTER
ガラガラ
CLATTER CLATTER

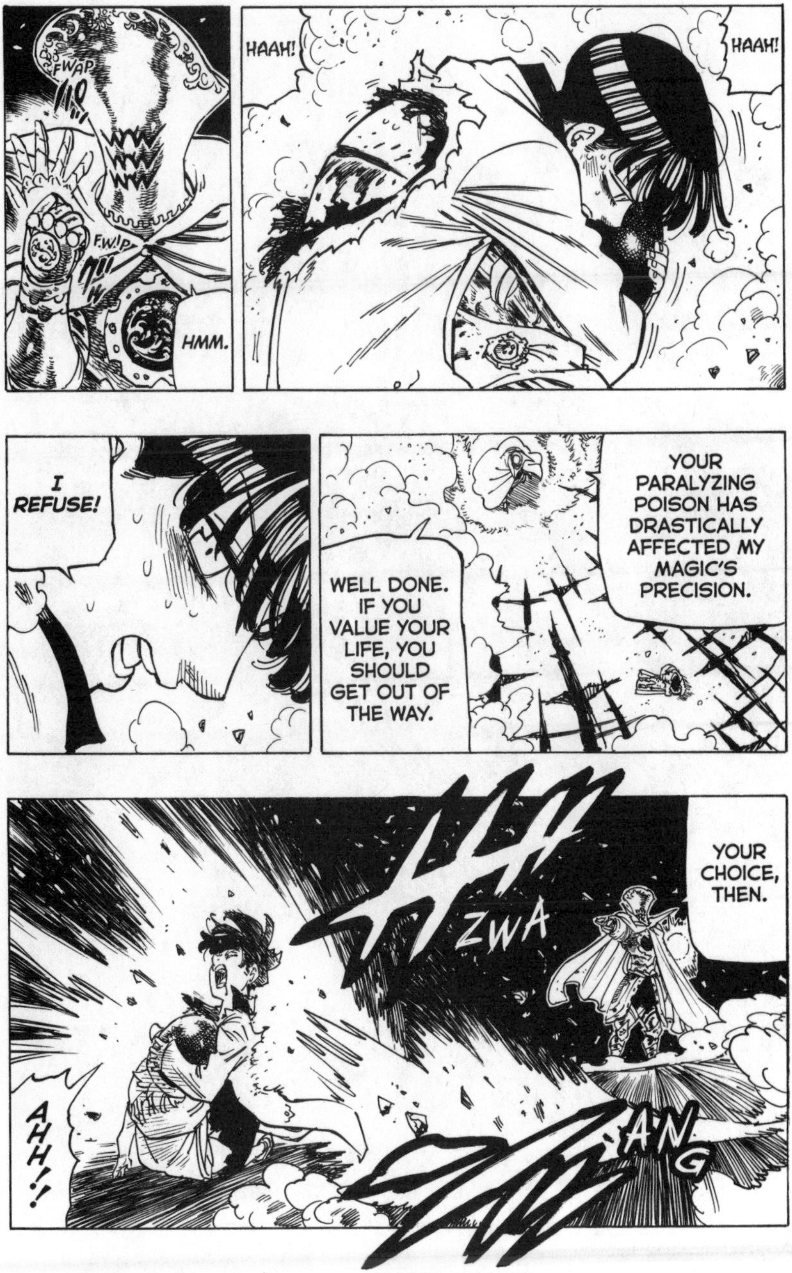
HAAH!
HAAH!
FWAP
FWIP
HMM.
YOUR PARALYZING POISON HAS DRASTICALLY AFFECTED MY MAGIC'S PRECISION.
WELL DONE. IF YOU VALUE YOUR LIFE, YOU SHOULD GET OUT OF THE WAY.
I REFUSE!
YOUR CHOICE, THEN.
ZWA
ANG
AHH!!

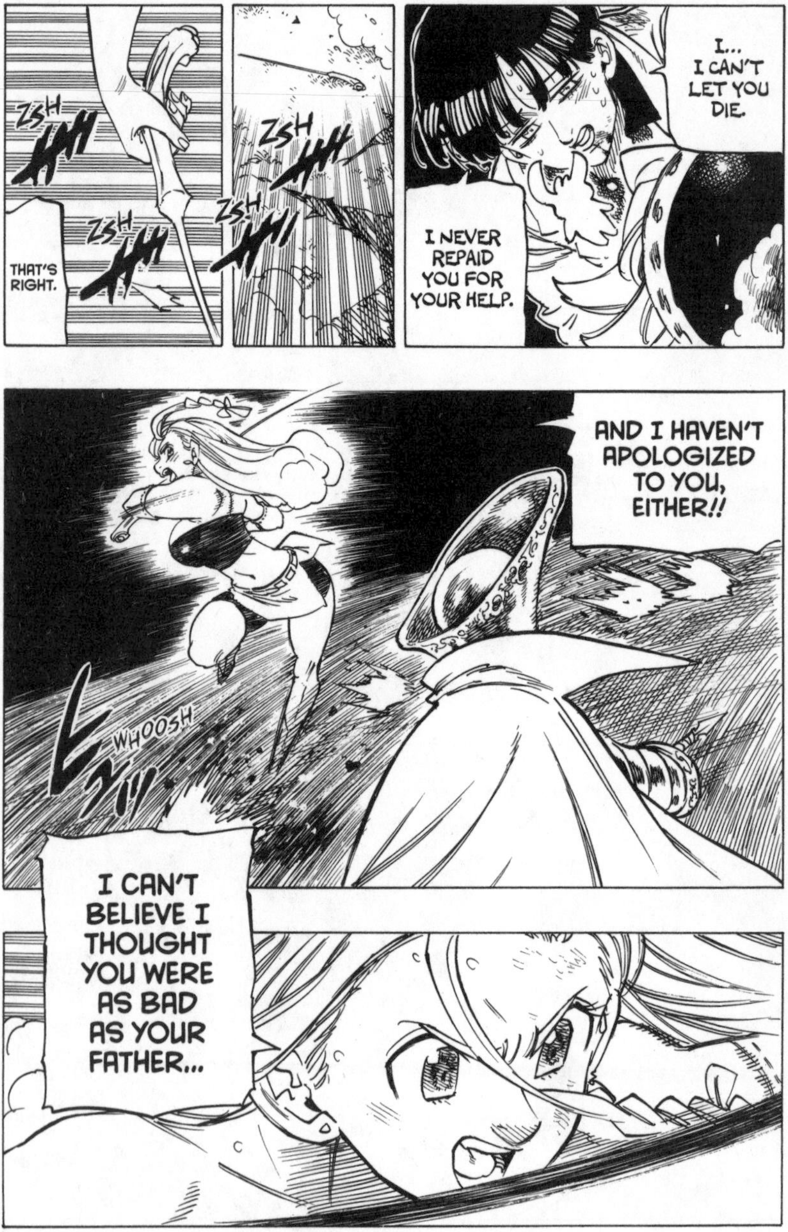
I... I CAN'T LET YOU DIE.
I NEVER REPAID YOU FOR YOUR HELP.
ZSH
ZSH
ZSH
ZSH
THAT'S RIGHT.
AND I HAVEN'T APOLOGIZED TO YOU, EITHER!!
WHOOSH
I CAN'T BELIEVE I THOUGHT YOU WERE AS BAD AS YOUR FATHER...

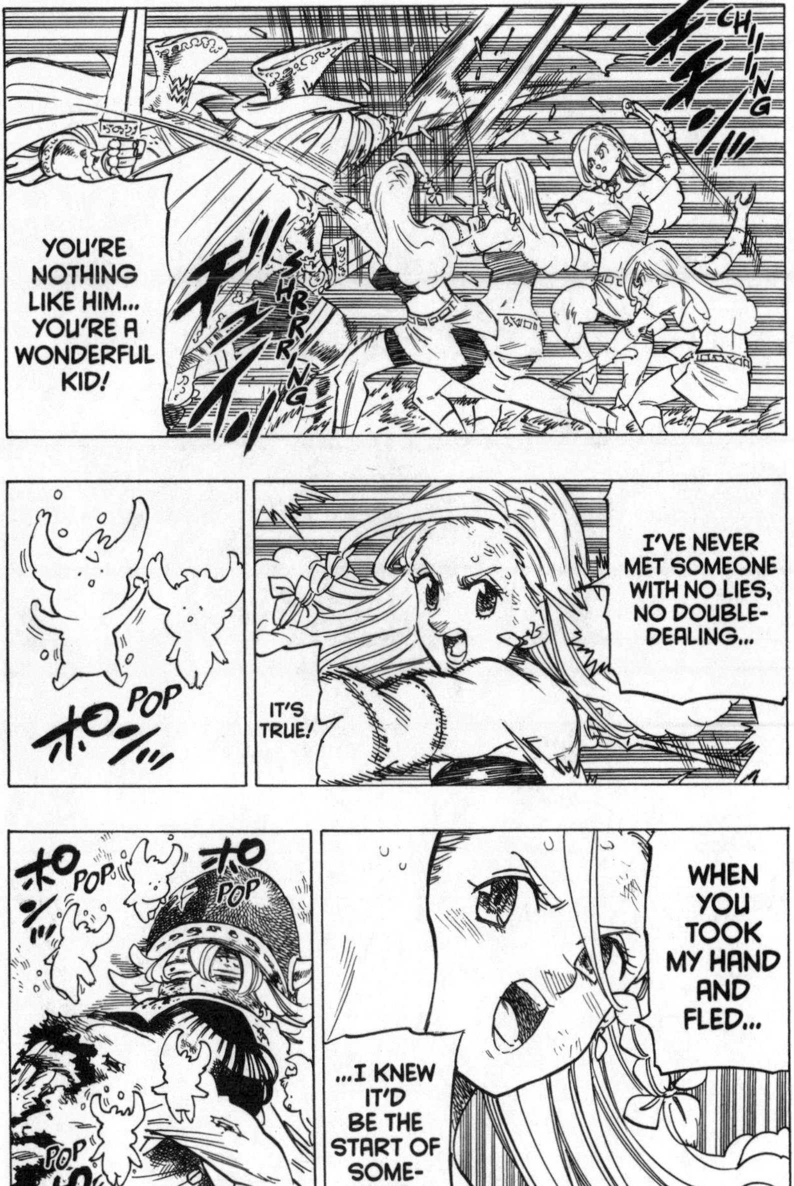
CHIIING
SHRRING
YOU'RE NOTHING LIKE HIM... YOU'RE A WONDERFUL KID!
I'VE NEVER MET SOMEONE WITH NO LIES, NO DOUBLE-DEALING...
IT'S TRUE!
POP
WHEN YOU TOOK MY HAND AND FLED...
...I KNEW IT'D BE THE START OF SOME-THING!
POP
POP
POP

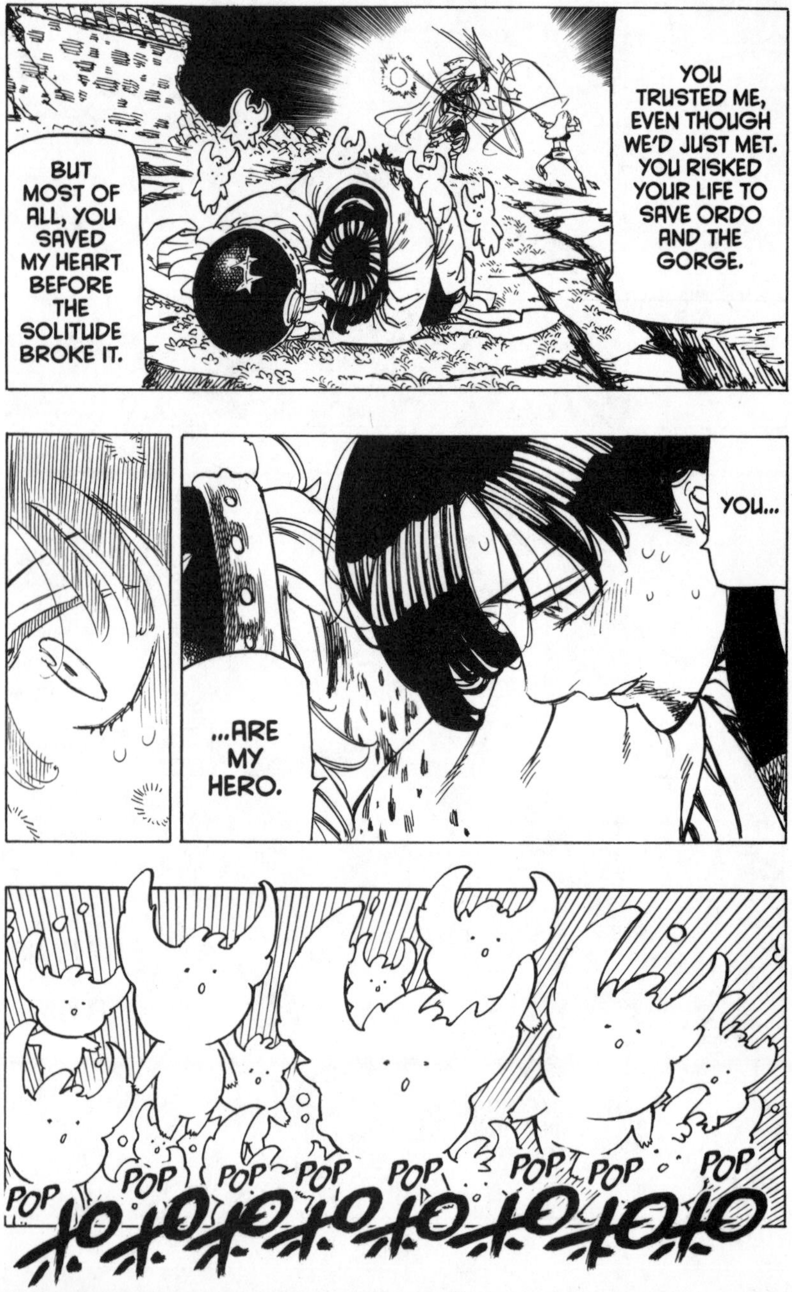
YOU TRUSTED ME, EVEN THOUGH WE'D JUST MET. YOU RISKED YOUR LIFE TO SAVE ORDO AND THE GORGE.
BUT MOST OF ALL, YOU SAVED MY HEART BEFORE THE SOLITUDE BROKE IT.
YOU...
...ARE MY HERO.
POP POP POP POP POP POP POP POP

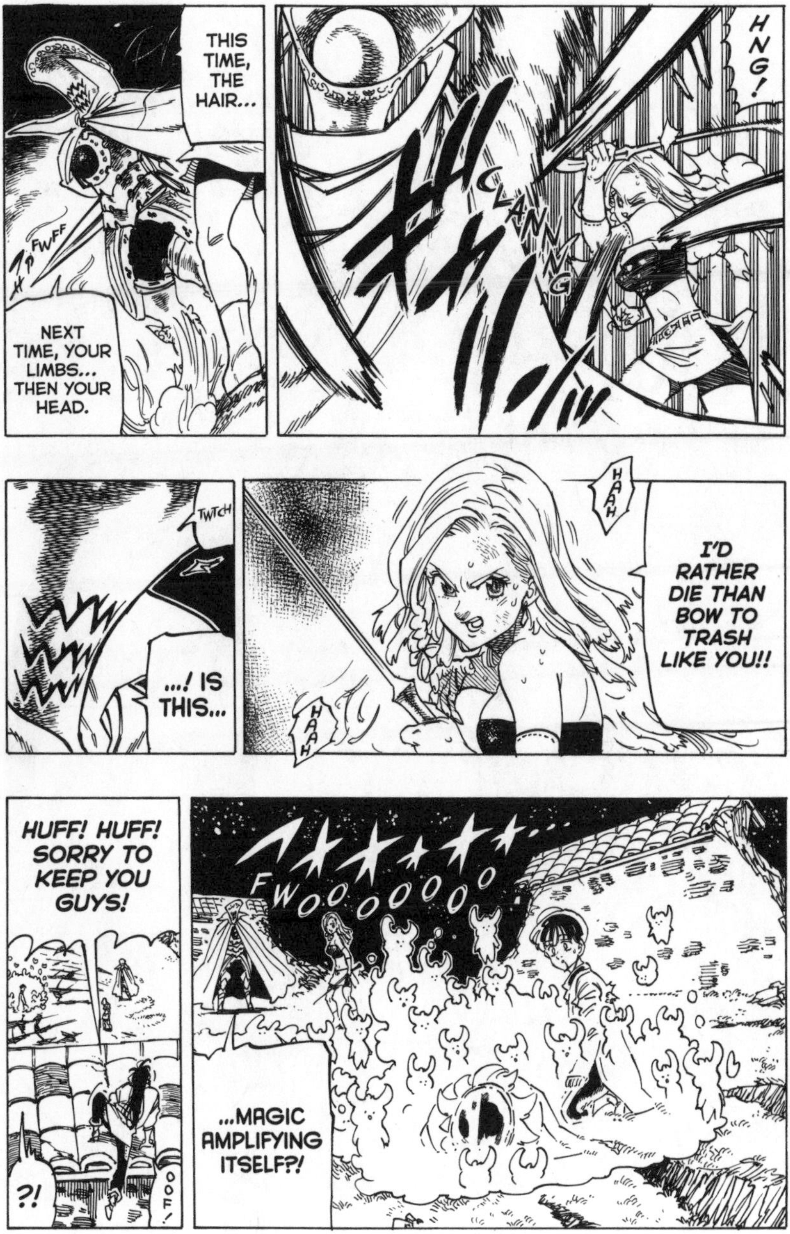
HNG!
CLANNNNG
THIS TIME, THE HAIR...
FWFF
NEXT TIME, YOUR LIMBS... THEN YOUR HEAD.
HAAH
I'D RATHER DIE THAN BOW TO TRASH LIKE YOU!!
HAAH
TWITCH
...! IS THIS...
FWOOOOOOO
...MAGIC AMPLIFYING ITSELF?!
HUFF! HUFF! SORRY TO KEEP YOU GUYS!
?!
OOF!

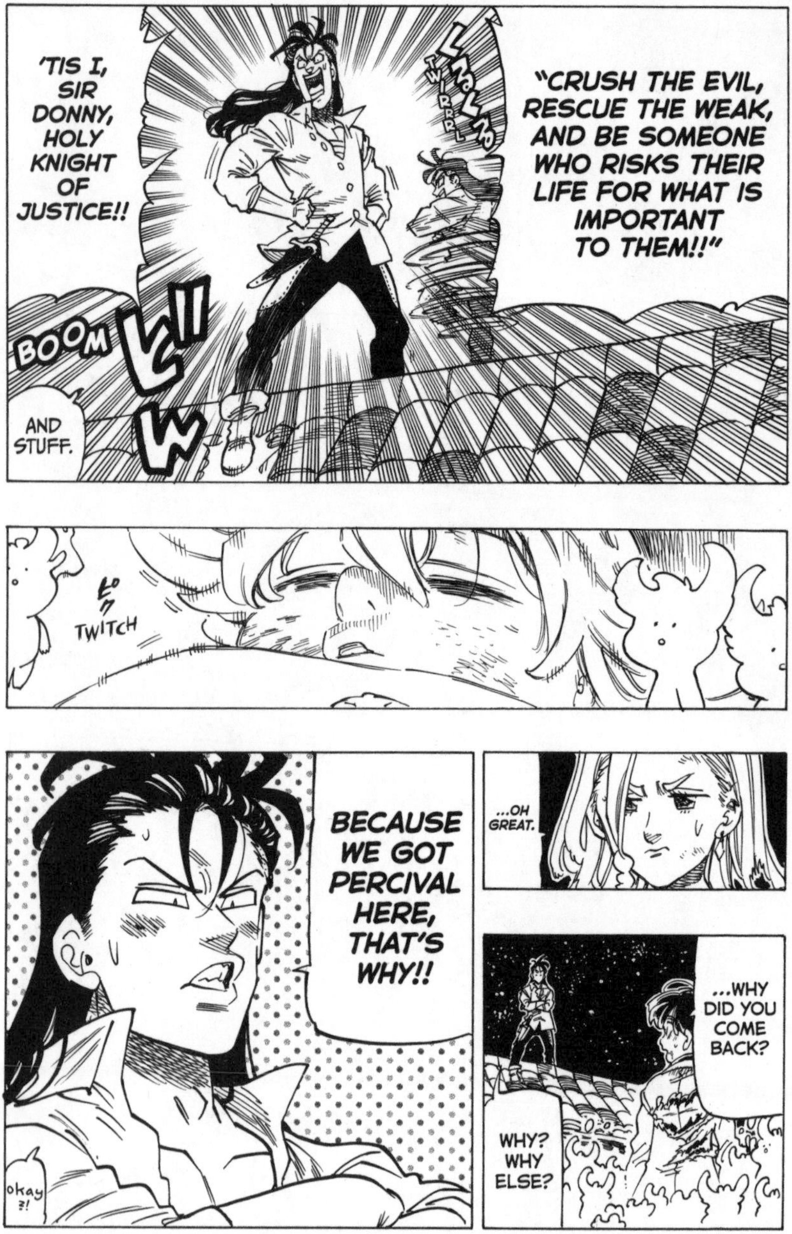
"CRUSH THE EVIL, RESCUE THE WEAK, AND BE SOMEONE WHO RISKS THEIR LIFE FOR WHAT IS IMPORTANT TO THEM!!"
TWIRRL
'TIS I, SIR DONNY, HOLY KNIGHT OF JUSTICE!!
BOOM
AND STUFF.
TWITCH
...OH GREAT.
...WHY DID YOU COME BACK?
WHY? WHY ELSE?
BECAUSE WE GOT PERCIVAL HERE, THAT'S WHY!!
okay?!

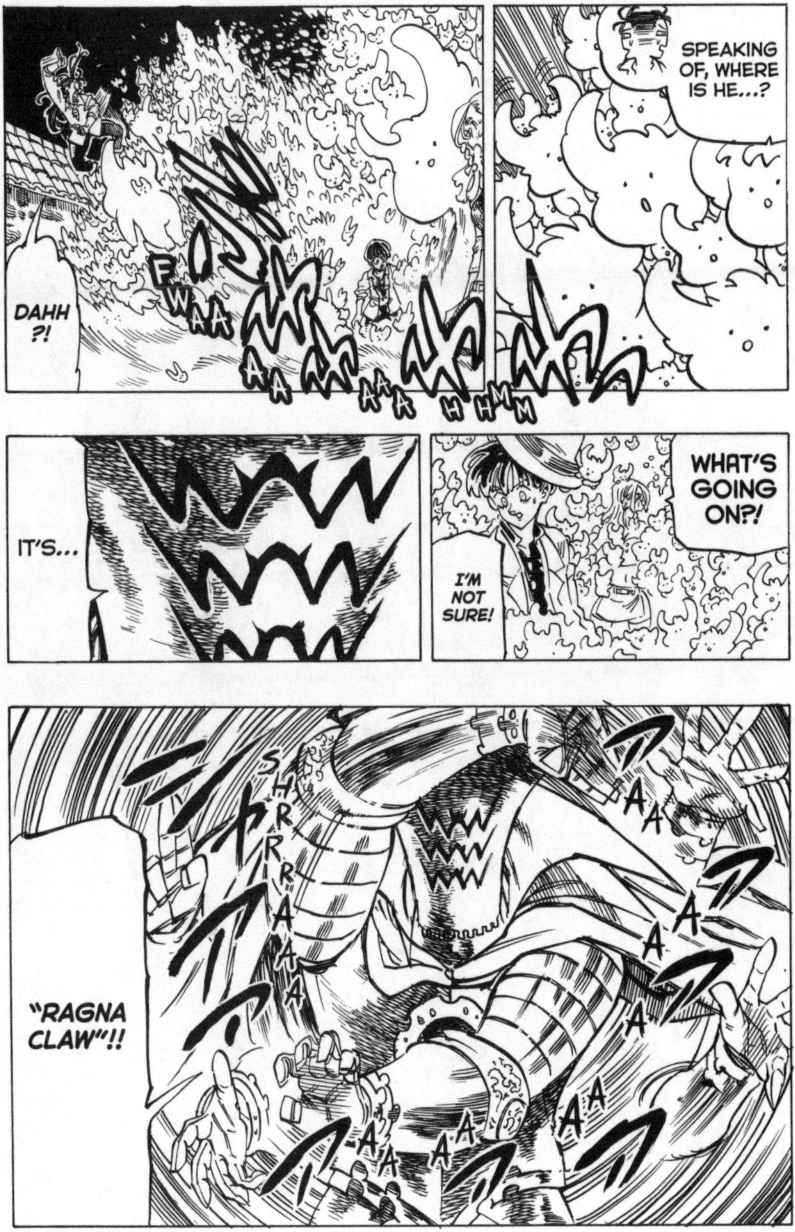

SPEAKING OF, WHERE IS HE...?
DAHH ?!
FWAAAAAAAAHHMMM
WHAT'S GOING ON?!
I'M NOT SURE!
IT'S...
SHRRRRAAAAA
"RAGNA CLAW"!!

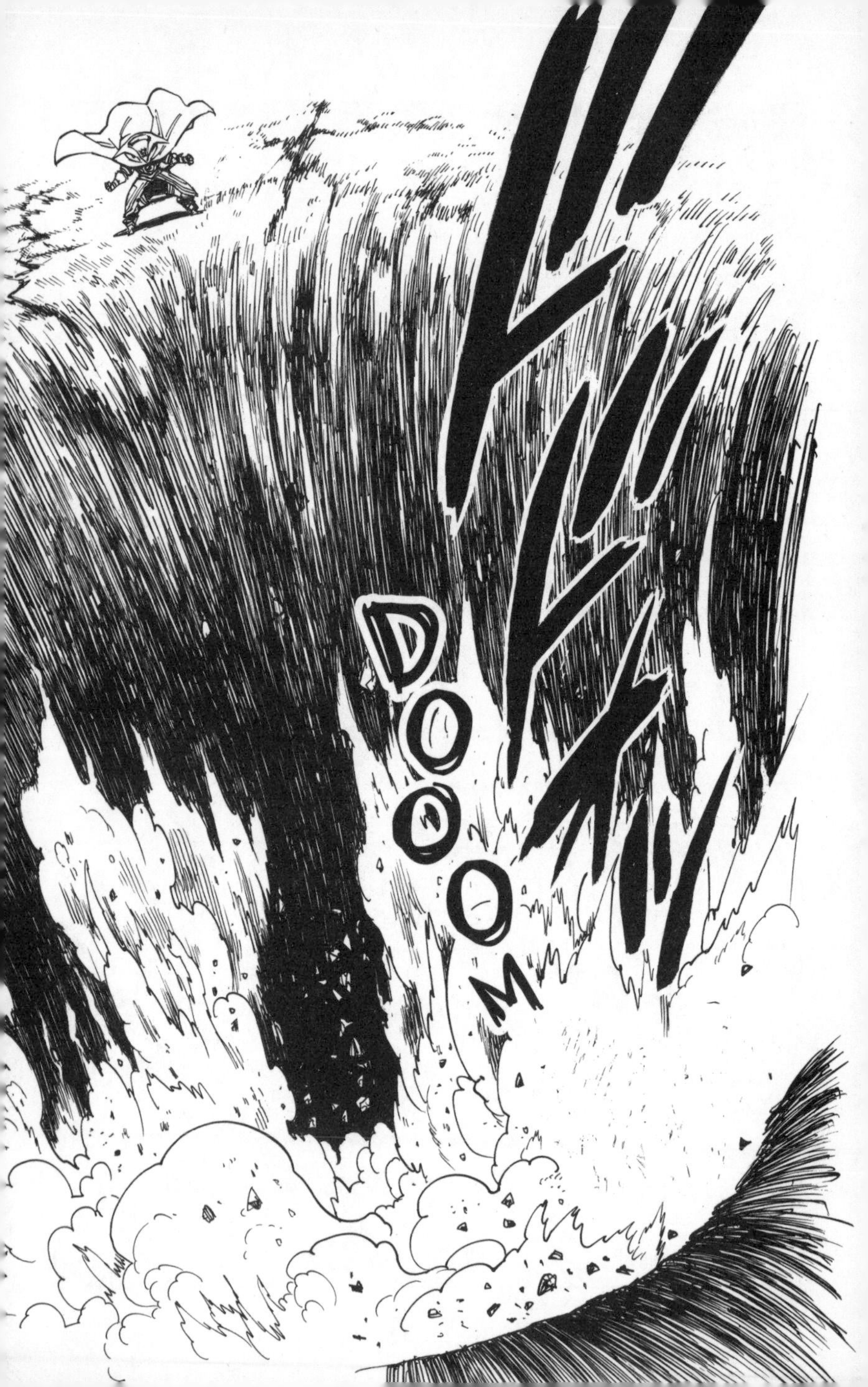
DOOOOM

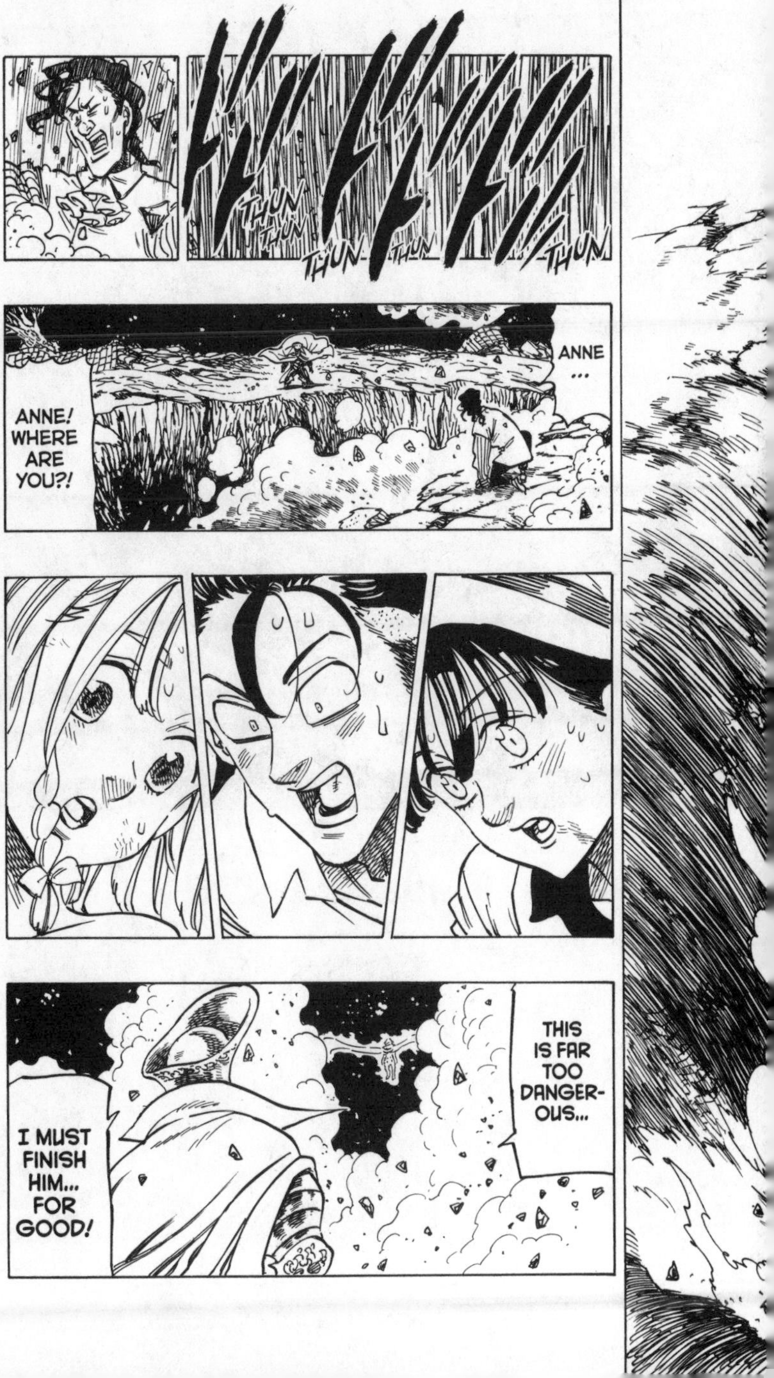
THUN THUN THUN THUN THUN THUN
ANNE ...
ANNE! WHERE ARE YOU?!
THIS IS FAR TOO DANGER-OUS...
I MUST FINISH HIM... FOR GOOD!

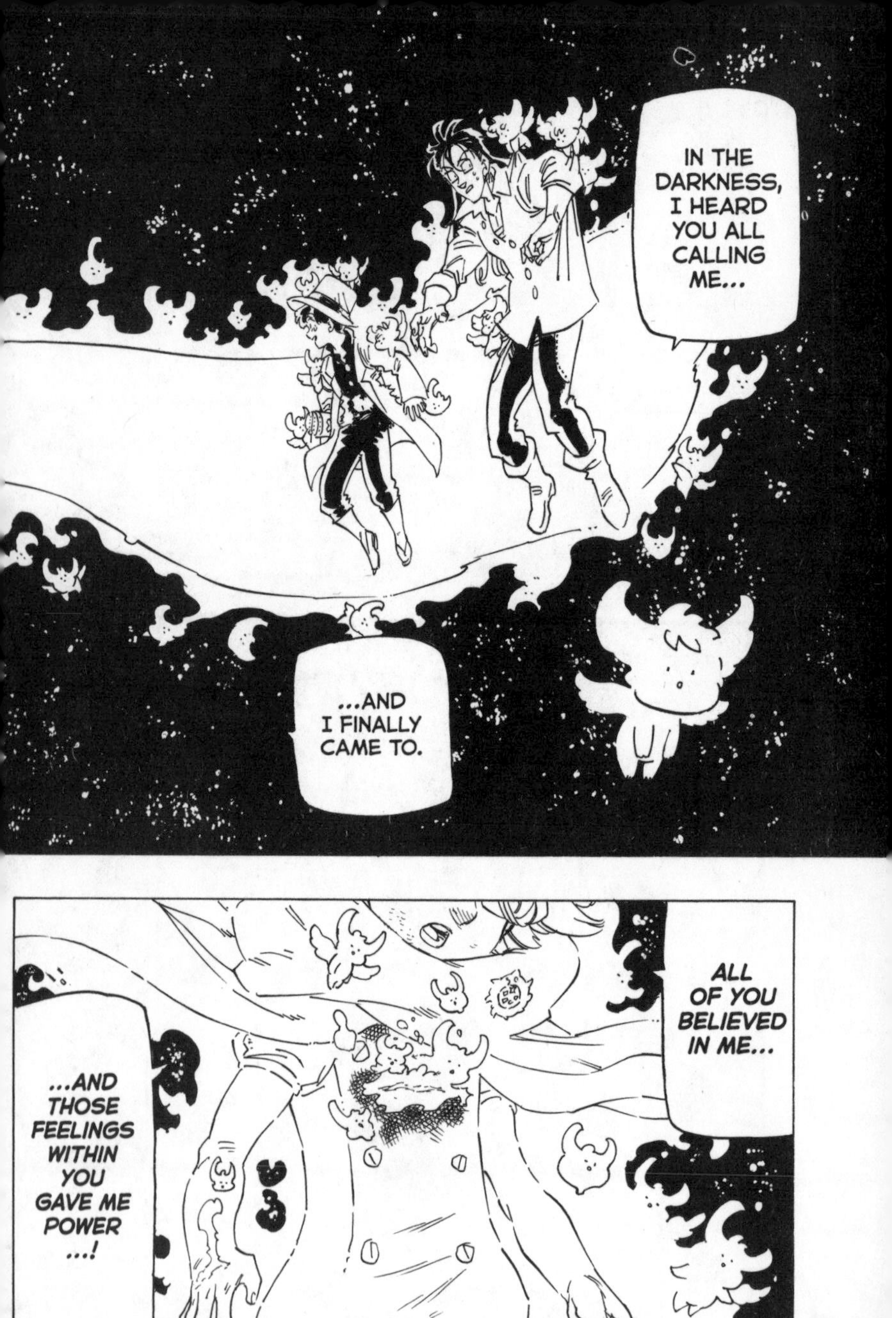
IN THE DARKNESS, I HEARD YOU ALL CALLING ME...
...AND I FINALLY CAME TO.
ALL OF YOU BELIEVED IN ME...
...AND THOSE FEELINGS WITHIN YOU GAVE ME POWER ...!

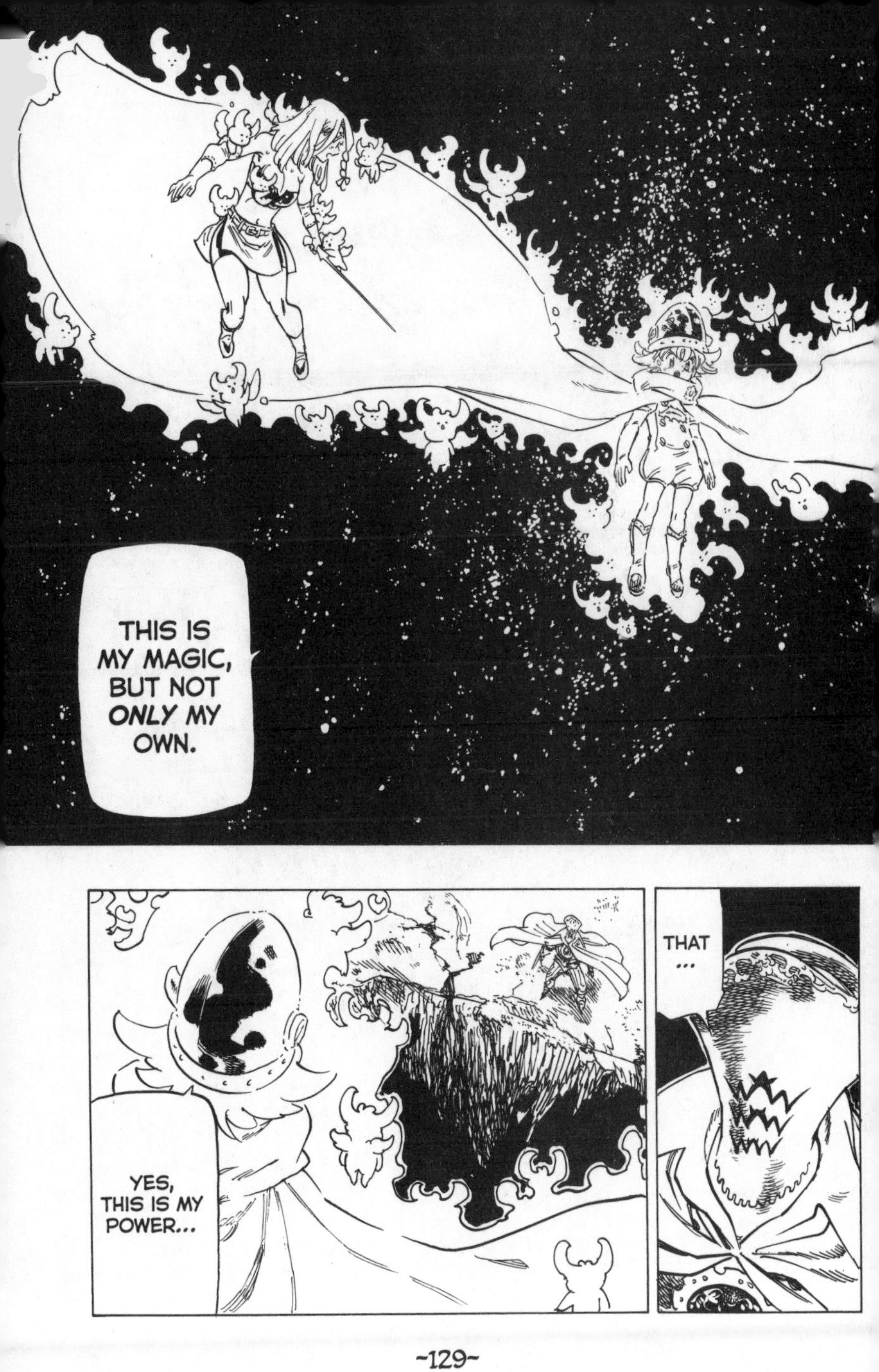
THIS IS MY MAGIC, BUT NOT *ONLY* MY OWN.
THAT ...
YES, THIS IS MY POWER...

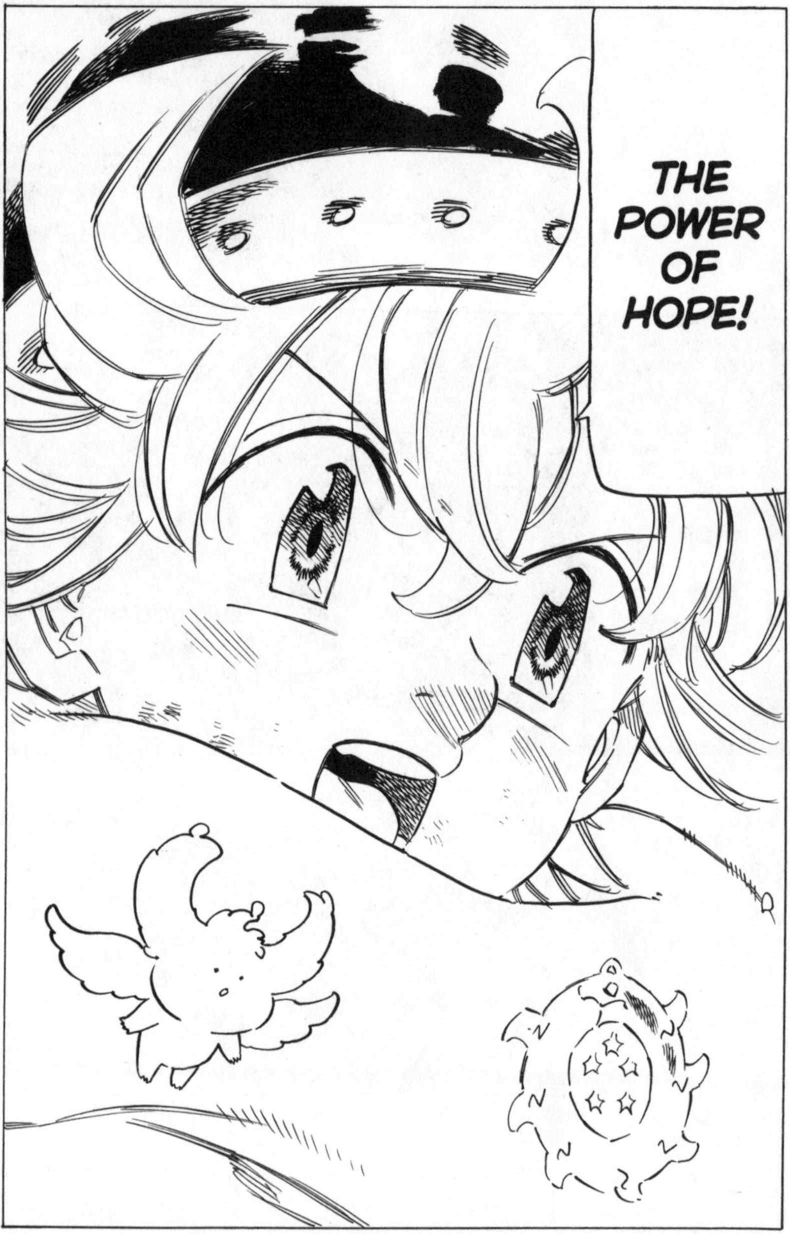
THE POWER OF HOPE!

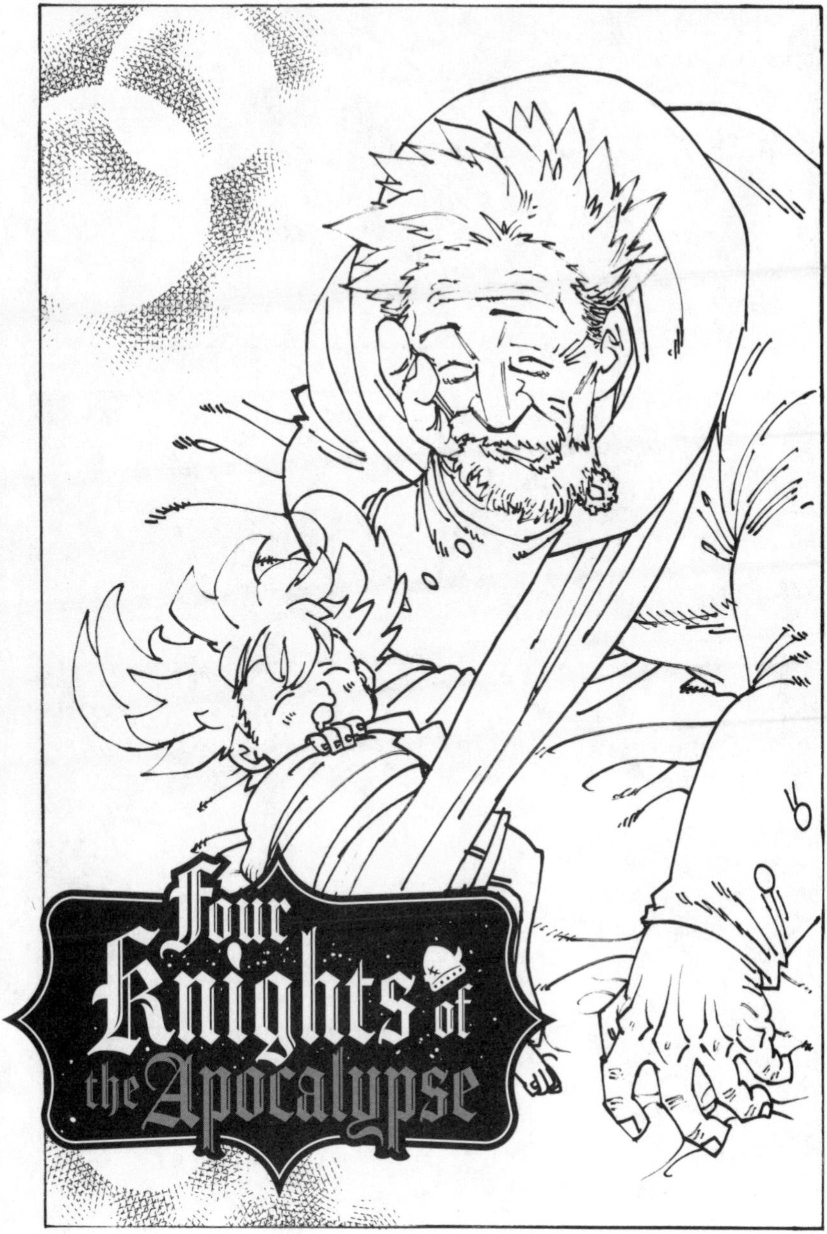
Four Knights of the Apocalypse

CHAPTER 21: HOPE

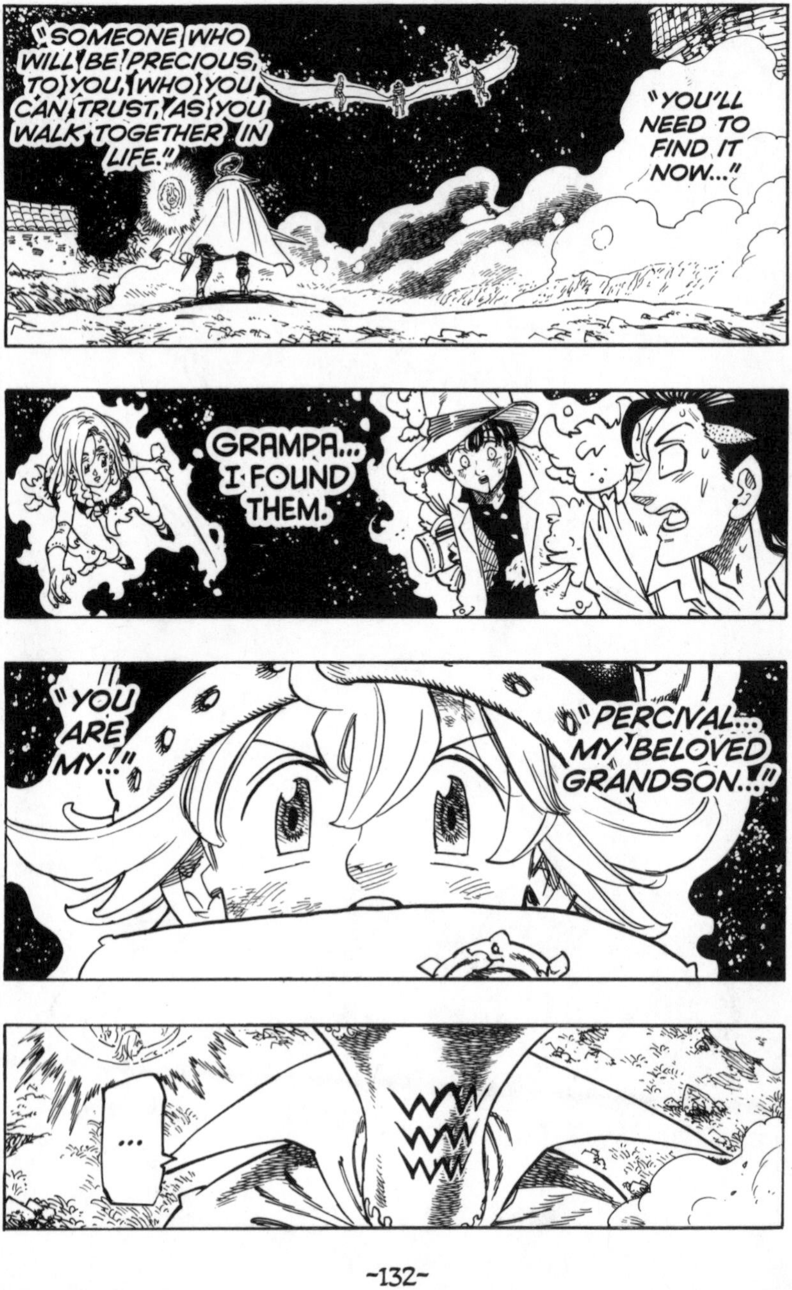
"YOU'LL NEED TO FIND IT NOW..."
"SOMEONE WHO WILL BE PRECIOUS TO YOU, WHO YOU CAN TRUST, AS YOU WALK TOGETHER IN LIFE."
GRAMPA... I FOUND THEM.
"PERCIVAL... MY BELOVED GRANDSON...!"
"YOU ARE MY...!"
...

"HOPE," YOU SAY?!
CONVERTING PEOPLE'S FEELINGS INTO YOUR POWER... PREPOSTEROUS!
DARAK! CAN YOU HEAR ME?!
WHY THE DELAY?! WHERE ARE MY SACRIFICES?!
I'VE SET THE STAGE FOR THE RITUAL!

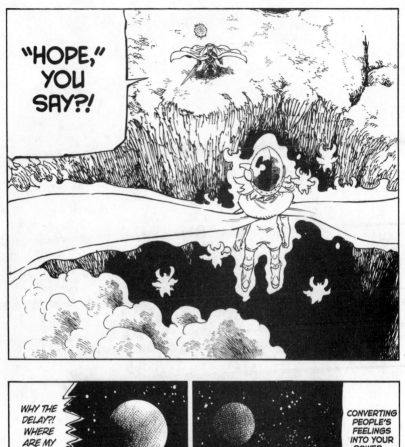

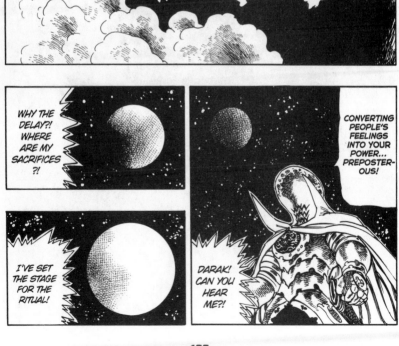

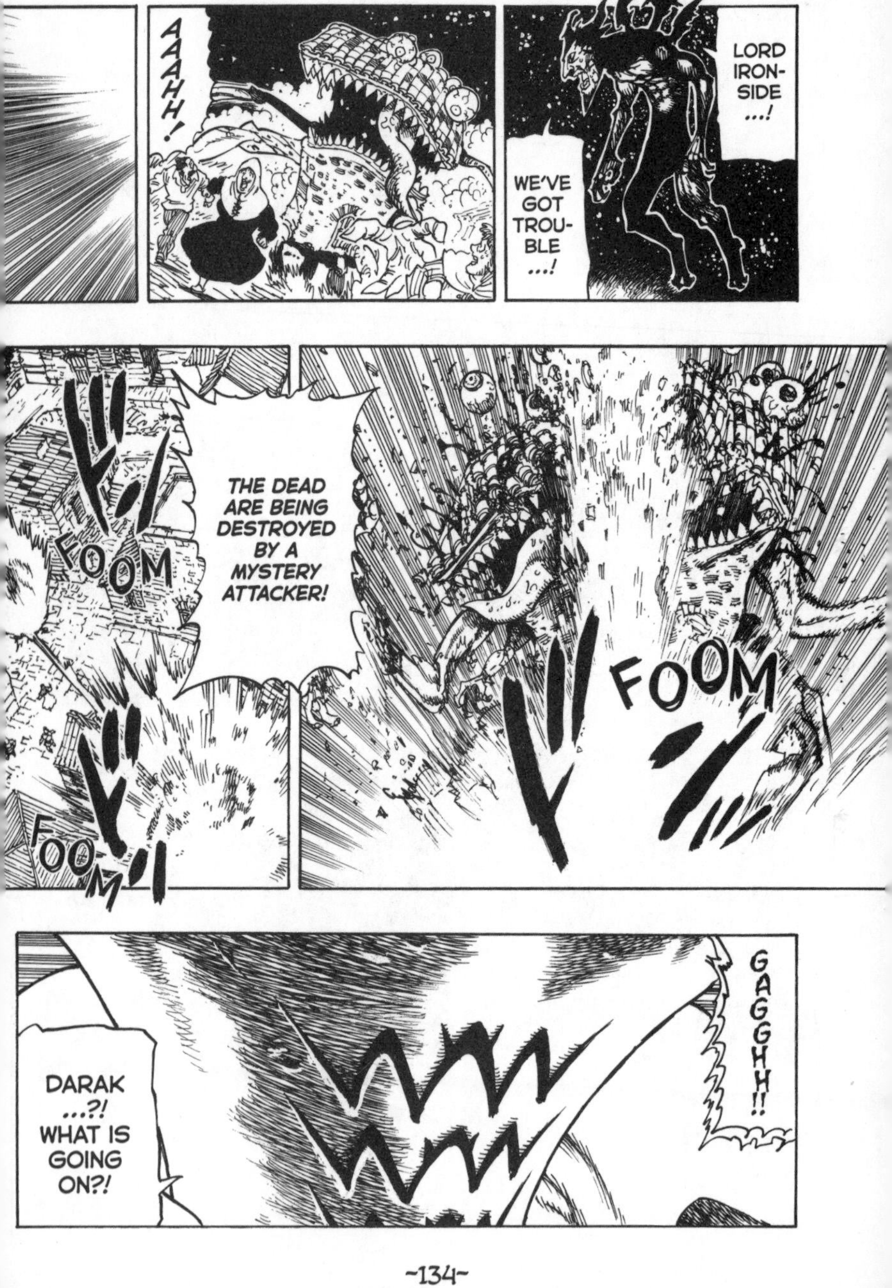
LORD IRONSIDE ...!
WE'VE GOT TROUBLE ...!
AAAHH!
FOOM
THE DEAD ARE BEING DESTROYED BY A MYSTERY ATTACKER!
FOOM
FOOM
GAGGHH!!
DARAK ...?! WHAT IS GOING ON?!

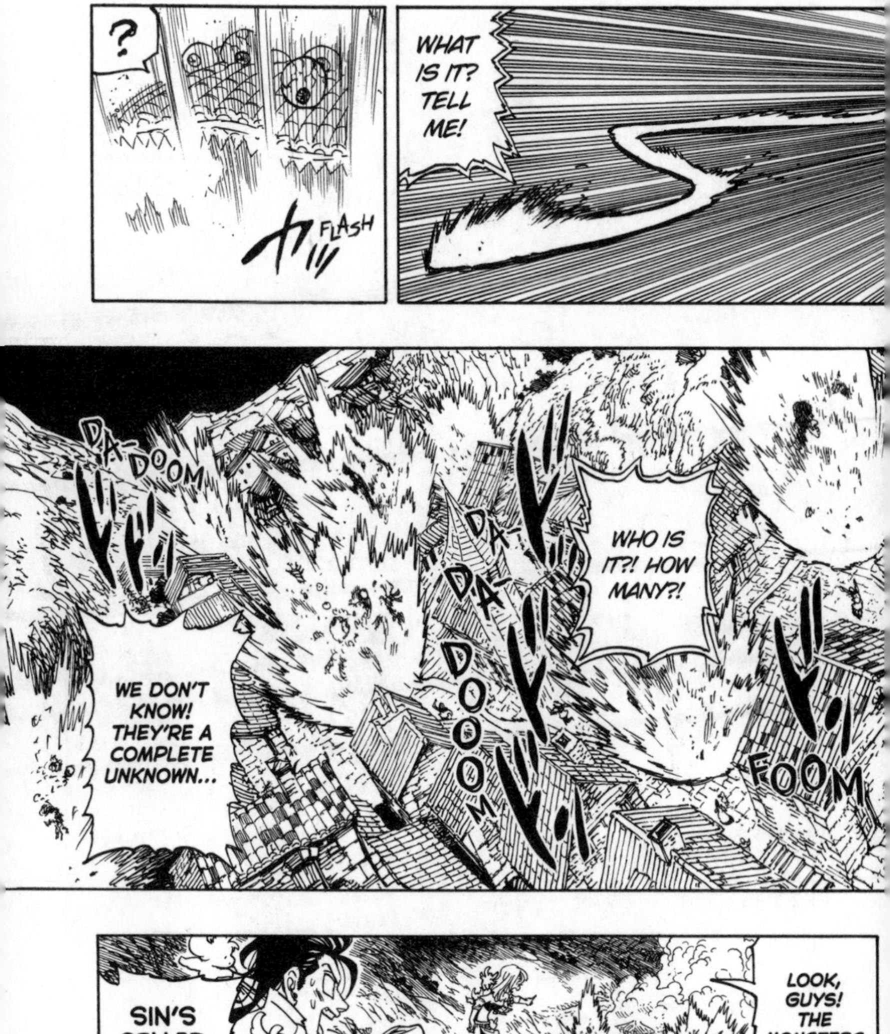
WHAT IS IT? TELL ME!
?
FLASH
WHO IS IT?! HOW MANY?!
FOOM
DA-DA-DOOOOM
DA-DOOM
WE DON'T KNOW! THEY'RE A COMPLETE UNKNOWN...
LOOK, GUYS! THE MONSTERS ARE FALLING!
IS IT SOME CORPS OF HOLY KNIGHTS?
SIN'S CALLED FOR BACKUP! I... I CAN'T BELIEVE IT!

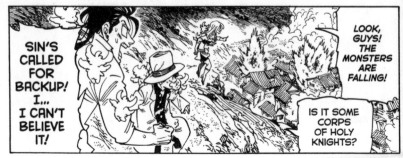

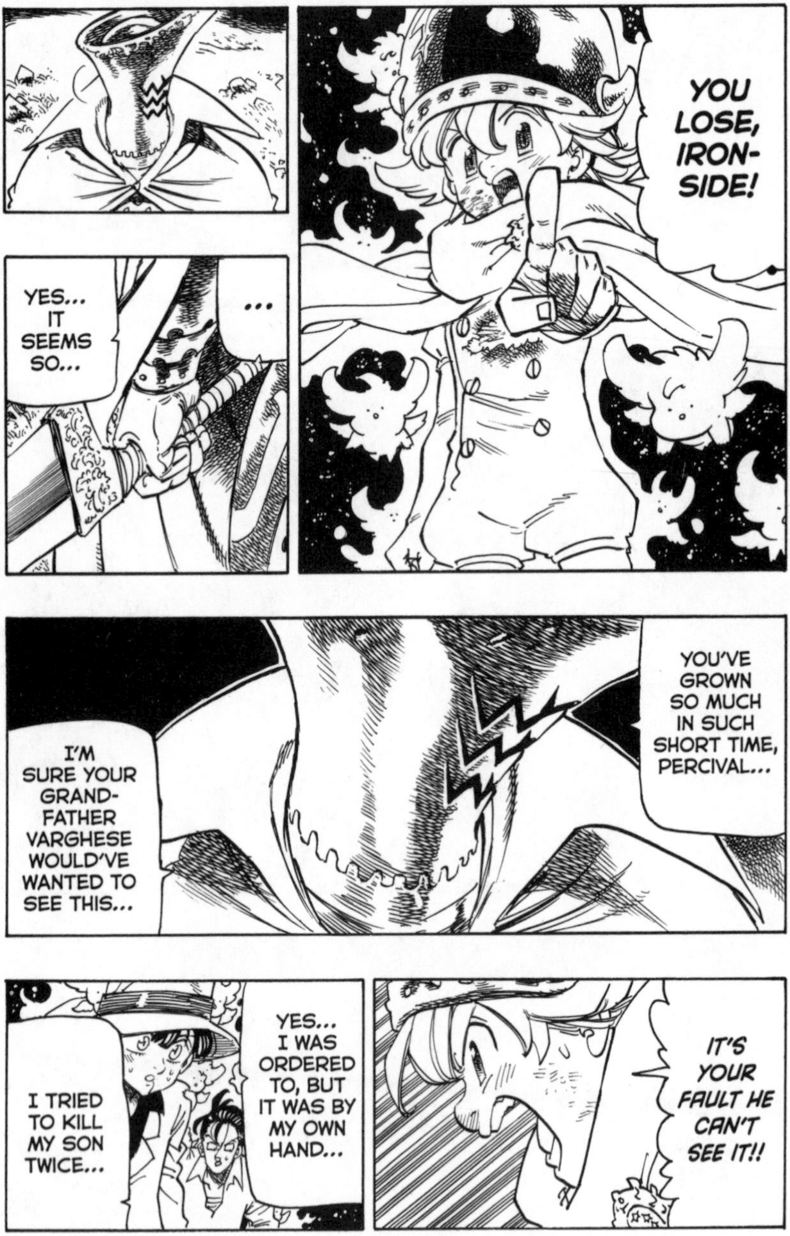
YOU LOSE, IRON-SIDE!
...
YES... IT SEEMS SO...
YOU'VE GROWN SO MUCH IN SUCH SHORT TIME, PERCIVAL...
I'M SURE YOUR GRAND-FATHER VARGHESE WOULD'VE WANTED TO SEE THIS...
IT'S YOUR FAULT HE CAN'T SEE IT!!
YES... I WAS ORDERED TO, BUT IT WAS BY MY OWN HAND...
I TRIED TO KILL MY SON TWICE...

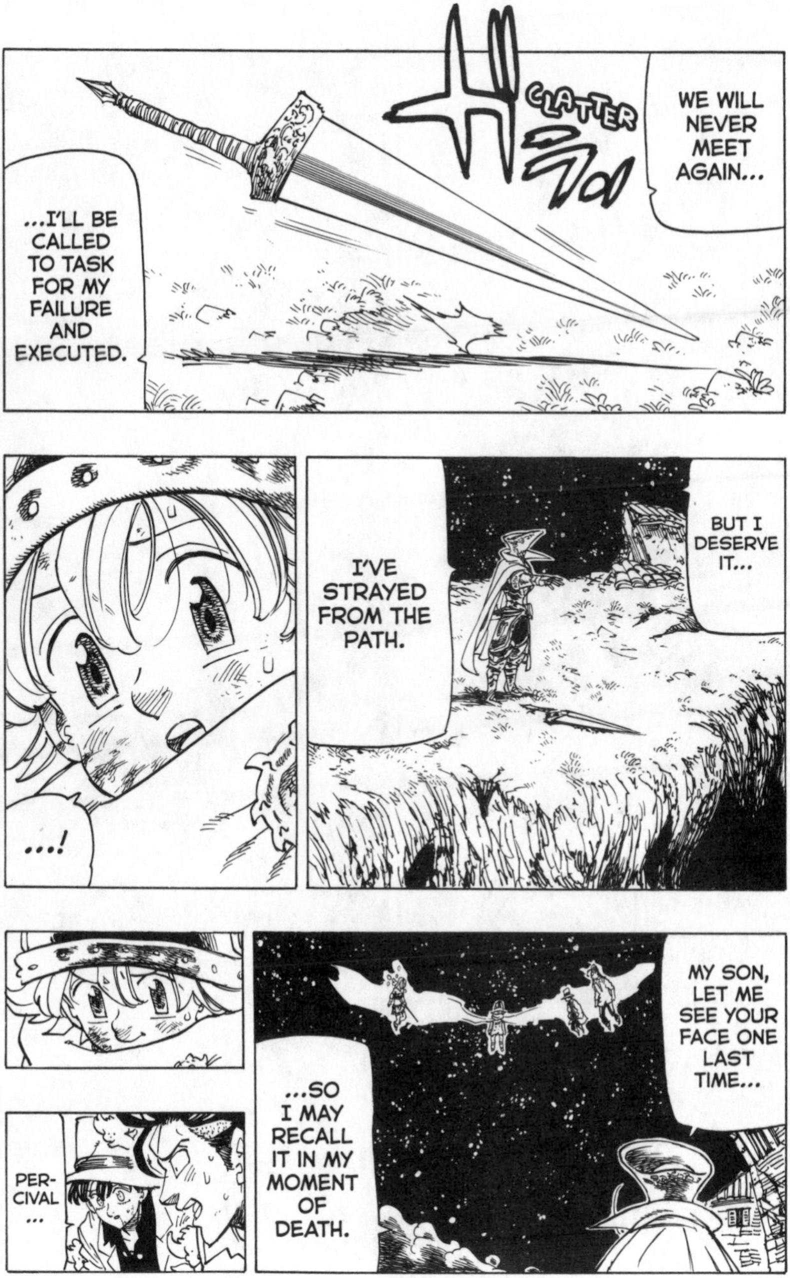
WE WILL NEVER MEET AGAIN...
CLATTER
...I'LL BE CALLED TO TASK FOR MY FAILURE AND EXECUTED.
BUT I DESERVE IT...
I'VE STRAYED FROM THE PATH.
...!
MY SON, LET ME SEE YOUR FACE ONE LAST TIME...
...SO I MAY RECALL IT IN MY MOMENT OF DEATH.
PER-CIVAL...

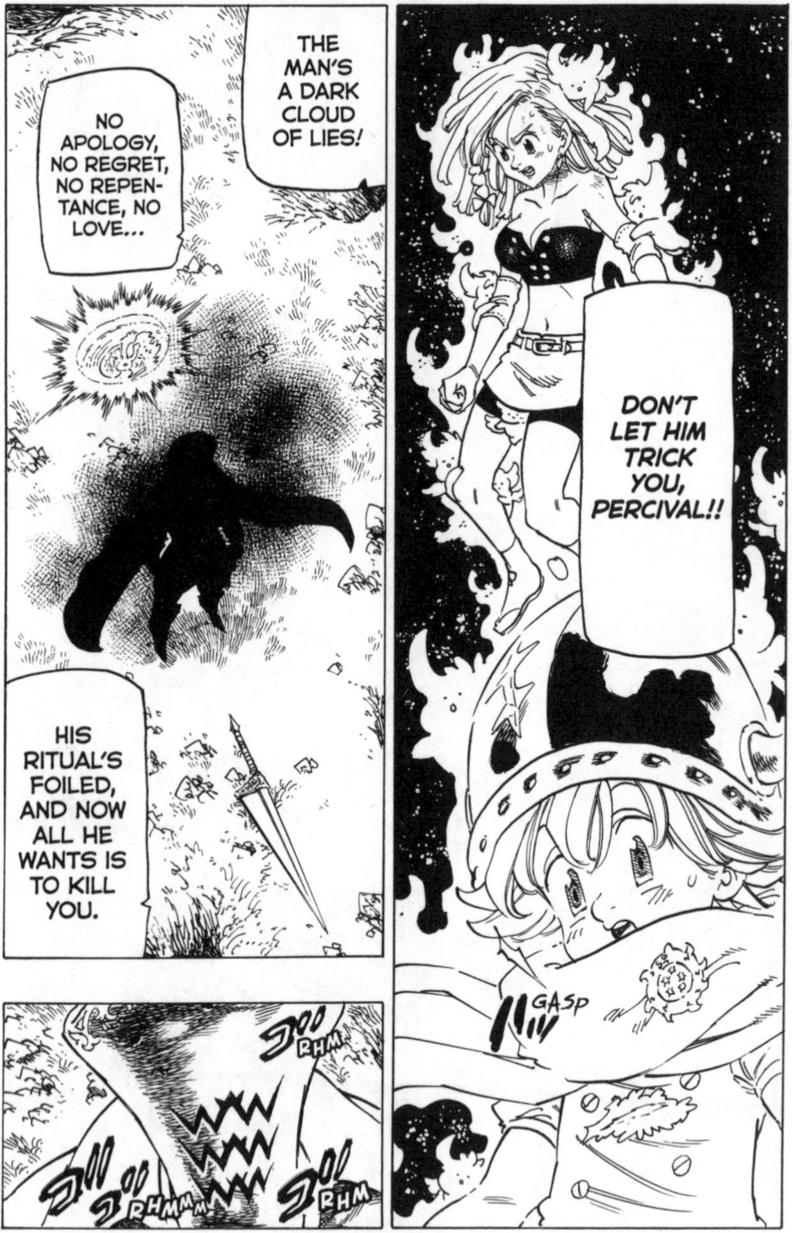
DON'T LET HIM TRICK YOU, PERCIVAL!!
GASP
THE MAN'S A DARK CLOUD OF LIES!
NO APOLOGY, NO REGRET, NO REPENTANCE, NO LOVE...
HIS RITUAL'S FOILED, AND NOW ALL HE WANTS IS TO KILL YOU.
RHM
RHM
RHMMM

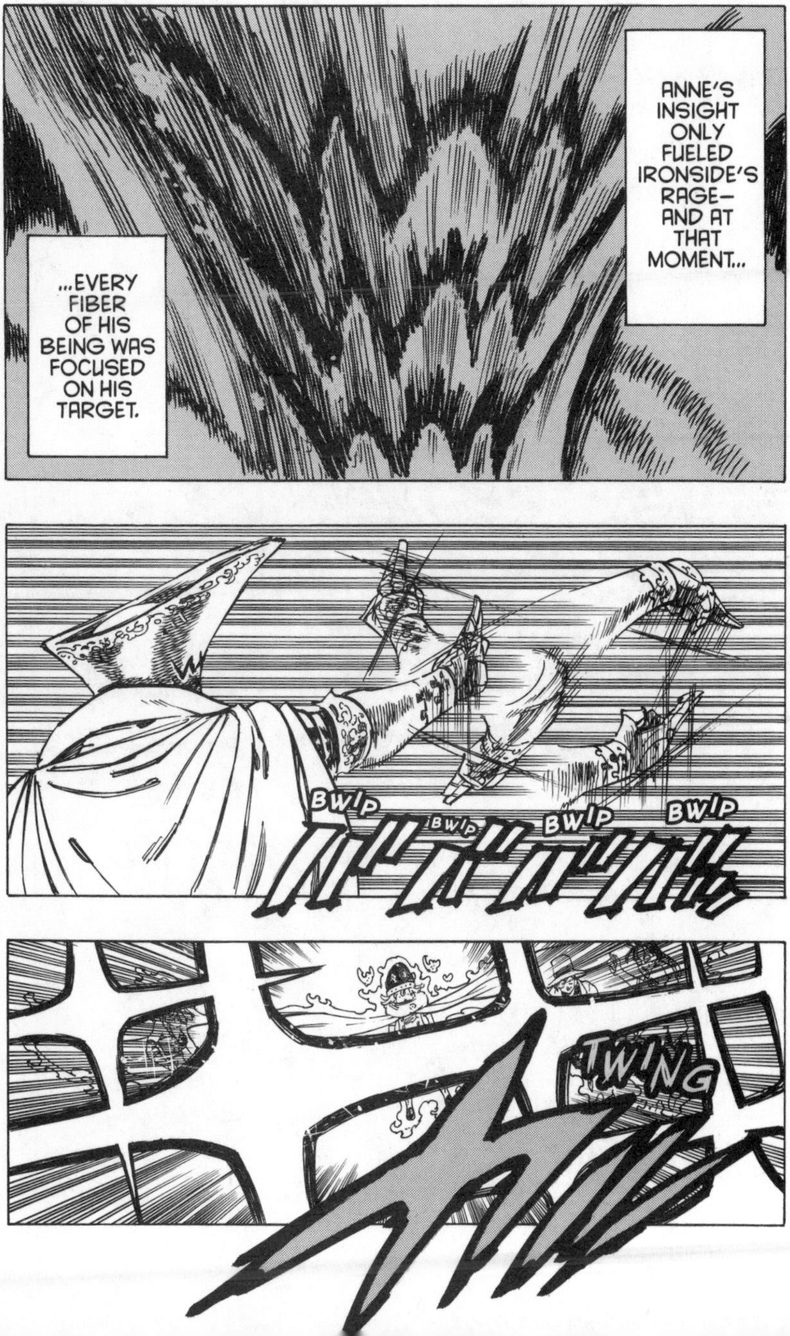
ANNE'S INSIGHT ONLY FUELED IRONSIDE'S RAGE— AND AT THAT MOMENT...
...EVERY FIBER OF HIS BEING WAS FOCUSED ON HIS TARGET.
BWIP
BWIP
BWIP
BWIP
TWING

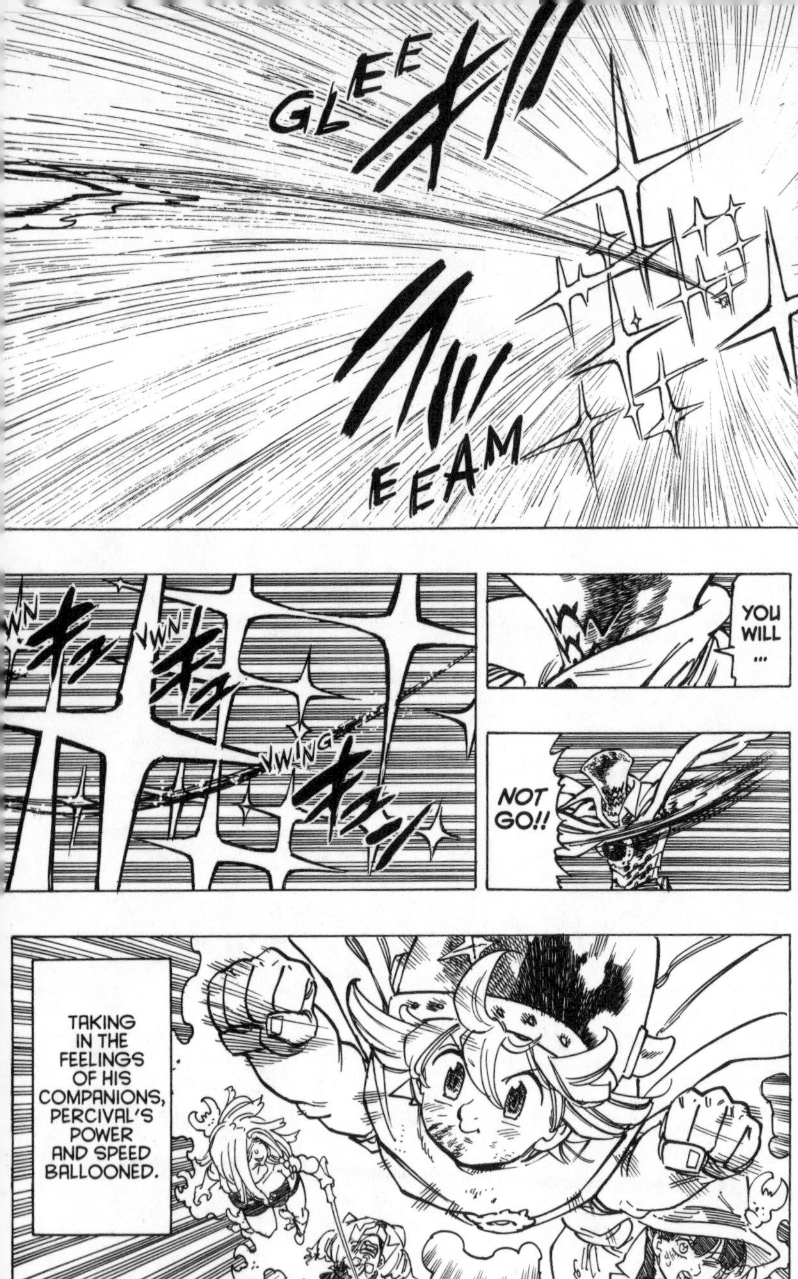
GLEE
EEAM
YOU WILL ...
NOT GO!!
VWN
VWN
VWING
TAKING IN THE FEELINGS OF HIS COMPANIONS, PERCIVAL'S POWER AND SPEED BALLOONED.

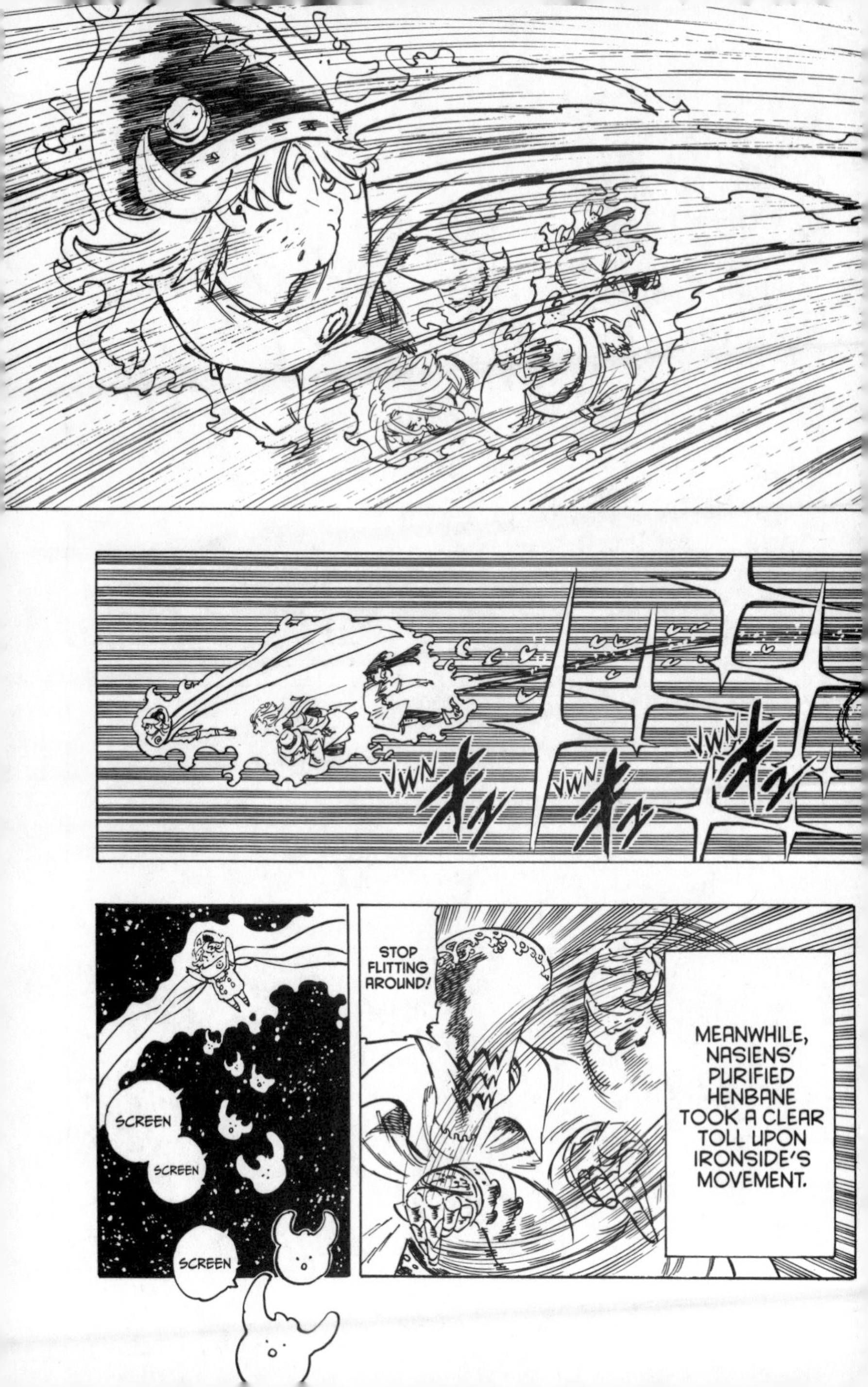
VWN
VWN
VWN
STOP FLITTING AROUND!
MEANWHILE, NASIENS' PURIFIED HENBANE TOOK A CLEAR TOLL UPON IRONSIDE'S MOVEMENT.
SCREEN
SCREEN
SCREEN

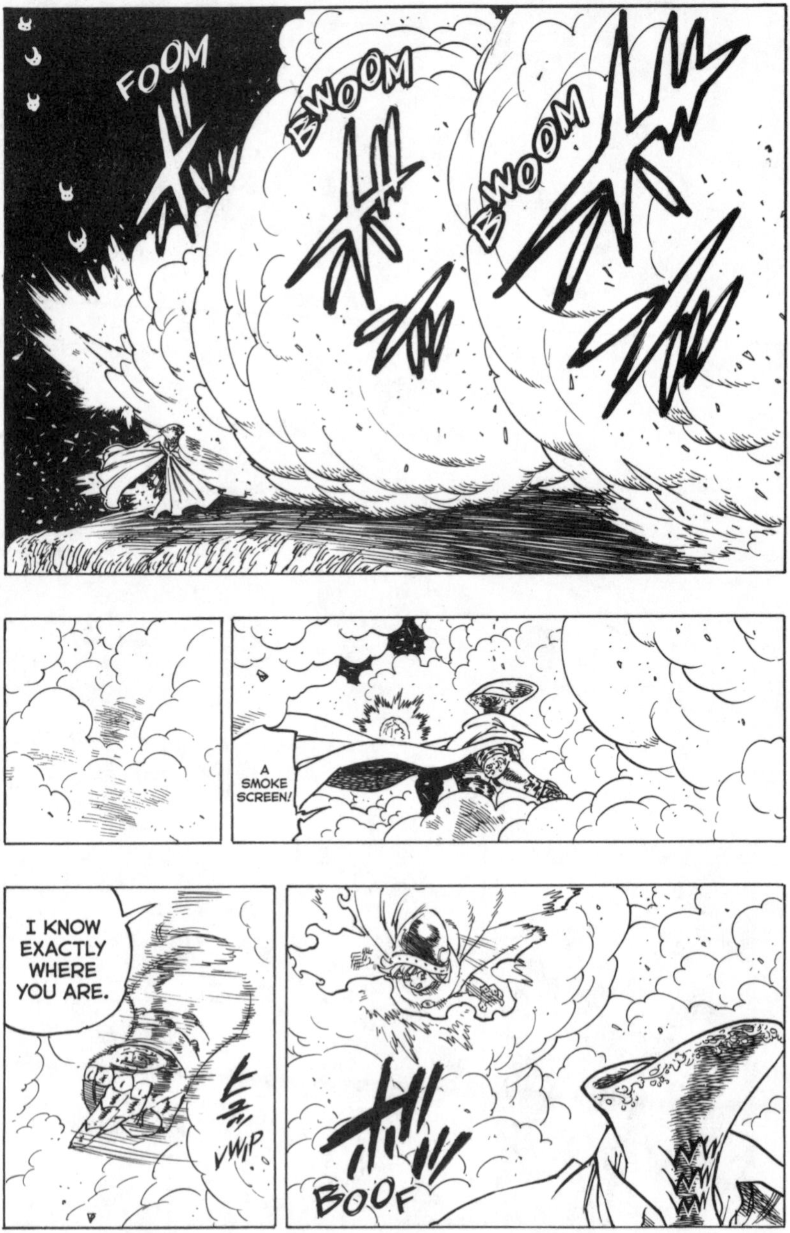
BWOOM
BWOOM
FOOM
A SMOKE SCREEN!
BOOF
I KNOW EXACTLY WHERE YOU ARE.
VWIP

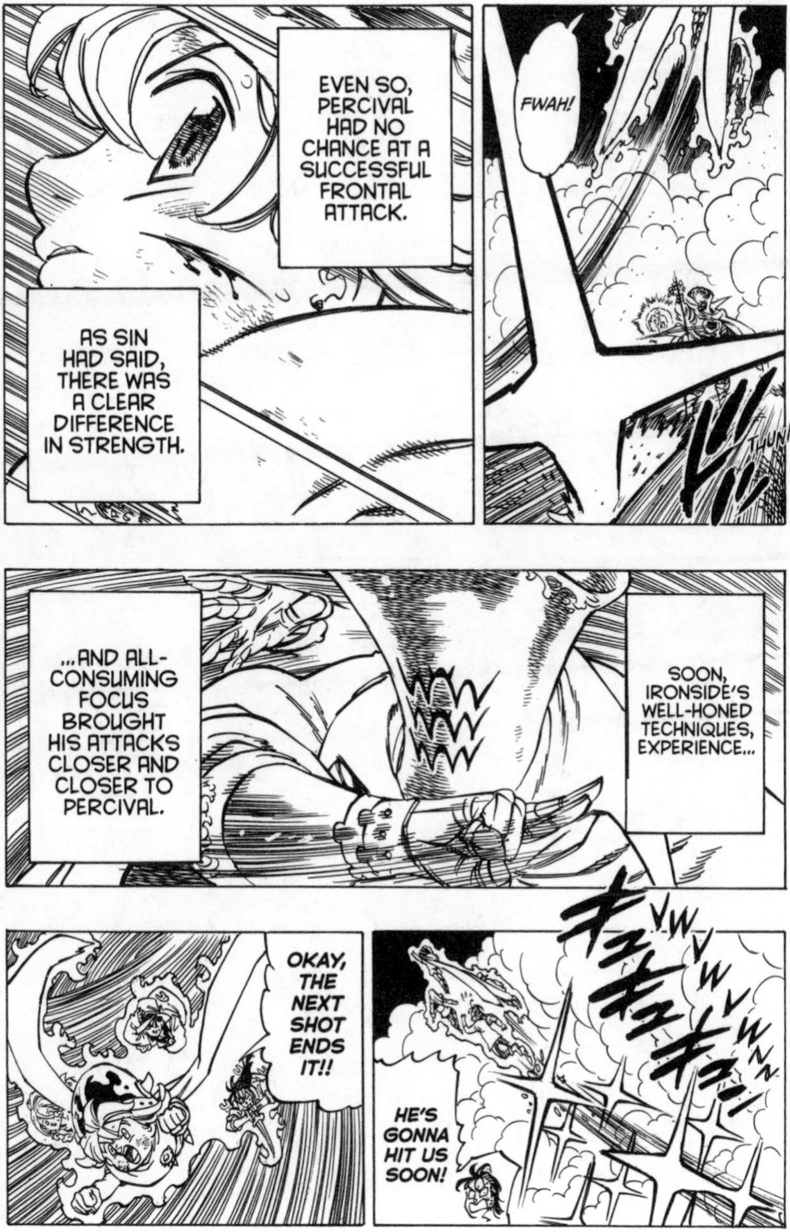
FWAH!
THUNN
EVEN SO, PERCIVAL HAD NO CHANCE AT A SUCCESSFUL FRONTAL ATTACK.
AS SIN HAD SAID, THERE WAS A CLEAR DIFFERENCE IN STRENGTH.
SOON, IRONSIDE'S WELL-HONED TECHNIQUES, EXPERIENCE...
...AND ALL-CONSUMING FOCUS BROUGHT HIS ATTACKS CLOSER AND CLOSER TO PERCIVAL.
VWVWVWNN
HE'S GONNA HIT US SOON!
OKAY, THE NEXT SHOT ENDS IT!!

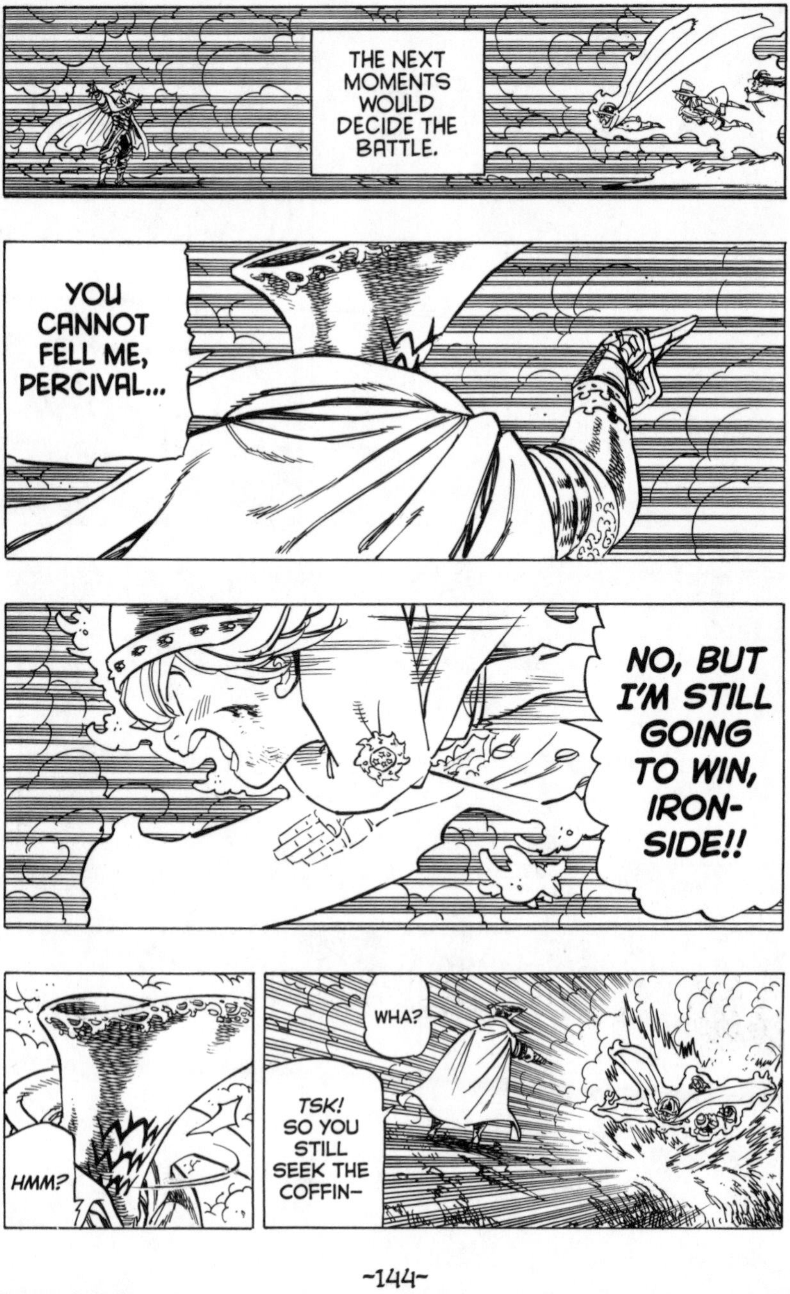
THE NEXT MOMENTS WOULD DECIDE THE BATTLE.
YOU CANNOT FELL ME, PERCIVAL...
NO, BUT I'M STILL GOING TO WIN, IRON-SIDE!!
WHA?
TSK! SO YOU STILL SEEK THE COFFIN–
HMM?

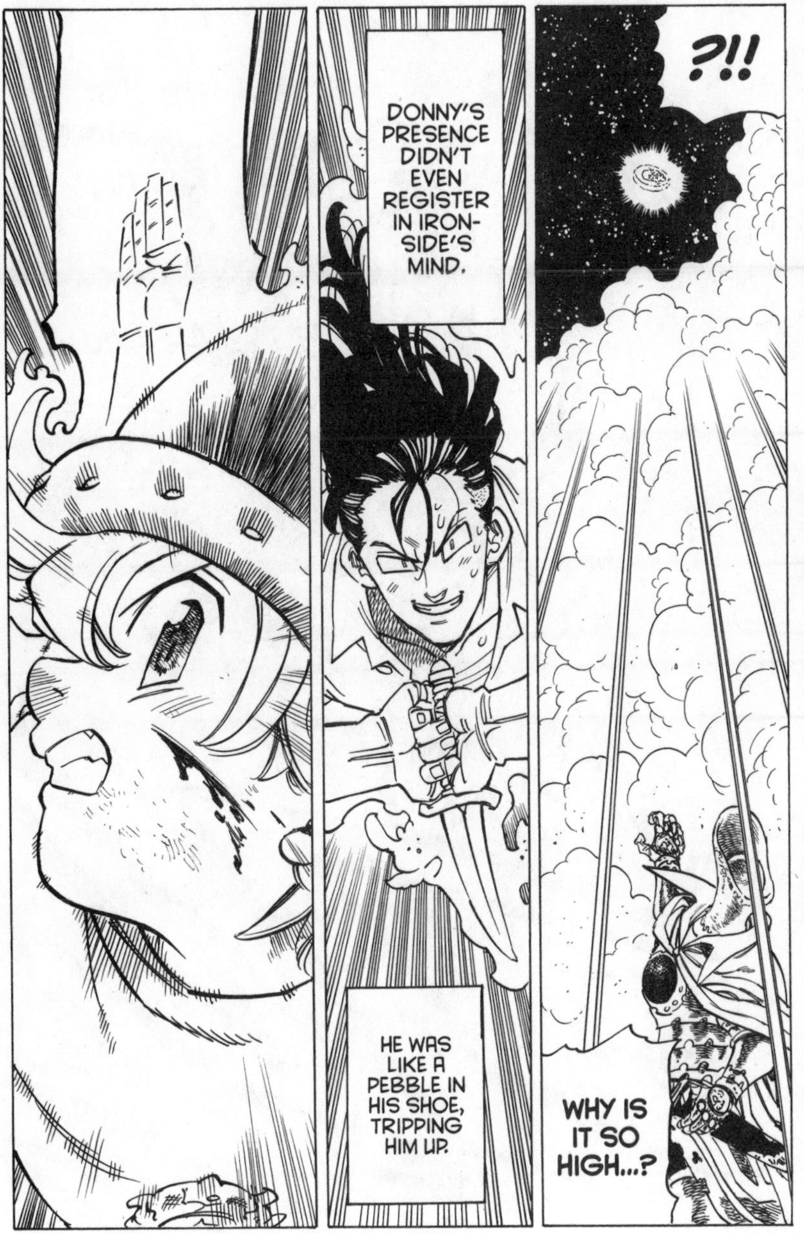
?!!
WHY IS IT SO HIGH...?
DONNY'S PRESENCE DIDN'T EVEN REGISTER IN IRON-SIDE'S MIND.
HE WAS LIKE A PEBBLE IN HIS SHOE, TRIPPING HIM UP.

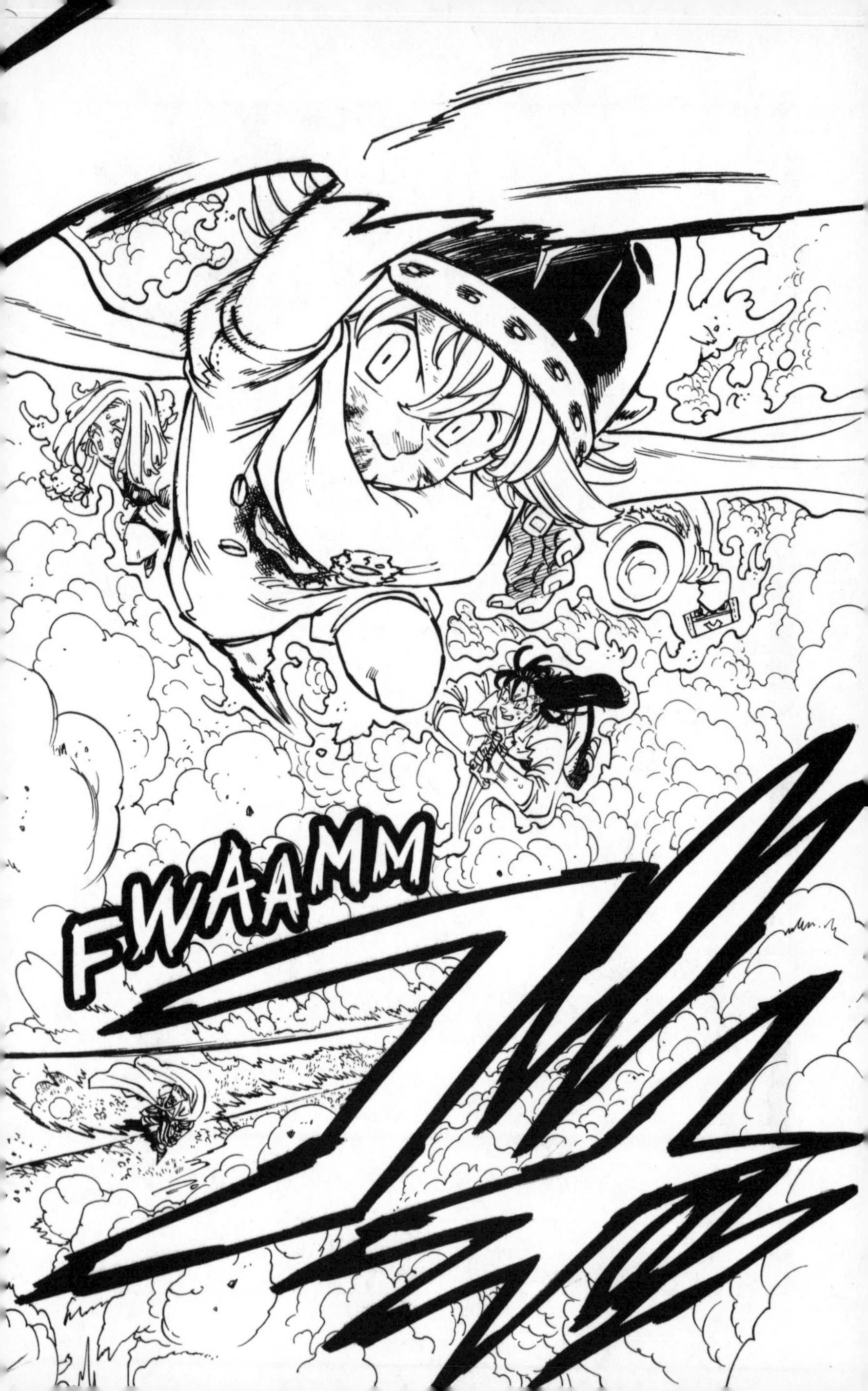
FWAAMM

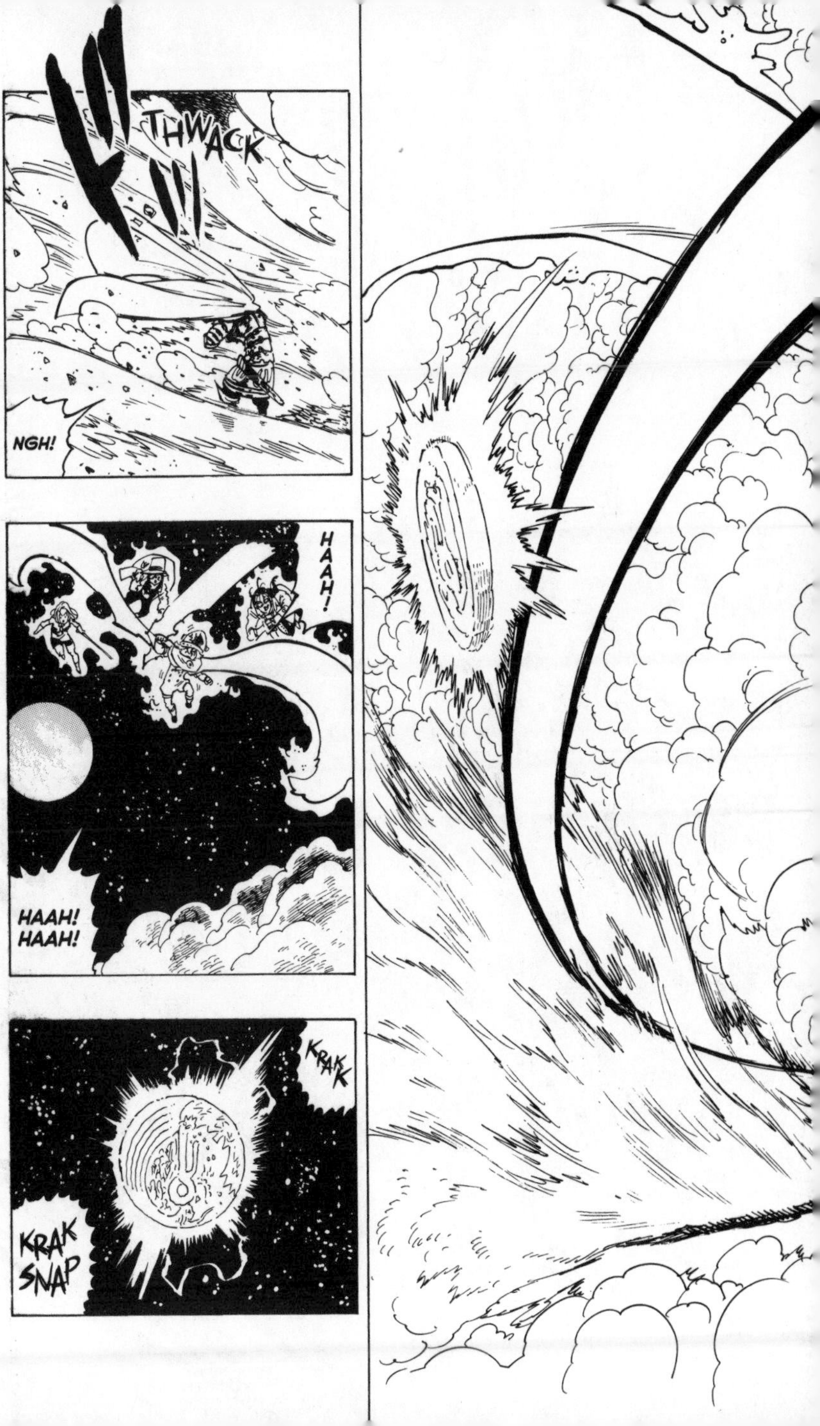
THWACK
NGH!
HAAH!
HAAH!
HAAH!
KRAKK
KRAK
SNAP

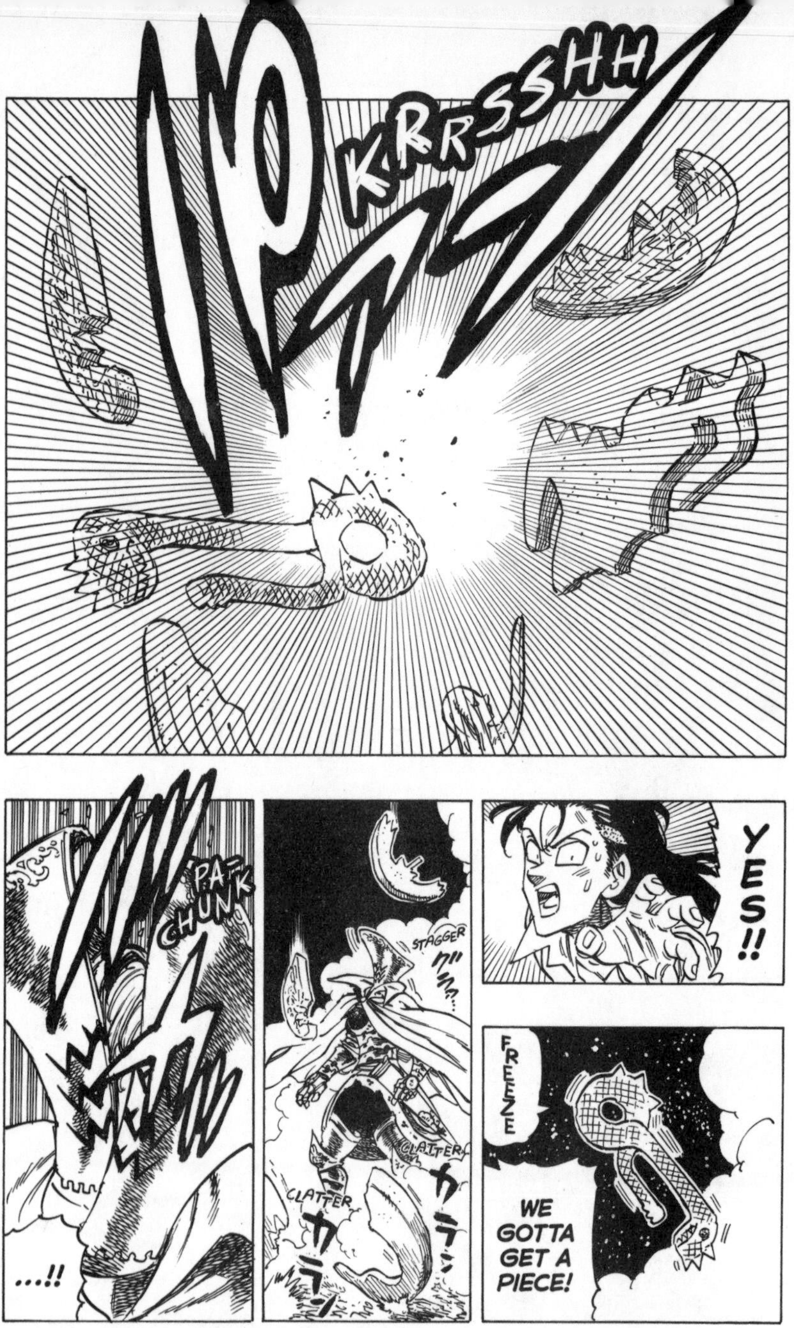
KRRSSHH
YES!!
FREEZE
WE GOTTA GET A PIECE!
STAGGER
CLATTER
CLATTER
PAK
CHUNK
...!!

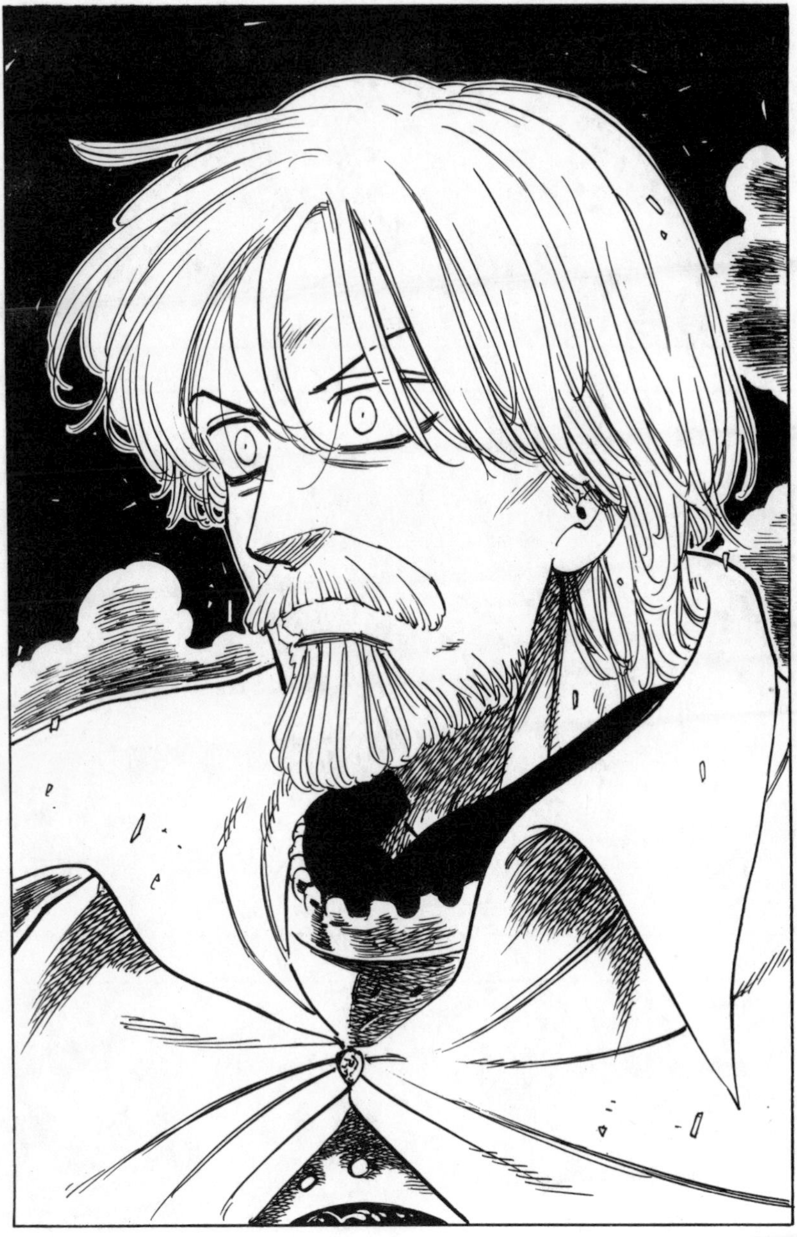

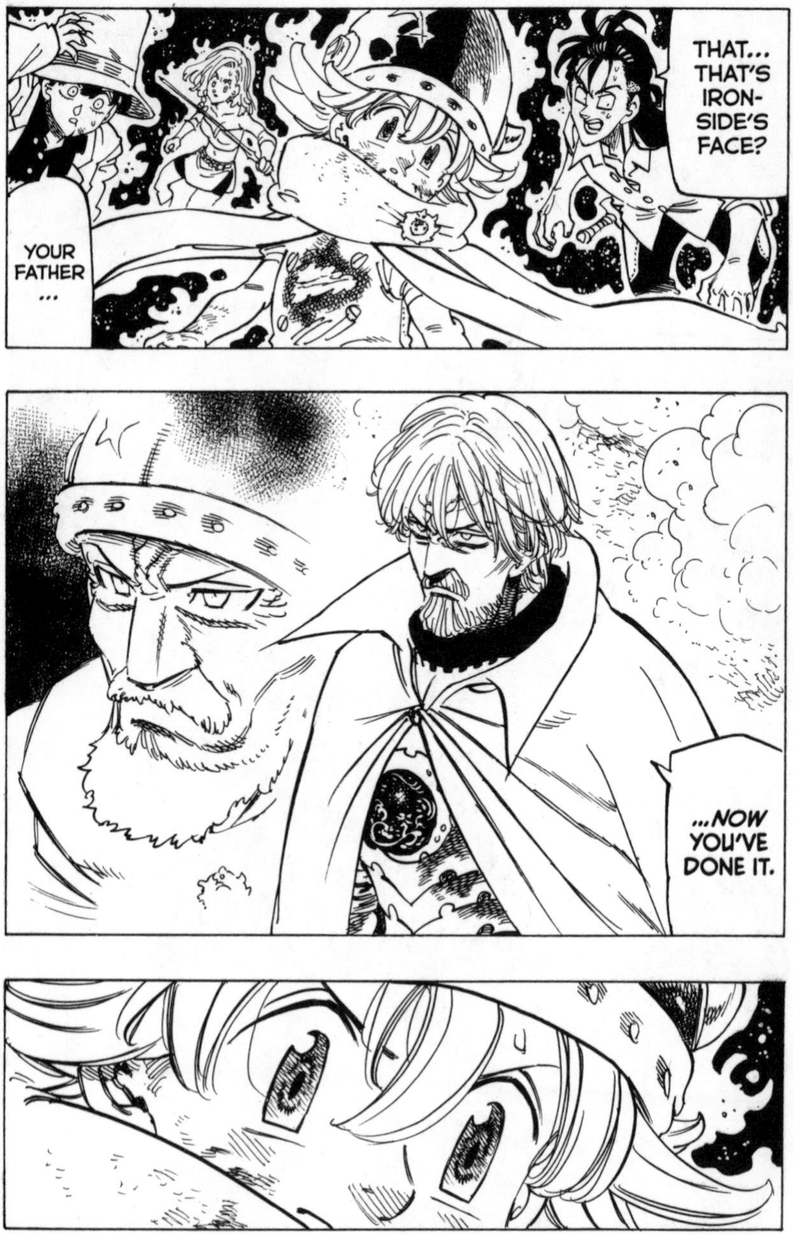
THAT... THAT'S IRON-SIDE'S FACE?
YOUR FATHER ...
...NOW YOU'VE DONE IT.

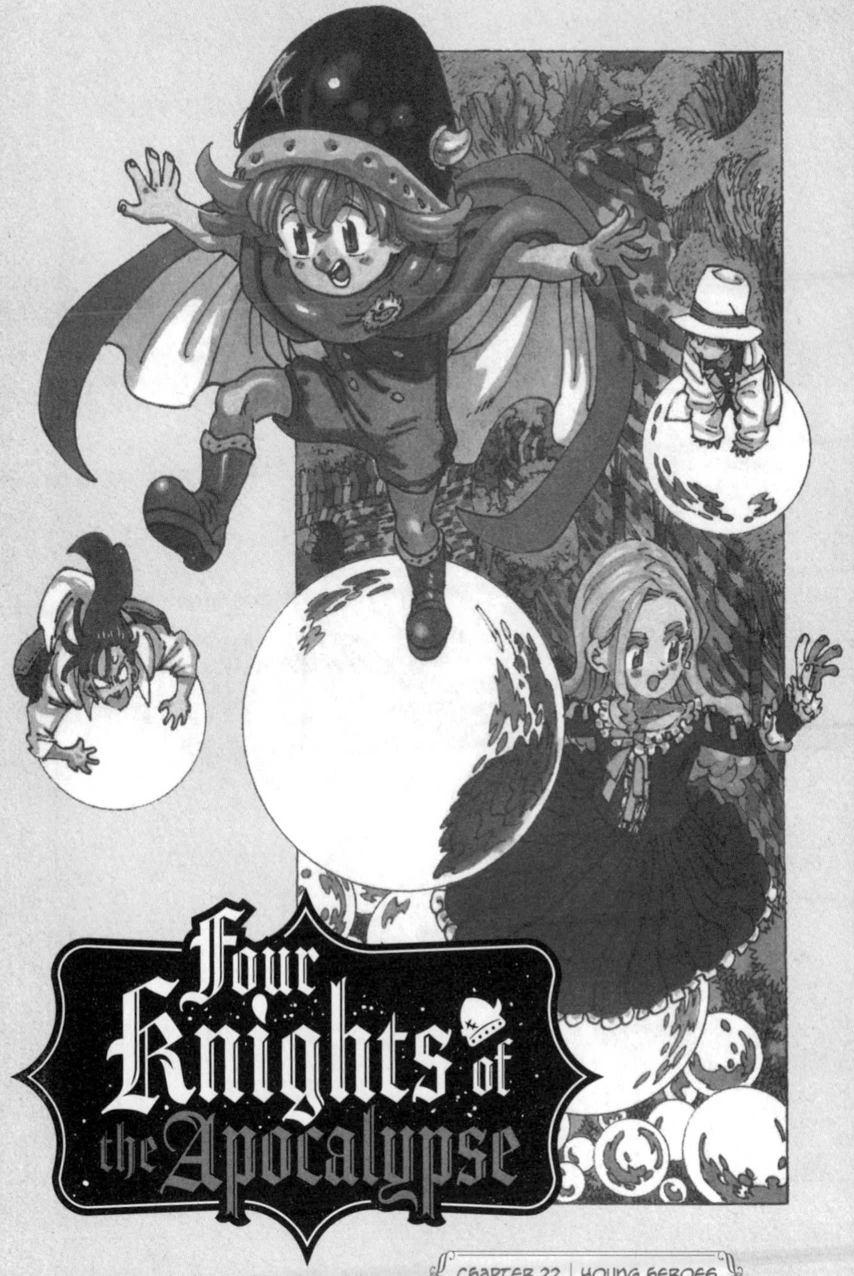
Four Knights of the Apocalypse
CHAPTER 22 | YOUNG HEROES

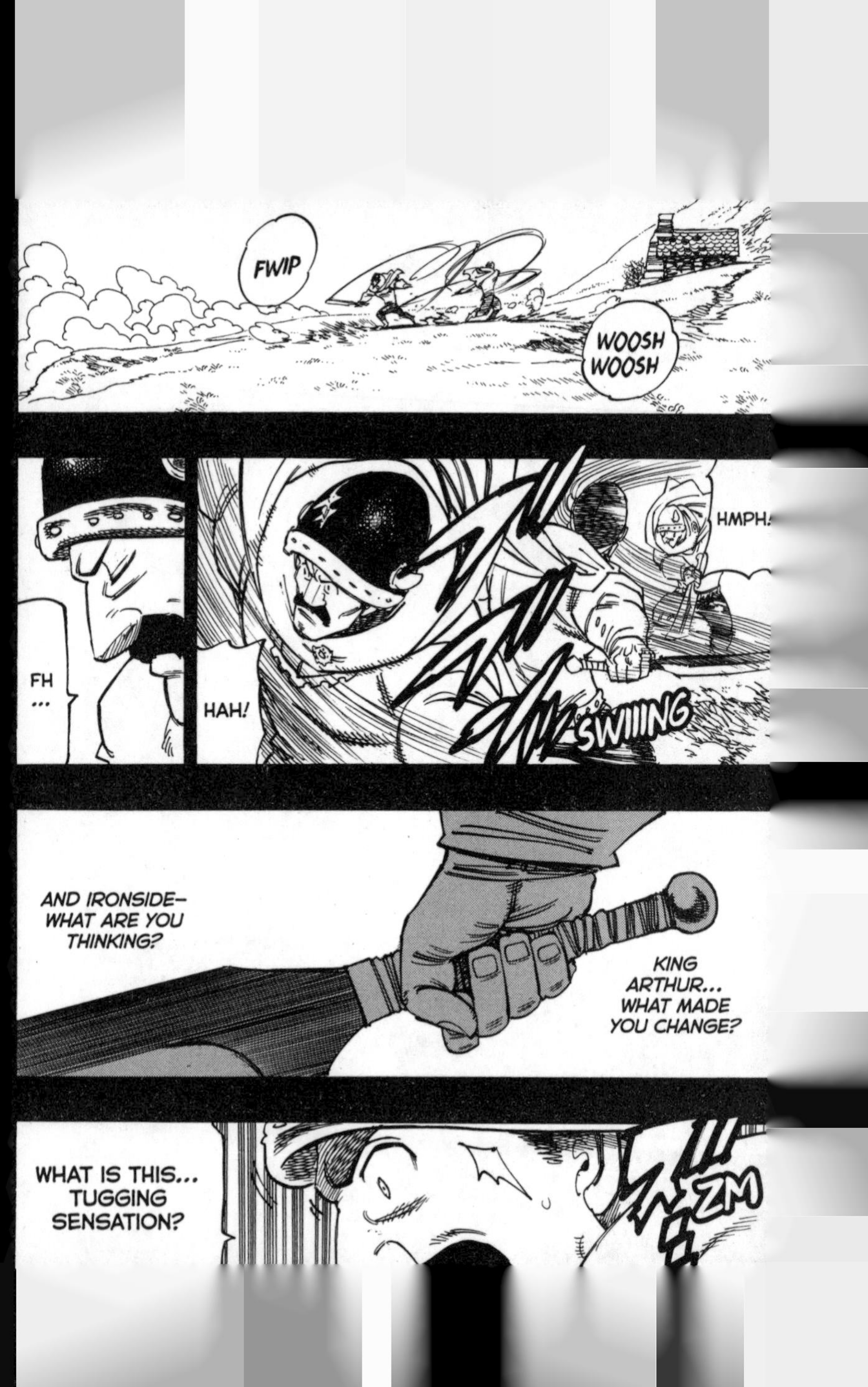
FWIP
WOOSH WOOSH
HMPH!
HAH!
SWIIING
FH ...
KING ARTHUR... WHAT MADE YOU CHANGE?
AND IRONSIDE— WHAT ARE YOU THINKING?
ZM
WHAT IS THIS... TUGGING SENSATION?

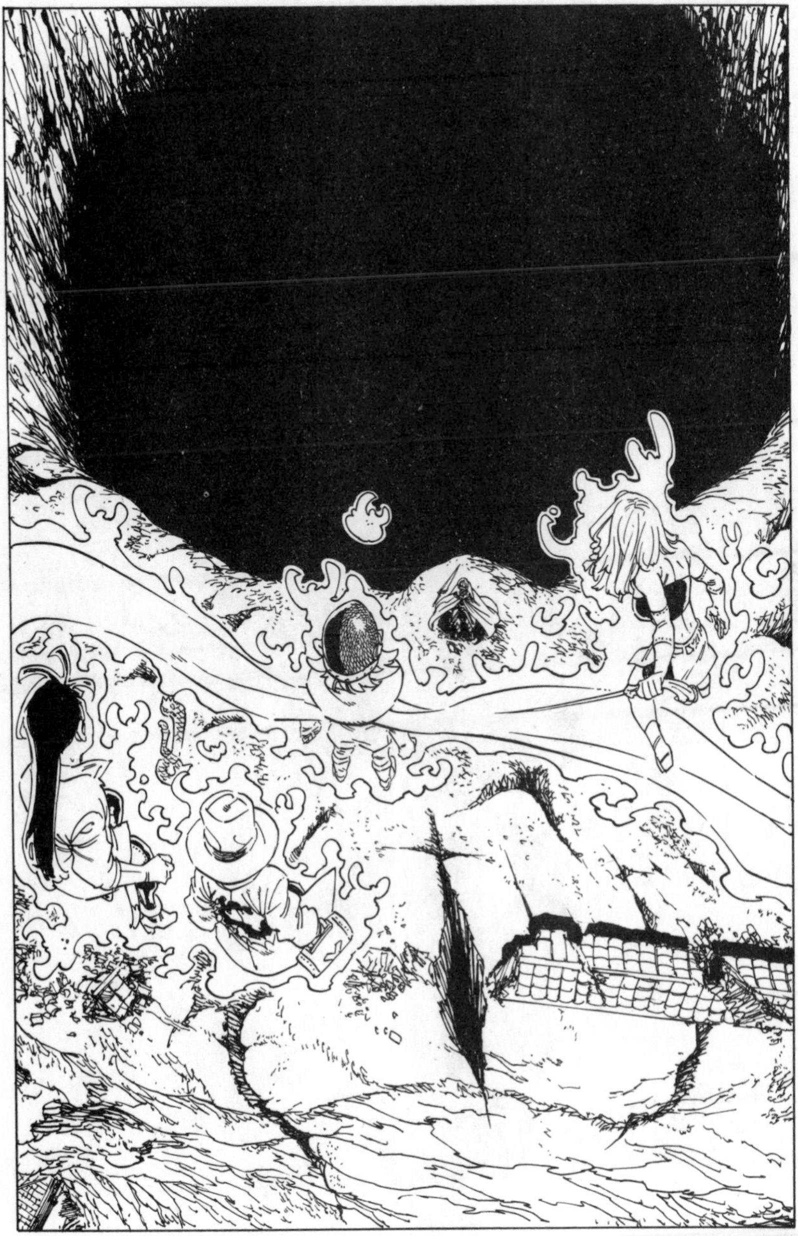

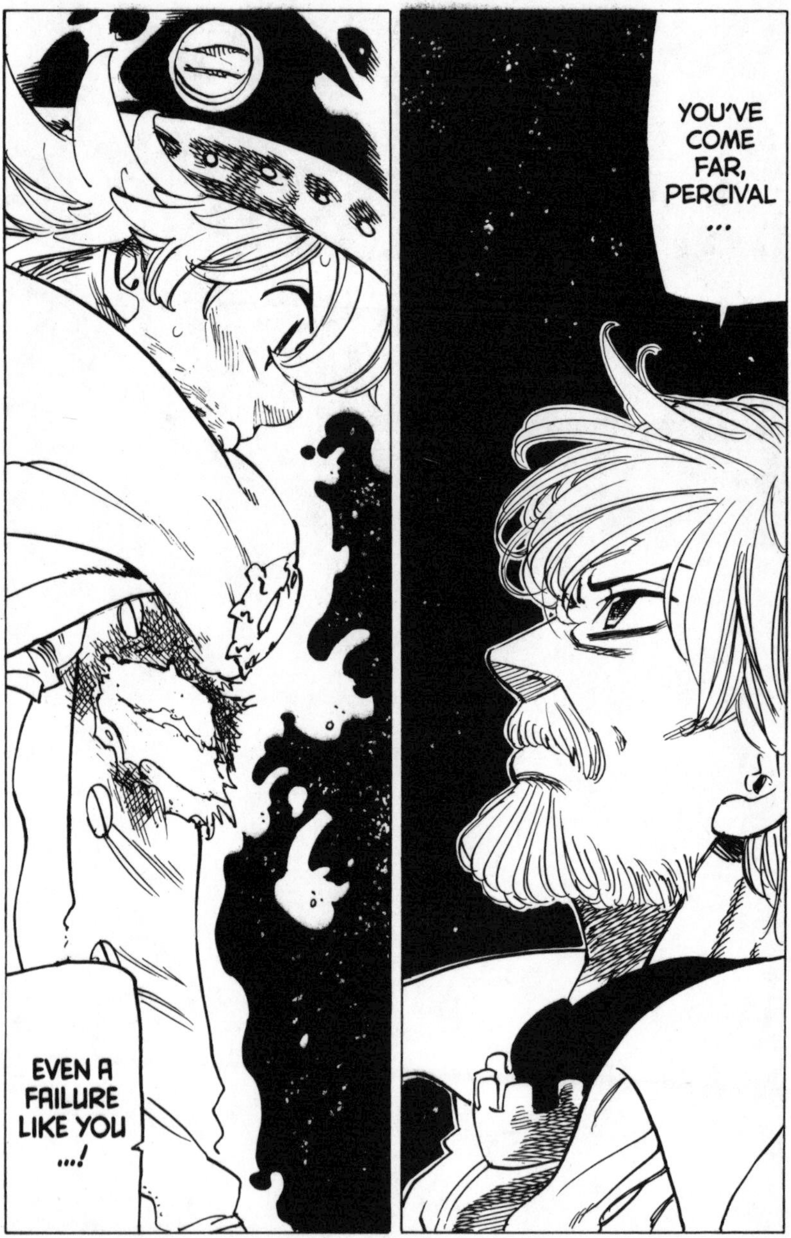
YOU'VE COME FAR, PERCIVAL ...
EVEN A FAILURE LIKE YOU ...!

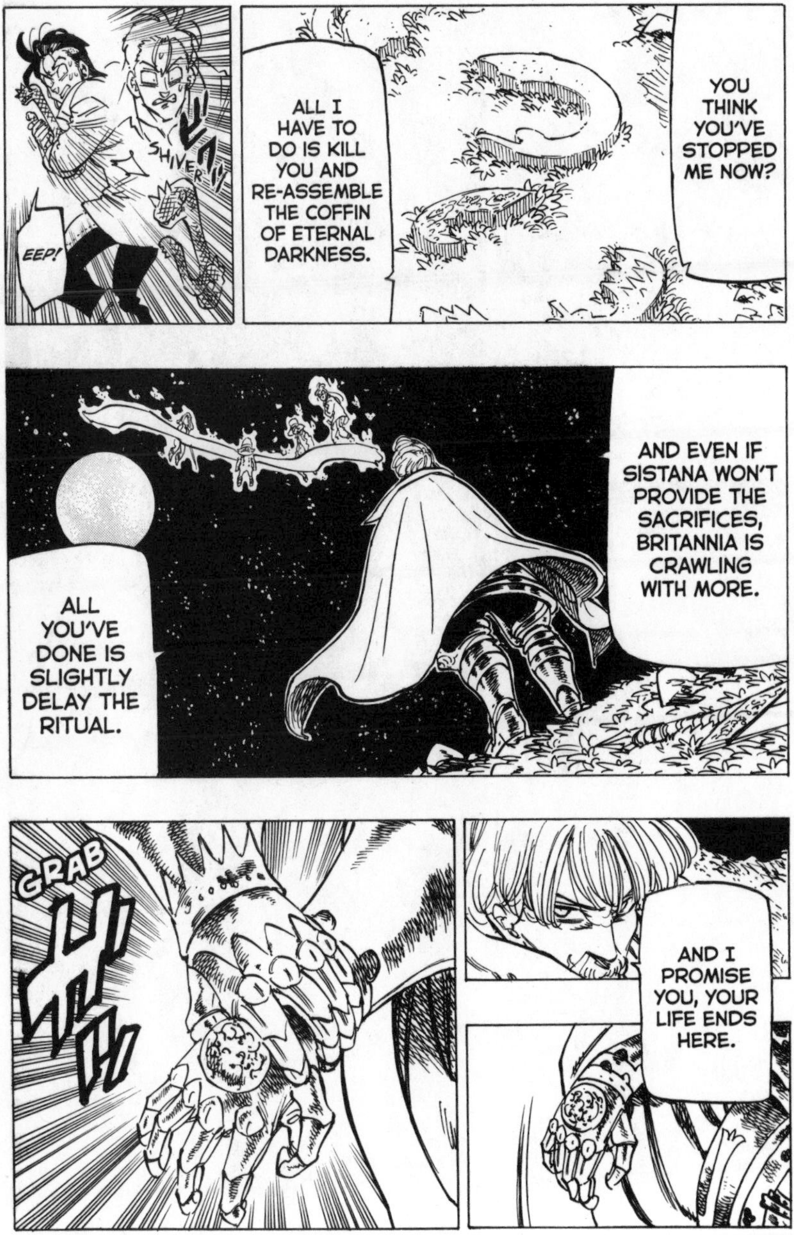
YOU THINK YOU'VE STOPPED ME NOW?
ALL I HAVE TO DO IS KILL YOU AND RE-ASSEMBLE THE COFFIN OF ETERNAL DARKNESS.
SHIVER
EEP!
AND EVEN IF SISTANA WON'T PROVIDE THE SACRIFICES, BRITANNIA IS CRAWLING WITH MORE.
ALL YOU'VE DONE IS SLIGHTLY DELAY THE RITUAL.
AND I PROMISE YOU, YOUR LIFE ENDS HERE.
GRAB

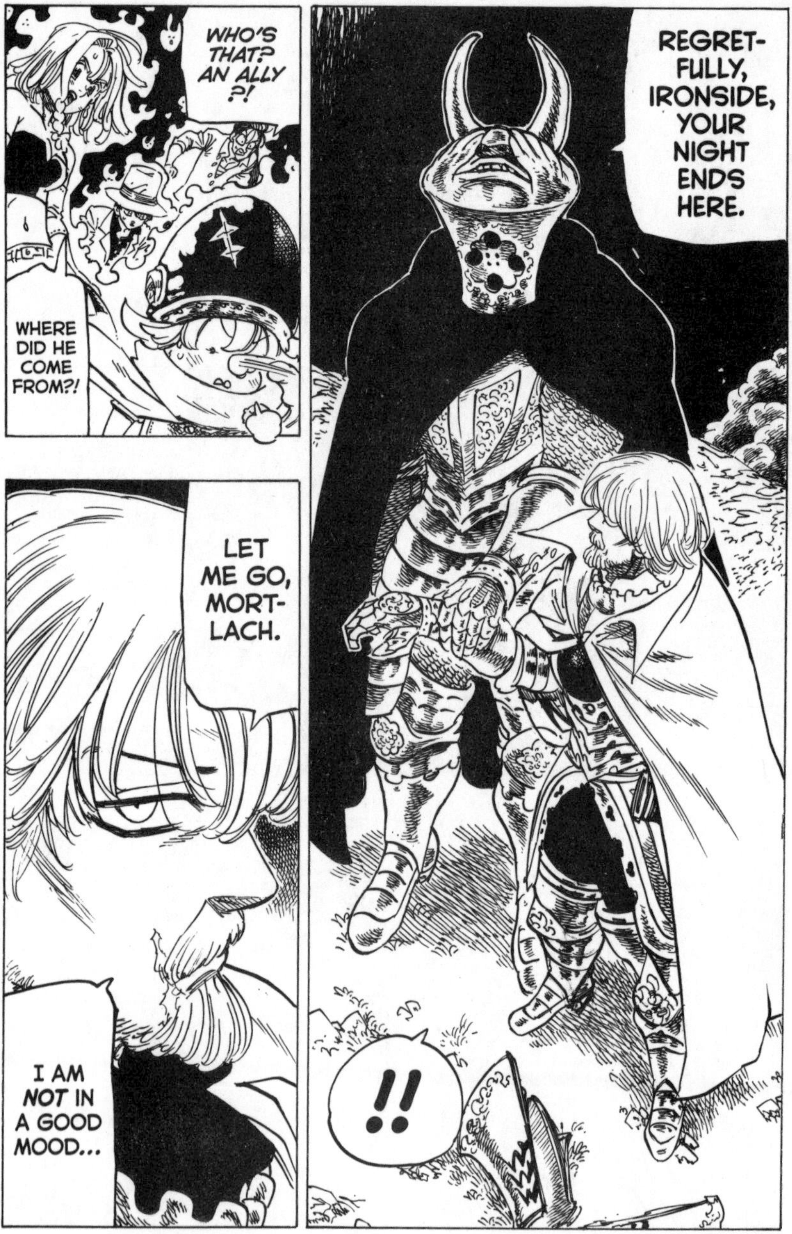
REGRETFULLY, IRONSIDE, YOUR NIGHT ENDS HERE.
!!
WHO'S THAT? AN ALLY?!
WHERE DID HE COME FROM?!
LET ME GO, MORTLACH.
I AM *NOT* IN A GOOD MOOD...

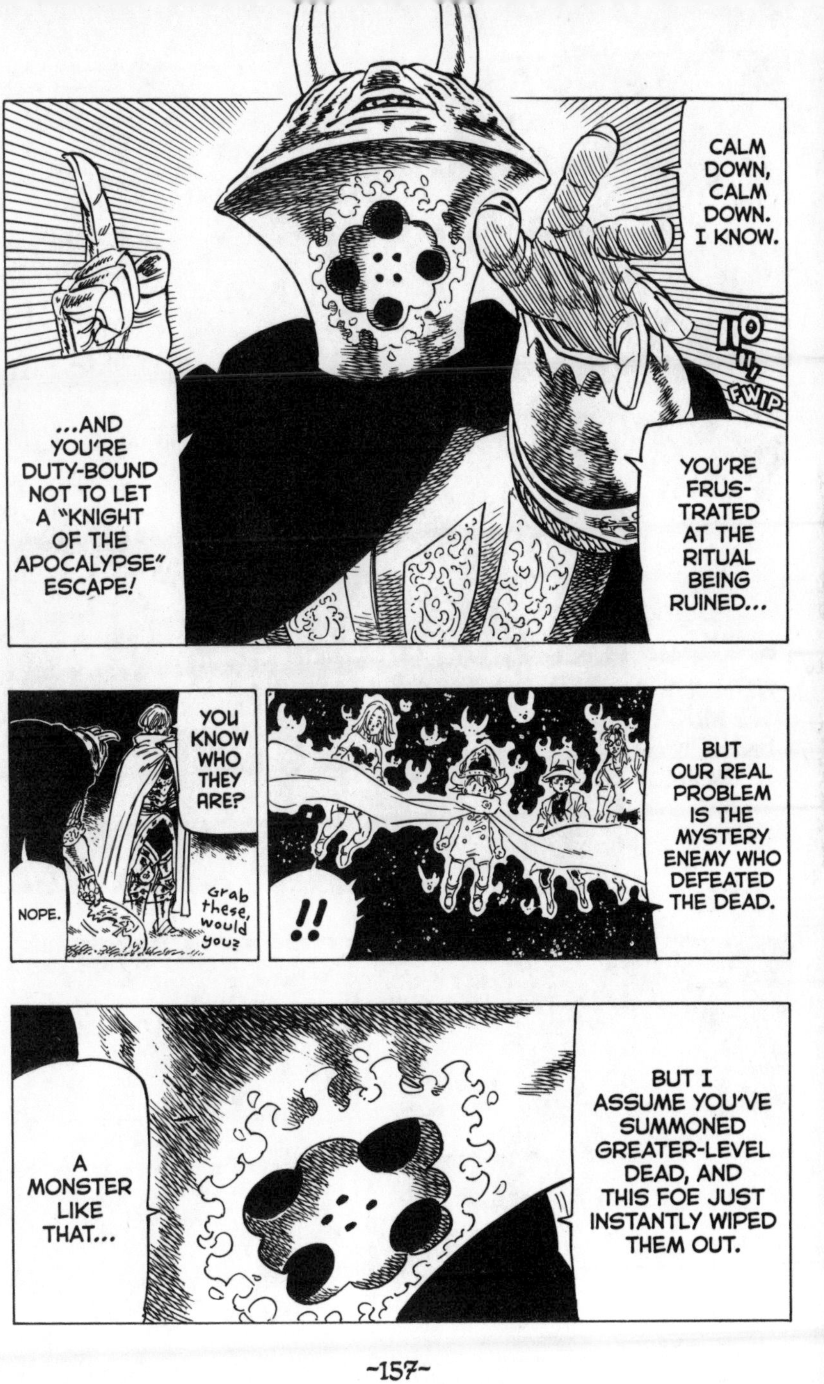
CALM DOWN, CALM DOWN. I KNOW.
FWIP
YOU'RE FRUS-TRATED AT THE RITUAL BEING RUINED...
...AND YOU'RE DUTY-BOUND NOT TO LET A "KNIGHT OF THE APOCALYPSE" ESCAPE!
BUT OUR REAL PROBLEM IS THE MYSTERY ENEMY WHO DEFEATED THE DEAD.
!!
YOU KNOW WHO THEY ARE?
Grab these, would you?
NOPE.
BUT I ASSUME YOU'VE SUMMONED GREATER-LEVEL DEAD, AND THIS FOE JUST INSTANTLY WIPED THEM OUT.
A MONSTER LIKE THAT...

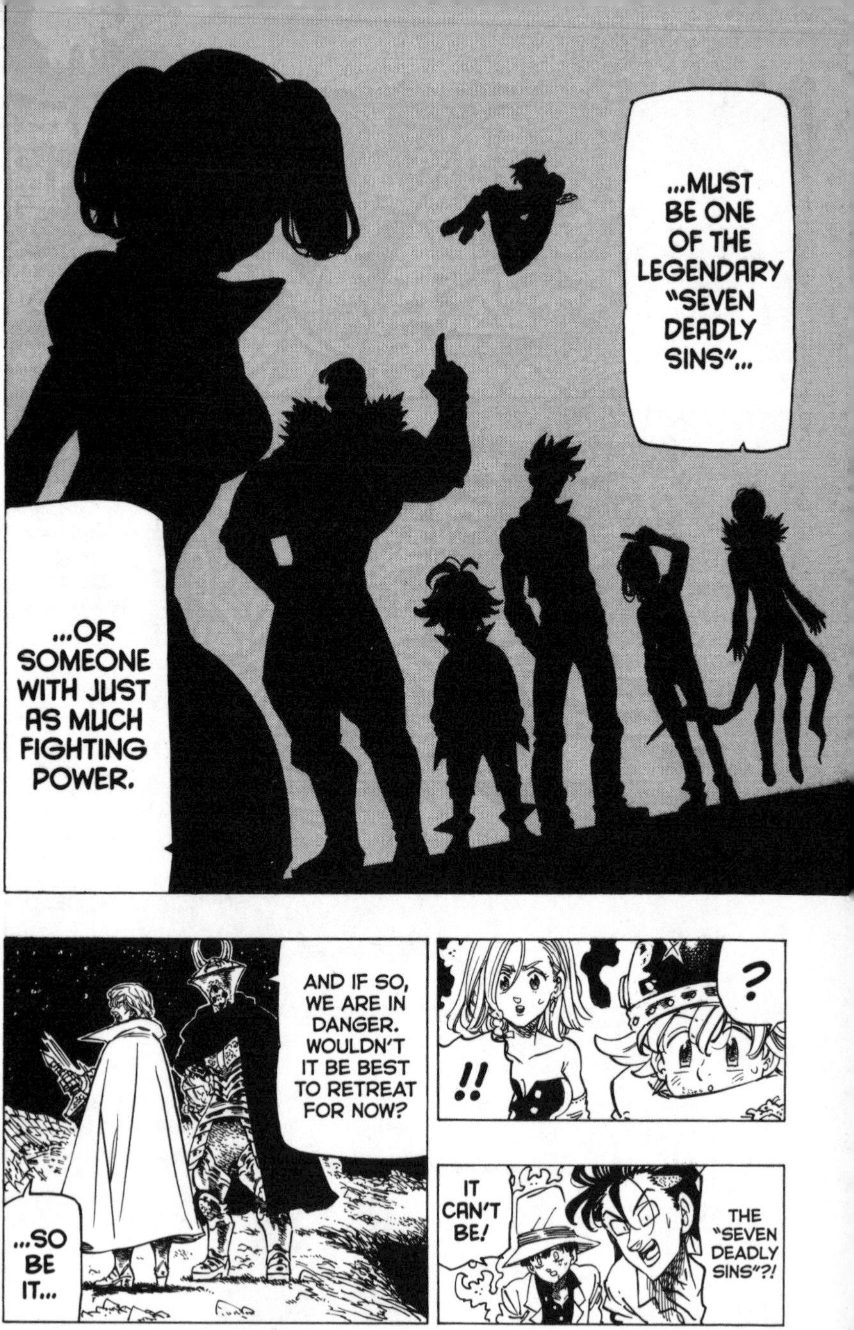
...MUST BE ONE OF THE LEGENDARY "SEVEN DEADLY SINS"...
...OR SOMEONE WITH JUST AS MUCH FIGHTING POWER.
?
!!
THE "SEVEN DEADLY SINS"?!
IT CAN'T BE!
AND IF SO, WE ARE IN DANGER. WOULDN'T IT BE BEST TO RETREAT FOR NOW?
...SO BE IT...

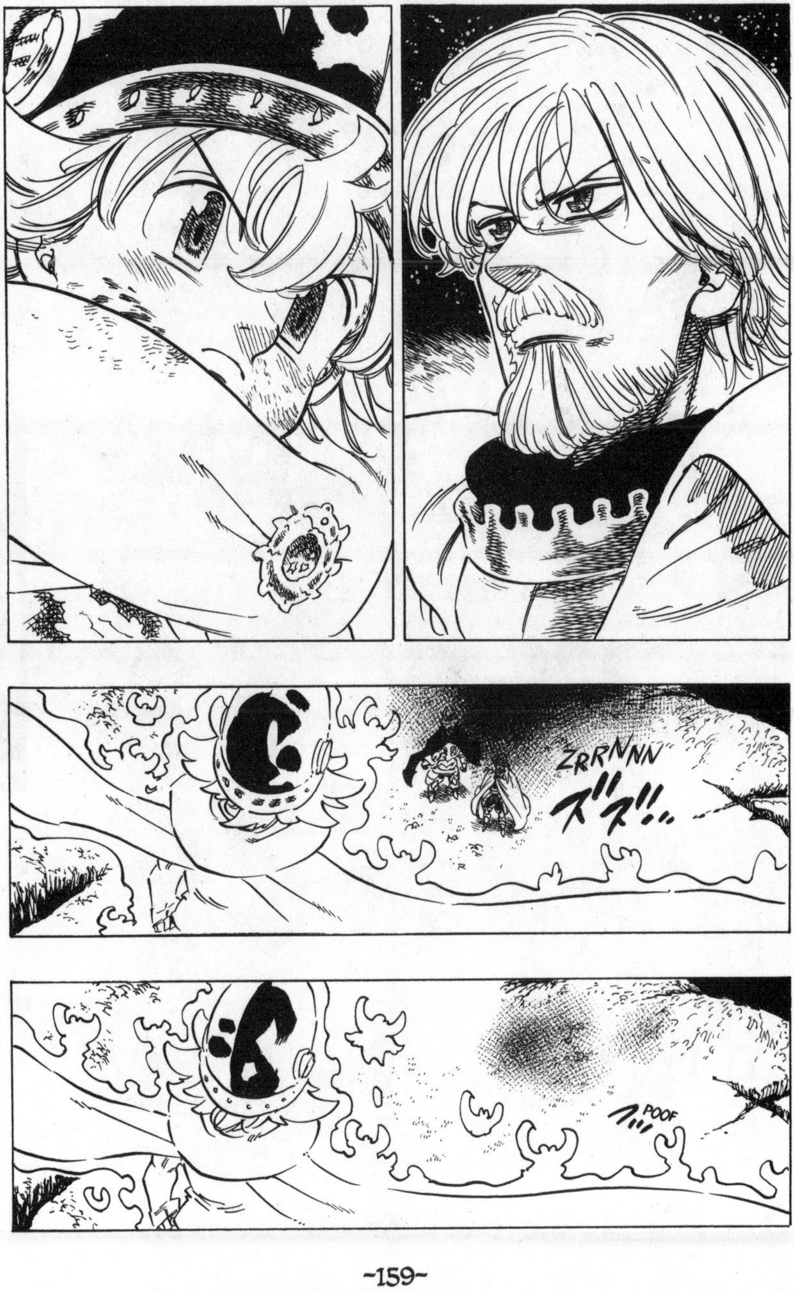
ZRRNNN
ズズ!!..
POOF
フ...

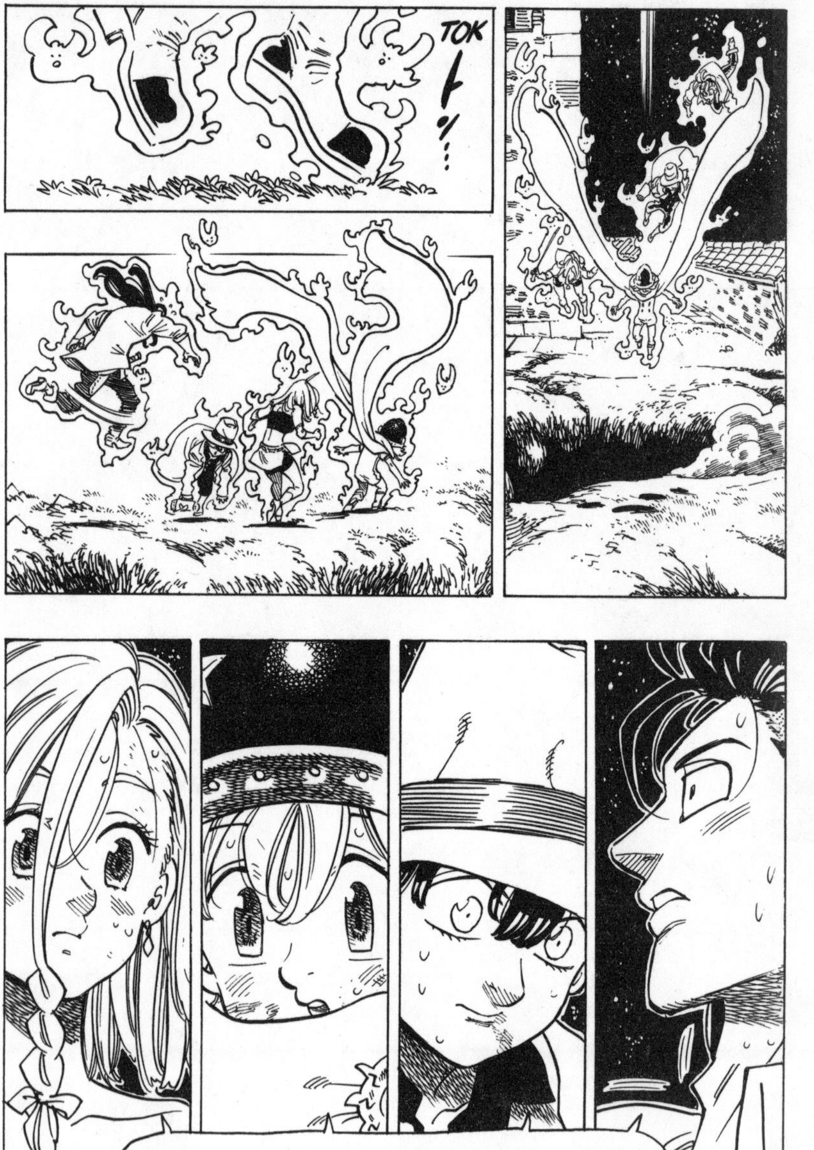

TOK
TOK...
... ...

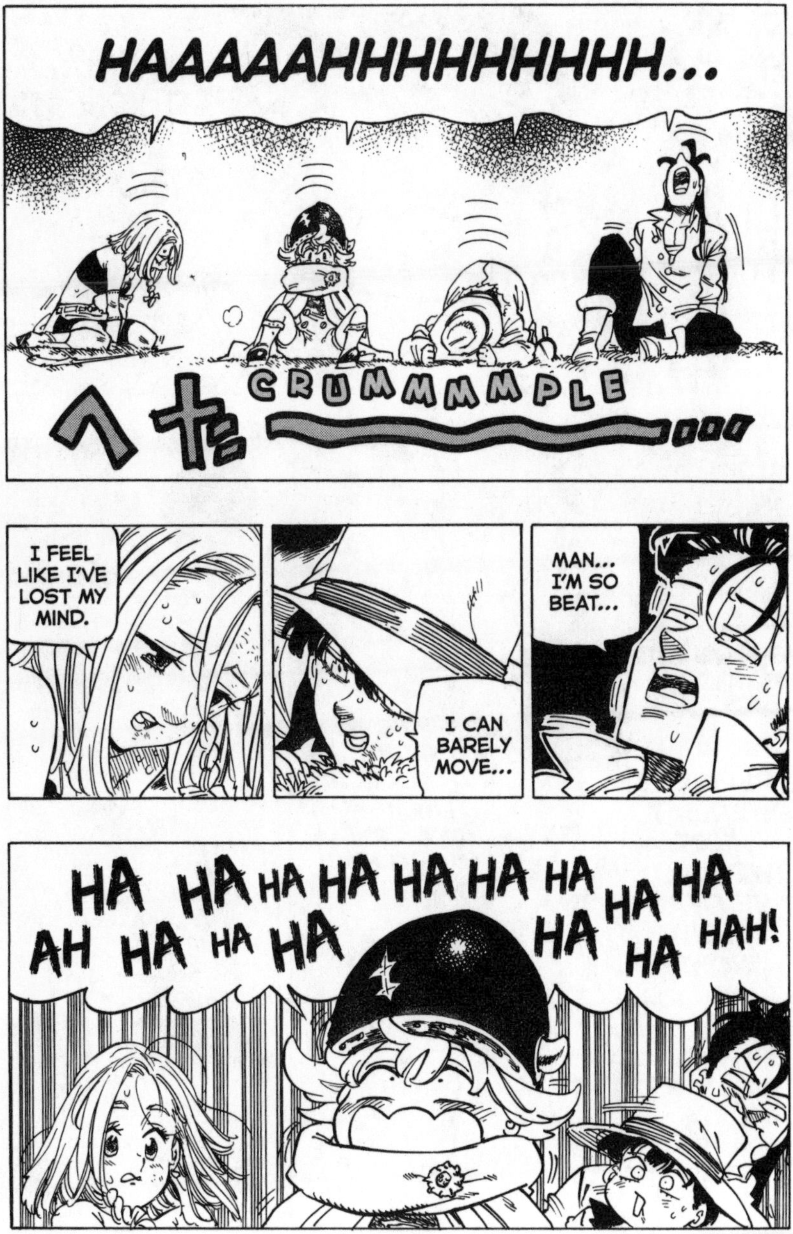
HAAAAAHHHHHHHHH...
CRUMMMMPLE
MAN... I'M SO BEAT...
I CAN BARELY MOVE...
I FEEL LIKE I'VE LOST MY MIND.
HA HA HA HA HA HA HA HA HA HA AH HA HA HA HA HA HA HAH!

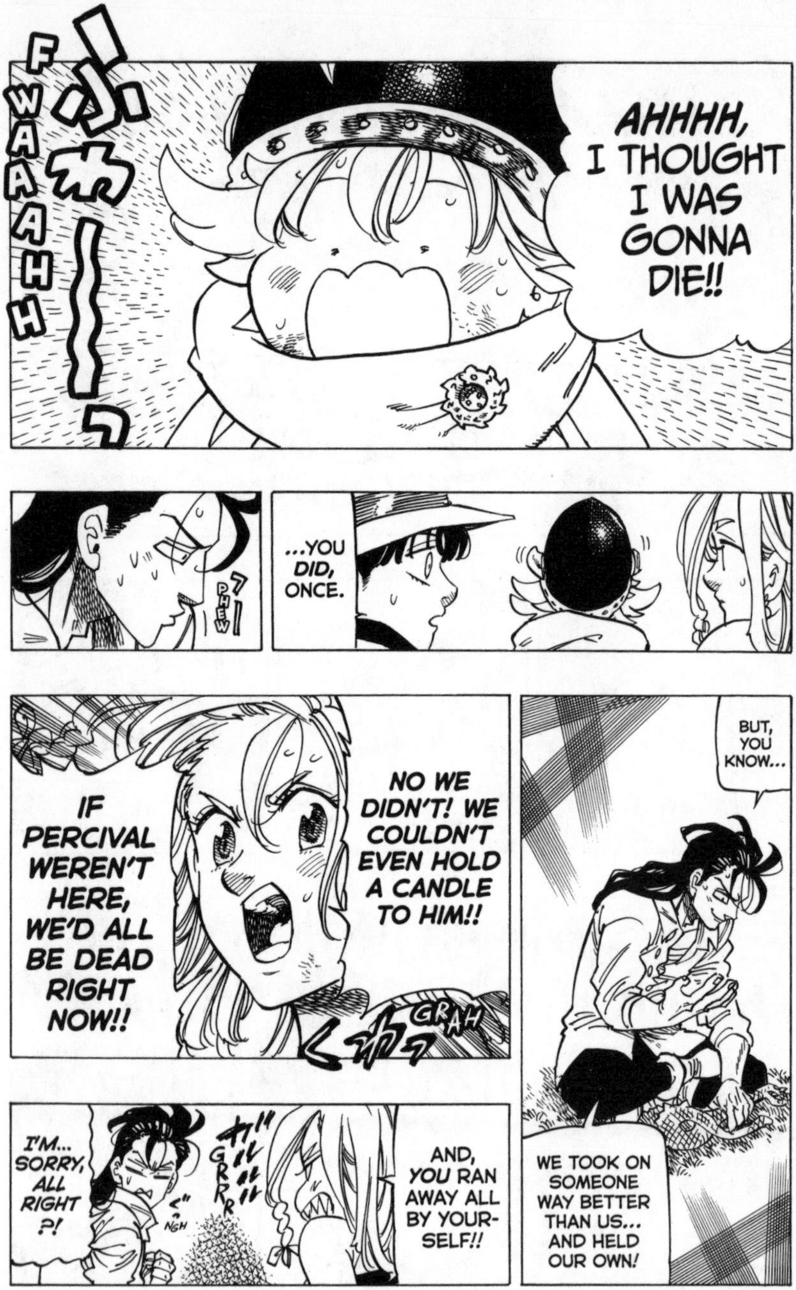
AHHHH, I THOUGHT I WAS GONNA DIE!!
FWAAAAHH
...YOU DID, ONCE.
PHEW
BUT, YOU KNOW...
WE TOOK ON SOMEONE WAY BETTER THAN US... AND HELD OUR OWN!
NO WE DIDN'T! WE COULDN'T EVEN HOLD A CANDLE TO HIM!!
IF PERCIVAL WEREN'T HERE, WE'D ALL BE DEAD RIGHT NOW!!
GRAH
AND, YOU RAN AWAY ALL BY YOURSELF!!
GRRR
I'M... SORRY, ALL RIGHT?!
NGH

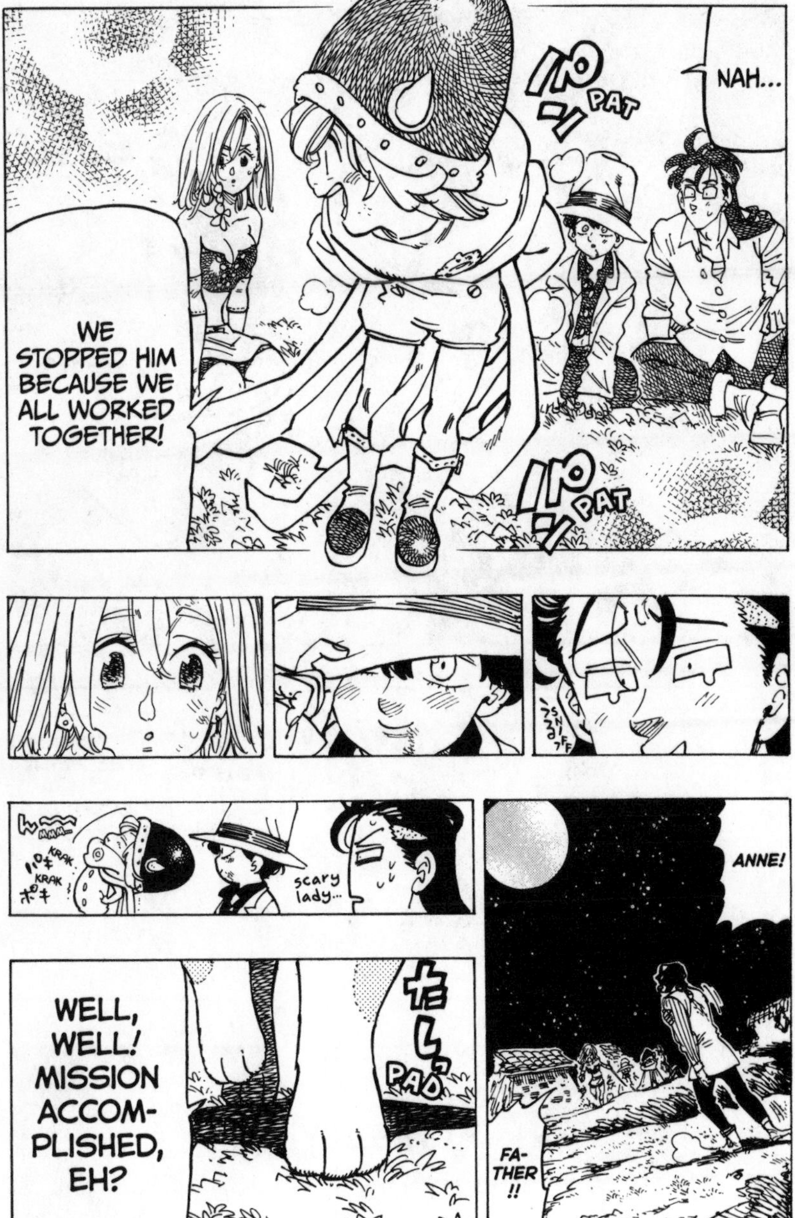
NAH...
PAT
PAT
WE STOPPED HIM BECAUSE WE ALL WORKED TOGETHER!
SNIFF
ANNE!
FA-THER!!
MMM...
KRAK
KRAK
scary lady...
WELL, WELL! MISSION ACCOMPLISHED, EH?
PAD

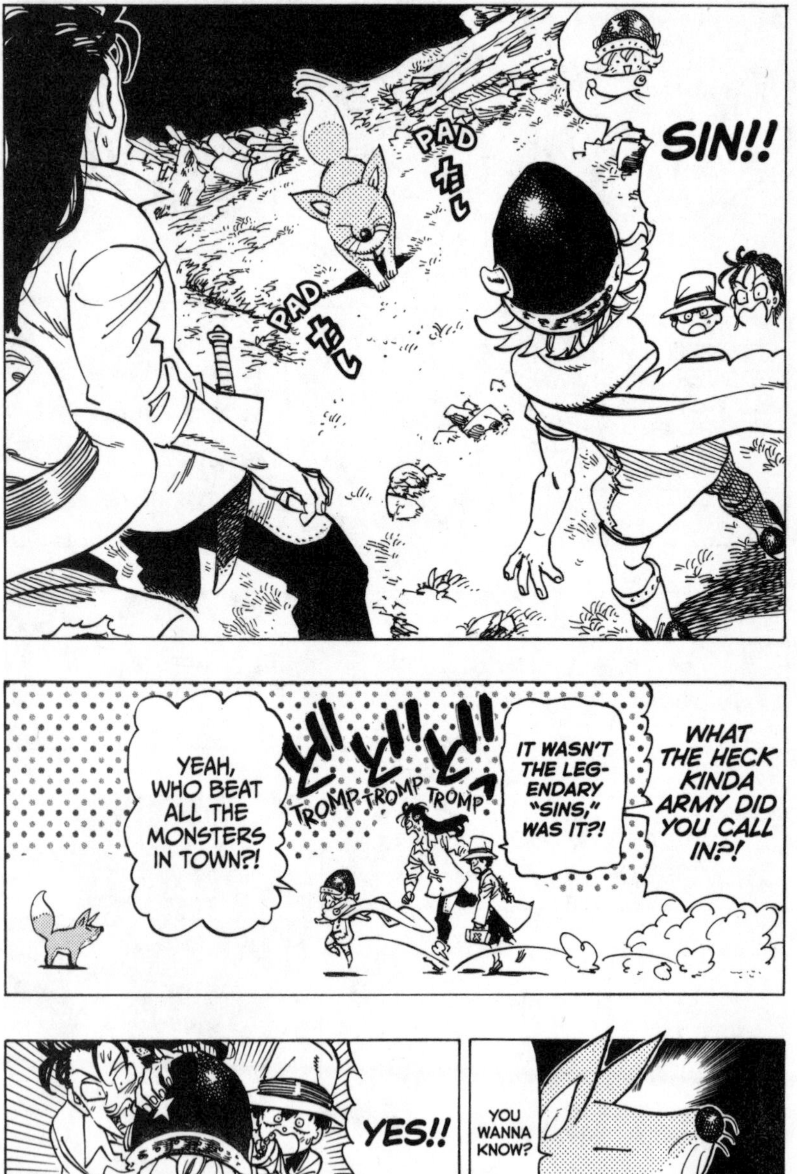
SIN!!
PAD
PAD
WHAT THE HECK KINDA ARMY DID YOU CALL IN?!
IT WASN'T THE LEG-ENDARY "SINS," WAS IT?!
TROMP TROMP TROMP
YEAH, WHO BEAT ALL THE MONSTERS IN TOWN?!
YOU WANNA KNOW?
YES!!

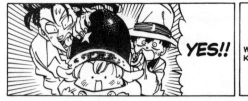

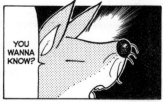

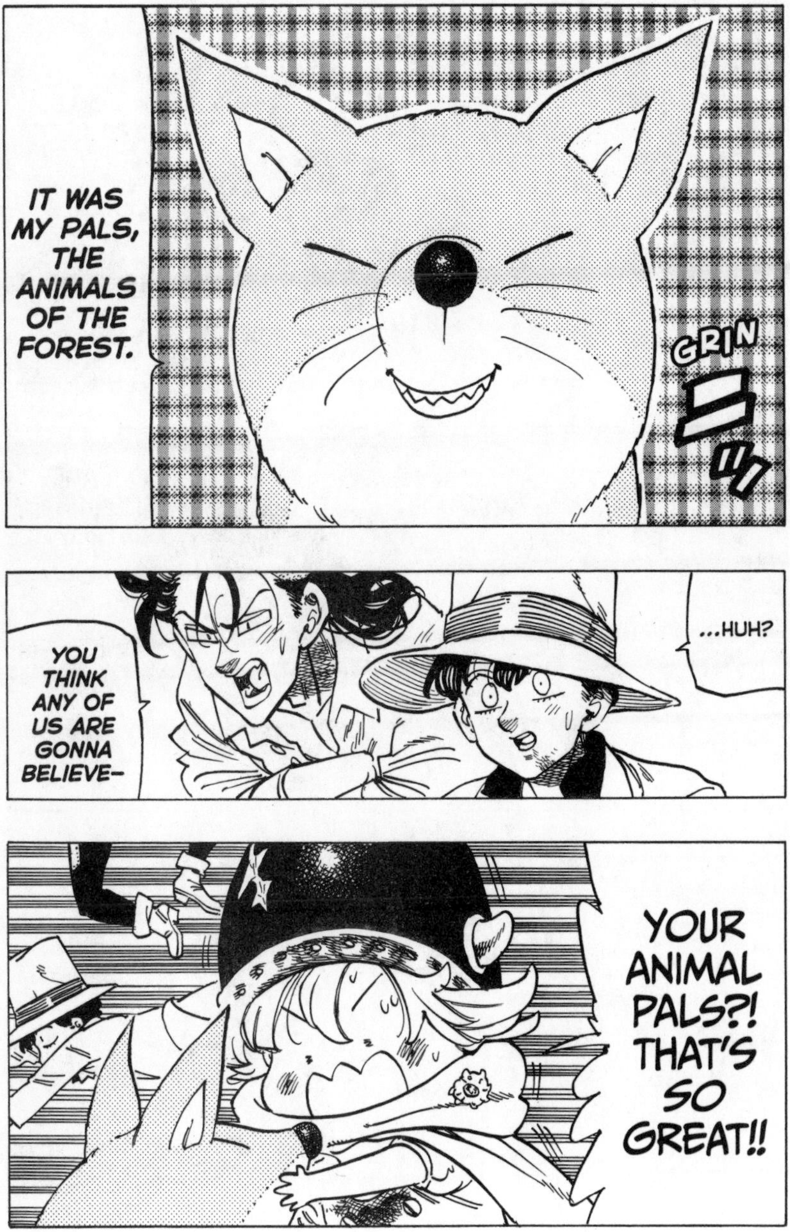
GRIN
IT WAS MY PALS, THE ANIMALS OF THE FOREST.
...HUH?
YOU THINK ANY OF US ARE GONNA BELIEVE-
YOUR ANIMAL PALS?! THAT'S SO GREAT!!

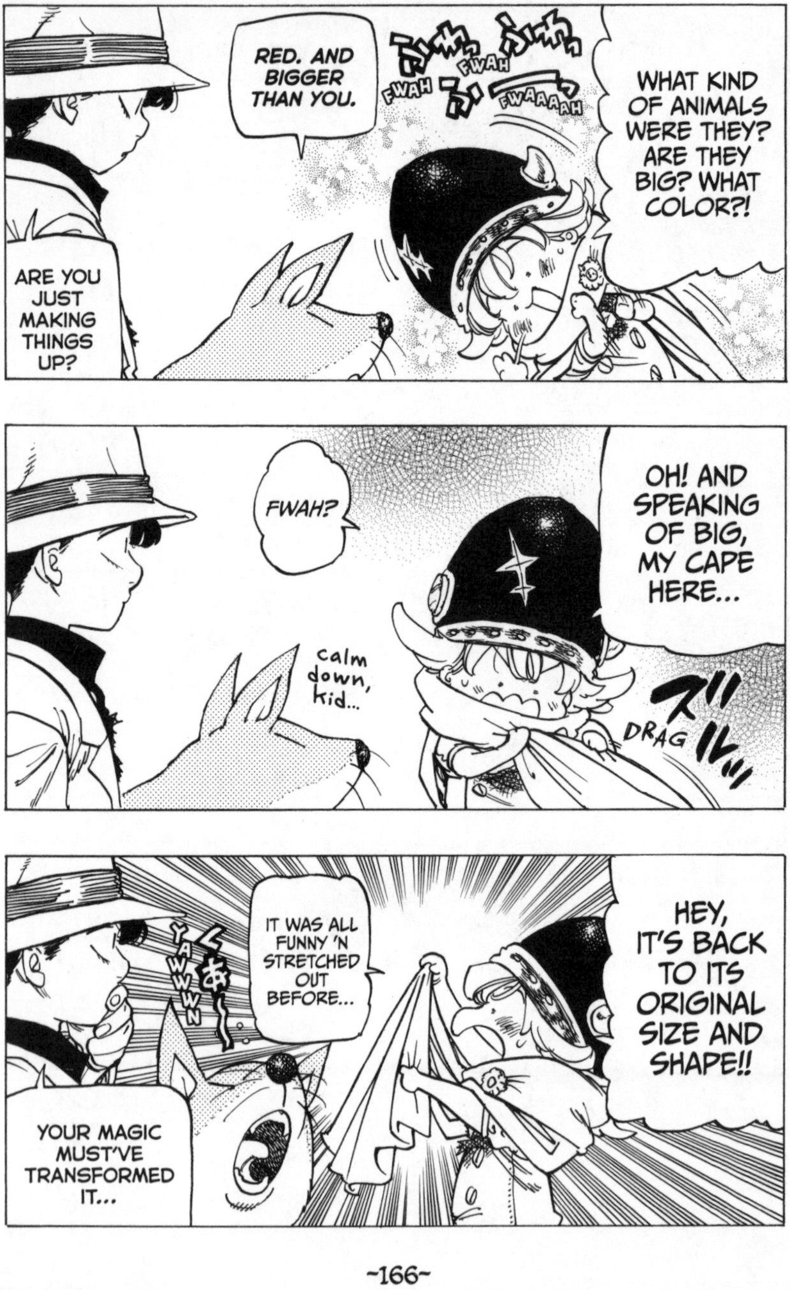
WHAT KIND OF ANIMALS WERE THEY? ARE THEY BIG? WHAT COLOR?!
FWAH
FWAH
FWAAAAAH
RED. AND BIGGER THAN YOU.
ARE YOU JUST MAKING THINGS UP?
OH! AND SPEAKING OF BIG, MY CAPE HERE...
DRAG
calm down, kid...
FWAH?
HEY, IT'S BACK TO ITS ORIGINAL SIZE AND SHAPE!!
IT WAS ALL FUNNY 'N STRETCHED OUT BEFORE...
YAWWWN
YOUR MAGIC MUST'VE TRANSFORMED IT...

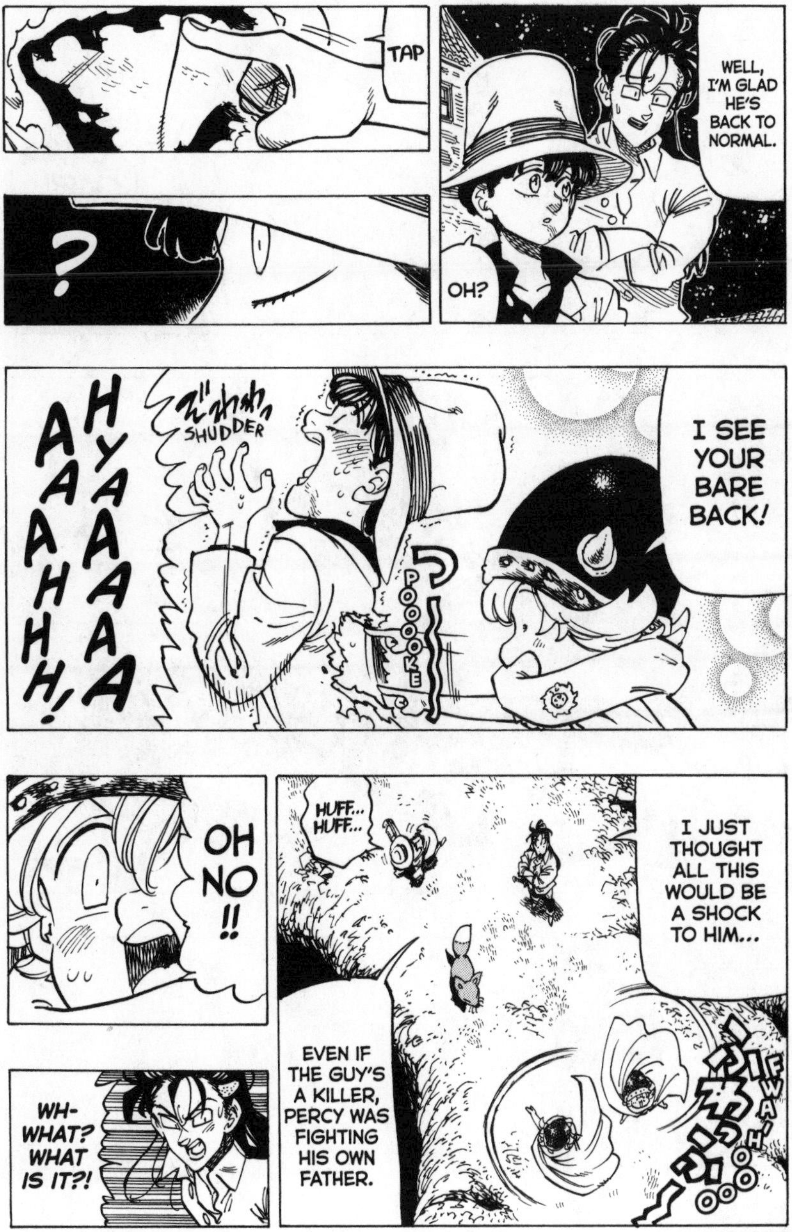
WELL, I'M GLAD HE'S BACK TO NORMAL.
OH?
TAP
?
I SEE YOUR BARE BACK!
POOOOKE
SHUDDER
HYAAAAAA AAAAHHH!
I JUST THOUGHT ALL THIS WOULD BE A SHOCK TO HIM...
HUFF... HUFF...
EVEN IF THE GUY'S A KILLER, PERCY WAS FIGHTING HIS OWN FATHER.
FWAH OOOO
OH NO!!
WH-WHAT? WHAT IS IT?!

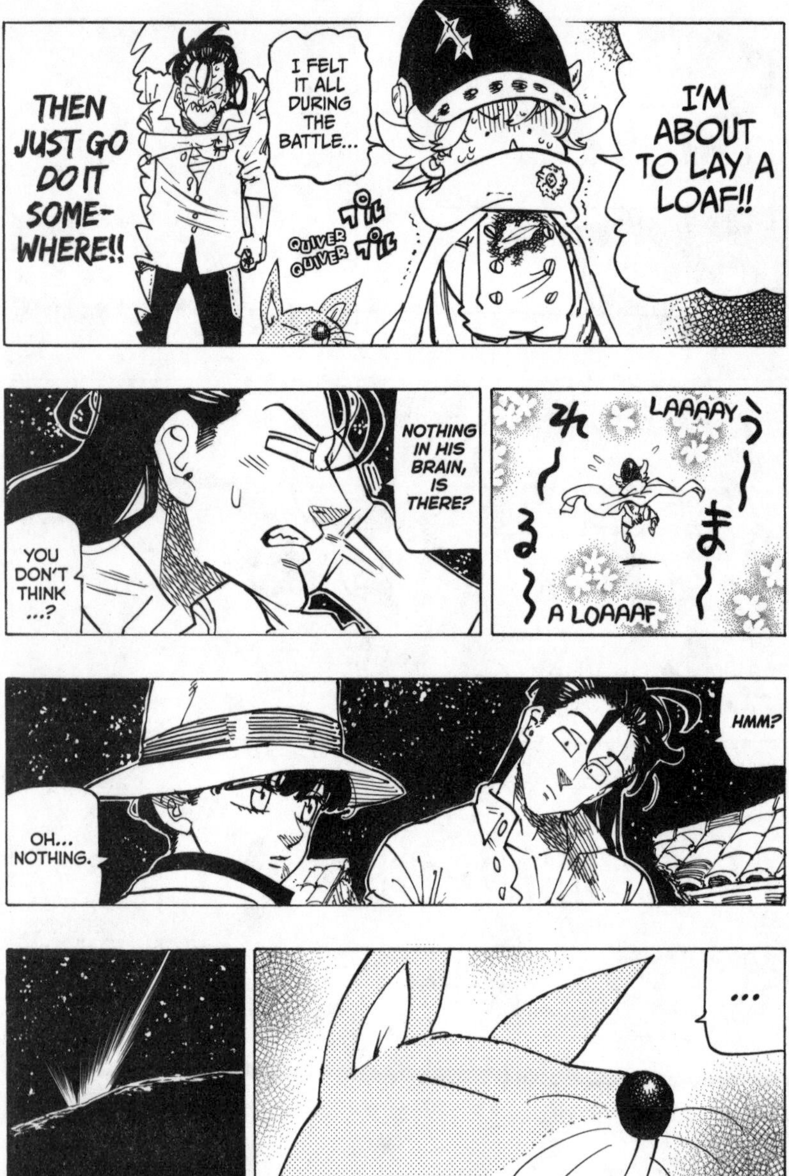
I'M ABOUT TO LAY A LOAF!!
I FELT IT ALL DURING THE BATTLE...
QUIVER QUIVER
THEN JUST GO DO IT SOME-WHERE!!
う〜ま〜
れ〜る〜
LAAAAY
A LOAAAF
NOTHING IN HIS BRAIN, IS THERE?
YOU DON'T THINK ...?
HMM?
OH... NOTHING.
...

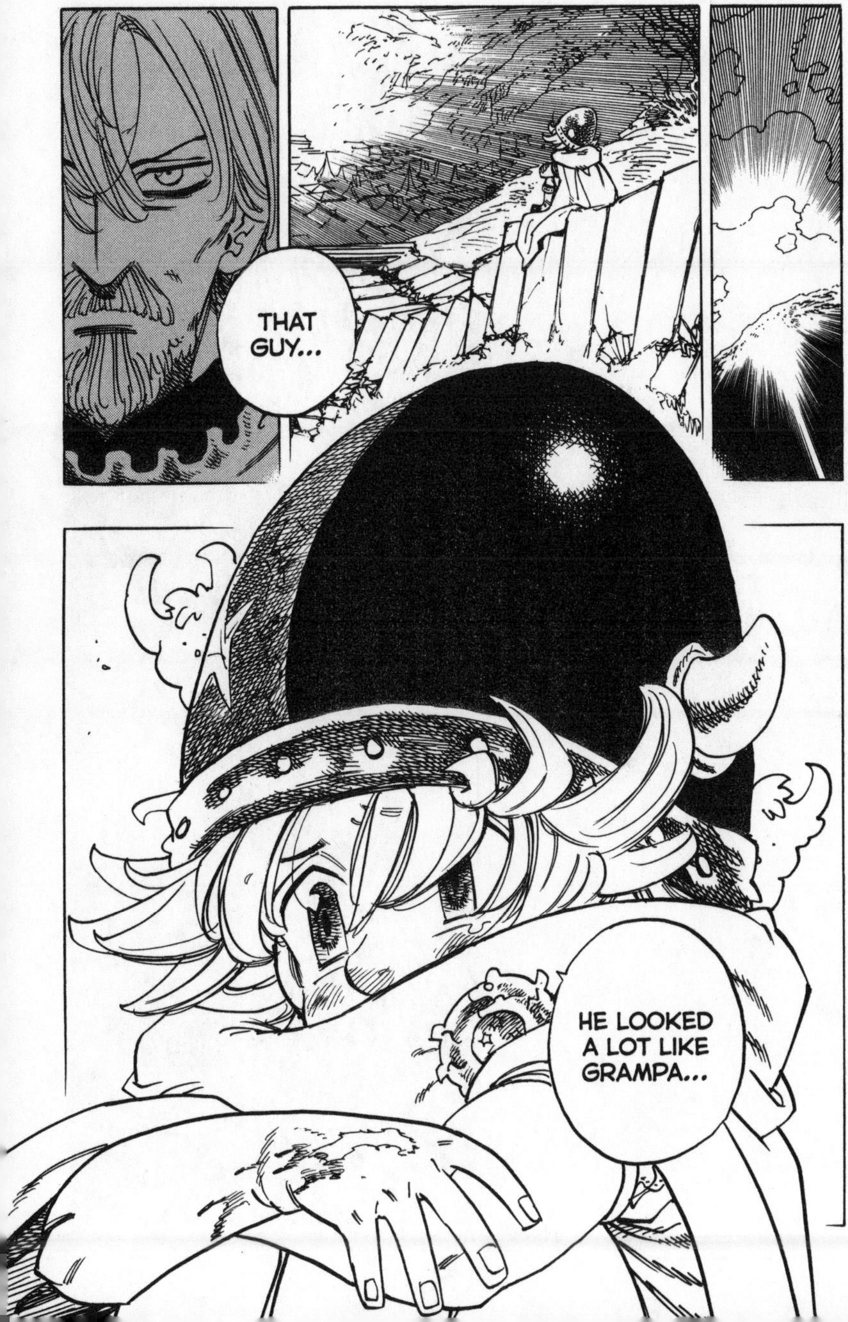
THAT GUY...
HE LOOKED A LOT LIKE GRAMPA...

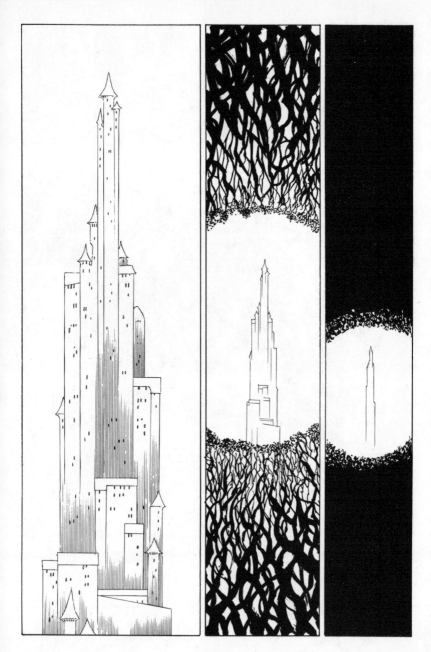

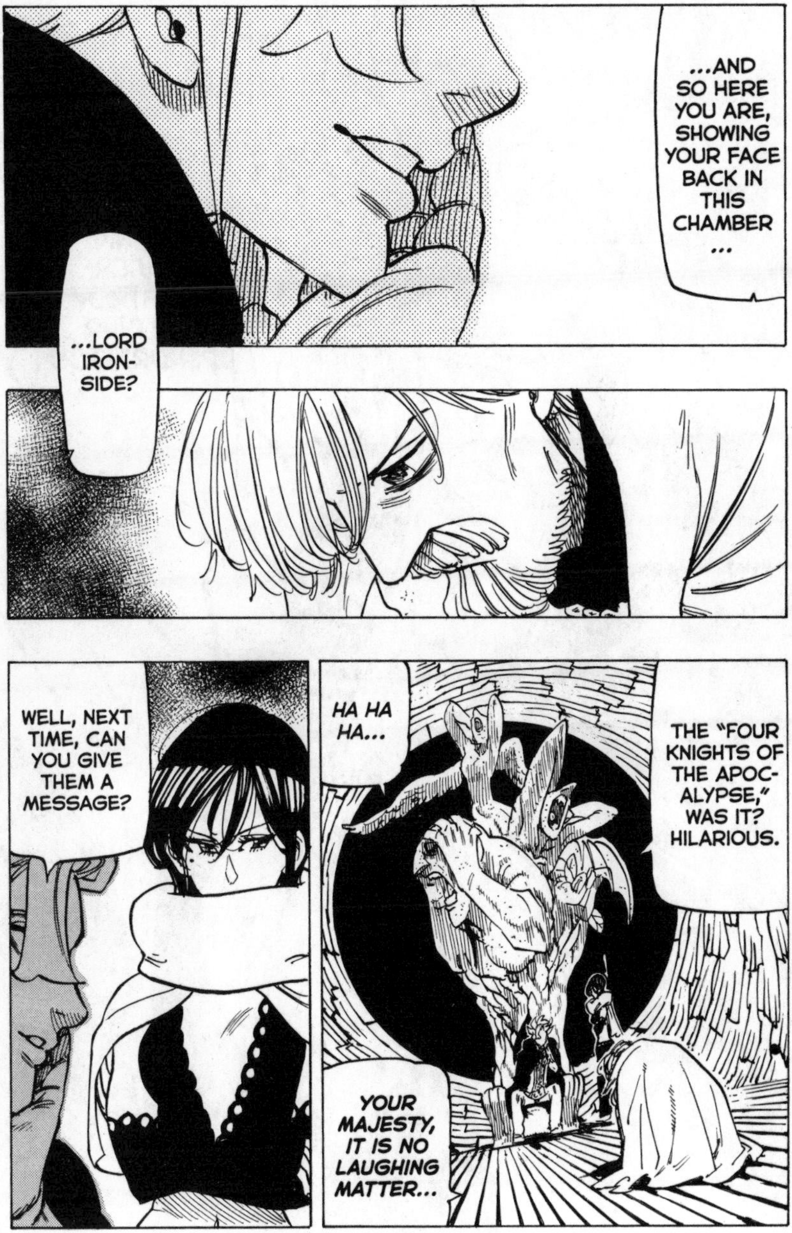
...AND SO HERE YOU ARE, SHOWING YOUR FACE BACK IN THIS CHAMBER...
...LORD IRON-SIDE?
THE "FOUR KNIGHTS OF THE APOC-ALYPSE," WAS IT? HILARIOUS.
HA HA HA...
YOUR MAJESTY, IT IS NO LAUGHING MATTER...
WELL, NEXT TIME, CAN YOU GIVE THEM A MESSAGE?

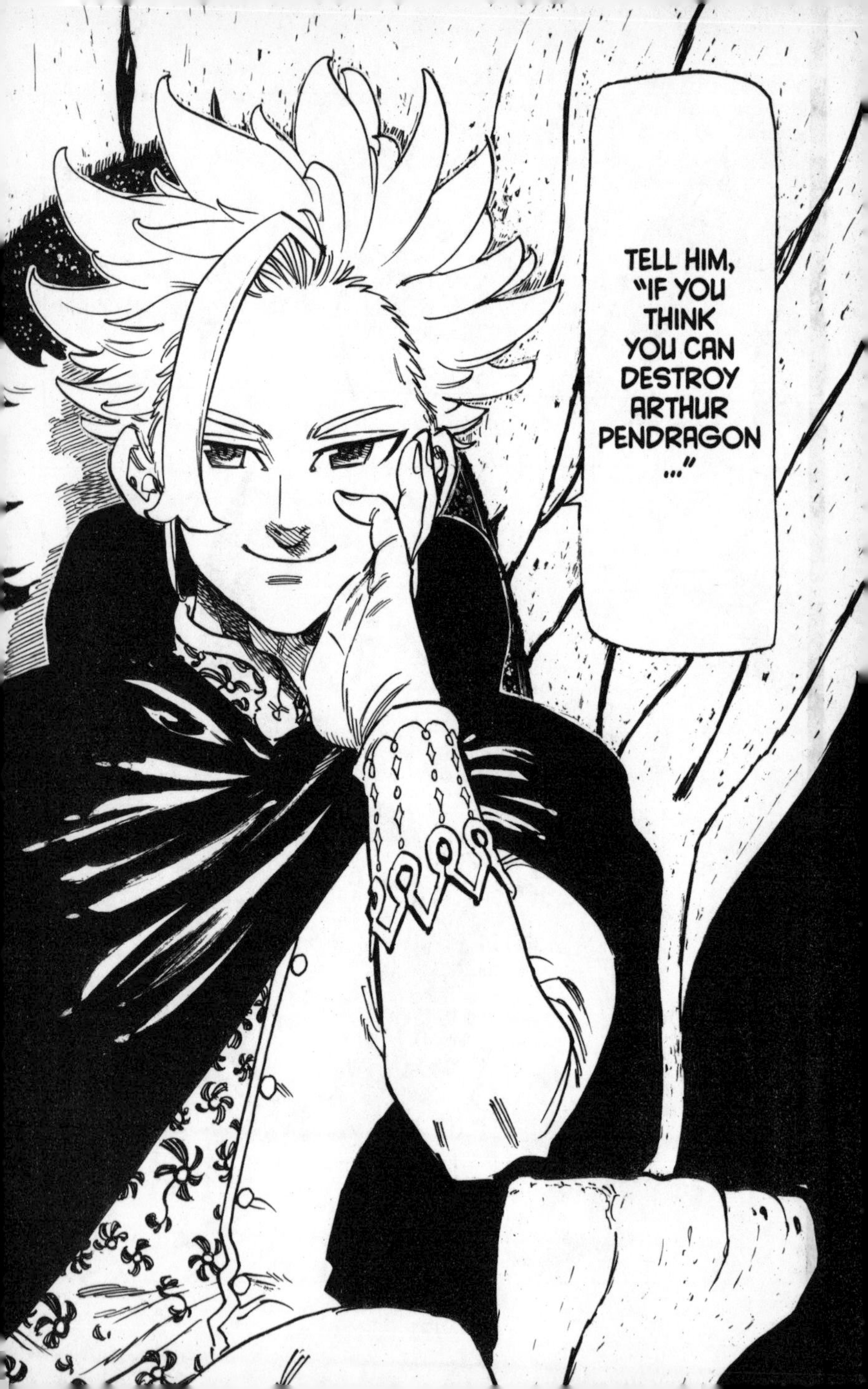
TELL HIM, "IF YOU THINK YOU CAN DESTROY ARTHUR PENDRAGON ..."

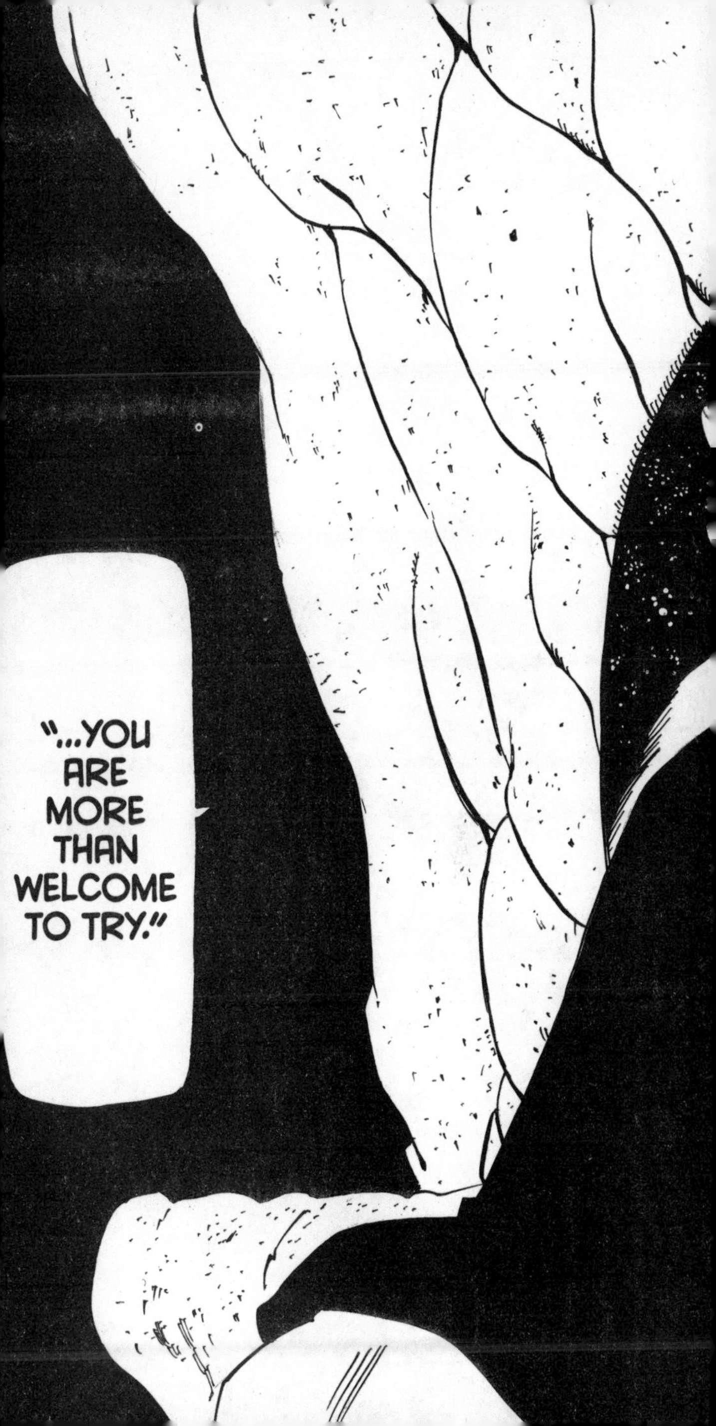
"...YOU ARE MORE THAN WELCOME TO TRY."

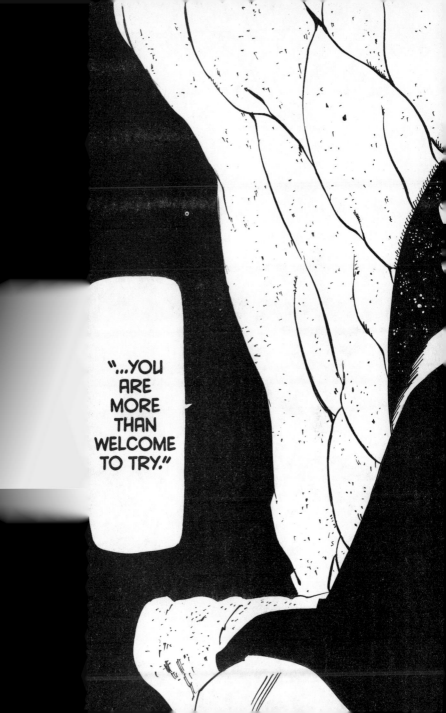

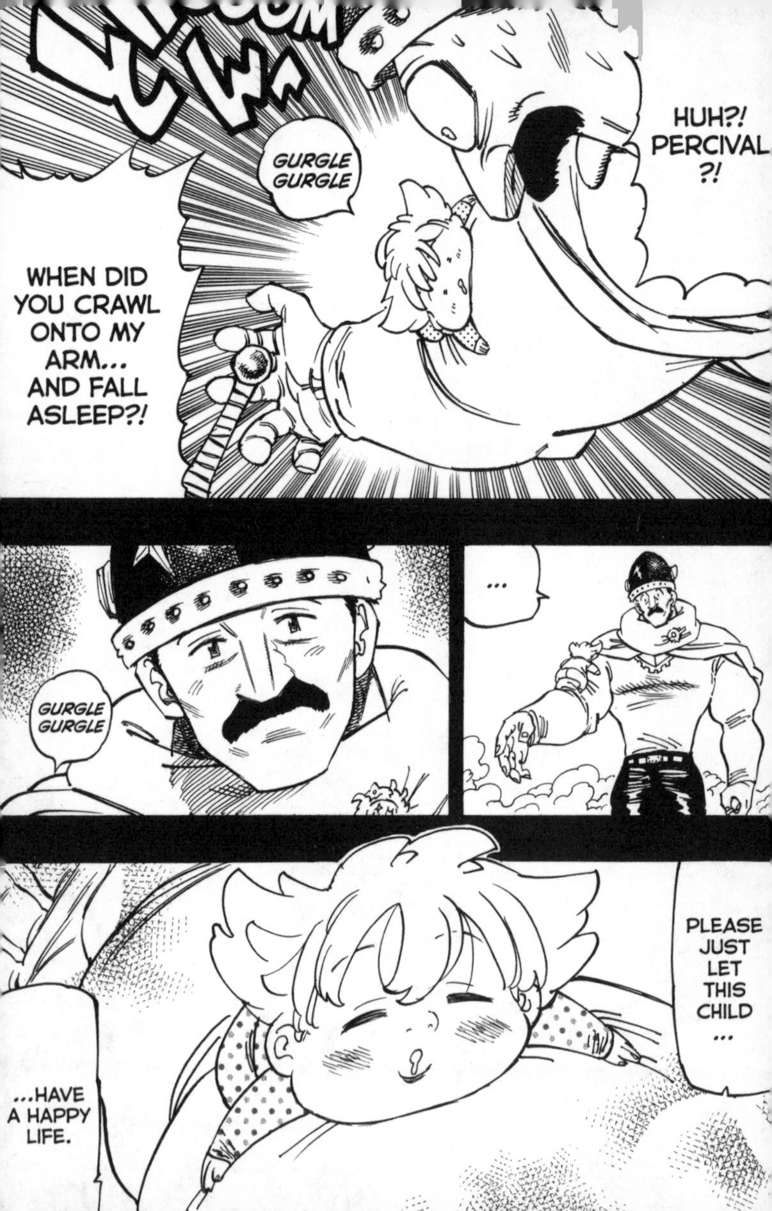
HUH?! PERCIVAL?!
GURGLE GURGLE
WHEN DID YOU CRAWL ONTO MY ARM... AND FALL ASLEEP?!
...
GURGLE GURGLE
PLEASE JUST LET THIS CHILD ...
...HAVE A HAPPY LIFE.

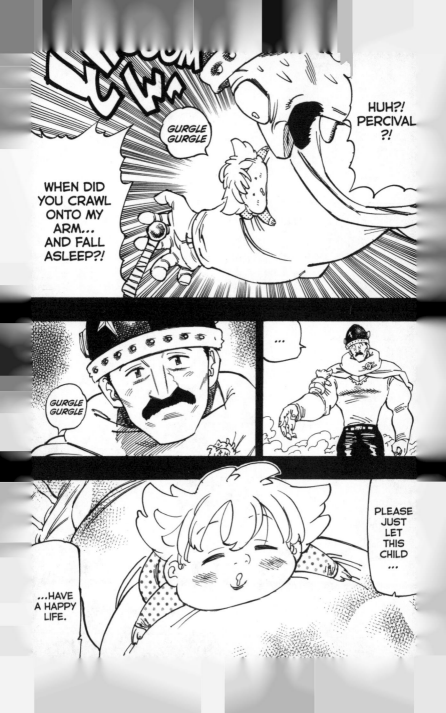

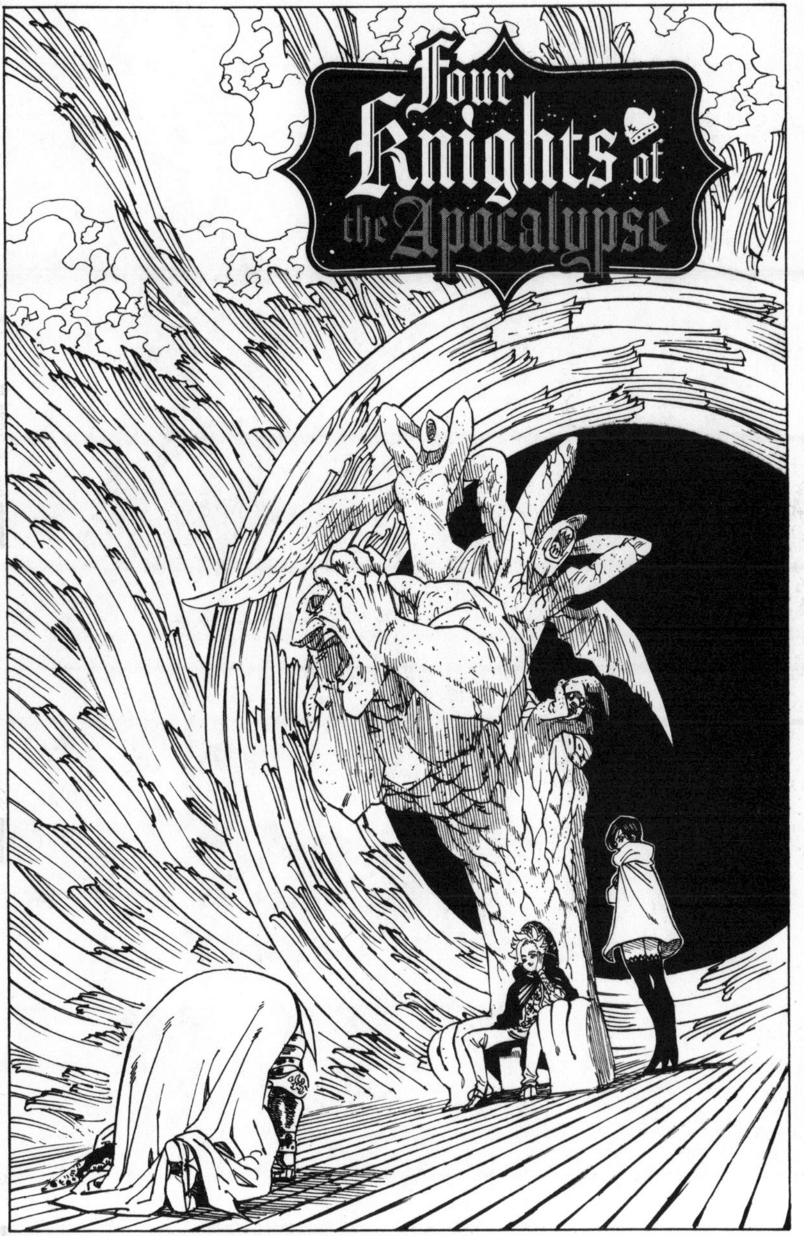
Four Knights of the Apocalypse

CHAPTER 23: ARTHUR PENDRAGON

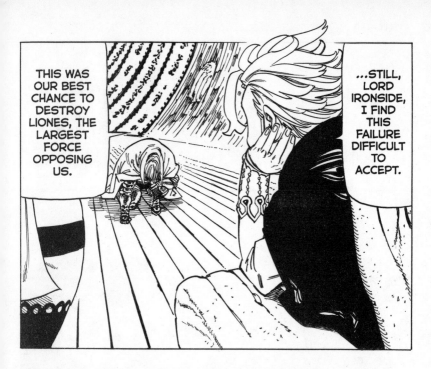

...STILL, LORD IRONSIDE, I FIND THIS FAILURE DIFFICULT TO ACCEPT.
THIS WAS OUR BEST CHANCE TO DESTROY LIONES, THE LARGEST FORCE OPPOSING US.
BUT YOU WERE BESTED BY A CHILD...EVEN IF HE WAS ONE OF THE "FOUR KNIGHTS OF THE APOCALYPSE."
OR SHOULD I SAY "ONE OF THE FOUR KNIGHTS, EVEN IF JUST A CHILD"?
I MAKE NO EXCUSES, YOUR MAJESTY.
YOU MAY PUNISH ME AS YOU PLEASE.

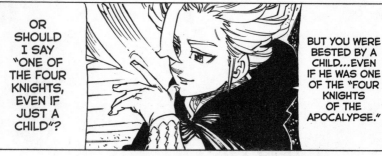

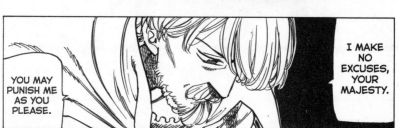

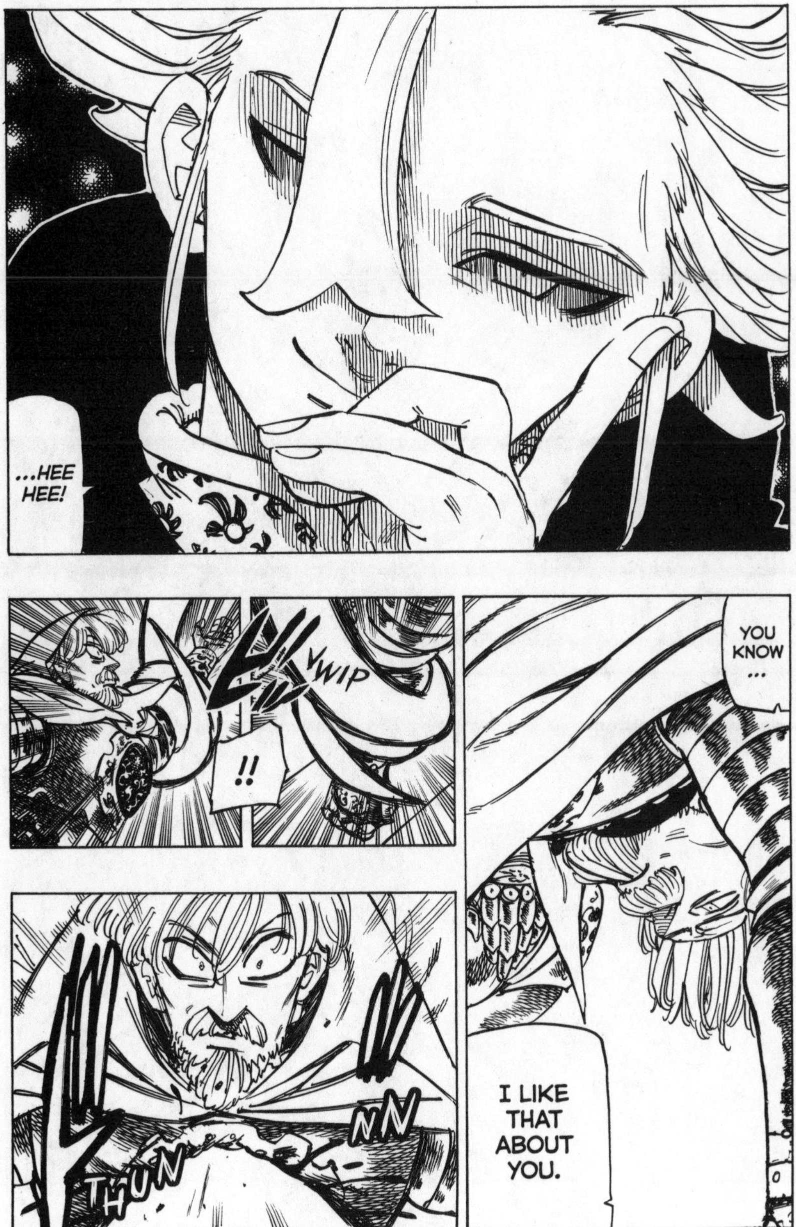
...HEE HEE!
YOU KNOW...
I LIKE THAT ABOUT YOU.
VWIP
!!
THUNNN

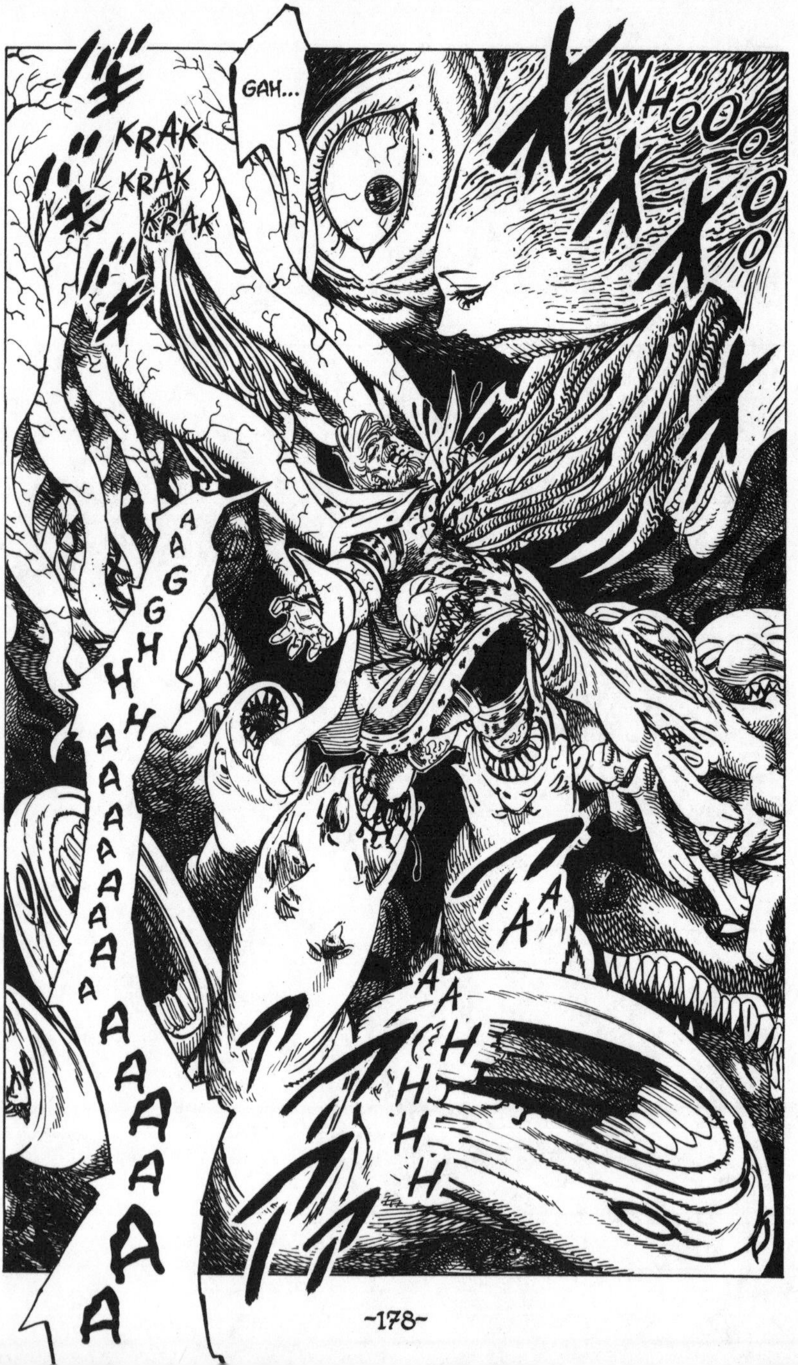
GAH...
WHOOOOOOO
KRAK KRAK KRAK
AAGGHHHAAAAAAAAAAAAAAAAA
AAA
AAHHHHHH

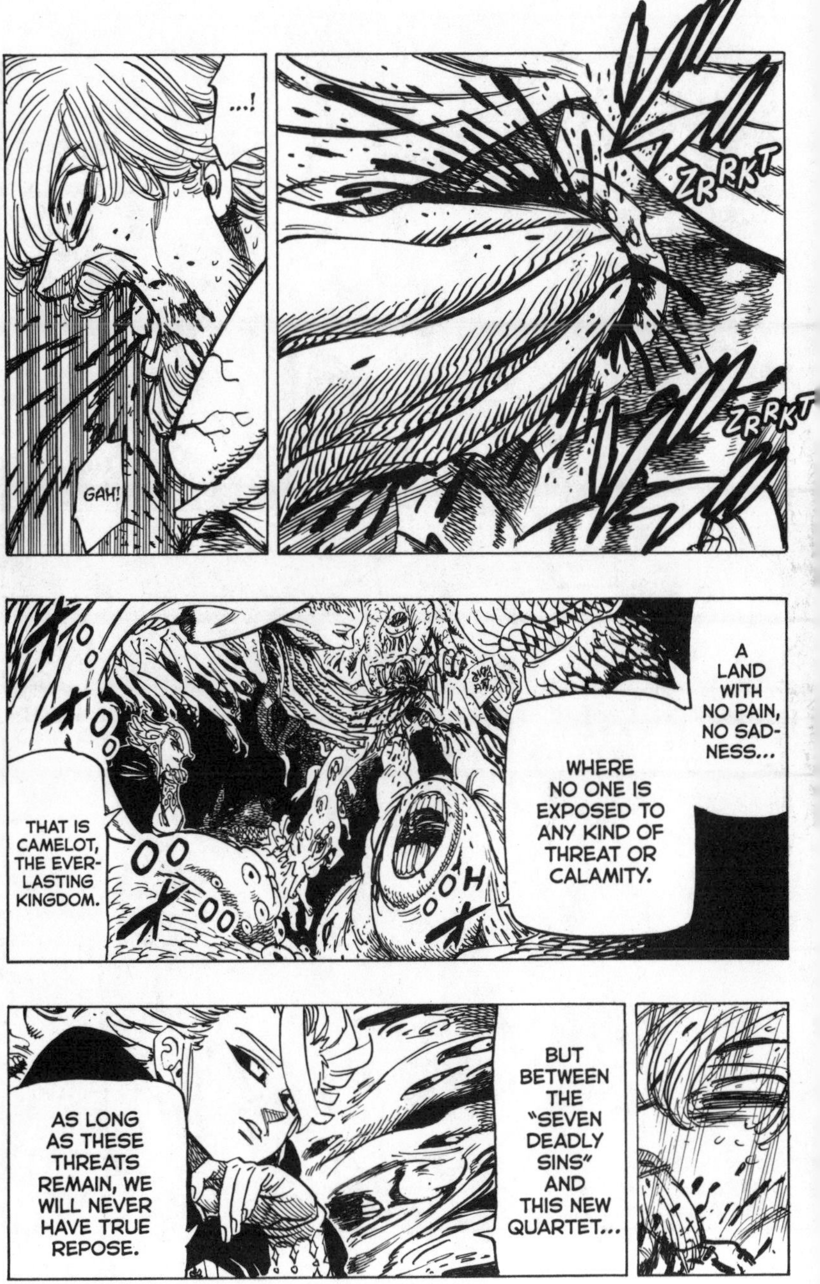
ZRRKT
ZRRKT
...!
GAH!
A LAND WITH NO PAIN, NO SADNESS...
WHERE NO ONE IS EXPOSED TO ANY KIND OF THREAT OR CALAMITY.
THAT IS CAMELOT, THE EVER-LASTING KINGDOM.
BUT BETWEEN THE "SEVEN DEADLY SINS" AND THIS NEW QUARTET...
AS LONG AS THESE THREATS REMAIN, WE WILL NEVER HAVE TRUE REPOSE.

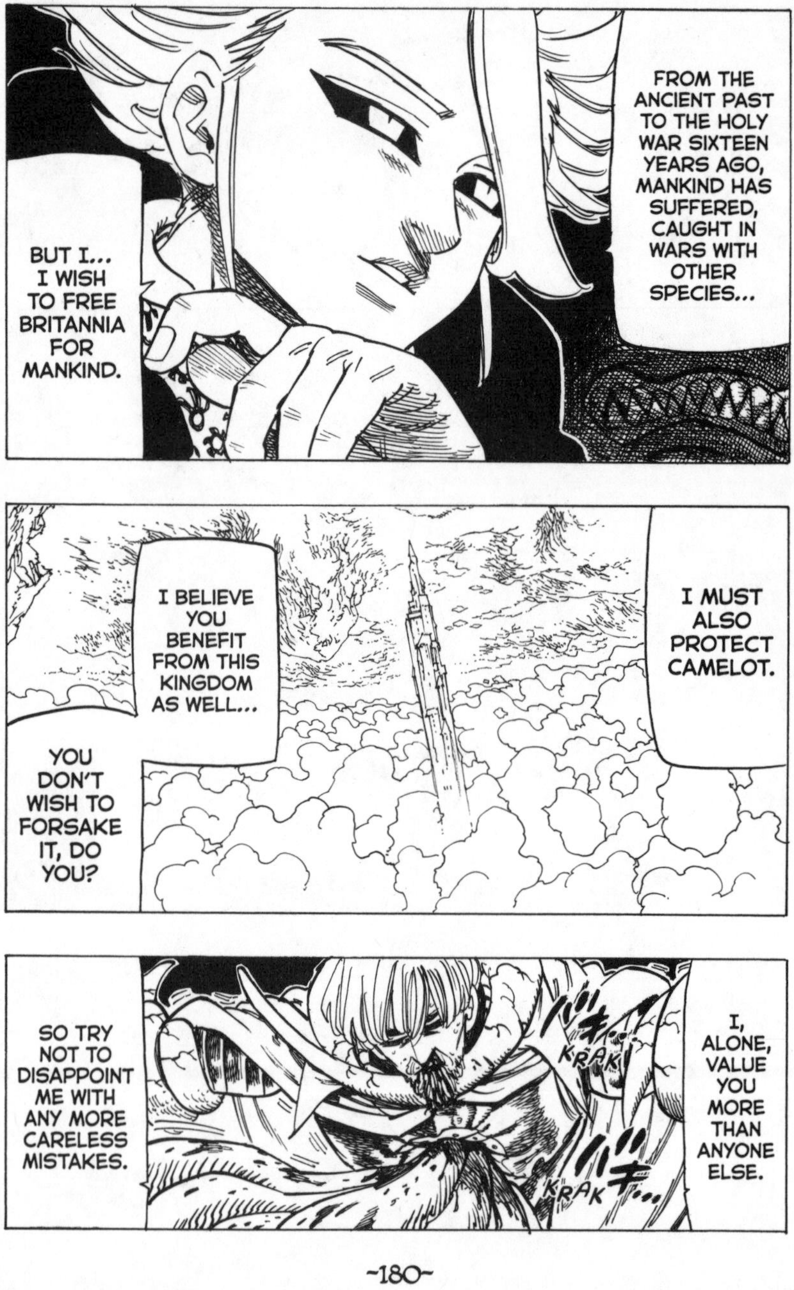
FROM THE ANCIENT PAST TO THE HOLY WAR SIXTEEN YEARS AGO, MANKIND HAS SUFFERED, CAUGHT IN WARS WITH OTHER SPECIES...
BUT I... I WISH TO FREE BRITANNIA FOR MANKIND.
I MUST ALSO PROTECT CAMELOT.
I BELIEVE YOU BENEFIT FROM THIS KINGDOM AS WELL...
YOU DON'T WISH TO FORSAKE IT, DO YOU?
I, ALONE, VALUE YOU MORE THAN ANYONE ELSE.
KRAK
KRAK
SO TRY NOT TO DISAPPOINT ME WITH ANY MORE CARELESS MISTAKES.

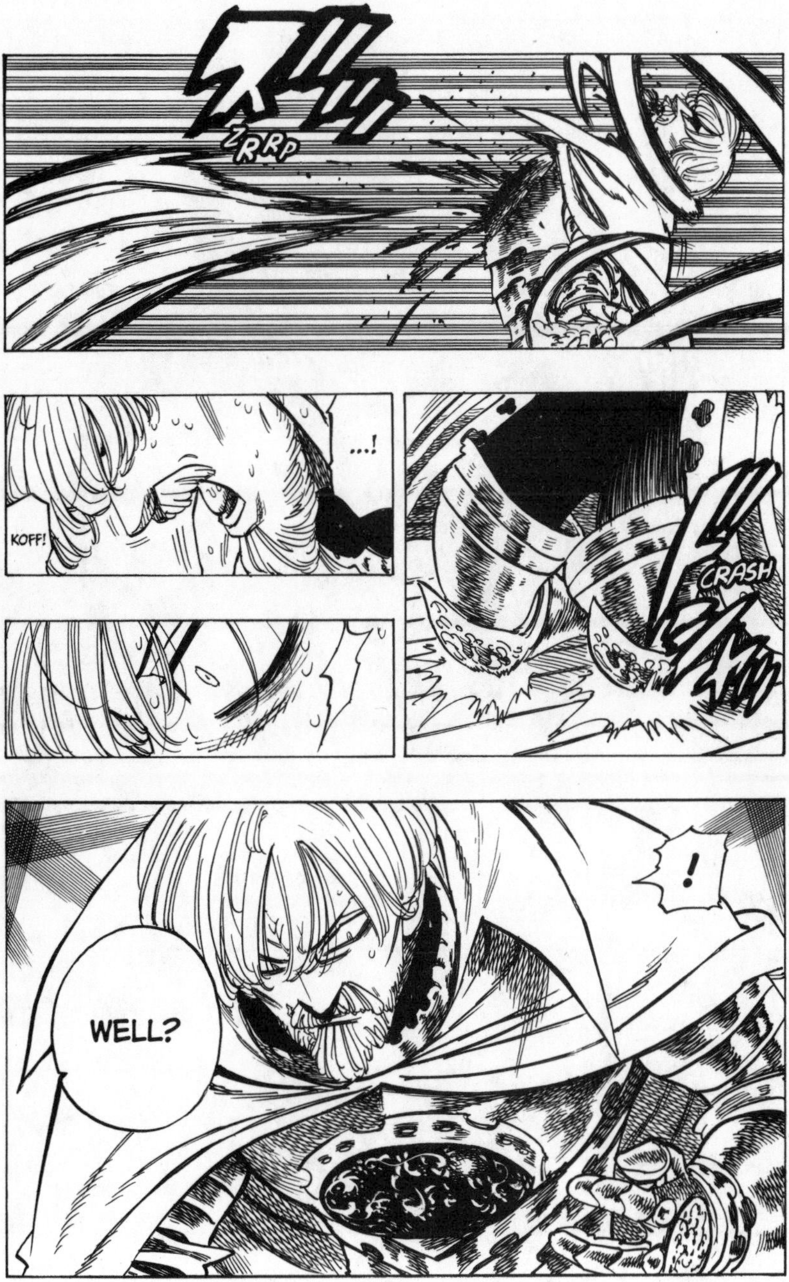
ZRRP
CRASH
...!
KOFF!
!
WELL?

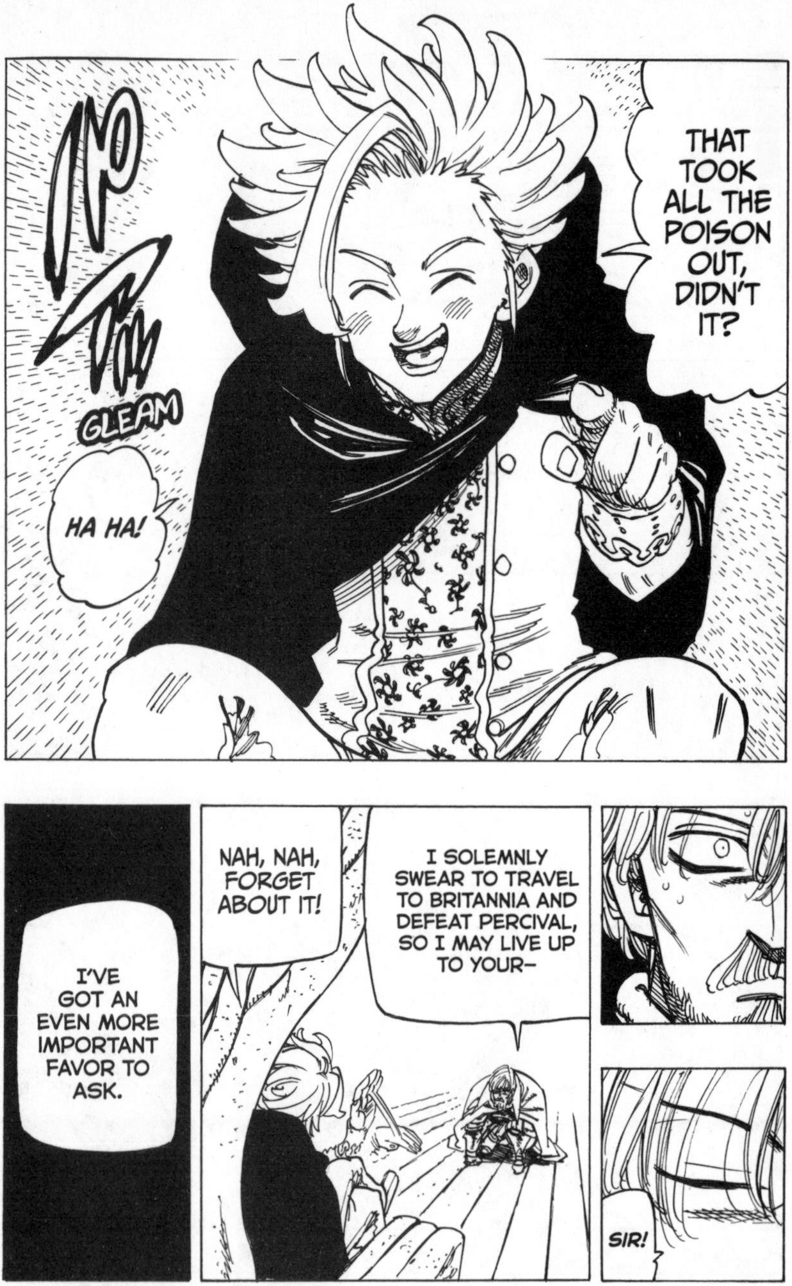
THAT TOOK ALL THE POISON OUT, DIDN'T IT?
GLEAM
HA HA!
SIR!
I SOLEMNLY SWEAR TO TRAVEL TO BRITANNIA AND DEFEAT PERCIVAL, SO I MAY LIVE UP TO YOUR–
NAH, NAH, FORGET ABOUT IT!
I'VE GOT AN EVEN MORE IMPORTANT FAVOR TO ASK.

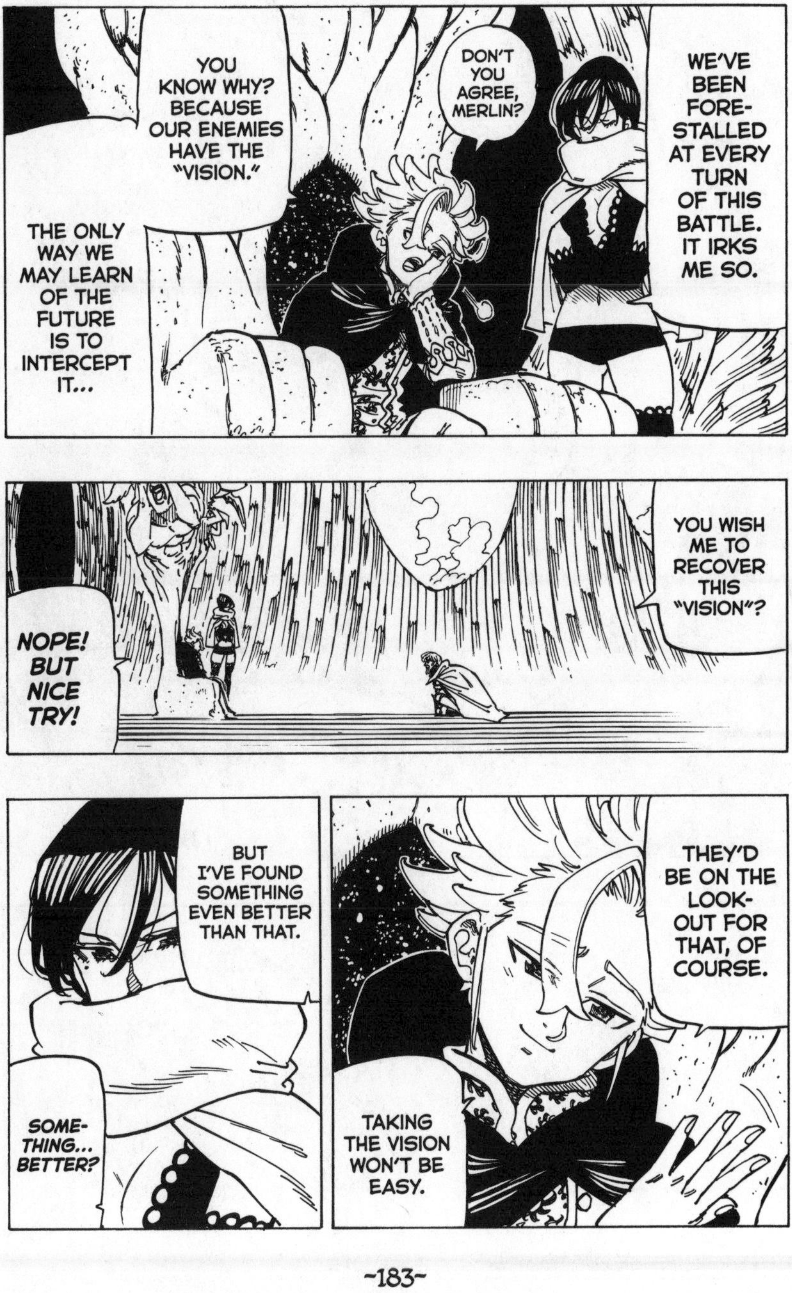
WE'VE BEEN FORE-STALLED AT EVERY TURN OF THIS BATTLE. IT IRKS ME SO.
YOU KNOW WHY? BECAUSE OUR ENEMIES HAVE THE "VISION."
THE ONLY WAY WE MAY LEARN OF THE FUTURE IS TO INTERCEPT IT...
DON'T YOU AGREE, MERLIN?
YOU WISH ME TO RECOVER THIS "VISION"?
NOPE! BUT NICE TRY!
TAKING THE VISION WON'T BE EASY.
THEY'D BE ON THE LOOK-OUT FOR THAT, OF COURSE.
BUT I'VE FOUND SOMETHING EVEN BETTER THAN THAT.
SOME-THING... BETTER?

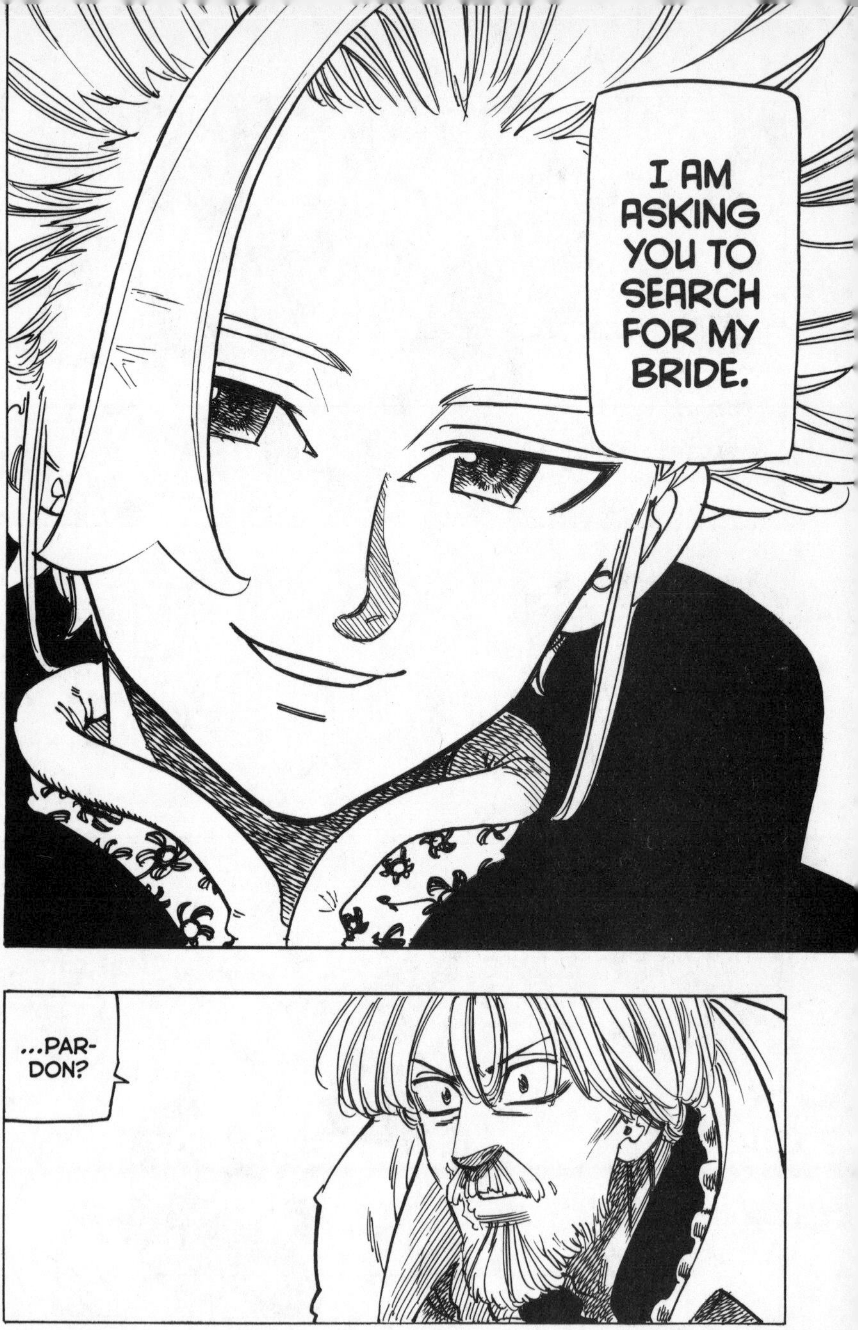
I AM ASKING YOU TO SEARCH FOR MY BRIDE.
...PAR-DON?

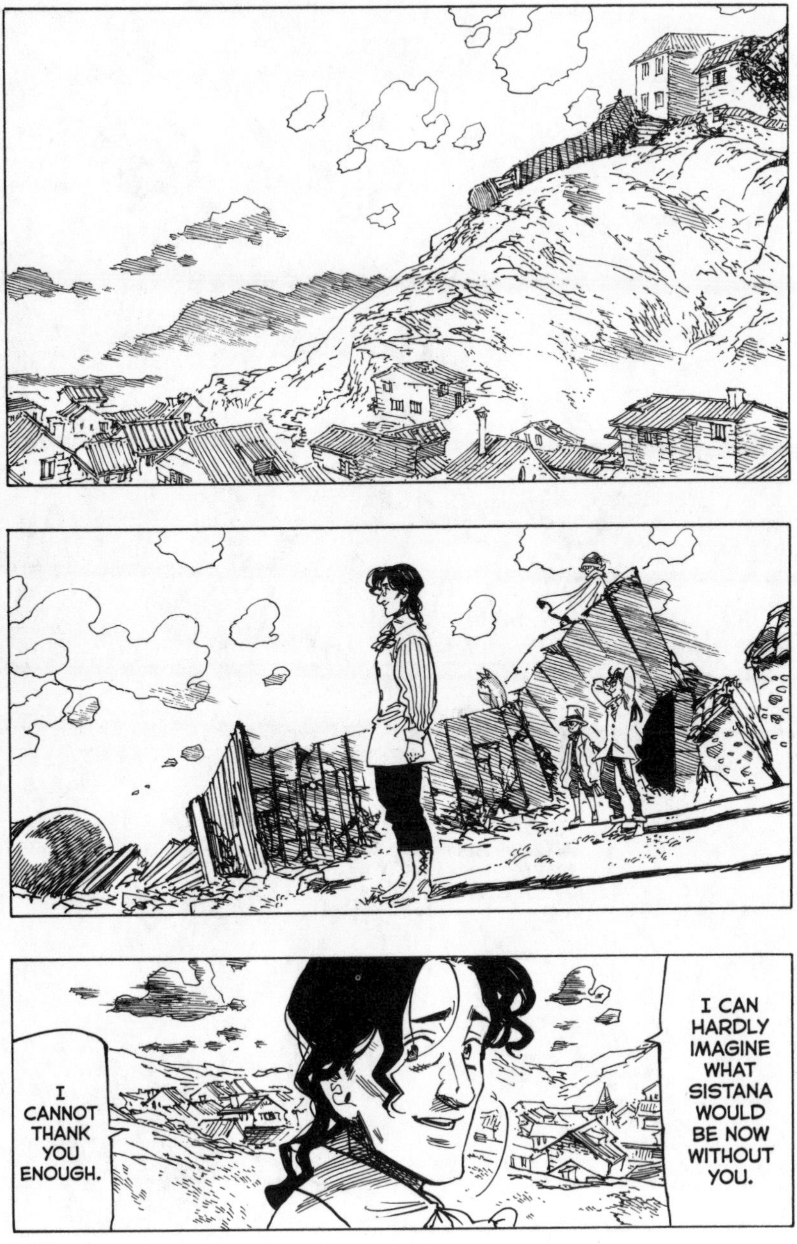
I CAN HARDLY IMAGINE WHAT SISTANA WOULD BE NOW WITHOUT YOU.
I CANNOT THANK YOU ENOUGH.

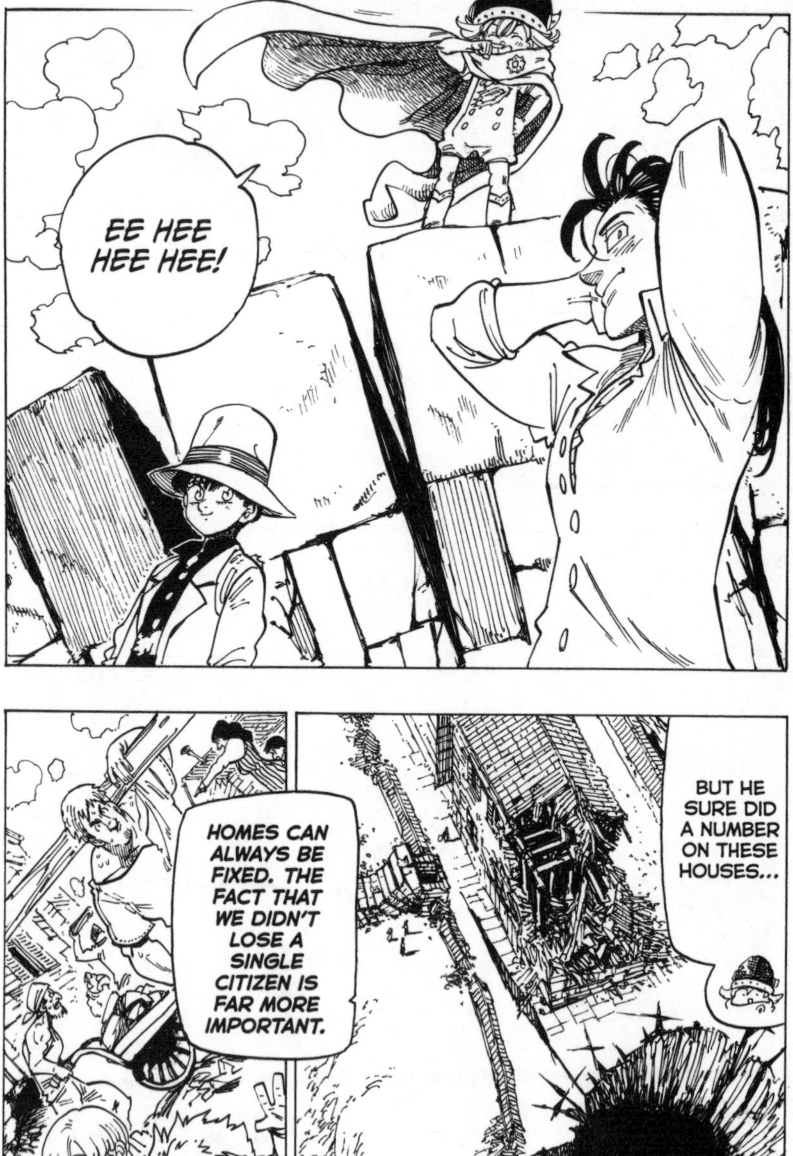
EE HEE HEE HEE!
BUT HE SURE DID A NUMBER ON THESE HOUSES...
HOMES CAN ALWAYS BE FIXED. THE FACT THAT WE DIDN'T LOSE A SINGLE CITIZEN IS FAR MORE IMPORTANT.

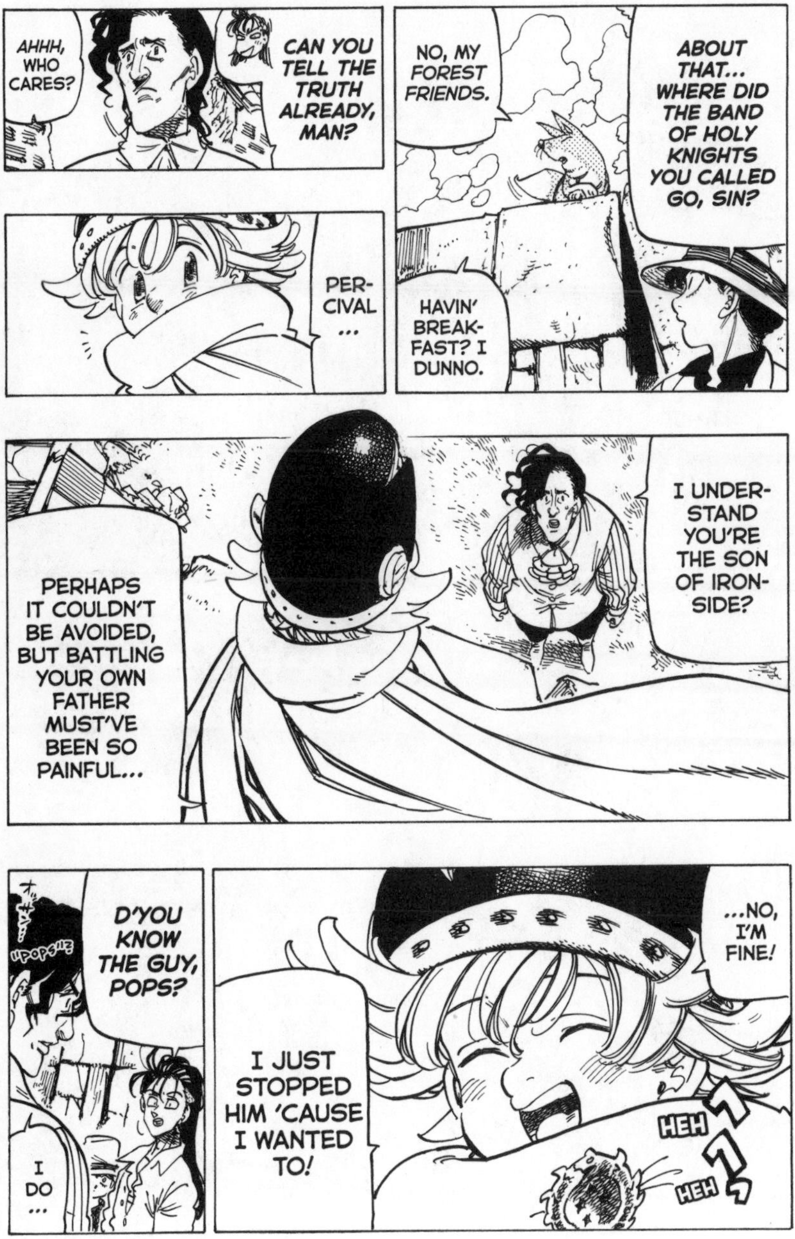
ABOUT THAT... WHERE DID THE BAND OF HOLY KNIGHTS YOU CALLED GO, SIN?
NO, MY FOREST FRIENDS.
HAVIN' BREAKFAST? I DUNNO.
CAN YOU TELL THE TRUTH ALREADY, MAN?
AHHH, WHO CARES?
PER-CIVAL...
I UNDER-STAND YOU'RE THE SON OF IRON-SIDE?
PERHAPS IT COULDN'T BE AVOIDED, BUT BATTLING YOUR OWN FATHER MUST'VE BEEN SO PAINFUL...
...NO, I'M FINE!
I JUST STOPPED HIM 'CAUSE I WANTED TO!
HEH HEH
D'YOU KNOW THE GUY, POPS?
POPS!?
I DO...

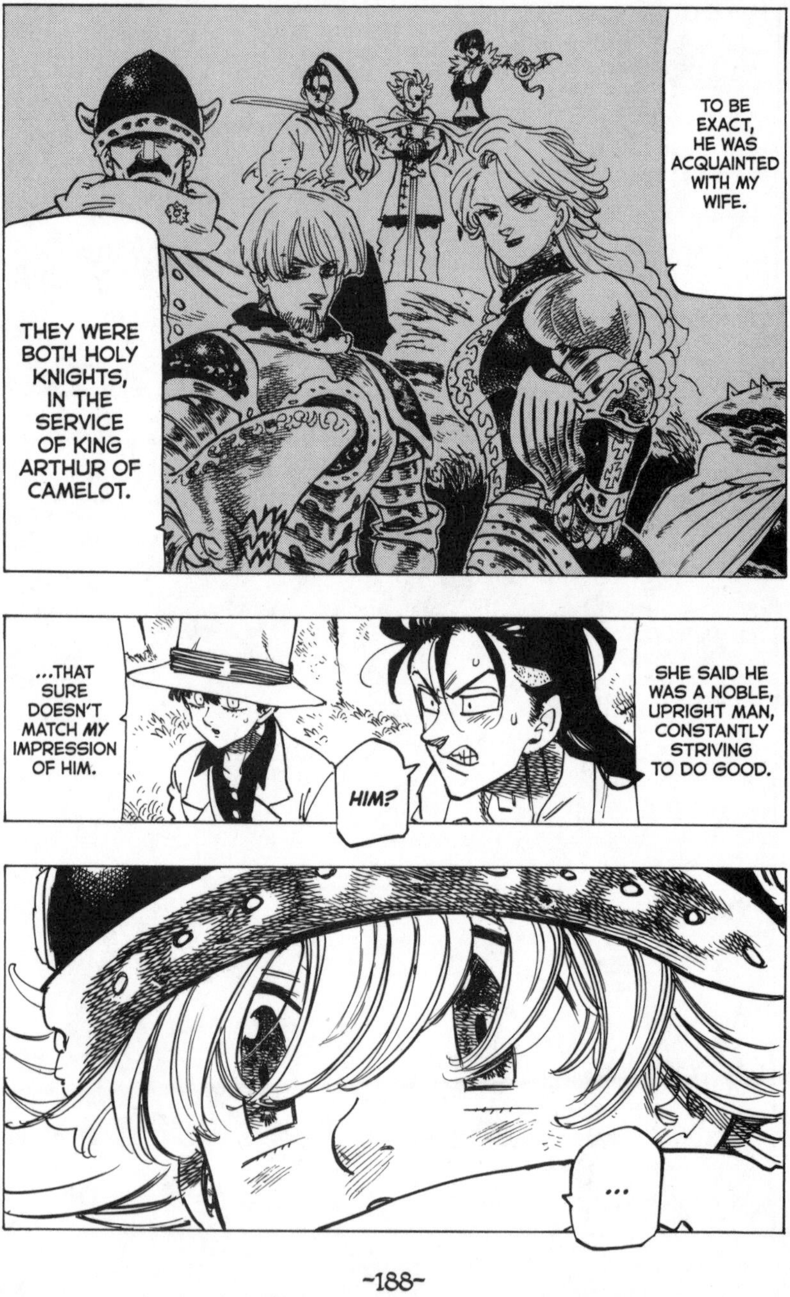
TO BE EXACT, HE WAS ACQUAINTED WITH MY WIFE.
THEY WERE BOTH HOLY KNIGHTS, IN THE SERVICE OF KING ARTHUR OF CAMELOT.
SHE SAID HE WAS A NOBLE, UPRIGHT MAN, CONSTANTLY STRIVING TO DO GOOD.
HIM?
...THAT SURE DOESN'T MATCH *MY* IMPRESSION OF HIM.
...

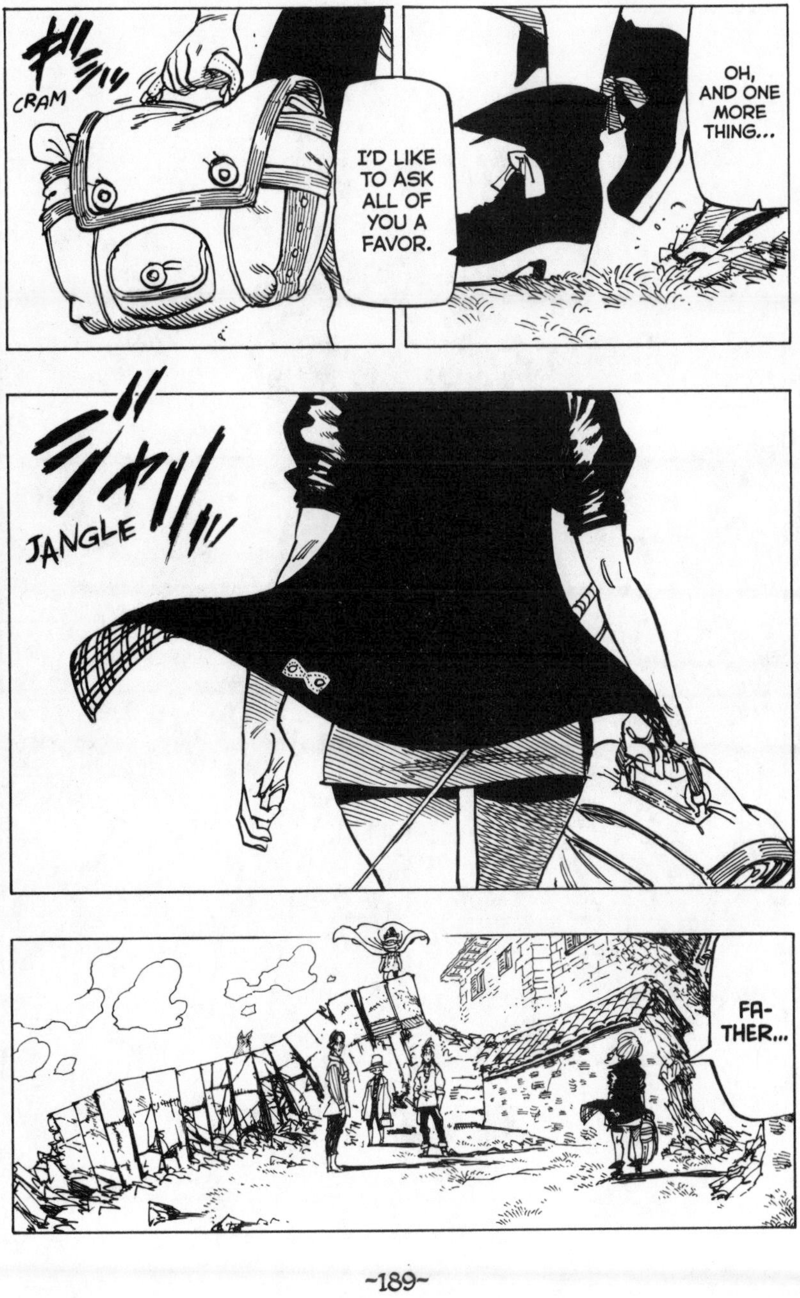
OH, AND ONE MORE THING...
I'D LIKE TO ASK ALL OF YOU A FAVOR.
CRAM
JANGLE
FA-THER...

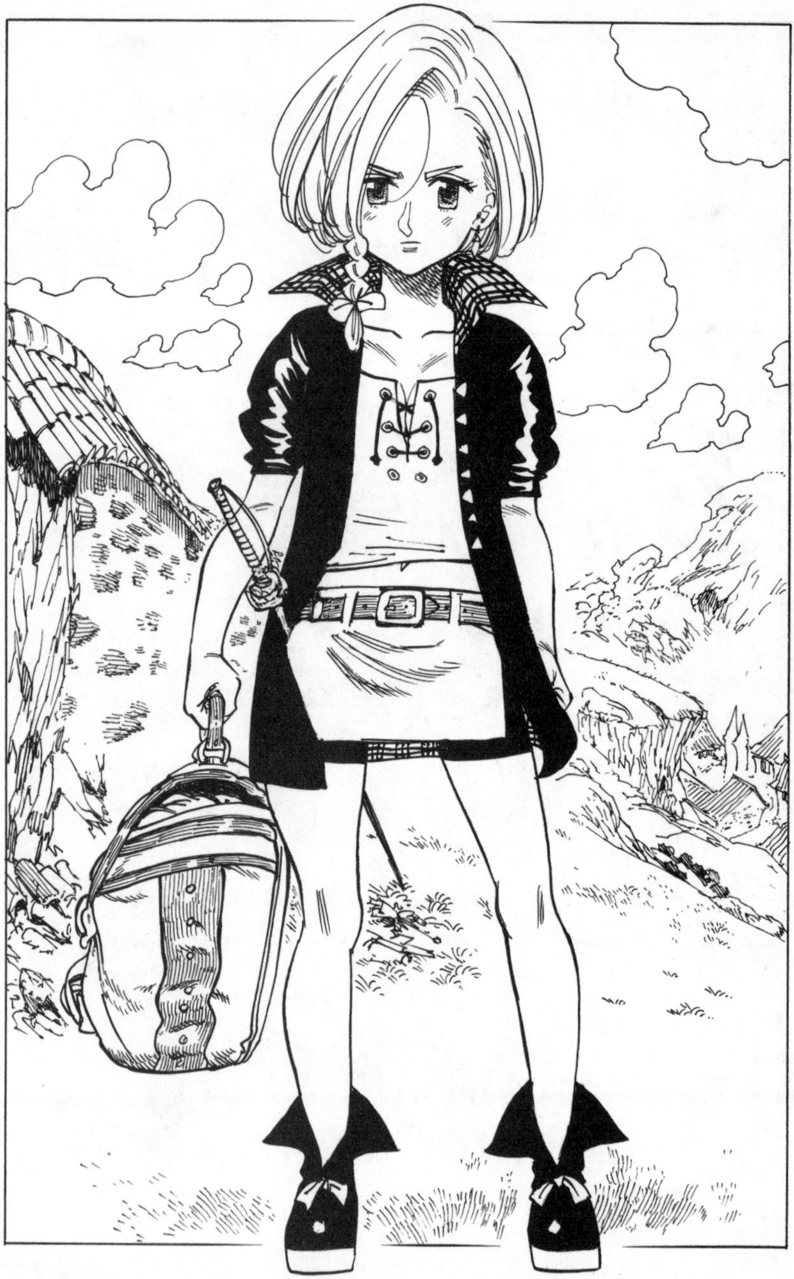

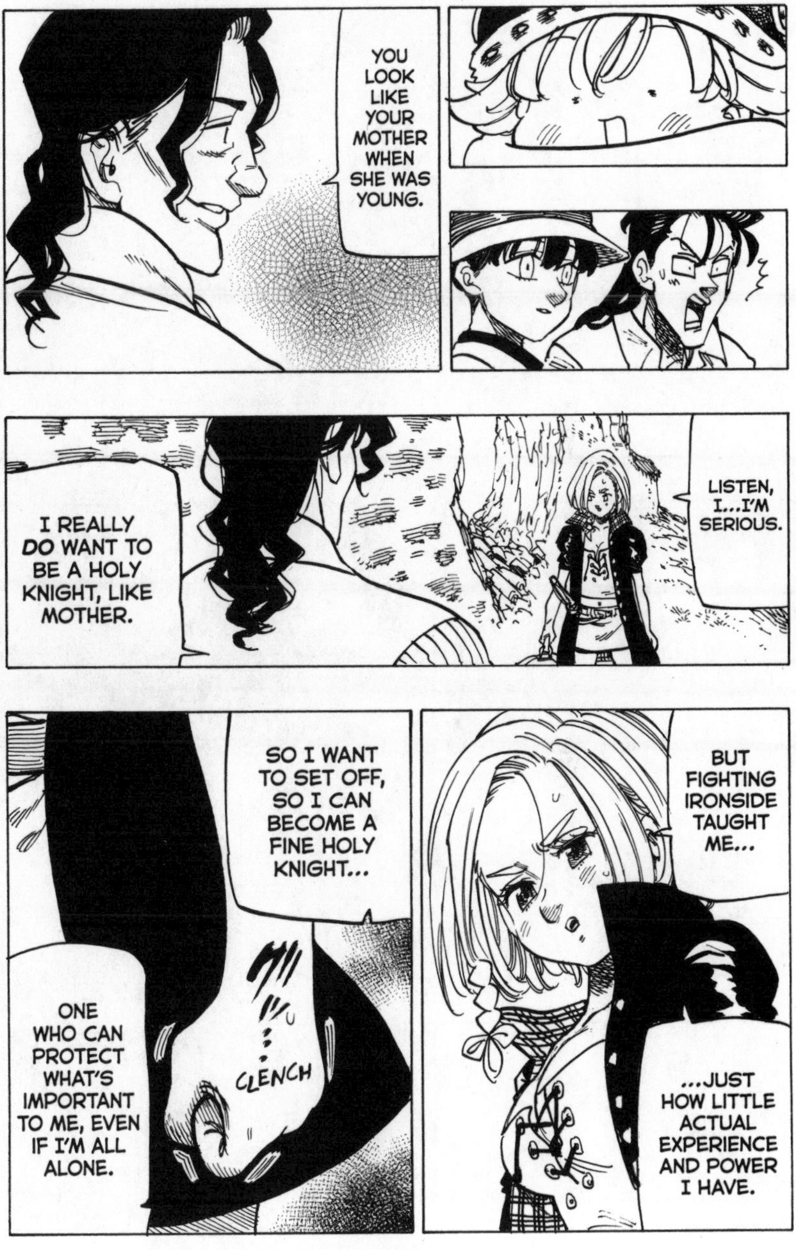
YOU LOOK LIKE YOUR MOTHER WHEN SHE WAS YOUNG.
LISTEN, I...I'M SERIOUS.
I REALLY *DO* WANT TO BE A HOLY KNIGHT, LIKE MOTHER.
BUT FIGHTING IRONSIDE TAUGHT ME...
...JUST HOW LITTLE ACTUAL EXPERIENCE AND POWER I HAVE.
SO I WANT TO SET OFF, SO I CAN BECOME A FINE HOLY KNIGHT...
CLENCH
ONE WHO CAN PROTECT WHAT'S IMPORTANT TO ME, EVEN IF I'M ALL ALONE.

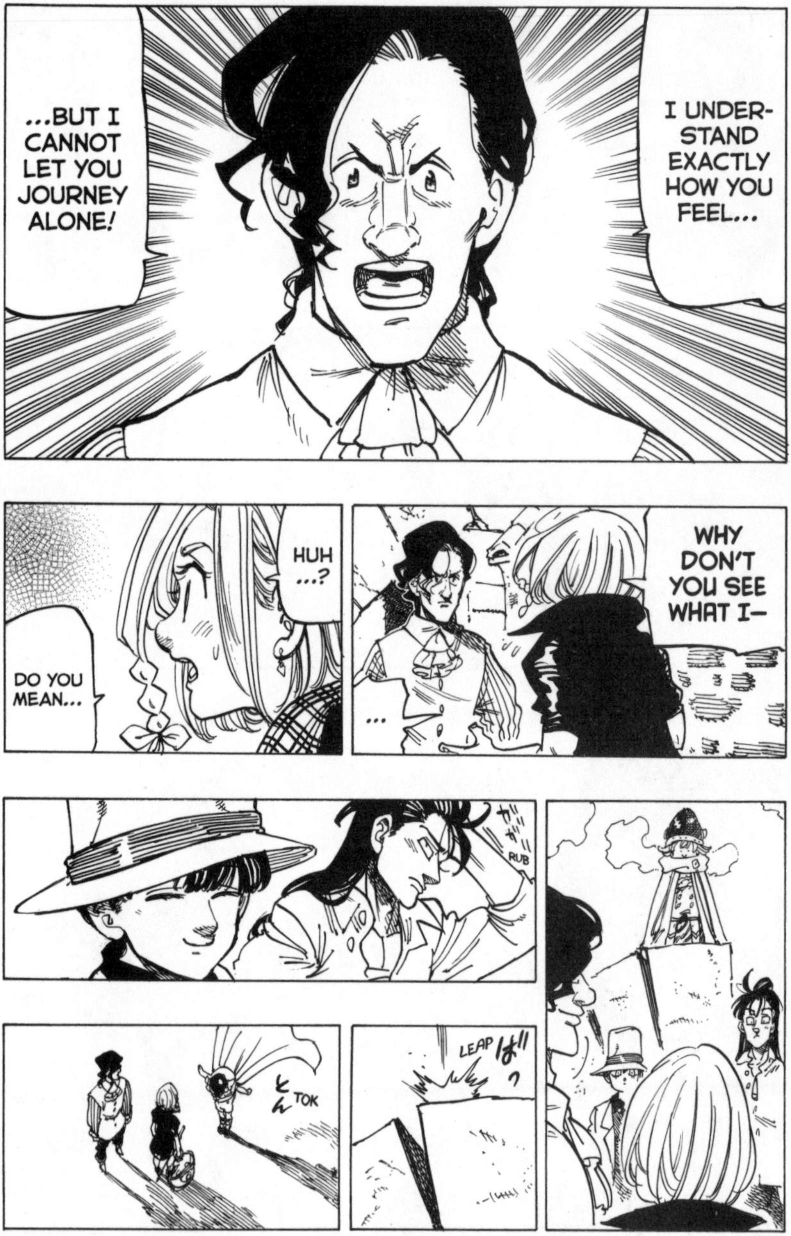
I UNDER-
STAND
EXACTLY
HOW YOU
FEEL...
...BUT I
CANNOT
LET YOU
JOURNEY
ALONE!
WHY
DON'T
YOU SEE
WHAT I—
...
HUH
...?
DO YOU
MEAN...
RUB
LEAP
ばっ
とん
TOK

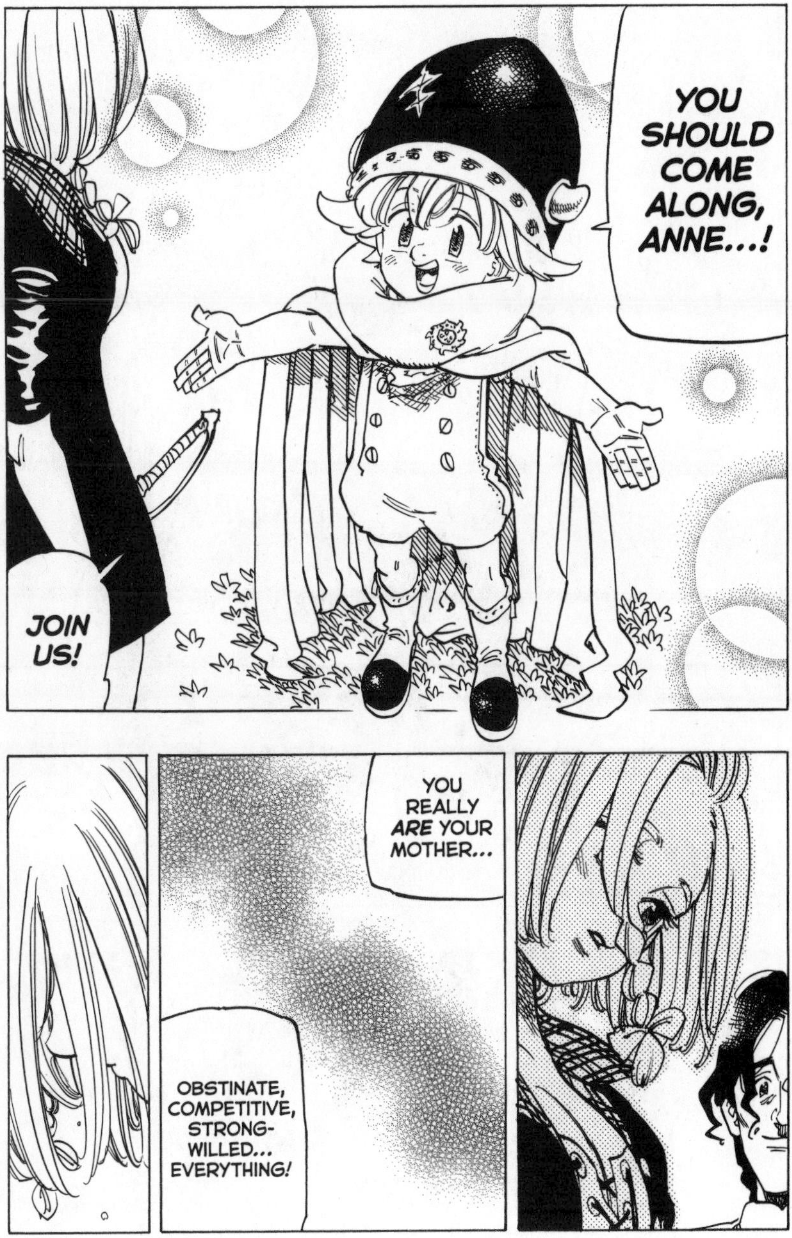
YOU SHOULD COME ALONG, ANNE...!
JOIN US!
YOU REALLY *ARE* YOUR MOTHER...
OBSTINATE, COMPETITIVE, STRONG-WILLED... EVERYTHING!

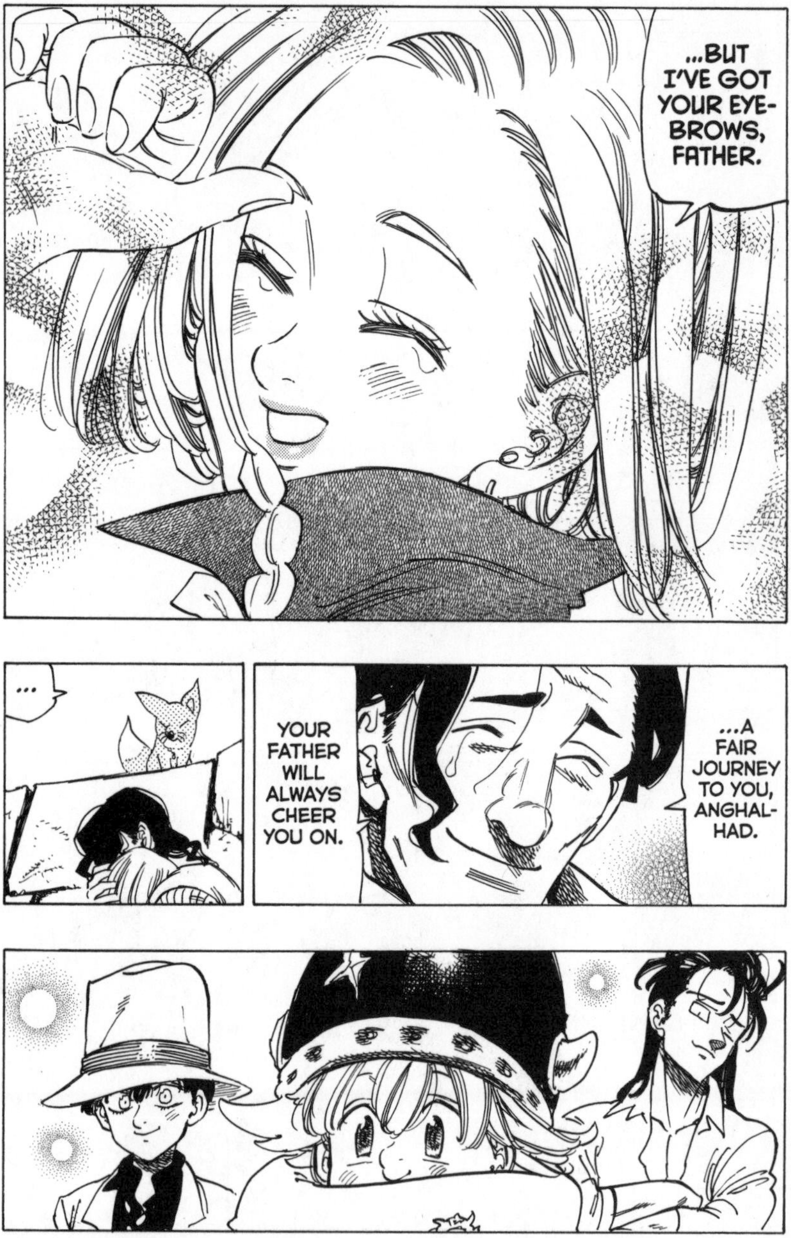
...BUT I'VE GOT YOUR EYE-BROWS, FATHER.
...A FAIR JOURNEY TO YOU, ANGHALHAD.
YOUR FATHER WILL ALWAYS CHEER YOU ON.
...

Four Knights of the Apocalypse Art Corner
Artist Knights' Chamber

DON'T FORGET TO INCLUDE YOUR NAME AND ADDRESS ON YOUR POSTCARD!

SPECIAL AWARD

P =

D =

S =

N =

...SNIFF...! GRAMPS AND I WILL ALWAYS BE TOGETHER...!

Kaeru – Kyoto Prefecture

N HEY, DONNY! DIDN'T YOU ALREADY HAVE SECONDS?

D I'M IN A GROWTH SPURT! AND THIS STUFF IS DELICIOUS!

Kocchi – Osaka Prefecture

P I WONDER WHAT THE OTHER THREE OF THEM ARE LIKE?

D HELL, I WOULDN'T KNOW.

Kuro-buta-don – Kagoshima Prefecture

Tatsuya Inaki – Chiba Prefecture

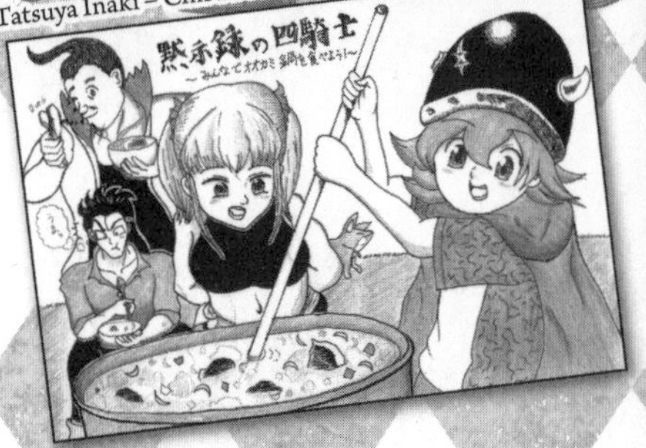
黙示録の四騎士

D WHO TAUGHT YOU TO COOK?

P UMM... GRAMPS AND SOME GUY WITH SPIKY HAIR.

P SIN ALMOST SEEMS HUMAN...

D A TALKING FOX. HE KINDA IS.

S ME, A HUMAN? DON'T BE SILLY.

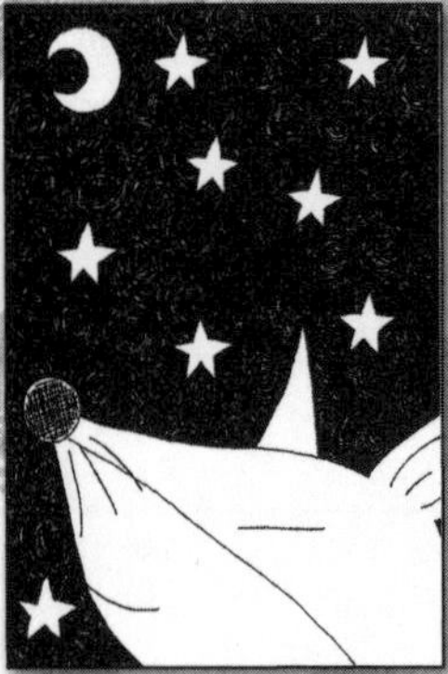

Haatan – Fukuoka Prefecture

P GRAMPS NEVER TALKED MUCH ABOUT HIS YOUNGER DAYS.

S WELL... I'M SURE HE HAD HIS REASONS.

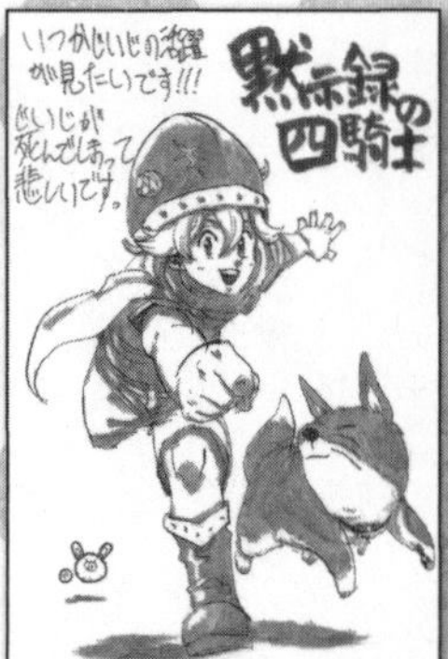
黙示録の四騎士

Yutaro Shige – Tokyo Prefecture

N THOSE MINI-PERCIVALS ARE CUTE... I'D LIKE ONE FOR MYSELF.

D Y-YOU WOULD?

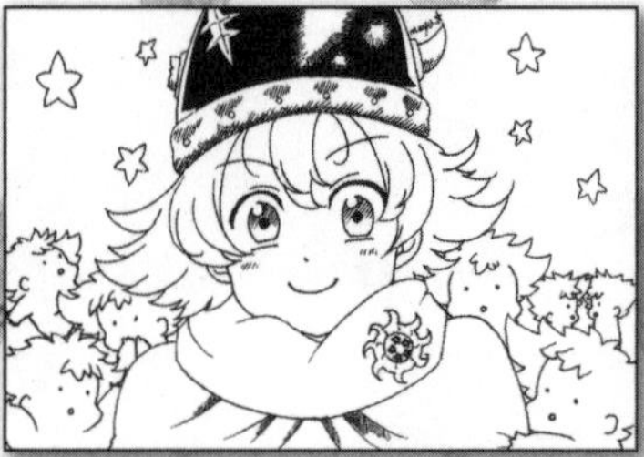

Mayu Aoba – Osaka Prefecture

P LET'S HAVE A CONTEST TO SEE WHO CAN EAT THE FASTEST!

D YOU REALLY LIKE CONTESTS, DON'T YOU...?

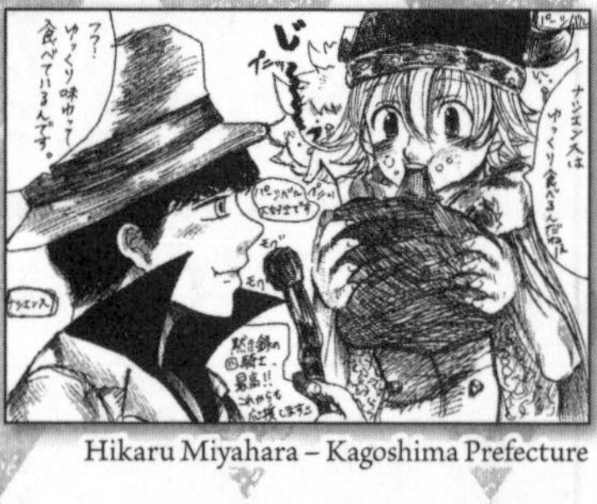

Hikaru Miyahara – Kagoshima Prefecture

P FUWWAA!~ ♫

N ARE YOU REALLY SIXTEEN?

D I'M STILL NOT CONVINCED...

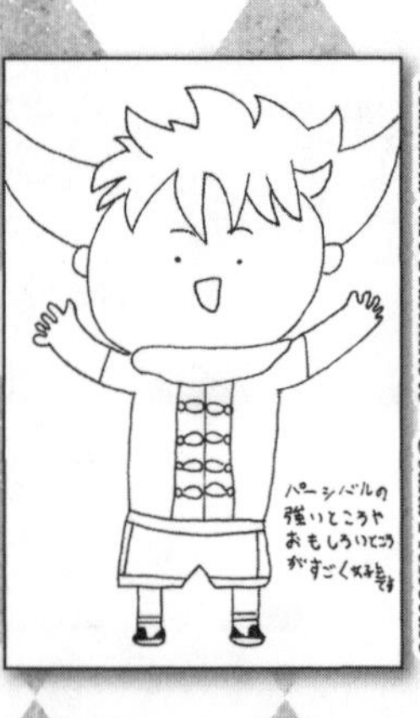

Hakama-taro Hashimoto – Osaka Prefecture

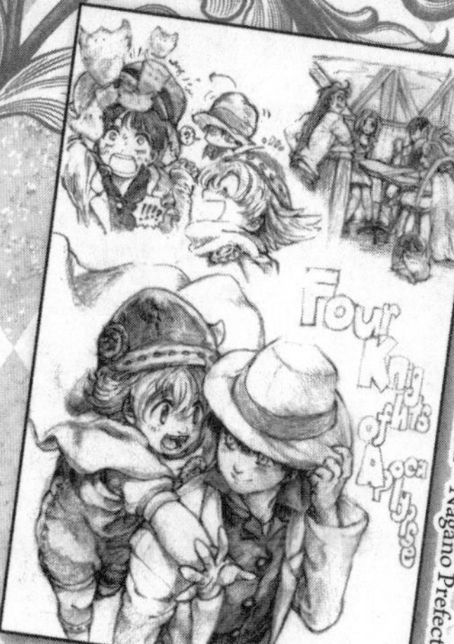
Four Knights of Apocalypse
Miwa Araki – Nagano Prefecture

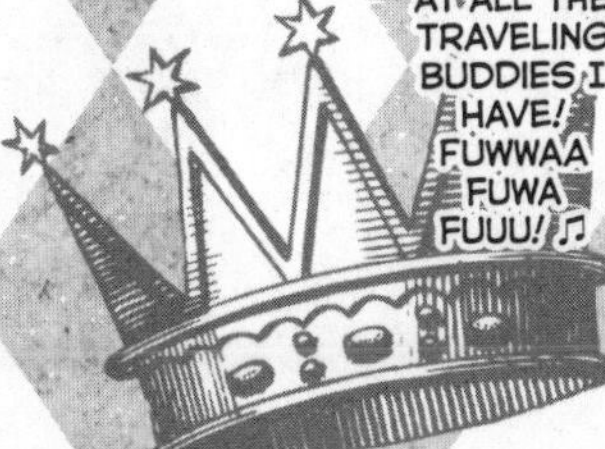

GRAMPS, YOU SEE ME?! LOOK AT ALL THE TRAVELING BUDDIES I HAVE! FUWWAA FUWA FUUU! ♫

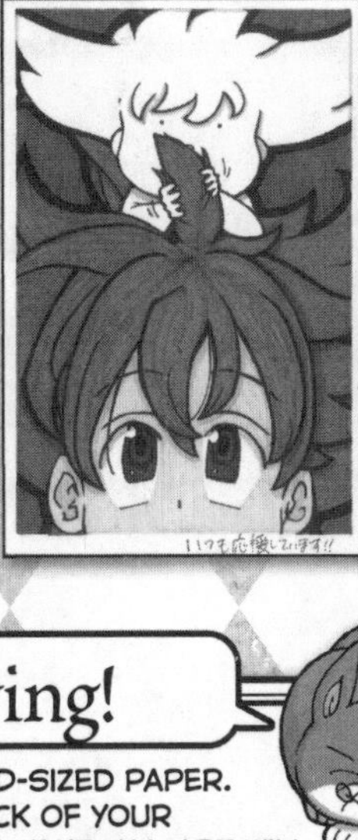
いつも応援しています!!
Misaki Ota – Kanagawa Prefecture

S I THINK HE'S STILL GOT SOME MAGIC LEFT IN HIM.

P YOU THINK SO?

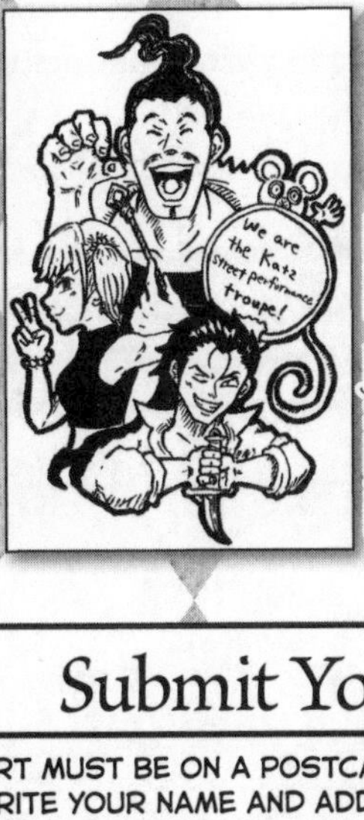
We are the Katz street performance troupe!
Kacchan – Tokyo Prefecture

S I WONDER HOW ELVA AND THE RING-MASTER ARE DOING...

P I'M SURE THEY'RE LIVING HAPPILY EVER AFTER!

Submit Your Drawing!

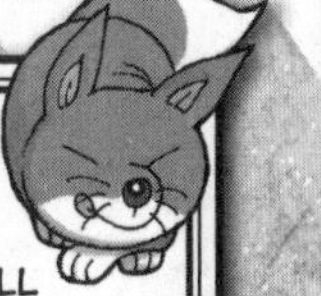

- ART MUST BE ON A POSTCARD OR POSTCARD-SIZED PAPER.
- WRITE YOUR NAME AND ADDRESS ON THE BACK OF YOUR PICTURE! YOU CAN INCLUDE COMMENTS IF YOU WANT. ALL ART WILL BE PRINTED IN BLACK AND WHITE, EVEN IF YOU SUBMIT IT IN COLOR.
- COPYING NAKABA SUZUKI'S ART STYLE IS FINE, OF COURSE, BUT COPYING PICTURES DRAWN BY OTHER FANS IS DEFINITELY NOT OKAY.

IF YOUR PIECE IS PRINTED, YOU'LL GET SPECIAL MERCH! THE BEST PIECE IN EACH VOLUME WILL RECEIVE THE "SPECIAL AWARD" AND AN AUTOGRAPH!

SEND SUBMISSIONS TO:
KODANSHA WEEKLY SHONEN MAGAZINE
ATTN: FOUR KNIGHTS OF THE APOCALYPSE ART TROOP
2-12-21 OTOWA, BUNKYO WARD, TOKYO PREFECTURE 112-8001

NOTE: SUBMISSIONS WILL BE GIVEN TO THE ARTIST. PLEASE UNDERSTAND THAT THIS INCLUDES ANY ADDRESS, NAME, OR OTHER PERSONAL INFORMATION WRITTEN ON SAID SUBMISSIONS.

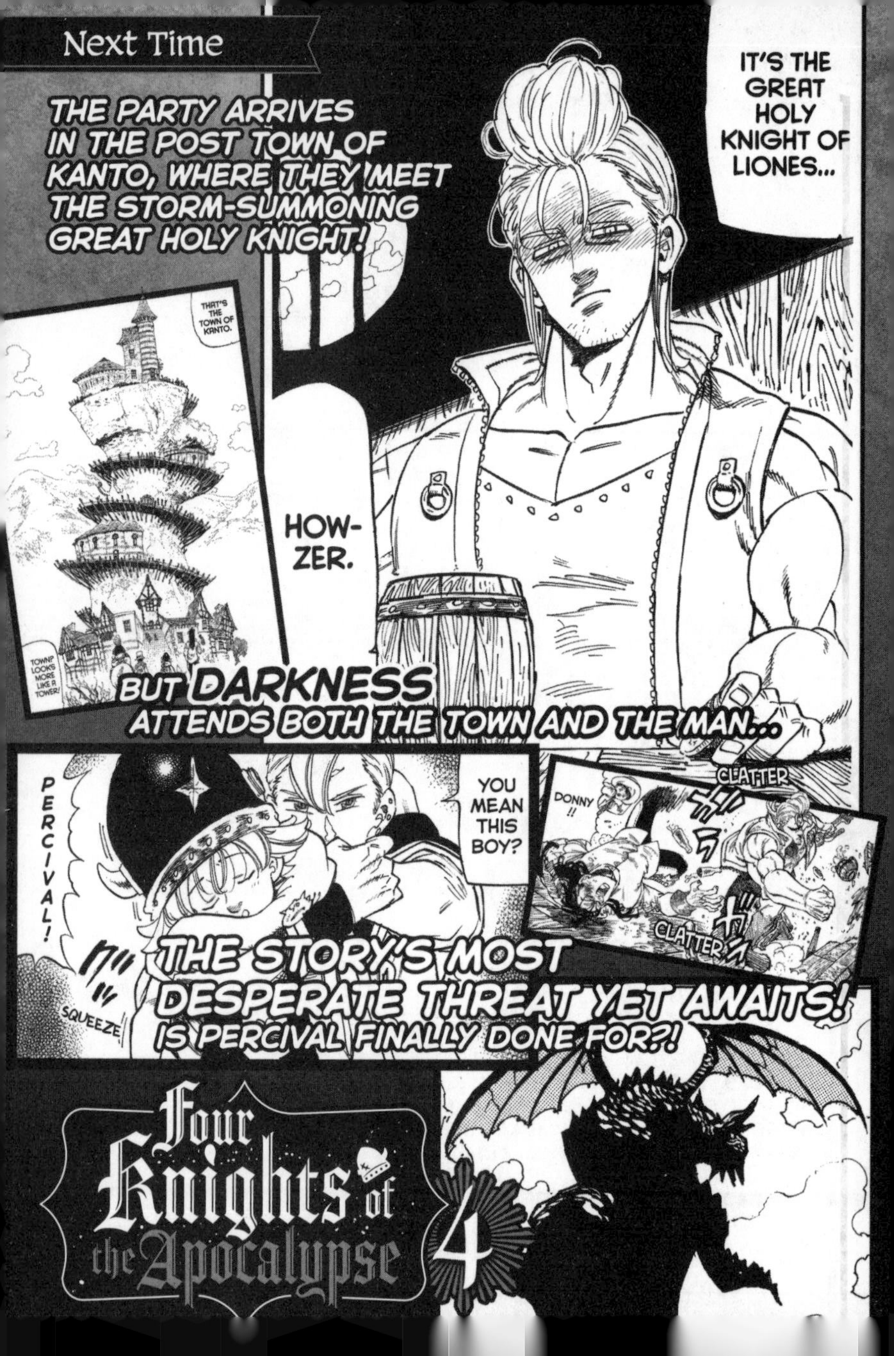
Next Time
THE PARTY ARRIVES IN THE POST TOWN OF KANTO, WHERE THEY MEET THE STORM-SUMMONING GREAT HOLY KNIGHT!
IT'S THE GREAT HOLY KNIGHT OF LIONES...
HOW-ZER.
THAT'S THE TOWN OF KANTO.
TOWN? LOOKS MORE LIKE A TOWER!
BUT DARKNESS ATTENDS BOTH THE TOWN AND THE MAN...
CLATTER
DONNY !!
CLATTER
YOU MEAN THIS BOY?
PERCIVAL!
SQUEEZE
THE STORY'S MOST DESPERATE THREAT YET AWAITS!
IS PERCIVAL FINALLY DONE FOR?!
Four Knights of the Apocalypse
4

Young characters and steampunk setting, like *Howl's Moving Castle* and *Battle Angel Alita*

Beyond the Clouds © 2018 Nicke / Ki-oon

A boy with a talent for machines and a mysterious girl whose wings he's fixed will take you beyond the clouds! In the tradition of the high-flying, resonant adventure stories of Studio Ghibli comes a gorgeous tale about the longing of young hearts for adventure and friendship!

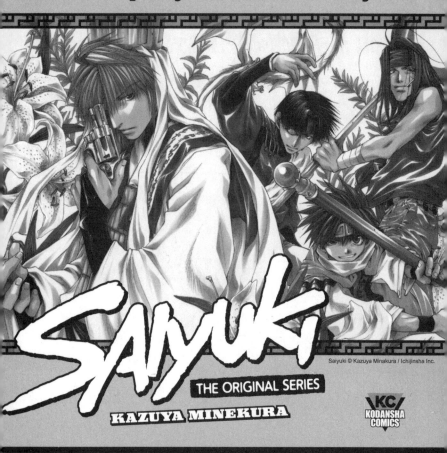

THE SWEET SCENT OF LOVE IS IN THE AIR! FOR FANS OF OFFBEAT ROMANCES LIKE *WOTAKOI*

Sweat and Soap © Kintetsu Yamada / Kodansha Ltd.

In an office romance, there's a fine line between sexy and awkward... and that line is where Asako — a woman who sweats copiously — meets Koutarou — a perfume developer who can't get enough of Asako's, er, scent. Don't miss a romcom manga like no other!

The adorable new odd-couple cat comedy manga from the creator of the beloved *Chi's Sweet Home*, in full color!

Praise for Chi's Sweet Home

"Nearly impossible to turn away... a true all-ages title that anyone, young or old, cat lover or not, will enjoy. The stories will bring a smile to your face and warm your heart."

~School Library Journal

Sue & Tai-chan
Konami Kanata

Sue is an aging housecat who's looking forward to living out her life in peace... but her plans change when the mischievous black tomcat Tai-chan enters the picture! Hey! Sue never signed up to be a catsitter! *Sue & Tai-chan* is the latest from the reigning meow-narch of cute kitty comics, Konami Kanata.

PERFECT WORLD

Rie Aruga

A TOUCHING NEW SERIES ABOUT LOVE AND COPING WITH DISABILITY

An office party reunites Tsugumi with her high school crush Itsuki. He's realized his dream of becoming an architect, but along the way, he experienced a spinal injury that put him in a wheelchair. Now Tsugumi's rekindled feelings will butt up against prejudices she never considered — and Itsuki will have to decide if he's ready to let someone into his heart...

"Depicts with great delicacy and courage the difficulties some with disabilities experience getting involved in romantic relationships... Rie Aruga refuses to romanticize, pushing her heroine to face the reality of disability. She invites her readers to the same tasks of empathy, knowledge and recognition."
—Slate.fr

"An important entry [in manga romance]... The emotional core of both plot and characters indicates thoughtfulness... [Aruga's] research is readily apparent in the text and artwork, making this feel like a real story."
—Anime News Network

KC KODANSHA COMICS

A Kodansha Trade Paperback Original

The Seven Deadly Sins: Four Knights of the Apocalypse 3 copyright © 2021 Nakaba Suzuki
English translation copyright © 2022 Nakaba Suzuki

Published in the United States by
Kodansha USA Publishing, LLC, New York.

Publication rights for this English edition arranged through
Kodansha Ltd., Tokyo.

First published in Japan in 2021 by Kodansha Ltd., Tokyo
as *Mokushiroku no Yonkishi 3*.

ISBN 978-1-64651-455-7

Printed in the United States of America.

1st Printing

Translation: Kevin Gifford
Additional translation: Kevin Steinbach
Lettering: Darren Smith
Additional lettering and layout: AndWorld Design
Editing: Aimee Zink
YKS Services LLC/SKY Japan, Inc.
Kodansha USA Publishing edition cover design by Matt Akuginow

Publisher: Kiichiro Sugawara

Director of Publishing Services: Ben Applegate
Director of Publishing Operations: Dave Barrett
Associate Director of Publishing Operations: Stephen Pakula
Publishing Services Managing Editors: Alanna Ruse, Madison Salters
Production Managers: Emi Lotto, Angela Zurlo

KODANSHA.US